MAILING ADDRESS

Maritime Studies Research Unit
Memorial University of Newfoundland
St. John's, Newfoundland A1C 5S7, Canada

RESEARCH IN MARITIME HISTORY
NO. 11

PRIZE AND PREJUDICE: PRIVATEERING AND NAVAL PRIZE IN ATLANTIC CANADA IN THE WAR OF 1812

Faye Margaret Kert

International Maritime Economic History Association

St. John's, Newfoundland
1997

ISSN -1188-3928
ISBN -0-9681288-1-5

Research in Maritime History is published semi-annually, in June and December.

Research in Maritime History is available free of charge to members of the International Maritime Economic History Association. The price to others is US$15 per copy.

Back issues of *Research in Maritime History* are available:

No. 1 (1991)	David M. Williams and Andrew P. White (comps.), *A Select Bibliography of British and Irish University Theses about Maritime History, 1792-1990*
No. 2 (1992)	Lewis R. Fischer (ed.), *From Wheel House to Counting House: Essays in Maritime Business History in Honour of Professor Peter Neville Davies*
No. 3 (1992)	Lewis R. Fischer and Walter Minchinton (eds.), *People of the Northern Seas*
No. 4 (1993)	Simon Ville (ed.), *Shipbuilding in the United Kingdom in the Nineteenth Century: A Regional Approach*
No. 5 (1993)	Peter N. Davies (ed.), *The Diary of John Holt*
No. 6 (1994)	Simon P. Ville and David M. Williams (eds.), *Management, Finance and Industrial Reslations in Maritime Industries: Essays in International Maritime and Business History*
No. 7 (1994)	Lewis R. Fischer (ed.), *The Market for Seamen in the Age of Sail*
No. 8 (1995)	Gordon Read and Michael Stammers (comps.), *Guide to the Records of Merseyside Maritime Museum*
No. 9 (1995)	Frank Broeze (ed.), *Maritime History at the Crossroads: A Critical Review of Recent Historiography*
No. 10 (1996)	Nancy Redmayne Ross (ed.), *The Diary of a Maritimer, 1816-1901: The Life and Times of Joseph Salter*

Research in Maritime History would like to thank Memorial University of Newfoundland for its generous financial assistance in support of this volume.

PRIZE AND PREJUDICE: PRIVATEERING AND NAVAL PRIZE IN ATLANTIC CANADA IN THE WAR OF 1812

Table of Contents

Tables / vi
Illustrations / vii
Acknowledgements / viii

INTRODUCTION / 1

CHAPTER 1: **RELUCTANT ENEMIES** / 11

Causes of the War of 1812 / 11
Popular Opinion / 15
The Atlantic Provinces to 1812 / 16
The Pursuit of Trade / 18
i) Smuggling / 19
ii) Specie / 22
iii) The Licensed Trade / 24

CHAPTER 2: **GOOD AND LAWFUL PRIZE** / 33

The Origins of Admiralty Law / 34
Prize Law Transformed / 36
The Role of the Admiral / 39
The Development of Prize Law / 41
Lawful Prize / 43
Refining the Rules / 46
Colonial Vice-Admiralty Courts / 48
United States Admiralty Courts / 52

CHAPTER 3: **PRIZEMAKING AND THE VICE-ADMIRALTY COURT AT HALIFAX** / 55

The Prelude / 56
The Practitioners / 59
i) Sir Alexander Croke / 59
ii) Richard John Uniacke / 61
The Problem / 62

The Process / 63
i) Prize Master's Affidavit / 63
ii) Petitions / 63
iii) Monition / 65
iv) Allegations / 67
v) Standing Interrogatories / 68
vi) Disposition / 68
Recaptures / 69
Appeals / 71
Prize Agency / 72
The Cost of Justice / 75

CHAPTER 4: **PUBLIC SERVICE, PRIVATE PROFITS** / 77

The Atlantic Privateers / 78
The Nature of Privateering / 80
A Dicey Business / 81
The Liverpool Experience / 83
Readying for Sea / 89
i) Affidavit of Sureties / 91
ii) Articles of Agreement / 92
iii) The Ship's Company / 93
Privateer Perquisites / 95
Generous Warfare / 96
Prisoners of War / 98
Cartel / 103
Prize and Reprise / 104

CHAPTER 5: **ON HIS MAJESTY'S SERVICE** / 109

The Atlantic Squadron / 110
The American Navy / 111
British Naval Problems at Sea and Ashore / 116
Manpower Shortages / 119
Naval Prize and the Profit Motive / 124
i) Head Money / 126
ii) Ransom / 126
iii) Joint Capture / 128
Gentlemen and Jack Tars / 129
Evaluating Naval Prize / 131

CHAPTER 6: **THE FORTUNES OF WAR** / 135

Commercial Warfare / 135
The Toll on America / 137
Strict and Rigorous Blockade / 140
Compulsory Convoy / 145
Maritime Risk: Insuring and Securing Trade / 148
Economic Impact / 151

CONCLUSION: PRIZEMAKING APPRAISED / 155

APPENDICES

APPENDIX 1: **Prize Cases Appearing before the Vice-Admiralty Court of Halifax from June 1812 to May 1815** / 159

APPENDIX 2: **Standing Interrogatories** / 204

APPENDIX 3: **Nova Scotia and New Brunswick Letter of Marque Vessels, 1812-1815** / 211

APPENDIX 4: **Investment in Privateering** / 215

APPENDIX 5: **Royal Navy Vessels and Their Prizes** / 223

APPENDIX 6: **Letters of Agency - RN Ships** / 232

APPENDIX 7: **Prize-Related Activity Among Merchants in Nova Scotia and New Brunswick** / 237

Bibliography / 243

List of Tables

3.1. *Court costs as a percentage of total custody costs and salvage awards* / 66

3.2. *Comparison of Court costs for Different Provincial Ports* / 76

4.1. *Comparative Tonnages for Private Armed Vessels from Baltimore, Captured American Privateers in Appendix 1, and Atlantic Privateers in Appendix 3* / 89

4.2. *Distribution of Provincial Privateer Vessel Types and their Prizes* / 90

4.3. *Prize Tonnages Captured by Nova Scotia and New Brunswick Privateers* / 106

4.4. *Atlantic Canadian Privateer Captures by Month* / 107

5.1. *Naval Captures by Month* / 131

5.2. *Prize Tonnages Captured by the Royal Navy* / 132

6.1. *A Comparison of Prize Tonnages Captured by Privateer and Royal Naval Vessels* / 154

List of Illustrations

1. Licence signed by Lt. Governor Sir John Coape Sherbrooke issued to John Moody, Halifax merchant / 27

2. Detail from the Map of the Seat of War in North America published by John Melish, ca. 1813-1815 (Hand-coloured engraving, National Archives of Canada, NMC-6760) / 32

3. Seal of the High Court of Admiralty / 54

4. Sir Alexander Croke, portrait by Robert Field (National Gallery of Canada) / 59

5. *Liverpool Packet*, ca 1815 (courtesy W. Wood Collection) / 79

6. Joseph Barss, portrait by unknown artist (Queen's County Museum, Liverpool, N.S.) / 86

7. Letter of Marque for the American privateer *Juliana Smith* / 88

8. HMS *Shannon* leading USS *Chesapeake* into Halifax Harbour (courtesy Maritime Museum of the Atlantic) / 119

Acknowledgements

Throughout the years it took to research and write this study, I was aided and abetted by family, friends, maritime history colleagues, co-workers and cats. While the final product, whatever its flaws, is my own, I could not have accomplished it without the encouragement and support of a great many people. To all of them I owe a debt of thanks.

At the National Archives of Canada, I would like to thank Pat Kennedy and Tim Dube for granting me access to the records of the Halifax Vice-Admiralty Court. Joyce Agnew at the Department of National Defense arranged a study grant for which I was truly grateful. Judge Arthur Stone of the Supreme Court of Canada critiqued an early draft of my chapter on prize law and John Telfer offered free legal research and advice as well as long-standing friendship. Dr. Carl Swanson of East Carolina University offered his advice and expertise even before he kindly took on the office of external adviser. Finally, I owe special thanks to Prof. Lewis Fischer of Memorial University of Newfoundland and the International Maritime Economic History Association for their role in publishing this work.

Prize and Prejudice is dedicated to my mother, without whom none of this would have been possible.

Introduction

Dismissed by many historians as a "strategical side show"[1] to the main event being fought in Europe, the War of 1812 between Great Britain and the United States seems to have been declared by the unprepared and fought by the unwilling for reasons that remain unexplained. Inconclusive and futile as a military exercise, the War of 1812 merits further study from an economic viewpoint as a war against trade. Not only did the War of 1812 mark an important turning point in the mercantile relationships between Great Britain and her current and former colonies in North America, it was the last international conflict in which commerce raiding or privateering played a major role.

As an economic weapon, the legalized seizure of enemy shipping has been praised, reviled, or ignored depending on the viewpoint of the writer. A review of the literature on the subject revealed a generally positive attitude toward private armed vessels or privateers among maritime historians and, not unexpectedly, less enthusiasm for their efforts among naval historians. Even fewer historians treated prizemaking as an important aspect of naval life.[2] The handful of legal historians concerned with prize emphasize the jurisdictional disputes surrounding the development of prize law while neglecting the wider economic and political issues. Such conflicting interests and perspectives contributed over time to a number of popular prejudices concerning privateers and prize.

For many people, privateering remained synonymous with piracy. Others recognized privateering's legal status but dismissed its effectiveness. To dispel some of these misconceptions, this study examines the economic, political, and social impact of both privateering and naval prize within the context of Atlantic Canada during the War of 1812. It relies heavily on the War of 1812 records of the Vice-Admiralty Court at Halifax that document the prizemaking activities of privateers from New Brunswick and Nova Scotia and Royal Navy vessels carrying prizes into provincial ports.[3] For this reason, the historical overview of prize law in Chapter 2 concentrates on the development of British admiralty law and its adaptation by colonial practitioners in the United States and British North America.

An obscure war fought by unlikely foes provides the setting for this study of prizemaking. The first chapter reviews the origins of the War of 1812 and the mixed feelings of those involved. The next two chapters discuss the legal evolution of prize law and its eventual interpretation in the colonial vice-admiralty courts of North America. Chapters 4 and 5 analyze how privateers from New Brunswick and Nova Scotia and both

---

[1]Paul M. Kennedy, *The Rise and Fall of the Great Powers: Economic Change and Military Conflict from 1500 to 2000* (New York, 1987), 137.

[2]One notable exception is Julian Gwyn's study *The Enterprising Admiral: The Personal Fortune of Admiral Sir Peter Warren* (Montreal, 1974).

[3]The manuscript series is PAC, RG8, Volume IV, Vice-Admiralty Court, Prize Court Records, Halifax, 1784-1818, Volumes 73 to 150.

American and British naval vessels applied, adapted, or avoided the rules governing prizemaking in the War of 1812. Chapter 6 evaluates the economic impact of the War of 1812 on the maritime communities involved. The final chapter appraises the role of prizemaking and privateering in the context of its last major international manifestation.

Many Americans waged the War of 1812 as a second War of Independence, a reaffirmation of American nationhood in the face of British interference with American shipping. The Royal Navy's policy of impressing "British" sailors off the ships of other nations at sea outraged the United States, especially when many of the sailors were Americans! Compounding this insult was Britain's insistence that neutral nations, like the United States, could not trade with France, with whom Britain was at war. In the face of Britain's intractable maritime policy, which threatened both the national pride and the commerce of the United States, President James Madison opted for war.[4] In spite of marked reluctance in many northern states, the United States finally went to war under the banner of Free Trade and Sailors' Rights.

Although the War of 1812 resolved none of the issues for which it was declared, it profoundly affected the participants. In two and a half years of war, the United States developed a small but potent navy capable of meeting, and even defeating, Royal Navy ships. Atlantic Canada established its economic independence and rebuffed the threat of American expansion once and for all. And Britain acquired a fuller understanding and respect for the United States.

As a case study of prizemaking, the War of 1812 signalled the culmination and the conclusion of six centuries of British privateering activity. Privateering or "guerre de course" was a form of commercial warfare against trade rather than territory. As the natural resource of a weaker against a stronger maritime power, privateering could be a potent weapon in the war against an enemy's commerce. It relied on privately-owned and armed ships of war acting first, as a substitute for, and then as an adjunct to, a state navy. Without a national fleet sovereigns were unable to police their own shores, let alone foreign seas. Changing alliances and frequent wars left maritime trade vulnerable to attack from enemy vessels. But, despite its expedience, the use of privateers as naval auxiliaries presented a sovereign with certain difficulties. A privateer crew's lack of discipline, over-enthusiasm, deliberate misinterpretation of regulations, or any of a number of transgressions against neutral shipping could provoke a state into declaring war. To prevent this, and ensure that the crown maintained an interest in the prizes, Britain passed a series of acts and orders-in-council over the years to regulate privateer activities. As William McFee points out, it is no coincidence that the laws of admiralty developed in the seventeenth century when privateering came of age.[5]

---

[4]For an explanation of the causes of the war, see Reginald Horsman, "The Conquest of Canada, a Tactical Objective," in Bradford Perkins, ed., *The Causes of the War of 1812* (New York, 1962), 100, and Kate Caffrey, *The Lion and the Union: The Anglo-American War 1812-1815* (London, 1978), 177. Canadian historian, George F. Stanley, *The War of 1812 - Land Operations* (Toronto, 1983), 12, attributes the War of 1812 to a clash between British insensitivity and American over-sensitivity resulting from the American Revolution.

[5]William McFee, *The Law of the Sea* (Philadelphia, 1950), 79.

Unfortunately for the business of privateering, many of the early practitioners under Queen Elizabeth I operated on their own account rather than the crown's. Their unsavoury reputation for piratical captures and the political problems they created prejudiced history's subsequent view of privateering. Despite the excellent work of many maritime historians, piracy and privateering remain confused in the popular mind. The result has been an ill-informed and incorrect perception of privateering as no more than legalized piracy. In fact, by the end of the eighteenth century, there was almost universal recognition that privateering was not only a legitimate pursuit in time of war, but a perfectly respectable one for members of mercantile society.

The inability of land-based courts to legislate beyond national boundaries frustrated attempts by maritime nations to protect and regulate their seaborne commerce. Issues such as seamen's wages, shipping contracts, insurance, salvage, fishing rights, and indemnity for loss at sea required laws that were internationally recognized and accepted. Nations also needed legal recourse against pirates, since "attacks upon seaborne trade were a persistent and important feature of the Atlantic empire established by European maritime powers in the early modern era."[6] Over time, the concept of international maritime law and the admiralty courts that administered it laid the foundation for Britain's role as a maritime and colonial power.

Prize law developed within the broad range of admiralty jurisdiction to govern the disposition of foreign property taken at sea. The difference between piratical seizure of merchant shipping and legal capture of a prize of war could often be extremely fine. The undisciplined behaviour of many early privateers resulted in abuses that tainted the reputations of both privateers and prizemaking. Once prize courts were universally recognized as the only way to determine whether a prize was "good and lawful" or not, the practice of privateering regained its legitimacy.

Britain's numerous eighteenth-century wars exported the concept of privateering to her American possessions. The struggle for sea power in the period involved denying the enemy access to cargoes of raw materials that would enable him to wage war.[7] By means of easily-obtained letters of marque, privately-owned colonial commerce raiders were encouraged to seize enemy merchantmen. An effective admiralty court system legally able to award prizes to their captors regularized the practice of privateering. Popular accounts of the periodic condemnation of valuable prizes in the press inspired would-be privateersmen and ensured that guerre de course would play a prominent role in future wars.

The privateers of Atlantic Canada in 1812 bore little resemblance to the Sea Dogs of the Elizabethan era. Those who owned, financed, and sailed letter of marque vessels from New Brunswick and Nova Scotia were part of a maritime community related by business and kinship. Honest and, for the most part, law-abiding, the merchants and shipowners of Atlantic Canada turned to privateering when war with the United States eliminated their regular commercial activities. Their practical combination of patriotism and profit-making continued only as long as prizemaking was commercially viable.

---

[6]David J. Starkey, "Pirates and Markets," *Research in Maritime History*, VII, (St. John's, Nfld., 1994), 59.

[7]D.P. O'Connell, *The Influence of Law on Sea Power* (Manchester, 1975), 114.

In the navy's case, national and private interests dovetailed so neatly that few questions arose concerning the legitimacy of naval prizemaking. The British shipping industry expected the navy to protect trade by clearing the seas of enemy naval vessels and letters of marque. While anxious to do their duty, Royal Navy commanders anticipated prize money just as eagerly as privateers. In comparing the motives of privateers and the Royal Navy during the War of 1812, naval historian Alfred Thayer Mahan denigrated one and exaggerated the other. He claimed: "the object of a privateer is profit by capture; to which fighting is only incidental, and where avoidable, blamable. The mission of a navy on the other hand is primarily military; and while custom permitted the immediate captor a share in the proceeds of his prizes, the taking of them was in conception not for direct gain, personal or national, but for injury to the enemy."[8] Mahan's analysis perpetuated misconceptions about both privateers and the navy that persisted for the next fifty years.

The study of prize law and the process of taking prize by both naval and private ships of war has received relatively little attention from either legal or maritime historians. Between 1897 and 1915, legal theorist R.G. Marsden compiled a series of documents explaining the evolution of English prize jurisdiction and admiralty law. His work, and the contributions of two of his legal contemporaries, E.S. Roscoe (a registrar of the British Prize Court) and H.C. Rothery, form the backbone of the present study. Although one or two legal historians took up the issue of admiralty law every decade, they all seemed to rely on Marsden for the basic interpretation of British maritime law.[9]

A similar cyclical historical spotlight focuses on privateering. During the nineteenth century, books by George Sheffield, Edgar Maclay, and former privateer George Coggleshall surveyed American privateers, while Gomer Williams chronicled the history of privateers from Liverpool, England. George Nichol's early account of privateering in Nova Scotia appeared in 1908 and was embellished by C.H.J. Snider in *Under the Red Jack* in 1927. J. Franklin Jameson first published his collection of colonial documents related to privateering and piracy in 1923. During the same period Ralph Eastman produced a booklet on New England privateers (1928), William Robinson examined Confederate privateering (1928), and Howard Chapin (1926 and 1928) surveyed privateering by Rhode Islanders during King George's War. Charles Wye Kendall's general history of privateers, *Private Men-of-War*, appeared in 1931, followed by Janet Mullins' article on privateering in Liverpool, Nova Scotia, in 1936. A study entitled *Men of Marque* by J.P. Cranwell and W.B. Crane marked the 1940s while the next decade saw Kenneth R. Andrews and H. Mouzon focus on Elizabethan privateers and South Carolina's 1812 privateers respectively. Historical interest in the War of 1812 seemed to revive in the 1960s, with the publication of Ulane Bonnel's *La France, Les*

---

[8]Alfred Thayer Mahan, *Sea Power in its Relations to the War of 1812* (Boston, 1905), II, 241.

[9]Key works on British admiralty law include: R.G. Marsden, ed., *Documents relating to Laws and Customs of the Sea*, 2 vols., (London, 1915) and *Select Pleas in the Court of Admiralty*, I, The Court of Admiralty of the West, A.D. 1390-1404, and II, The High Court of Admiralty, A.D. 1547-1602 (London, 1897); E.S. Roscoe, *A History of the English Prize Court* (London, 1924); H.C. Rothery, *Prize Droits* (London, 1915). A recent publication for the Selden Society by M.J. Pritchard and D.E.C. Yale, eds., *Hale and Fleetwood on Admiralty Jurisdiction* (London, 1993) has a very useful introduction on the history of admiralty law, but does not deal with prize jurisdiction.

États-Unis et la guerre de course (1797-1815), one of the first major studies of privateering in an international economic context, along with several fine papers on eighteenth-century French, Dutch, and English privateering traditions by J.S. Bromley. Later works by Joyce Harman and Melvin Jackson dealt only with American privateering and focused on the pre- and post-Revolutionary periods respectively.[10]

The 1970s saw the first serious revival of historical interest in privateering typified by the reissue of Jameson's colonial documents nearly fifty years after their original publication. James G. Lydon's *Pirates, Privateers, and Profits* and Captain Donald Macintyre's *The Privateers* fuelled popular interest in privateering. In 1975, participants at the Tenth International Congress for Maritime History in San Francisco, California, presented papers on numerous aspects of privateering and piracy. Among the speakers were Kenneth Andrews, Ulane Bonnel, J.S. Bromley, Jaap R. Bruijn, Patrick Crowhurst, James Lydon, Walter Minchinton, and David Walker, whose papers inspired subsequent research on privateering throughout the maritime history community. In 1977 Jerome Garitee published his landmark study of the business aspects of privateering in Baltimore during the War of 1812. In 1978, John Leefe published a small book on the privateers of Atlantic Canada, with special emphasis on the War of 1812. Patrick Crowhurst's major work on French privateering appeared in 1989, followed closely by David J. Starkey's *British Privateering Enterprise* and Carl E. Swanson's study of

---

[10]Prior to the Second World War, the most comprehensive study of British privateering covering the 1812-15 period was Gomer Williams, *History of the Liverpool Privateers* (London, 1897). For an insight into American privateering activities in various periods and places see George Coggleshall, *The American Privateers* (New York, 1861); William P. Sheffield, *Rhode Island Privateers and Privateersmen* (Newport, R.I., 1883); Edgar Stanton Maclay, *A History of American Privateers* (New York, 1899); J. Franklin Jameson, ed., *Privateering and Piracy in the Colonial Period: Illustrative Documents* (1923; reprint, New York, 1970); Ralph Eastman, *Some Famous Privateers of New England* (Boston, 1928); William Morrison Robinson, Jr., *The Confederate Privateers* (1928; reprint, Columbia, S.C., 1990); Howard M. Chapin, *Privateering in King George's War, 1739-1748* (Providence, R.I., 1928) and *Rhode Island Privateers in King George's War, 1739-1748* (Providence, R.I., 1926); Charles Wye Kendall, *Private Men-of-War* (London, 1931); and W.B. Crane and J.P. Cranwell, *Men of Marque* (New York, 1940). The relatively few authors examining Canadian privateering include George E.E. Nichols, "Notes on Nova Scotia Privateers," *Nova Scotia Historical Society*, XX, (1908; reprint, Halifax, N.S., 1981), 111-152; C.H.J. Snider, *Under the Red Jack* (Toronto, 1927); Janet E. Mullins, *Liverpool Privateering, 1756-1815* (1936; reprint, Liverpool, N.S., 1996); *Some Liverpool Chronicles*. (1941; reprint, Liverpool, N.S., 1980), and "The Liverpool Packet," (n.d.; reprint, Liverpool, N.S., 1966). Between 1950 and 1970, Kenneth R. Andrews published some important work on Elizabethan privateering including *Elizabeth Privateering: English Privateering During the Spanish War, 1585-1603* (Cambridge, 1964). In 1961, Ulane Bonnel created new interest in privateering with *La France, Les États-Unis et la guerre de course (1797-1815)* (Paris, 1961). J.S. Bromley published a number of articles on eighteenth-century privateering and naval topics between 1950 and 1986, which were subsequently collected in *Corsairs and Navies, 1660-1770* (London, 1987). Works on American privateering in this period included: Harold Alwyn, *Privateers of Charleston in the War of 1812* (Charleston, S.C., 1954); Joyce Harman, *Trade and Privateering in Spanish Florida, 1732-1763* (St. Augustine, Fla., 1969), and Melvin H. Jackson, *Privateers in Charleston, 1793-1796* (Washington, 1969).

eighteenth-century American privateers, *Predators and Prizes*. The present work owes a debt to all these historians, and many more.[11]

There is no doubt that England's restrictive Navigation Acts generated increasing friction with seagoing American commerce between 1803 and 1812, as Britain and France sought to cripple each other's colonial economy with a series of embargoes and anti-trade acts. In 1806 Britain ordered a blockade of Europe. France retaliated with the Berlin Decree of January 1807 forbidding any ship visiting a British port to enter a French harbour. Britain countered in November with an order-in-council extending the blockade and requiring neutral ships (including American vessels) to clear from a British port, obtain a licence, and pay duties. Napoleon's Milan Decrees of December 1807 threatened neutral vessels with confiscation for complying with the British regulations. As a neutral nation, the United States was caught in the middle. In 1807, in response to the virtual elimination of the American carrying trade, President Thomas Jefferson had Congress enact a fourteen-month embargo against Britain. Unfortunately for Jefferson, American trade suffered serious disruption. Economic depression deepened in the northeastern states while British trade escaped unscathed. Escalating Anglo-American commercial antagonism allowed the pro-war lobby in the United States to focus growing public resentment against Britain rather than France.[12]

Britain's conflict with Napoleon in Europe finally sparked into war in North America in 1812. For Britain, an overseas war meant stretching tight resources and lines of communication to the breaking point. For America, it was a matter of pride and self-identification. But for the Canadians in Nova Scotia and New Brunswick, the War of 1812 presented a golden opportunity to capitalize on declining American markets. In the pre-war round of embargoes and non-importation acts between Britain and France, American merchants, ship-owners, and seamen found themselves squeezed out of their regular avenues of trade. The maritime merchants of Halifax and Saint John were more than happy to fill the vacuum left by the United States in the triangular trade between Great Britain, North America, and the West Indies.

---

[11]Those who kept American privateering traditions alive included James Lydon. *Pirates, Privateers, and Profits* (Upper Saddle River, N.J., 1970); Capt. Donald Macintyre, *The Privateers* (London, 1975); Jerome R. Garitee, *The Republic's Private Navy: The American Privateering Business as Practiced by Baltimore during the War of 1812* (Middletown, Conn., 1977); and Carl E. Swanson, *Predators and Prizes: American Privateering and Imperial Warfare, 1739-1748* (Columbia, S.C., 1991). International interest in privateering and prize was piqued after the publication of papers from the Commission Internationale d'Histoire Maritime. *Course et piraterie: Études présentées à la Commission Internationale d'Histoire Maritime à l'occasion de son XVe colloque international pendant le XIVe Congrès International des Sciences historiques* (San Francisco, août 1975). 2 vols. (Paris, 1975). Patrick Crowhurst published a thorough examination of French privateering activity in *The French War on Trade: Privateering 1793-1815* (Brookfield, Conn., 1989). David J. Starkey's study, *British Privateering Enterprise in the Eighteenth Century* (Exeter, 1990), applied computerized data analysis to British privateering with excellent results. The sole work on Canadian privateering, prior to F. Kert's work in the 1980s, was John Leefe, *The Atlantic Privateers* (Halifax, 1978).

[12]For a discussion of the events leading to Jefferson's embargo see Donald R. Hickey, *The War of 1812: A Forgotten Conflict* (Urbana, Ill., 1989). J.C.A. Stagg offered the political background to the War of 1812 from a Republican standpoint in *Mr. Madison's War: Politics, Diplomacy, and Warfare in the Early American Republic, 1783-1830* (Princeton, N.J., 1983).

In June 1812, neither side was in a position to undertake a naval war. Financially and militarily overextended after nearly twenty years of conflict with France, Britain could ill afford the men and resources necessary for a war in North America. Similarly, American coffers were far from full, the navy had been left to rot after the Revolution by the same southern states who now supported the war, while the communities closest to the Canadian border were prepared to use fair means or foul to maintain business as usual. In 1811 Britain had over 1,000 warships, seventy percent of them in commission, but only twenty-seven could be spared for the North American station.[13] Moreover, all but one ship-of-the-line usually departed for Bermuda from November to July leaving Canada's poorly-defended maritime provinces vulnerable to attack.[14]

The United States Navy, on the other hand, had 150 vessels, no ships-of-the-line, and only seven frigates, several of them dating from the American Revolutionary War. American naval strategy was based on Thomas Jefferson's gunboat system. These were small vessels, variously rigged, with a crew of twenty and a couple of small cannon. Compared to the $30,000 to $40,000 cost of a frigate, a gunboat could be launched for a few thousand dollars.[15] A contemporary analysis reprinted in Niles' *Weekly Register* recommended that the American navy be either enlarged or laid by.

Preoccupied with fighting Napoleon in Europe, and anxious to defuse mounting tensions in America, Britain finally repealed her orders-in-council on 16 June 1812. Unfortunately, the slow communications of the day prevented the news from reaching President Madison in time to forestall his 18 June Declaration of War. Whether the United States would have reconsidered going to war if Britain had acted sooner is a moot point. Certainly, the decision divided the country and left the New England states (most likely to be affected by the war) soundly opposed to it.[16]

According to international law, a declaration of war had to be enacted before a nation could proclaim a prize act to regulate the capture of enemy shipping by naval or private armed vessels. Without such an act, the Admiralty could not issue letters of marque to would-be privateers, nor could the vice-admiralty court begin dispensing maritime justice concerning prize. Britain's initial reluctance to declare war denied the merchants and shipowners of New Brunswick and Nova Scotia a means of avenging their losses against American privateers, who had begun taking prizes the day war was

---

[13]H. Niles, ed., *The Weekly Register*, (Baltimore, 7 Sept. 1811). Published every Tuesday in the city of Baltimore, Maryland, from 1 Sept. 1811, *Niles Weekly Register* offered readers a selection of articles from various American and foreign newspapers, shipping news, advertisements, and editorial comment throughout the War of 1812.

[14]Walter Ronald Copp, "Military Activities in Nova Scotia During the War of 1812," *Collections of the Nova Scotia Historical Society*, XXIV (1938), 59.

[15]W.B. Crane and J.P. Cranwell, *Men of Marque*, 26. See also Gene A. Smith, *"For the Purposes of Defense": The Politics of the Jeffersonian Gunboat Program* (Newark, Del., 1995).

[16]American support for the War of 1812 was strongest in the agrarian states of the South, which had traditionally been opposed to naval defence. J. Mackay Hitsman, *The Incredible War of 1812* (Toronto, 1965), 39-42.

declared. Nova Scotia's Lieutenant Governor, Sir John Coape Sherbrooke, tried to resolve this problem by issuing his own commissions. The subsequent repercussions entangled the Halifax Court of Vice-Admiralty and the British High Court of Admiralty in legal wrangles that outlasted the war.[17]

The privateering ventures undertaken by the merchants, investors, and sailors of New Brunswick and Nova Scotia during the War of 1812 followed six centuries of British practice. Legislation and usage had defined the relationship between the admiralty courts and private vessels commissioned to capture enemy commerce. The British government's rigorous efforts to eliminate piracy and regulate the adjudication of prize provided her colonies with a legal framework within which to operate. Thanks to a firmly established vice-admiralty court system in North America, experienced privateers had become well acquainted with the prize court process.

Although the objective of privateering was the capture and condemnation of enemy shipping, the transfer of ownership via a prize court had economic rather than strategic implications for both the victim and captor. Once the limited firepower of private armed vessels could no longer match a naval broadside, privateering lost its value as an offensive weapon. Although, as a means of waging war against an enemy's commerce by harassing trade and interrupting communications, privateering had a nuisance value that could be offensive in the extreme.

Lured by visions of windfall profits, merchants, investors, ship owners, and sailors looked to privateering as a commercial opportunity, an outlet for investment, a means of defence managed at the local level, and gainful – even lucrative – employment in an otherwise flat economy. In addition, "privateering employed the fishermen and all those who depended upon shipping, taught daring seamanship, and strengthened our maritime aptitude and tradition." Alongside its redeeming social, economic and military values, privateering also paid better wages, and was "safer and more fun than the army or navy."[18]

Unlike the Royal Navy, privateers could not be obliged to attack enemy vessels; in fact, most of them took great care to avoid combat situations. This was not a lack of courage on their part, but rather a realization that exposing themselves or their prizes to damage could result in time-consuming repairs ashore and reduce their profits. As Cranwell states, "hard knocks, blood and glory" had small commercial value for an investor. While battle honours may have held an appeal for naval commanders, privateersmen kept an eye on the ledger.[19]

---

[17]Sir John Coape Sherbrooke (1764-1830) served as lieutenant governor of Nova Scotia from 1811 to 1816. The owners and crew of the privateer *Liverpool Packet* had to wait five to six years for their share of prize money from their first nineteen prizes.

[18]Samuel Eliot Morison, *The Maritime History of Massachusetts, 1783-1860* (Boston, 1921), 29 and 199. See also John K. Mahon, *The War of 1812* (Gainesville, Fla., 1972), 24.

[19]Crane and Cranwell, *Men of Marque*, 19. Naval historians such as Mahan perpetuated this naval prejudice against privateers, acknowledging their role as commerce raiders as little more than a nuisance force in any maritime conflict. Alfred Thayer Mahan, *The Influence of Sea Power upon History, 1660-1783*, (1890; reprint, London, 1965), 132.

The War of 1812 ended much the way it began – haphazardly and half-heartedly. President Madison did not approve the Treaty of Ghent, signed 24 December 1814, until 16 February 1815. On 8 January 1815 the Battle of New Orleans gave America its most decisive victory – two weeks after the war was officially over! After three years of war over free trade, impressment, territorial issues, and assorted affronts to American dignity, the peace treaty "provided for little more than the cessation of hostilities, return of prisoners and resumption of the territorial status quo ante."[20] It is interesting to note that the War of 1812, ostensibly fought under the banner of Free Trade and Sailors' Rights, concluded with a treaty that ignored both issues. Unprepared and under-resourced, neither side could have endured a war of attrition. Britain was dependent on American foodstuffs for her troops in Spain and North America, and the United States needed British manufactured goods. In fact, it was fortunate for both sides that the citizens of New England "had their hands but not their hearts in the war."[21]

Although the peace treaty failed to identify a victor, the people of Atlantic Canada actually profited most from the war. Buoyed by wartime speculation, military contracts, a steady supply of prize cargoes, and a populace willing to engage in trade under licence or under cover, the provinces of New Brunswick and Nova Scotia prospered. Instrumental in their success was the vice-admiralty court system that streamlined the judicial procedure and enabled men such as Judge Alexander Croke, Richard Uniacke, and scores of privateersmen to fill judicial and political coffers as well as their own.

The War of 1812 provides the historical context for this study of prizemaking by both naval and privateer vessels. In the Public Archives of Canada, the records of the Nova Scotia Court of Vice-Admiralty in Halifax revealed a fascinating and previously untapped vein of historical data on the prizemaking activities of both naval and privateer vessels of the period. The privateering experience of the British colonies of New Brunswick and Nova Scotia illustrates the successful transformation of prizemaking from the seizure of enemy ships and cargoes by semi-piratical amateurs to a well-orchestrated legally-sanctioned process undertaken by experienced merchant vessels and crews. Just as the capture of prizes often redeemed the fortunes of their captors, it is hoped that the present study will redeem the reputation of prizemaking.

---

[20]Major James Ripley Jacobs and Glenn Tucker, *War of 1812* (New York, 1969), 191.

[21]W.M. Whitelaw, *The Maritimes and Canada before Confederation* (Toronto, 1966), 59.

Chapter 1
Reluctant Enemies

Sharing the same colonial roots and inextricably linked by both trade and tradition, the provinces of New Brunswick and Nova Scotia were America's most unlikely enemies. Not only were they near neighbours, but many inhabitants of Atlantic Canada were former New Englanders, whose loyalty to King George III during the American Revolution had forced them to relocate northwards. While continuing to support Great Britain politically, many displaced merchants maintained their business connections with the United States through a variety of stratagems, not the least of which was smuggling.

Thinly populated and poorly endowed with agricultural resources, the Atlantic provinces traditionally relied on fishing, lumbering, and the coasting trade for their livelihood. Unable to produce enough food for their own inhabitants, New Brunswick and Nova Scotia enjoyed a mutually beneficial trade with their American neighbours, exchanging food for British manufactured goods. This traditional economic interdependence refused to recognize national borders in spite of political manoeuvring elsewhere in Europe. When the War of 1812 threatened to interrupt their longstanding commercial relationship, inhabitants on both sides turned to licences, smuggling, and subterfuge to maintain the flow of trade. Throughout the war, military contractors at Halifax had little difficulty purchasing American goods, while British manufactures imported by Halifax merchants continued to find their way across the border. Once war was declared, Lieutenant Governor Sherbrooke of Nova Scotia was quick to issue licences enabling provincial merchants to import emergency supplies of foodstuffs from any American port. As long as their so-called enemies were willing to pay, American shipmasters had no intention of allowing anyone to starve. Only the most rigorous patriots found anything odd about American farmers supplying the British fleet that was blockading their coasts.

This chapter focuses on the economic, political, and social forces that initiated such an unpopular war and its ultimate failure to engage the maritime and merchant interests for whom it was declared. Forced into reluctant enmity, the maritime communities of New Brunswick and Nova Scotia sought to circumvent or subvert the war by fair means or foul.

Causes of the War of 1812

Unnecessary, unpopular, and inconclusive, the War of 1812 was declared in response to American political and economic agendas related to national ambition, regional self-interest, and political opportunism. A.T. Mahan roots the origins of the war "in the principles governing commercial, colonial and naval policy, accepted almost universally prior to the French Revolution." Later historians, such as A.L. Burt, Julius Pratt, and George Rogers Taylor have identified at least six reasons for the war: Britain's violation of American rights to uninterrupted commerce on the high seas, impressment of American seamen, incitement and arming of Indians on the American frontier, American annexationist ambitions for Florida and Canada, conviction that Britain was somehow responsible for the economic depression in the American South, and finally, accumulated British insults to American honour.[1] The official American declaration of war listed four reasons for war: impressment, British harassment of neutral American commerce, blockade of United States ports, and restriction of American trade through orders-in-council. While none can be considered more than a serious provocation, taken together they generated sufficient political heat to ignite a war.

Since the seventeenth century, Britain had relied on a series of Navigation Acts to defend her carrying trade. These acts protected British merchants from foreign competition by ensuring that foreign goods from Asia, Africa, and America reached British ports in British bottoms.[2] Especially resented by the American colonies, many of the most restrictive acts were regularly ignored or circumvented. Having won independence from Great Britain, the United States refused to recognize any British or French trade injunctions and decrees that threatened to interfere with America's right to trade as neutrals. President Jefferson's attempt to impose a retaliatory embargo against British ships in 1807 not only failed to hinder British shipping, but actually caused severe economic hardship in the northeastern states and contributed to their lack of enthusiasm for war.

British impressment of sailors right off the decks of American ships outraged the American public. In June 1807 the two nations edged to the brink of war when the captain of HMS *Leopard* forcibly removed four Royal Navy deserters (one British-born and three Americans) from aboard the U.S. *Chesapeake* just off the American coast. Humiliated and furious, Americans in nearby Norfolk rioted, while the outcry against Britain in the rest of the country was violent enough to cause concern within naval circles. In August, Vice- Admiral of the White, Sir George Berkeley, wrote to Lord Bathurst, president of Britain's Board of Trade and Plantations, advocating a surprise naval attack on New York City. He argued that destroying 12,000 - 14,000 American fishing boats returning from Newfoundland and Labrador would "prevent their seamen from subsequently becoming privateers!" To the credit of both sides, cooler heads prevailed.[3]

The accusation that Britain was inciting the Indians along the frontier likely relied more on propaganda than proof. Although relatively few in number, the Indians

---

[1]Alfred Thayer Mahan, *Sea Power in its Relation to the War of 1812* (Boston, 1905), I, 1. See A.L. Burt, "Issues and the Evolution of Causes of the War of 1812," Julius W. Pratt, "Expansionists of 1812," and George Rogers Taylor, "Agrarian Discontent in the Mississippi Valley Preceding the War of 1812," in George Rogers Taylor, ed., *The War of 1812: Past Justifications and Present Interpretations* (Boston, 1963), vi.

[2]There were approximately two thousand acts affecting British trade by 1820, added to and adapted from the original navigation laws dating from 1660. Marion Gilroy, "Customs Fees in Nova Scotia," *Canadian Historical Review*, XVII (1936), 9.

[3]J. Mackay Hitsman, *Safeguarding Canada 1763-1871* (Toronto, 1968), 68. Two of the four men taken from the *Chesapeake*, John Strachan and Daniel Martin, were eventually restored to their ship after five years. One sailor died in prison, and one was hanged as a deserter. William S. Dudley, ed., *The Naval War of 1812, A Documentary History*, I, (Washington, D.C., 1985), 190, hereafter cited as *Naval Docs*.

in the Great Lakes region were reputed to be fierce warriors. Indicative of Britain's healthy respect for the native population was Lord Castlereagh's opinion: "We are to consider not so much their use as allies, as their destructiveness if enemies." Certainly, as Lord Bathurst confided in a letter to Sir John Coape Sherbrooke, he preferred not to involve the Indians in the present war, but he was afraid that if the Indians did not fight for them, they might fight against them.[4] As American expansion into the Ohio Valley pushed the Indian population farther westward, many native leaders realized that sooner or later they would have to fight for their lives. John Randolph of Virginia acknowledged American responsibility for inciting the Indians: "It is our own thirst for territory that has driven these sons of nature to desperation."[5] This did not stop British strategists from exploiting the very real American fear of Indian attacks to their own advantage.

Similarly, the extent of American annexationist designs on both Florida and Canada remains unclear. In a speech to the Congress in December 1811, Randolph rejected maritime rights and proclaimed his support for American expansionism. He urged, "Canada! Canada! Canada! Not a syllable about Halifax which unquestionably should be our great object in a war for maritime security."[6]

Canadian historians such as Thomas Raddall and G.F.G. Stanley interpret the American attitude to the conquest of Canada as a bit of unfinished business left over from the American Revolution. On the American side, historian Julius Pratt counters that Florida, not Canada, was the real focus of American expansion. The South had agrarian, commercial, and strategic reasons for annexing Florida, while the acquisition of Canada, according to the correspondence of Secretary of State James Monroe was something "he never really desired or expected." In Mahan's opinion, Monroe saw the invasion of Canada not as an object of the war, but as a means of ending it. J.C.A. Stagg's study of the Madison administration suggests "the purpose of the War of 1812 was to break various manifestations of the British navigation system." Capturing Canada would restrict British access to raw materials and provide the United States with an economic lever to force Britain to respect America's neutral rights.[7]

In 1811, the entire population of Canada comprised some 500,000 inhabitants, roughly seven percent of the United States' population. Widely dispersed and weakly

---

[4]Kate Caffrey, *The Lion and the Union: The Anglo-American War of 1812-1815* (London, 1978), 126. John K. Mahon, *The War of 1812* (Gainesville, Fla., 1972), 15, estimates warrior strength at 1,500. *Report of the Department of Public Archives*, "Appendix: Nova Scotia State Papers," Bathurst to Sherbrooke, [No. 6, 206, 26 Aug. 1812, 128], (Ottawa, 1946), 118-189.

[5]Thomas H. Raddall, *The Path of Destiny: Canada from the British Conquest to Home Rule: 1763-1850* (Toronto, 1957), 182.

[6]Donald P. Hickey, *The War of 1812 - A Forgotten Conflict* (Urbana, Ill., 1989), 72, argues that Randolph exaggerated the importance of territorial issues over maritime ones.

[7]Raddall, *Path of Destiny*, xx, and Pratt, "Expansionists," in G.R. Taylor, ed., *Past Justifications*, 35, and Mahan, *War of 1812*, I, 293. G.F.G. Stanley, *The War of 1812 - Land Operations* (Toronto, 1983), 35, claims America declared war "to satisfy national honour and to acquire control over Canada." J.C.A. Stagg, *Mr. Madison's War: Politics, Diplomacy, and Warfare in the Early American Republic, 1783-1830* (Princeton, N.J., 1983), 5-7.

defended, Canadian settlements must have seemed like easy pickings to the annexationists. Yet the New England states, which stood to gain the most from any territorial expansion, were unable to recruit enough militia men. On the day war was declared, the governor of Massachusetts proclaimed a day of fasting, and both he and the governor of Connecticut flatly refused to furnish state military quotas.[8] Some, who refused to bear arms themselves, hired others to fight their battles for them. In 1813, one man complained to his brother: "this war is two hundred dollars out of pocket to me. I was drafted for a minute man and I have to hire a man in my name and give him five dollars per month beside our government give him seventy dollars in cash as soon as he got home."[9] Opting to trade goods rather than blows with their American neighbours, Canadian entrepreneurs undertook to conduct their business with as little interference from the war as possible.

An even more specious cause for war is the claim by Southern War Hawks that war with England would somehow "remedy commercial and agrarian distress." If, as Kate Caffrey points out, British markets absorbed at least 80 percent of Southern cotton production until 1811, the chances of a war with Britain improving trade were slight. Moreover, the cost of a prolonged war and possible defeat made the argument for war as cure for the South's economic ills even less valid.[10]

The last, and most likely, cause of the War of 1812, was Britain's repeated affronts to American pride. G.F.G. Stanley claims that the twin legacies of the American Revolutionary War, namely, "callousness in Britain and oversensitivity in the United States" led to the War of 1812. George Coggleshall, an American privateersman, articulated the patriotic rhetoric of the period when he stated, "The mad ambition, the lust of power, and commercial avarice of Great Britain, arrogating to herself complete dominion of the ocean and exercising over it an unbounded and lawless tyranny, have left to neutral nations an alternative only between the base surrender of their rights and a manly vindication of them."[11] President Madison and the pro-war propagandists argued that to continue allowing British violation of American freedom on the high seas undermined the independence for which the American Revolution had been fought and reduced Americans to no more than "colonists and vassals." Appeals to common sense, from the newspaper or the pulpit, failed to quell the tide of righteous indignation.

Ironically, by 18 June, when Congress declared war, British diplomatic efforts had already eliminated the first two ostensible causes of the war. Although the orders-in-council restricting American trade had finally been repealed two days earlier, by then, Anglo-American relations had deteriorated to the point that Congress was unwilling to

---

[8]Hitsman, *Safeguarding Canada*, 88. J. MacKay Hitsman, *The Incredible War of 1812* (Toronto, 1965), 44, places the American population at 7.5 million. See also Mahon, *War of 1812*, 32, 15.

[9]PAC, RG 8, IV, *Hero*, Edward Quinsy Weeks to his brother, 12 Nov. 1813.

[10]Caffrey, *The Lion and the Union*, 50. Norman K. Risjord, "1812: Conservatives, War Hawks and the Nation's Honor," in Taylor, ed., *Past Justifications*, 107.

[11]Stanley, *Land Operations*, 12. George Coggleshall, *The American Privateers* (New York, 1861), xxiv. Also Mahan, *War of 1812*, I, 41.

relent. Facing re-election, Madison needed the support of the anti-British faction in Congress, which contributed to the American decision to declare war.[12]

Popular Opinion

Public reaction to war in Britain and the United States mirrored the political uncertainty. Despite the United States' aggressive posturing, the British government was convinced that Congress would stop short of actual hostilities. Madison's war message caught both Britain and her North American colonies by such surprise that the Royal Navy was not put on alert until late July. Even then, Admiralty orders were to capture and detain American vessels in port, but not to proceed against them in court.[13] In August, Lord Bathurst advised Nova Scotia Lieutenant Governor Sir John Coape Sherbrooke, "His Royal Highness still retains an anxious hope that our amicable relations with the United States may shortly be restored on a permanent basis."[14] Britain clung to the hope of negotiating a diplomatic settlement until 13 October 1812 when Parliament finally issued an official declaration of war.

From mid-June until October Governor Sherbrooke walked a tightrope between war and peace. On 1 July 1812, he issued a public proclamation containing the American declaration of war. This was followed three days later by a second proclamation urging residents of New Brunswick and Nova Scotia "to abstain from molesting the inhabitants living on the shores of the United States" as long as they refrained from similar acts of aggression. In a letter the next day to Lord Liverpool, British secretary of state for the Department of War and the Colonies, Sherbrooke explained that he hoped to encourage "a friendly disposition which appears to manifest itself in some of the states in our more immediate neighbourhood." In Baltimore, *Niles Weekly Register* indignantly reprinted Sherbrooke's second proclamation under the headline "TO ENCOURAGE TREASON."[15]

---

[12]Stanley, *Land Operations*, 7, quotes a letter from Major General Hunter to Lord Liverpool that speculates that declaring war was Madison's "only chance of remaining in power."

[13]In passing judgement on a petition from Admiral Sir John Borlase Warren, his successor, Vice-Admiral Herbert Sawyer, and others regarding such captures, Judge Croke of the vice-admiralty court in Halifax pronounced that the 31 July order-in-council directed His Majesty's ships to bring in American ships, but preserve them and their cargoes until an official declaration of war. James Stewart, *Reports of Cases argued and determined in the Court of Vice-Admiralty at Halifax in Nova Scotia from the commencement of the War in 1803 to the end of the year 1813 in the time of Alexander Croke LLD., Judge of that Court* (London, 1814), 328.

[14]W. Wood, ed., *Select British Documents of the Canadian War of 1812* (Toronto: Champlain Society, XIII, 1920. Reprint, New York: Greenwood Press, 1968), 232, Bathurst to Sherbrooke, 10 Aug. 1812.

[15]*Nova Scotia Royal Gazette*, 1 July 1812, also 3 July 1812. Margaret Ells, ed., *A Calendar of Official Correspondence and Legislative Papers, Nova Scotia, 1802-1815* [Vol. 62, doc. 6], (Halifax, N.S., 1936) 260. Colonial affairs were the responsibility of the secretary of state for war and the colonies until the creation of the Colonial Office in 1820. Lord Liverpool succeeded Lord Castlereagh in this position in late 1809. In 1812, Castlereagh was succeeded by Henry, third Earl Bathurst, who held the position until 1827. *Niles Weekly Register*, 1 Aug. 1812.

A review of newspaper articles published in England, America, and Nova Scotia preceding and just after Madison's call for war reveals dismay, confusion, and bravado among the respective citizenry. American editorialists blamed the war on the cumulative effects of British restrictions on America's neutral trade, aggravated by the Royal Navy's policy of impressment. Popular resentment was fuelled by articles, such as the one in *Niles Weekly Register* in April 1812, that claimed there were 6,257 known cases of pressed American seamen listed in state documents. The writer went on to speculate that there was not a Royal Navy vessel afloat without an impressed American sailor or two.[16] This ongoing affront to American sovereignty was a major propaganda issue for those in favour of war.

Britain's justification for its actions was reflected in an article in the *London Courier* of 5 June 1812, accusing the United States of inciting her citizens to war with the following: "we have not provoked it, unless it be called provoking to resort to acts of retaliation against an enemy and refuse to withdraw them until the enemy have withdrawn the measures that rendered them necessary."[17] London's *Morning Post* in 1812 confidently assured its readers that "a war of a very few months, without creating to England the expense of a single additional ship would be sufficient to convince America of her folly by a necessary chastizement of her insolence and audacity."[18] On a more sober note, the *Connecticut Courant* bemoaned a war "commenced in folly ... to be carried on in madness ... and unless speedily terminated, will end in ruin."[19] An anonymous citizen of Halifax expressed similar puzzlement in a letter to the *Nova Scotia Royal Gazette* within the first few weeks of the war: "It is so evidently unnecessary, impolitic, unnatural and wicked, that there is still a difficulty in realizing it as the solemn act of a deliberate body."[20] Although patriots on both sides supported their leaders, most merchants north and south of the border had no intention of abandoning long-standing and mutually profitable commercial arrangements for the sake of a war they did not want.

The Atlantic Provinces to 1812

Unlike the American colonies, which had originated as proprietary colonies or corporate grants, commercial units, or religious refuges, Nova Scotia was established as a Crown Colony in 1749 for purely strategic purposes, to offset the French presence in

---

[16]E.B. Potter, ed., *Sea Power - A Naval History* (New York, 1960), 207. Potter suggests that as many as 10,000 American sailors were pressed during the Napoleonic Wars. *Niles Weekly Register*, 18 Apr. 1812.

[17]*Niles Weekly Register*, 1 Aug. 1812. Niles probably reprinted this article from a London paper expressly to arouse his readers.

[18]Stanley Bonnet, *The Price of Admiralty* (London, 1968), 22.

[19]Caffrey, *The Lion and the Union*, 147.

[20]*NS Royal Gazette*, 15 July 1812.

Louisbourg. Derided by Edmund Burke shortly after its establishment as "an ill-thriven, hard-visaged and ill-favoured brat," Nova Scotia soon developed a viable maritime economy and a colonial infrastructure that included a legislative assembly and a vice-admiralty court.[21] When New Brunswick was created in 1784 to accommodate American loyalists seeking political refuge under the Union Jack, it too acquired a provincial legislature whose first session was held in January 1786.[22]

Closely linked by commerce and kinship to the northeastern United States, the inhabitants of New Brunswick and Nova Scotia faced the prospect of an Anglo-American war with mixed feelings. On one hand, there were the inevitable opportunities for those who were willing to risk their ships or their capital in blockade running, privateering, or trading with the enemy under licence; on the other, war threatened smaller entrepreneurs whose livelihoods in the fishing and coastal trade were vulnerable to attack by American privateers. For most Atlantic Canadians, however, there was little to fear in terms of an American attack because the northeastern states opposed the war and refused to undertake offensive operations by land.[23]

Protected by the Royal Navy, commercial interdependence, and geography, New Brunswickers and Nova Scotians regarded the war with a certain insouciance. A month after the war was declared, Elkanah Morton, a veteran of the American Revolutionary War, expressed his concerns to Nova Scotia's deputy provincial secretary. While convinced that the Americans were far more likely to smuggle than fight, he did fear the depredations of American privateers along the coast. Having lost a leg in the Revolution, Morton was "cordially willing to risk the other" in any way necessary![24]

Before the American Revolution there had been regular movement between the British colonies of New England and Nova Scotia. The economic opportunities in the new colony of Nova Scotia had lured New Englanders north to settle in communities like Yarmouth, Liverpool, and Halifax.[25] After the Revolution, those Americans who had remained loyal to the crown were forced to find new homes, and many joined their former compatriots in Atlantic Canada.

Simeon Perkins, a Connecticut entrepreneur who moved to the tiny Atlantic community of Liverpool in 1762, was typical of the early settlers of Nova Scotia. Enterprising and energetic, he was soon involved in shipping, trading, fishing,

---

[21] Thomas H. Raddall, *Halifax, Warden of the North* (Toronto, 1971), 76-77. Burke's criticism was part of his larger attack on the Board of Trade and Plantations made in Parliament in 1780 during the Revolutionary War.

[22] Peter Waite, Sandra Oxner, Thomas Barnes, eds., *Law in a Colonial Society: The Nova Scotia Experience* (Toronto, 1984), 1. The first 2,600 settlers in Nova Scotia were mostly veterans of the British army or navy. Brian Cuthbertson, *The Old Attorney General* (Halifax, N.S., 1980), 9.

[23] Walter Ronald Copp, "Military Activities in Nova Scotia During the War of 1812," *Collections of the Nova Scotia Historical Society*, XXIV (1938), 63.

[24] *NS Leg. Papers*, [Vol. 256, doc. 18], 269.

[25] Clement Crowell, *NovaScotiaman* (Halifax, N.S., 1979), 1. In the 1760s, New Englanders from Cape Cod and Cape Ann settled in Yarmouth.

lumbering, shipbuilding, and privateering. Perkins' diary, written over forty-five years, chronicles the early political and commercial life of Nova Scotia and provides invaluable insights into the attitudes of the day. While some of Nova Scotia's colonists may have flirted briefly with American revolutionary ideals, most, like Perkins, clung to the security of the British imperial system. Related by business or marriage to most of Liverpool's commercial elite by the time of his death in 1812, Perkins represents the vitality and versatility of Nova Scotia's mercantile community, its support for British institutions, and its strong cultural and commercial links with the United States.[26]

By 1812, Halifax was a bustling little provincial capital with schools and churches of several denominations, numerous merchant houses, a booming naval dockyard, one of the best natural harbours in North America, and scores of seasoned mariners who had sailed the Atlantic coast almost since infancy. Flush with the profits from military contracts and the sale of French prizes throughout the previous decade, Halifax's population doubled from 5,000 inhabitants around 1800 to 10,000 by 1812.

Seemingly unperturbed by an almost non-existent militia, naval protection that was only on-station from July to November, and "dilapidated" and "untenable" fortifications around the main port of Halifax, defenses that Sir George Provost had condemned in 1808 as "in such a state of ruin, as to allow nothing short of total reform,"[27] the inhabitants of Canada's Atlantic provinces looked forward to further expansion of the profitable wartime economy they had enjoyed throughout the Napoleonic Wars. Having profited handsomely from England's imperial trade policy and naval supremacy over the years, the people of New Brunswick and Nova Scotia no sooner saw war clouds gathering than they began to look for silver linings.

In both provinces mercantile considerations far outweighed political concerns. Wartime exigencies interfered as little as possible with the status quo, and commercial relations between Atlantic Canada and the northeastern United States remained generally cordial. Faced with the prospect of increased restrictions on their regular trade, shipowners examined alternative ways of supplying their regular customers on both sides of the border with foodstuffs, manufactured goods, and specie, all of which were always in short supply in a wartime economy.

The Pursuit of Trade

By June 1812, a volatile combination of politics, economics, and bruised national feelings catapulted North America into a state of war. Those enterprising merchants of New Brunswick and Nova Scotia who converted their vessels to privateers for commissioned warfare will be dealt with in a later chapter. Merchants of a less adventurous turn sought

---

[26]John Leefe, *The Atlantic Privateers* (Halifax, 1978), 18. In 1780, Perkins and William Freeman were co-owners of Liverpool's first privateer, the *Lucy*. Charles Bruce Fergusson, ed., *The Diary of Simeon Perkins 1797-1803* (Toronto, 1967), 1, xix.

[27]Ibid., *NS Leg. Papers*, [Vol. 58, doc. 6], Provost to Castlereagh, 28 May 1808, 148. Sir George Provost served as captain general, Governor in chief, vie-admiral, lieutenant governor and commander of His Majesty's forces in Upper and Lower Canada, Nova Scotia, New Brunswick, Prince Edward Island, Cape Breton, and Newfoundland during the War of 1812. Prevost was lieutenant governor of Nova Scotia from 1808 to 1811 until Sir John Coape Sherbrooke succeeded him in 1812.

to arm themselves with licences to protect their trade. Finally, there were those ready to resort to what had been "a normal by-occupation since the border was created" – smuggling.[28]

i) Smuggling

The close commercial relationships between New Brunswick and Nova Scotia entrepreneurs and their American neighbours in Vermont, New York, and Massachusetts (now Maine) had evolved through years of conspiring to evade British duties. While the Americans ultimately expressed their defiance of Britain's colonial rule in rebellion, the inhabitants of Atlantic Canada did not share the same sense of oppression. Perhaps, as Dave McIntosh's study of Canadian customs and excise suggests, people of the Maritime provinces were such skilled smugglers that imperial duties weighed much less heavily on their pockets! Certainly, according to historian Gordon Blake, "there was a notable lack of coordination of naval and customs establishments and this fact suggests that collusion between the smugglers and those whose duty it was to prevent illicit trade would not be difficult."[29]

By forcing American merchants to choose between bankruptcy and smuggling, Jefferson's Embargo Act of 1807 boosted the pre-war economy of maritime Canada from "merely prosperous to booming and buoyant."[30] Yet this prosperity was undoubtedly at the expense of New England. Samuel Eliot Morison blames the embargo for suspending half the commerce of Massachusetts, worth $15.5 million per year in freight money alone, and rendering the other half "more furtive, difficult and hazardous."[31]

In an attempt to circumvent the smuggling trade and capitalize on the commercial vacuum resulting from the closure of American markets in 1808, Nova Scotia Attorney General Richard J. Uniacke urged the Board of Trade and Plantations to open up Halifax, Shelburne, and Saint John, New Brunswick, as free ports. Not unexpectedly, an even larger smuggling network developed "with American vessels bringing provisions and fish into the free ports to exchange for British manufactures and West Indian rum and sugar."[32] So widespread was this illicit trade before the war that in April 1811 William Goodall of Nova Scotia complained to Nathaniel Atcheson, agent to the colonial committees of trade: "Unless some steps are taken to prevent the smuggling trade from the American states, we shall soon be without a customer for the

---

[28]J. Heaton, "The Erosion of Economic Warfare," in Taylor, ed., *Past Justifications*, 38.

[29]Gordon Blake, *Customs Administration in Canada* (Toronto, 1957), 29. Dave McIntosh, *The Collectors. A History of Canadian Customs and Excise* (Toronto, 1984), 34.

[30]W.S. MacNutt, *The Atlantic Provinces: The Emergence of a Colonial Society, 1712-1857* (Toronto, 1965), 131.

[31]Samuel E. Morison, *The Maritime History of Massachusetts, 1783-1860* (Boston, 1961), 188.

[32]MacNutt, *Atlantic*, 132. On 26 Oct. 1808, Halifax, Shelburne, and Saint John were designated as ports for the admission of enumerated articles. This was extended by an order-in-council on 1 Oct. 1811. St. Andrews, New Brunswick, was opened to limited trade in 1809. Cuthbertson, *Old Attorney General*, 58.

principal part of the articles that we deal in; ever since the removal of the embargo and the non-intercourse acts, great quantities of teas and all sorts of India goods ... gin, American rum and many other articles, are daily & illicitly brought into this province by the Americans as well as by British subjects residing in this country."[33]

In November 1811, a British order-in-council attempted to regularize some of this illegal commerce. It extended the 1808 Act (which allowed trade between Saint John, St. Andrews, and Halifax and any American port from which British vessels were excluded) providing that the vessel carried a customs certificate stating that the goods were imported into New Brunswick or Nova Scotia in a British ship from a British port. Similarly, American products could be imported from American ports with the appropriate documentation.[34]

Comparing import and export figures between 1807 and 1812, W.S. MacNutt calculates that although official figures for American imports from Britain dropped roughly fifty percent, actual British exports for the same period recorded a slight decline of only seven percent. According the Blake's estimates, illicit colonial importation at the end of the eighteenth century accounted for "nearly all the tea; three quarters of the wine; nine tenths of the spirits; seven eighths of the soap and candles; most of the indigo, starch, mustard, tobacco and cottons; all the nankeens, sailcloth, cordage and anchors."[35] With the cost of American flour at $3 per barrel as compared to $12 in New Brunswick, a smuggler could easily make back the $47 it cost to hire and man a boat to carry the contraband to Canadian soil. Shippers in Liverpool, Nova Scotia, openly acknowledged their preference for the free port of Saint Andrews over Saint John because of their increased likelihood of encountering American smugglers.[36]

The American-owned warehouses of Eastport, Maine, on Moose Island were not only larger than those in Saint John, New Brunswick, according to McIntosh, but more business was conducted off Moose Island in one day than went through Saint John in two months! Although British officials disputed American ownership of the island following the Peace of Amiens in 1803, New Brunswick Collector of Customs William Wanton recognized the American claim and treated the waters around Moose Island as neutral territory right up to the War of 1812. Historian W.S. MacNutt refers to Eastport, an American settlement established in 1791, as a haven for deserters from both the army and the navy, and suggests that much of New Brunswick's produce, as well as specie, found its way out of the province during the war via the channel between Moose Island

---

[33]*NS Leg. Papers*, [Vol. 62, doc. 11], 230.

[34]*Niles Weekly Register*, 21 Dec. 1811.

[35]Blake, *Customs Administration*, 29.

[36]W.S. MacNutt, *New Brunswick, A History: 1784-1867* (Toronto, 1963), 148. He cites the papers of Edward Winslow, a loyalist and judge of the New Brunswick Supreme Court.

and Campobello Island.[37] The dubious potential of Passamaquoddy Bay was certainly recognized by contemporary observers. After reconnoitring the area in 1808, a British Royal Engineer captain advised Lieutenant General Sir George Prevost that Moose Island's growing population was due to "the facility its situation affords to smuggling" and the fact that the harbour at Eastport was "within the range of Gun shot, from Campo-Bello, Deer, Marvel & Indian Islands," which were British territory. Despite the scattered presence of provincial militia units, Captain Nicolls cautioned with considerable foresight, "I do not think that much reliance should be placed on the militia of any of these islands."[38]

In the 26 October 1811 issue of the *Weekly Register*, editor Niles demanded the repeal of the non-importation law or its renaming as "An Act for the Better Encouragement of Roguery and Other Purposes," since so many goods were feloniously entering the United States via Canada, "which has prospered beyond example by it."[39] Some stratagems used by smugglers before and during the war included transferring cargoes from British to American ships in secluded coves, landing British goods on Campobello or other islands to be picked up by "fishermen," and obtaining false neutral Swedish or Spanish clearance papers to carry goods as neutrals into American ports.[40] The pilot of the licensed ship *Cuba* admitted to falsifying the ship's log to deceive American cruisers and conceal its real destination. Another wartime ruse involved having American vessels arrange to be captured by Canadian privateers or blockading forces and carried into Saint John or Halifax. There, the American owners could petition the vice-admiralty court for permission to sell the cargo to defray expenses and in this roundabout way find a market for their goods. Although illegal, such collusion was apparently so commonplace in the waters between the Maine - New Brunswick border that Stanley feels many so-called captures were likely "prearranged shipments to Maritime importers."[41]

Once war broke out, smuggling efforts redoubled to maintain the steady supply of American foodstuffs on which the Canadian colonies depended and to ensure the

---

[37]McIntosh, *Collectors*, 235-236. Moose Island is located in Passamaquoddy Bay about twenty miles from St. Andrews, New Brunswick. Raddall, *Path of Destiny*, 315, calls Eastport a "cheerful smugglers' nest." British forces under Sir Thomas Hardy captured Moose Island on 12 July 1814 during the Passamaquoddy Expedition. When offered the choice of swearing an oath of allegiance to King George III or leaving Moose Island, two-thirds of the inhabitants became British subjects. The Treaty of Ghent returned the island in Jan. 1815. See Stanley, *Land Operations*, 367-369.

[38]Wood, *Select British Documents*, I, 141, 143, Captain Gustavus Nicolls to Sir George Prevost, 30 June 1808.

[39]*Niles Weekly Register*, 26 Oct. 1811.

[40]For an example, see PAC, RG 8, IV, Vol. 81, *Diamond*, Examination of Joseph Greely, chief mate, 31 Aug. 1812.

[41]PAC, RG 8, IV, Vol. 80, *Cuba*, Examination of Henry Rider, pilot and mate, 10 June 1812. Mahon, *War of 1812*, 226. Stanley, *Land Operations*, 363. The lieutenant governor of New Brunswick finally stopped issuing letters of marque because so many of the so-called privateers were simply staging captures to obtain smuggled goods. Leefe, *Atlantic Privateers*, 46.

return flow of British manufactured goods southward. Historian Charles W. Kendall asserts that "during the war there was a tacit treaty on the Maine and New Brunswick frontier for the interchange of goods between the United States and Canada. Customs officials did not recognize it but American and British merchants did."[42] Widespread and well organized, such covert trade was not unique to North America. American seamen strove to keep the long arm of the customs establishment out of their pockets wherever they sailed. For example, in a letter found aboard the American schooner *Hiram* captured by HMS *Belvidera*, John Lamed, in Gibraltar, cautioned his wife, Lucinda, in Providence, Rhode Island, to say nothing about a trunk containing clothing, glassware, and other luxuries he shipped to her: "Be careful my love to have as little said as possible about all these things -- as they must be *smuggled* and unpleasant consequences would result were any of our Custom House Officers to get news of them."[43]

Although McIntosh argues that most wealthy Nova Scotians made money from smuggling, the very nature of the activity means that there is no way of knowing just how extensive or lucrative the practice actually was.[44] Nevertheless, trade increased after June 1812 as American flour was smuggled across the border for the use of British soldiers in Canada. British manufactured goods continued to reach American markets through licensed traders who smuggled them "past the often conniving customs officials into the ports of northern Maine."[45] It is likely, however, that most merchants and shipowners on both sides of the border preferred the security of trading under a British licence.

ii) Specie

In an era when there were no banks in Atlantic Canada, one of the most difficult commodities to obtain was hard currency needed by the provincial governments for public works and military contracts. In a letter to the British secretary of state for war (Lord Liverpool) in July 1812, Lieutenant Governor Sherbrooke included the American declaration of war, described his preparations, requested authority to issue letters of marque, urged Liverpool to send reinforcements for provincial troops, and concluded that a remittance of specie would fill an urgent need.[46]

Along the U.S./Canadian border, illicit trade provided one source of specie. According to Mahon, "large quantities of British goods were smuggled downward from Quebec into New England in return for specie."[47] Chronically short of hard currency

---

[42]Charles Wye Kendall, *Private Men-of-War* (London, 1931), 282.

[43]PAC, RG 8, IV, Vol. 124, *Hiram*, ship's papers.

[44]McIntosh, *Collectors*, 236.

[45]Blake, *Customs Administration*, 29. W.B. Crane and J.P. Cranwell, *Men of Marque* (New York, 1940), 32. MacNutt, *Atlantic*, 132.

[46]*NS Leg. Papers*, [Vol. 59, doc. 49], 260.

[47]Mahon, *War of 1812*, 330.

(which trickled steadily out of the country due to the adverse balance of trade), British military and naval contractors in Halifax were especially grateful for specie no matter how it arrived. Although smuggling enterprises meant profits for both parties, the amount of cash generated by such small scale operations could not match the windfall of prize specie captured by the Royal Navy after June 1812.

Motivated by poor pay and worse conditions, the navy made the most of prize making opportunities, especially when there was specie at stake. The captain of HMS *Plumper* wrote to Vice-Admiral Herbert Sawyer concerning a prize that was later recaptured by the Americans: "Finding some few dollars in the brig which I have taken, I thought it wise to take them out as there is no difficulty in sharing them and our people are very poor, some of them having had no money for these nine years past."[48] In several cases, British officials unsuccessfully petitioned the vice-admiralty court for access to specie captured on board various prizes. As early as August 1812, Lieutenant Governor Sherbrooke wrote Lord Bathurst for an order to release specie for provincial use. He also recommended that the government promote the existing traffic in British manufactures, which would lead to an illegal trade of great benefit to Nova Scotia. Of course that would require cooperation from naval and customs officials to protect the smugglers and encourage this trade. There is no record of Bathurst's response to Sherbrooke's second suggestion, but in a letter dated 30 September 1812, Bathurst agreed to the province's sequestering money captured from prizes since there was no specie available from Britain.[49]

Nor were the amounts of cash at stake inconsequential. For example, in July 1812, *Mary Elizabeth* was captured carrying $2,313 in specie, *Maria* had $32,000 on board, and *Cordelia* $21,144. *Hiram* and *Four Sisters* carried $12,800 and $1,000 respectively. In August, *Bolina* was taken with $13,550 aboard, while *Eastern Star* carried $21,000. *Melantho*, with $45,000, was the only prize in September carrying specie. All these prizes and their cargoes, captured before England's official declaration of war in October, were condemned to the Crown *jurae coronae*. Not until 1814 were the colonies permitted to import specie.[50]

Prizes captured by American privateers and naval vessels contributed a similar volume of specie to the early prosecution of the war. G. Auchinleck calculates that between 18 June and 31 December 1812, Americans sent in 305 prizes worth $10,000 each. Twenty-one of the vessels carried $1,850,000 in specie for a total prize value of $5 million, not to mention the 45,000 seamen taken in the first six months of the war.

---

[48] *Niles Weekly Register*, 25 July 1812.

[49] *NS Leg. Papers*, [Vol. 59, doc. 61], Sherbrooke to Bathurst, 7 Aug. 1812, 265, 129.

[50] Prizes captured before an official declaration of war or seized without a proper letter of marque, belonged to the crown rather than the captor, and were condemned in right of the crown or *jure corone*. PAC, RG 8, IV, Vol. 120, *Bolina*, Examination of John Fairfield, master, 24 Aug. 1813; Vol. 121, *Cordelia*, Affidavit of Lieutenant John Newton, 22 July 1812; and *Eastern Star*, Examination of Collin Hughes, mate, 1 Sept. 1812; Vol. 122, *Four Sisters*, Affidavit of Henry John Hall, 25 July 1812; Vol. 124, *Hiram*, Examination of Josiah Orne, master, 23 July 1812; Vol. 125, *Maria*, Examination of Jabez Norton, 20 July 1812; *Mary Elizabeth*, Affidavit of Lieutenant William Philip Delafons, 25 Aug. 1812; and *Melantho*, Affidavit of Edmund Marley, midshipman, 10 Oct. 1813.

By 1814, the British naval blockade of the American coast had virtually swept American shipping from the sea, and money was in short supply on both sides of the border. As Auchinleck comments, "American merchants being thus unable to settle their debts in kind were now forced to pay in coin, and Nova Scotian shippers were anxious that they should be permitted to pay."[51]

iii) The Licensed Trade

To assure a steady supply of flour and foodstuffs to the duke of Wellington's troops in Spain from 1803 onward, Britain permitted unarmed vessels of over 100 tons from any nation (except France) to obtain a licence of nine months' duration to transport flour and grain.[52] A licence protected American vessels from zealous Royal Navy cruisers strictly enforcing the acts by ordering "all captains and commanders of His Majesty's ships and vessels of war, which may fall in with any American or other vessel bearing a neutral flag, laden with flour, bread, corn and pease, or any other species of dried provisions, bound from America to Spain or Portugal, and having this protection on board, to suffer her to proceed without unnecessary obstruction or detention in her voyage; provided she shall appear to be steering a due course for those countries." An order-in-council of 8 April 1812 confirmed the issuing of licences and extended the cargo permitted to include wheat, grain, bread, biscuit, flour, pitch, tar, and turpentine.[53]

Instead of abruptly halting the licensed trade, the American declaration of war had surprisingly little effect. Enemies or not, Britain still needed American food supplies. In anticipation of a speedy end to the war, the British government issued special licences to safeguard American vessels carrying provisions to ports in New Brunswick, Nova Scotia, and the West Indies, as well as to Spain and Portugal. The United States attempted to deter this trade by forbidding American vessels from accepting British licences to trade with the enemy in any port in the British dominions. The penalty for such an offence was the forfeiture of a sum double the value of the vessel and cargo, conviction of a misdemeanour, up to twelve months in prison, and a fine not to exceed one thousand dollars.[54] Although some shipowners may have been intimidated by these penalties, American sailors were more afraid of the Royal Navy. Two typical crewmen

---

[51] G. Auchinleck, *A History of the War between Great Britain and the U.S.A. During the Years 1812, 1813 & 1814* (1855; reprint, Toronto, 1972), 78. W.R. Copp, "Nova Scotian Trade During the War of 1812," *CHR*, XVIII (1937), 94.

[52] The Prize Act of 1809 (49 Geo. III, c. 49) refers to this licensed trade. E.S. Roscoe, *Reports of Prize Cases determined in the High Court of Admiralty before the Lords Commissioners of Appeals in Prize Cases and before the Judicial Committee of the Privy Council from 1745-1859* (London, 1905), II, 210, the case of the *Actaeon*. See also Michael J. Crawford, "The Navy's Campaign against the Licensed Trade in the War of 1812," *American Neptune*, XLVI (1986), 165.

[53] Hitsman, *Incredible*, 50. Licences based on 49 Geo. III, c. 49 were reinforced by 52 Geo. III, c. 20. Stewart, *Reports*, 455.

[54] Crawford, "Licensed Trade," *Am. Nep.*, XLVI (1986), 165. See also Reginald Horsman, *The War of 1812* (London, 1969), 57. The full text of the law was published in *Niles Weekly Register*, 18 July 1812.

insisted on seeing *Victory*'s licence before signing on in Lisbon "because we objected to ship on board any vessel which was not protected from capture."[55]

Available from the Board of Trade in London, the lieutenant governor of Nova Scotia, the naval commander of the British North American station, Vice-Admiral Herbert Sawyer, and various former British consuls in America, hundreds of licences of varying legitimacy were issued in the first few months of the war. The advantage of a licence was that it not only allowed trade in certain commodities, it was also supposed to protect the bearer from capture by British naval vessels. Unfortunately, as the owners of fifty-four licensed vessels discovered, this protection was not consistently recognized by the Halifax Court of Vice-Admiralty. Judge Croke disliked and distrusted such licences. In his lengthy judgement of the *Economy*, a vessel carrying a licence from Lieutenant Governor Sherbrooke, captured by the *Liverpool Packet*, 17 November 1812, Croke accused America of trying "to ruin our commerce and shipping, to deprive us of all the benefit which the operation of the navigation laws for so many years has procured us, and to compel us to weaken, to depart from, and even to abandon that system which he has found to be the only bulwark which he could not subvert." Granting licences, he argued, "is in opposition to the system of navigation laws, and, as protecting the property of an enemy, is contrary to the established maxims of law." Although most licensed captures were eventually restored to their owners, either by the court or on appeal, nine were wholly or partly condemned by the vice-admiralty court when Judge Croke deemed their licences invalid.[56]

As a rule, only those licences issued by a properly constituted authority, such as the Board of Trade, were considered valid. Known as "Sidmouths," these licences bore the signature of Lord Sidmouth, one of the principal secretaries of state.[57] While fundamentally opposed to licences, Judge Croke recognized their strategic value and occasionally allowed a more liberal interpretation of their terms. For example, in the case of the *Abigail*, whose licence bore the name of the Liverpool agent instead of the owners, Croke decided that since the vessel had complied with the basic terms of the licence, the vessel should be restored. He explained: "Of late, when the extraordinary mode of warfare carried on against this country had required new expedients to counteract it, licences to a great extent have been granted to relieve the stagnant trade

---

[55]PAC, RG 8, IV, Vol. 99, *Victory*, Testimony of Christopher Williams and Ephraim Simonds, 31 Mar. 1813.

[56]Stewart, *Reports*, 455. In the case of the *Economy*, Croke argued that the order in council of 13 October 1812 which declared war against the United States invalidated licences such as the *Economy*'s, previously issued under an order in council in April 1812. The general reprisals granted in October against the vessels and goods of the United States exempted licensed trade or special cases carrying grain and flour to Spain or Portugal and no one else. In condemning the *Economy* as a droit of Admiralty, Croke's judgement also reflected the fact that the *Liverpool Packet*, having no letter of marque specifically against the United States, was not a properly commissioned vessel. The prize was eventually condemned to the privateer. PAC, RG 8, IV, Vol. 119, also PRO, HCA 46/11.

[57]London *Times*, 22 Sept. 1812. Although described as "mild, sincere, benevolent and incorruptible" Sidmouth's administration was, according to the *Times*, "a display of narrow views, of feeble measures and of honest blunders."

of the country, and this measure so highly beneficial, or even necessary has been facilitated by the adoption of a still more liberal latitude of construction."[58]

Such was the case with the licensed vessel *Mary*, brought in by the *Wolverine* privateer for carrying "cigarroes." Cigars were not a licensed commodity because they could be obtained from the British West Indies. Suspecting that the contraband cigars along with the rest of the cargo were not likely destined for Halifax, the captain of the privateer justified sending the vessel in since "the articles found is not agreeable with the tenor of her licence." In Croke's opinion, even though cigars were prohibited, they did not invalidate the licence.[59] Accordingly, *Wolverine* was awarded the contraband, but the rest of the cargo and the vessel were restored to the owner.

On the other hand, licences signed by Vice-Admiral Sawyer really had no force of law except on naval vessels under Sawyer's command as vice-admiral of the North American station. Licences signed by Andrew Allen, His Majesty's former consul for Massachusetts, New Hampshire, Rhode Island, and Connecticut, were accompanied by a letter from Admiral Sawyer asking vessels under his command not to detain bona fide vessels bearing Allen's passport. Such licences were found aboard *Friendship*, *Expedition*, *Nymph*, and *Reward* when they were captured.[60]

Once Baltic ports were reopened to trade in November 1812 and North American food and ships' stores were not so urgently required for the troops in Europe, the British government ceased issuing licences. Nonetheless, Lieutenant Governor Sherbrooke continued to grant licences under his own seal. The *Economy* of Boston, mentioned earlier, claimed protection under a Sherbrooke licence, but her case collapsed in court because she had the misfortune to fall into the hands of a privateer and not a naval ship. The solicitor general of the vice-admiralty court, James Stewart, argued on behalf of the *Economy* that the licence was granted by the governor-in-council in compliance with 49 George III, c. 49, and with the intent of the ministers "who have expressed the strongest desire that a friendly and commercial intercourse should be preserved with the neighbouring states of America." A decision on 12 October 1812 by Dr. Charles Robinson of Doctors' Commons in the High Court of Admiralty found Sherbrooke's policy of issuing licences to be "perfectly correct." Accordingly, Sherbrooke licences were available to various Halifax merchants such as John Moody and Company and William K. Reynolds.[61] These licences, usually good for a three-month period, enabled merchants to import wheat, grain, bread, biscuit, flour, tar, pitch, and turpentine into Halifax from any American port from which British vessels were excluded. The licence had to be deposited in the customs house upon the completion of the voyage.

---

[58]Stewart, *Reports*, 360. PAC, RG 8, IV, Vol. 73, *Abigail*.

[59]PAC, RG 8, IV, Vol. 90, *Mary*, Letter from Captain Shea, 9 Sept. 1812. Stewart, *Reports*, 465.

[60]PAC, RG 8, IV, Vol. 119, *Economy*; Vol. 117, *Friendship*, *Expedition*; Vol. 118, *Reward*; Vol. 91, *Nymph*.

[61]Stewart, *Reports*, 446. As well as being a court official, James Stewart recorded all Croke's judgements. PAC, RG 8, IV, Vol. 119, *Star*, *Economy*; Vol. 77, *Arab*.

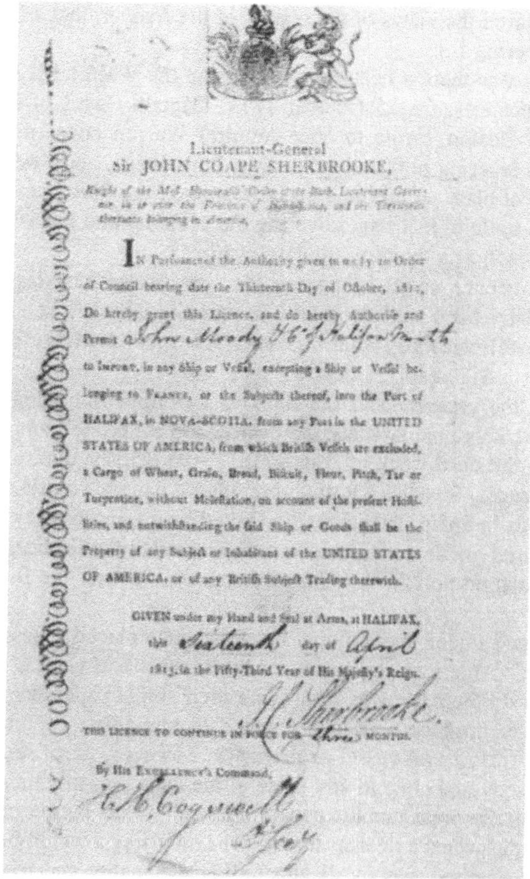

Lieutenant-General
Sir JOHN COAPE SHERBROOKE,

IN Pursuance of the Authority given to me by an Order of Council bearing date the Thirteenth Day of October, 1812, Do hereby grant this Licence, and do hereby Authorise and Permit John Moody

to IMPORT, in any Ship or Vessel, excepting a Ship or Vessel belonging to FRANCE, or the Subjects thereof, into the Port of HALIFAX, in NOVA-SCOTIA, from any Port in the UNITED STATES OF AMERICA, from which British Vessels are excluded, a Cargo of Wheat, Grain, Bread, Biscuit, Flour, Pitch, Tar or Turpentine, without Molestation, on account of the present Hostilities, and notwithstanding the said Ship or Goods shall be the Property of any Subject or Inhabitant of the UNITED STATES OF AMERICA, or of any British Subject Trading therewith.

GIVEN under my Hand and Seal at Arms, at HALIFAX, this Sixteenth day of April 1813, in the Fifty-Third Year of His Majesty's Reign.

J. C. Sherbrooke.

THIS LICENCE TO CONTINUE IN FORCE FOR three MONTHS.

By His Excellency's Command,
H. H. Cogswell

Figure 1: Licence signed by Lt. Governor Sir John Coape Sherbrooke issued to John Moody, Halifax merchant.

Suspicious of the licensed trade from the outset, Judge Croke was particularly contemptuous of Reynolds and Moody. In his verdict on the *Arab*, which restored half the cargo, Croke accused both men of profiteering. "It is notorious that both Reynolds and Moody were engaged in licence jobbing, that they procured them from the government and afterwards disposed of them as they could find purchasers, some in this country and others were transmitted for sale to the United States."[62] Given the restrictions war imposed on regular merchant shipping, it would appear that Reynolds and Moody sought to take advantage of every available profit-making opportunity. Not only were they active in the licensed trade, Reynolds and Moody also had money invested in eight privateers. Many others involved in maritime trade, including many

---

[62]Stewart, *Reports*, 549. The prize-related activities of various merchants are listed in Appendix 7.

crew members, shared the views of the master of the *Nymph*, that a British licence was better than privateering.[63]

Not only was there a licensed trade during the War of 1812, there was also a thriving trade in licences. On 25 October 1813, Captain Hayes of HMS *Majestic*, on blockade duty off Boston, wrote to Vice-Admiral Warren concerning the number of suspicious vessels entering port under Spanish, Portuguese, and Swedish flags: "I find the licences are sent blank to be filled up in Boston ... the Portuguese consul is said to be making quite a trade of that flag, covering the property and furnishing the necessary papers for any person at a thousand dollars a ship."[64]

Since a licence could cost more than the vessel carrying it, the perceived advantages must have been considerable. For example, *Hiram*'s licence cost its owners one dollar per barrel of cargo, while *Monsoon*'s owners paid $1,133 for a licence to carry a cargo worth $12,000.[65]

Despite the expense and the dubious morality of trading with the enemy, licences were extremely popular since they worked to everyone's advantage. According to one source, by the third week of August 1812, the British Admiralty had issued 180 licences to American, Swedish, Portuguese, and Spanish vessels to carry grain to Wellington's troops in Spain. In return, the United States purchased £5 million worth of British manufactured goods during the war. In fact, until the licences were withdrawn, virtually every Atlantic port in the United States traded with the British forces under licence.[66]

As defined under international law, a licence placed a vessel in a temporary state of neutrality.[67] American ships arrested by British naval vessels or privateers were obliged to deliver up their licences along with their ship's papers as soon as they were boarded. Failure to produce a licence resulted in immediate capture. The same ship hailed by an American naval vessel or privateer, however, faced seizure for treason if a licence were discovered. Just to add spice to the situation, maritime law decreed that if a captain voluntarily presented his papers, the captor was not permitted to search the vessel, even if he suspected a licence aboard. The only way a would-be captor could find out if a ship was licensed was by disguising his nationality and tricking the captured vessel into presenting its licence.

At a time when vessels were captured under one flag and recommissioned immediately under another, and when seamen of every nationality were hired or pressed as crews, it was often difficult to distinguish one country's ships from another's. Non-standard naval uniforms and the common practice of carrying flags of various nations

---

[63]PAC, RG 8, IV, Vol. 91, *Nymph*, Examination of Joseph Dixon, seaman, 15 June 1813.

[64]Mahan, *War of 1812*, II, 171.

[65]Crawford, "Licensed Trade," *Am. Nep.*, XLVI (1986), 166. PAC, RG 8, IV, Vol. 124, *Hiram*; Vol. 74, *Monsoon*.

[66]Mahon, *War of 1812*, 55; Horsman, *War of 1812*, 58; Morison, *Massachusetts*, 205.

[67]Stewart, *Reports*, 493. [*Henry*, captured 28 Apr. 1813.]

further complicated the identification of a ship met at sea. Captain Eldred of the American ship *Frederick Augustus* was hailed by a vessel flying the American flag. Presuming her "to be an American privateer as she was under American colours and her officers were in American uniforms" Eldred rushed to the "caboose" and burned his licence. Imagine his dismay when he discovered the captor was actually the Nova Scotia privateer *Sir John Sherbrooke* and his only protection had just gone up in smoke! Fortunately, for Captain Eldred, the vice-admiralty court admitted his claim and the vessel and cargo were restored.[68]

Although Judge Croke regarded every licence as "a nail driven into the coffin of the British empire,"[69] Thomas Jefferson, a loyal American and proponent of the war, took a more pragmatic view. Jefferson justified the licensed trade in a letter to James Ronaldson in 1813. His main argument ran that America could not starve Britain by refusing to supply foodstuffs, "and if she is to be fed at all events, why not we have the benefit of it as well as others?"[70] He also argued that profits from trade contributed to the war coffers and kept the conflict popular by keeping the markets open. Jerome Garitee's study of Baltimore privateers reveals a further advantage. Ironically, many merchants who profited from the lucrative flour trade reinvested their earnings in privateers, which contributed enormously to the American war effort.[71] In Crawford's judgement, carrying supplies to British troops in Spain was really only indirect trade with a distant enemy, but transporting American provisions to sustain British military forces in Canada was "clearly treasonous."[72]

One aspect of licensing not lost on enterprising ship owners was the fact that the same licence that protected ships importing goods to Nova Scotia from vigilant British naval vessels and privateers could also be used to shelter the American carrying trade from Boston or New York up to Maine. In his examination of licensing in the case

---

[68]PAC, RG 8, IV, Vol. 84, *Frederick Augustus*, Examination of John Rowez, mate, 19 Apr. 1813, Claim and Affidavit of Nathaniel Eldred, 26 May 1813, letter from Sir Thomas Hardy, 19 Apr. 1813. Although prize regulations demanded that vessels hoist their true colours before engaging, the privateer may not have done more than hail the prize as a fellow "American." An affidavit by the captain of *Frederick Augustus* indicates his ship had been boarded earlier that day by HMS *Ramilies* and warned that the American government condemned all vessels with British licences. He acknowledged that the weather was foggy and he could not see very clearly. Thinking any vessel so near the American coast in that weather had to be an American vessel and seeing the American colours, he feared the worst and burnt his licence. His captors let him off near Bedford, Massachusetts, to find Sir Thomas Hardy, the commander of HMS *Ramilies*, who provided him with a deposition confirming that Hardy had seen the licence and allowed Captain Eldred to proceed. It was likely this letter that persuaded the court to restore the ship upon payment of costs.

[69]Stewart, *Reports*, 467.

[70]Crawford, "Licensed Trade," *Am. Nep.*, XLVI (1986), 166.

[71]Jerome R. Garitee, *The Republic's Private Navy: The American Privateering Business as Practiced by Baltimore during the War of 1812* (Middletown, Conn., 1977), 51.

[72]Crawford, "Licensed Trade," *Am. Nep.*, XLVI (1986), 171.

of the *Economy*, Judge Croke acknowledged: "That they [licences] are employed to cover the coasting trade of the United States, or for other fraudulent purposes, is evident because of above one hundred licences which have been granted within the last eight months, not more than twenty have found their way with cargoes of corn and provisions into the port of Halifax."[73]

Whether condemned or condoned, licences fulfilled a variety of economic and strategic needs on both sides. In addition to food, American vessels carried another important cargo – news. With communications rendered more erratic by war, any information on current events and the state of American politics or public opinion was an important source of intelligence for Atlantic Canada. Lieutenant Governor Sherbrooke recognized another tactical advantage of licences in a letter to the Colonial Secretary Lord Bathurst dated 17 August 1813. Noting that American ships trading under licence were less likely to become privateers, Sherbrooke shrewdly observed: "In this way, I think the licensed trade has operated more to our security than an additional force of several thousand men."[74]

As the war progressed and Britain tightened her naval blockade along the American coast, the U.S. Navy watched the licensed trade with increasing frustration. In July 1813, the secretary of the navy issued orders against "the palpable and criminal intercourse" with the enemy, not only by foreigners but "with great subtlety and treachery by profligate citizens, who ... find means to convey succours or intelligence to the enemy, and elude the penalty of law."[75] To discourage this trade with the enemy, by late 1813 the United States instituted a sweeping embargo against food and contraband. This crackdown, combined with renewed British access to continental ports, meant the virtual disappearance of New England's licensed trade. The effect was apparent in the decrease in ship captures from 1814 onward. Not only were there fewer prizes taken overall (roughly half of the 1813 figures), but the presence of licensed ships declined dramatically. Of the 186 captures in 1814, only the Swedish vessels *Falun* and *Magdalena* carried licences, and both were restored by Judge Croke.[76]

The War of 1812 proved that while governments could make war, they could not make enemies. Despite the best efforts of both British and American authorities, trade continued throughout the War of 1812. Whether smuggled or licensed, goods moved over borders and across the ocean because the merchants who engaged in this trade refused to allow politics to interfere with profits. Longstanding business and family ties between New England and the Maritime provinces proved more persuasive than either maritime grievances or annexationist dreams, especially when Britain was so reluctant to declare war. For the first few months of the war, British troops in Spain relied on the licensed trade in American foodstuffs while provincial interests welcomed

---

[73]Stewart, *Reports*, 452.

[74]Copp, "Nova Scotian Trade," *CHR*, XVIII (1938), 90.

[75]Mahan, *War of 1812*, II, 174.

[76]PAC, RG 8, IV, Vol. 105, *Falun*, captured by *Liverpool Packet* and *Retaliation*, 21 Jan. 1814; Vol. 109, *Magdalena*, captured by HMS *Martin*, 5 June 1814.

all American specie, whether captured or contraband. Even privateers, who had a vested interest in prolonging the war, regarded prizemaking as more of an alternative to trade than a patriotic exercise.

The letters of marque carried by New Brunswick and Nova Scotia privateers were the final descendants of a long line of international sea customs and laws surrounding prize that ended with the War of 1812. To put prizemaking within its historical context, chapter 2 examines the origins of maritime law, the development of the English High Court of Admiralty and the creation of Britain's colonial vice-admiralty courts to administer the international law of prize in North America.

Figure 2: Detail from the Map of the Seat of War in North America published by John Melish, ca. 1813-1815.

Source: (Hand-coloured engraving, National Archives of Canada, NMC-6760).

Chapter 2
Good and Lawful Prize

Basic to the study of privateering and prizemaking as practised by the Royal Navy and the privateers of New Brunswick and Nova Scotia during the War of 1812 is an understanding of the history and development of English prize law. The regulations under which colonial prize courts operated formed part of a continuum of admiralty law that was firmly anchored in the seafaring traditions of the ancient world. Descended from the maritime customs of such mercantile nations as Rhodes, Phoenicia, and Rome,[1] English admiralty law developed to resolve commercial or civil disputes that arose at sea, often involving conflicting usages of different nations.

By the eighteenth century, virtually all maritime nation states had established some form of admiralty jurisprudence to deal with mercantile disputes beyond their shores.[2] Ironically, the strongest prejudice against admiralty law in Britain came from within the legal profession itself. Proponents of the common law vehemently opposed the exercise of civil or international law in a struggle that lasted well into the eighteenth century. Prize law, on the other hand, remained relatively untouched by this judicial jealousy. Legal historian R.G. Marsden traces the development of prize law within the admiralty structure from the first use of the term letter of marque in 1404 until the mid-eighteenth century when prize procedures for both the Royal Navy and privateers were well established. According to Marsden, the instructions to privateers issued in 1585 set the precedent for subsequent royal instructions "which until recently, have been issued at the commencement of every war." Changes from war to war illustrate how England's admiralty system gradually curbed the excesses of the Elizabethan era and exerted more control over private armed warships.[3]

Prize Acts followed a similar evolutionary process, especially during the eighteenth century, with each new act incorporating elements of earlier acts along with new clauses to clarify or correct regulations. Studies of eighteenth century privateering by James G. Lydon, Carl E. Swanson, and David J. Starkey demonstrate how the British government helped popularize privateering by decreasing the fees owing to the crown and the court and offering incentives such as head money.[4] This chapter provides a brief background for the international law of prize emphasizing its development within British admiralty law and the colonial vice-admiralty courts such as Halifax that furnished the

---

[1]G. de Forest Lord and G.C. Sprague, *Cases on the Law of Admiralty* (St. Paul, Minn., 1939), 1.

[2]John Colombos, *A Treatise on the Law of Prize* (London, 1949), 16.

[3]R.G. Marsden, ed., *Documents relating to Laws and Customs of the Sea* (London, 1915), I, 236, and II, 112, 403-435.

[4]James G. Lydon, *Pirates, Privateers, and Profits: New York Privateering, 1689-1763* (Upper Saddle River, N.J., 1970), 86. Under 6 Ann, c. 4, XV (1740) naval and privateer crews were entitled to "five pounds for every man which was living on board any ship or ships so taken, sunk, burnt or otherwise destroyed at the beginning of the engagement." Carl E. Swanson, *Predators and Prizes: American Privateering and Imperial Warfare, 1739-1748* (Columbia, S.C., 1991). David J. Starkey, *British Privateering Enterprise in the Eighteenth Century* (Exeter, 1990).

legal framework for naval and privateer operations. Following the British declaration of war in October 1812, the prize act of 3 June 1813 extended the acts proclaiming general reprisals against the Italian and Ligurian Republics (17 August 1803) and Spain (27 June 1805) to American prizes.[5] With centuries of experience to draw from, both prize law and prizemakers were ready for the War of 1812.

The Origins of Admiralty Law

English admiralty courts and the law they administered grew out of the medieval struggles of English kings to exert their power, both executive and judicial, over often reluctant and occasionally rebellious subjects. Attempts to achieve control over law and order within the realm were matched by similar efforts to establish sovereignty on the seas. The high cost of building and arming a large fleet of warships deterred the creation of a state navy, despite the fact that hiring foreign vessels was even more costly and requisitioning merchant ships was both slow and unreliable. Only King John and Henry V maintained large enough fleets to put to sea early in the season and take the initiative quickly before their enemy had time to prepare. Yet, even with these options available, in the absence of a national navy, there was little a king could do to guarantee the safety of seaborne trade from those who were determined to attack it.[6]

Like their brethren throughout history, the Channel pirates of the twelfth and thirteenth centuries targeted weaker, well-laden merchant vessels without regard to nationality or alliance. As a result, "their acts were as often an excuse for war as for judicial action, and as often settled by a peace treaty as by a criminal court."[7] One of the chief reasons for this was that demands for restitution through English courts from their non-English victims ran aground on the inability of the existing common law either to hear foreign claims or order compensation (i.e. equity). At the risk of crediting pirates with inspiring the legal system that eventually led to their demise, it is probably fair to suggest that a king's continued failure to curb piratical attacks on maritime trade implied a lack of power that could have serious economic and political repercussions. Frederic L. Cheyette described the historic role of pirates and admirals in the Middle Ages as "bringing terror to the sea and its coasts, but also bringing forth ... a doctrine of sovereignty and an institution to embody it that were destined to become major features of the European world."[8]

Piracy typified the endemic lawlessness of the late Middle Ages. Life at sea in the fourteenth century was "a sort of cold war" between England and her former Franco-

---

[5]The prize acts were 53 Geo. III, c. 63 (1813), 49 Geo. III, c. 123 (1805), and 45 Geo. III, c. 72 (1803).

[6]John B. Hattendorf, R.J.B. Knight, A.W.H. Pearsall, N.A.M. Rodger, and Geoffrey Till, eds., *British Naval Documents, 1204-1960* (London, 1993), 33.

[7]Frederic L. Cheyette, "The Sovereign and the Pirates, 1332," *Speculum: A Journal of Medieval Studies*, XLV (1970), 46.

[8]Ibid., 68. Marsden, *Select Pleas in the Court of Admiralty* (London, 1897), I, xiv, agrees that the real impetus to the creation of admiralty courts was the difficulty of trying to resolve the claims of foreign sovereigns in cases of spoil or piracy.

Castilian allies, "marked by piracy tolerated, if not officially inspired by both governments."[9] Pirates preyed indiscriminately on both English and foreign trade in the Narrow Seas of the English Channel and the Bay of Biscay. Their crimes are described in lawyers' Latin as "rapinas, invasiones, depredaciones, prisias, reprisilias, marchas, et alia maleficia et illicita."[10] Robbery at sea, at least until the latter part of the fourteenth century, seems to have been regarded by the king's courts as no worse a crime than robbery on land, and similarly for maritime murder and assault.[11] The legal concept of pirates as enemies of humanity did not really emerge until the sixteenth century, after which point they were generally hanged, if caught.

In the absence of national systems of taxation, customs duties on imported goods were one of the king's chief sources of revenue. Thus, protecting English markets while encouraging international trade figured prominently in the interest of the realm. Achieving this in law, however, pitted the nationalism of ownership against the internationalism of commerce.[12] From very early times, any English merchant suffering damages at the hands of foreign ships or pirates during peacetime could petition the crown for a legal remedy. He would be granted a licence or commission to exact a personal reprisal without involving the sovereign in war. The licence, however, applied just to ships of the offending nation and allowed the holder to recoup only the value of property lost.[13] Wartime indemnity was a different matter. Once war was declared, the king issued general reprisals, and all ships and cargoes at sea or in port were identified as the property of either allies, enemies, or neutrals. Needless to say, the identification of which was which, and from what date it became so, occasioned considerable dispute. When a seizure might be piracy one day and lawful capture the next, it became crucial to have an impartial judicial tribunal to decide the issue.

Of necessity, admiralty law was international in scope -- reflecting diplomatic alliances, mercantile agreements, and international treaties between England and her neighbours. As part of this admiralty system, prize law was distinctly different in both jurisdiction and procedure from English common law, which dealt with civil and criminal law within the realm. Admiralty law held sway from the low water mark seaward and was originally concerned with regulating commercial issues such as freight, wreck, insurance, salvage, contracts, wages, and piracy. When war upset the status quo, the commerce of one nation became fair game for the other. The determination of whether ships and cargoes captured by either naval vessels or private armed ships were legitimate prizes required independent, impartial adjudication. Accordingly, within the admiralty system, at the same time and under the same judges and officials, prize law gradually established its own jurisdiction.

---

[9]Hattendorf, *et al.*, eds., *Naval Documents*, 5.

[10]Cheyette, "Sovereign and Pirates," *Speculum*, XLV (1970), 46.

[11]Marsden, *Laws and Customs*, I, 99.

[12]William McFee, *The Law of the Sea* (Philadelphia, 1950), 29.

[13]Richard Pares, *Colonial Blockade and Neutral Rights, 1739-1763* (Oxford, 1938), 2.

Key to an understanding of prize law is the fact that any prize, once condemned as "good and lawful," belonged to the sovereign *jurae coronae* as part of his ancient fiscal prerogative.[14] Prize courts applied the international law of prize to determine whether the prize was enemy property and if so, to transfer legal ownership from the crown to the captor by means of an Act of Condemnation.[15]

The forms of law that emerged borrowed heavily from the tribunal procedures of civil suits and canon or religious law, rather than those of trial by jury, which was an integral part of the common law. As early as the twelfth century, English courts were divided into civil or civilian courts and courts of common law. Relying on codified systems of law derived from ancient Roman law or canon law, civilian courts included the courts martial, ecclesiastical courts, and admiralty courts. Although the jurisdiction of each court was different, they all dispensed law that was international in scope. In 1592, Sir Julius Caesar proudly defended the use of civil law: "The civil laws imperial were best suited for the sea: which for that by long continuance in the most flourishing commonwealth of Rome, they have been, many ages since, the most perfect and equal laws of the world and are generally received throughout all nations about us."[16] In contrast, the common law of England remained largely unwritten and was based on custom and past practice within the realm. Clearly, the people best suited to exercise maritime jurisdiction, including questions of piracy or spoil, were those familiar with the application of international law – a skill found among "civilian" rather than "common" lawyers.[17] Although its progress was slow and somewhat intermittent, by the end of the seventeenth century, "the English Prize Court [had] become a properly constituted legal tribunal of far-reaching commercial, financial and international importance."[18] From its earliest cases, English prize law developed its own expertise and procedures to respond to a specialized legal role within the context of admiralty law.

Prize Law Transformed

The evolution of prize law from an assortment of regulations attempting to exert judicial control over medieval maritime trade to a smoothly functioning system of international law required several centuries. From the eleventh century onward, merchants engaged in maritime trade from the Baltic to the Levant began codifying their various common

---

[14]James Stewart, *Reports of cases argued and determined in the Court of Vice-Admiralty at Halifax in Nova Scotia from the commencement of the war, in 1803, to the end of the year 1813, in the time of Alexander Croke LLD., Judge of that Court* (Halifax, N.S., 1813), 317.

[15]George Coggleshall, *The American Privateers* (New York, 1861), 92. An Act of Condemnation was significant since no vessel could be legally purchased or registered under English maritime rules until it had been properly condemned as prize. Otherwise it had the same status as a vessel captured by pirates; it still legally belonged to its original owners.

[16]Nicholas Tracy, *Attack on Maritime Trade* (Toronto, 1991), 11.

[17]E.S. Roscoe, *A History of the English Prize Court* (London, 1924), 21.

[18]Charles Wye Kendall, *Private Men-of-War* (London, 1931), 69. In 1825, the English High Court of Admiralty absorbed the Scottish Prize Court dating from 1566. Colombos, *Law of Prize*, 16.

customs and usages into law. Historical sources refer to early maritime tribunals such as the Consuls of the Sea at Trani (1063), the Court of the Chain at Jerusalem (1099), the Tables of Amalfi, the Consula Maris at Pisa (1233), and the Catalan Consolato del Mare. By the end of the thirteenth century, the latter had become the commercial code of the northern coast of the Mediterranean.[19] The incentive to commit these rules to writing apparently arose during the Crusades, when European princes found themselves trying to administer the political and economic activities of eastern cities on the basis of nothing more than oral tradition.[20] Similarly, the emergence of northern European codes such as the Jugements de Damme, the Purple Book of Bruges, and the Laws of Wisby, indicates that shipmen of the Low Countries and the Baltic attempted to regularize their own maritime trade.

Among the earliest maritime codes and the one that had the most profound effect on England's law of the sea was the Laws (Rolls or Rôles) of Oleron.[21] The island of Oleron near La Rochelle, off the western coast of France, belonged to the Duchy of Aquitaine or Guienne and was the centre of the Gascon wine trade in the thirteenth century. Sir Travers Twiss suggests that the marriage of Eleanor of Acquitaine and Henry II may have brought both her duchy and her laws to England by the end of the twelfth century.[22] Basically a codification of the decisions made in the maritime courts of Oleron, the Rolls covered all aspects of a shipping venture, including wreck, and ensured that merchants, ship owners, and crew had a stake in the enterprise's success. Castile, Brittany, Normandy, Flanders, and the Baltic States as well as England eventually adopted the Rolls, which were imported like the Gascon wine. England's admiralty court may well have begun, as Timothy J. Runyan suspects, because one of the intermittent wars with France in the mid-fourteenth century rendered the Oleron court inaccessible and obliged England to create its own administrative structure for resolving maritime disputes.[23]

Convenience and dispatch had always been the goals of mercantile courts because tide, not law, was the main regulator of trade. Customary port courts tended to limit deliberations to one or two tides, and the early admirals' courts continued this tradition by conducting their business close to the water's edge, often below the high water mark. In fact, London's first admiralty court was located at Horton's Quay in Southwark in 1410.[24] With speed came precision, and constant usage refined maritime

---

[19]William Senior, *The History of Maritime Law* (London, n.d), 261-262; Sir Travers Twiss, ed., *The Black Book of Admiralty*, 4 vols., (1857; reprint Weisbaden, 1965).

[20]Lord and Sprague, *Cases*, 2. See also Twiss, *Black Book*, IV, xcvi.

[21]Twiss refers to these northern codes as does Senior in *Maritime Law*, 261.

[22]Twiss, *Black Book*, IV, xxi.

[23]Timothy J. Runyan, "The Rolls of Oleron and the Admiralty Court in the Fourteenth Century," *American Journal of Legal History*, XIX (1975), 101. Runyan, among other authors, dismisses the Eleanor of Aquitaine theory but does not dispute the links between the Roles of Oleron and English maritime law.

[24]Twiss, *Black Book*, I, 348, cites the act (11 H IV) referring to the admiral's office "a Loundres a le Key de William Horton, Suthwerk" within the flux and reflux of the tide.

rules into law or *lex maritima*. For example, the original practice of granting personal reprisals differentiated between losses in territorial waters (for which the victim petitioned the king for a letter of reprisal) and damages incurred beyond national seas (which engendered a letter of marque).[25] Eventually, special peacetime licences became obsolete, and "general" licences were standardized as letters of marque and reprisal to be issued by the crown to owners of private armed vessels only during wartime. Within a century or so, letters of marque were simply bought from the admiralty court.[26] Of course, the development of such licensed warfare was not without incident. In 1242 Henry III issued general commissions to merchants of the Cinque Ports against France. The response was so enthusiastic that captors got out of hand, and Henry was forced to hang thirty of them to restore order![27] While likely far from the first, the earliest extant letter of marque was issued to a merchant of Bayonne in 1295. Included in these early royal grants were rules specifying the sharing of prize, ransom of prisoners, court fees, and the role of the admiral, all of which became basic regulations for subsequent wartime prize acts.[28] Compliance with these rules represents "the foundation of the right of the captors, whether they manned a ship of war or a privateer, to prizes captured by them at sea."[29]

The gradual application of general laws of war to the capture of trade was a fairly *ad hoc* process. Maritime powers squabbling about the law of war at sea had to recognize the rights of neutral nations to continue trading during war, or risk converting a non-combattant into an enemy. The Dutch East India Company commissioned Dutch jurist and philosopher Hugo Grotius to prepare a brief on prize law. In 1609 he published *Mare Liberum*, the twelfth chapter of his brief, which defended the freedom of the sea for use by neutral commerce, and therefore, their right to take prize. In 1625, Grotius' tried to explain belligerent rights in terms of the laws of war and peace in *De Jure Belli ac Pacis*, but he failed to resolve the legal confusion over sovereignty at sea. In 1635, John Selden rebutted Grotius in *Mare Clausum*, claiming that England had established sovereignty over the sea by dint of long usage. The status of neutral ships and cargoes and why or when they were liable to capture remained a subject of debate throughout the seventeenth and eighteenth centuries. When the newly created United States of America began drafting its maritime laws in 1776, neutral rights figured prominently. Britain

---

[25]Jerome Garitee, *The Republic's Private Navy: The American Privateering Business as Practiced by Baltimore during the War of 1812* (Middletown, Conn., 1977), 4. Eventually the two became synonymous, and all privateer commissions were known as letters of marque. Marque may be derived from the High German "marcha" meaning boundary or frontier. At one stage, letters of marque covered injury on land or sea, and such licences may have enabled holders to cross international boundaries to exact reprisals. Kendall, *Private Men-of-War*, 6.

[26]Captain Donald Macintyre, *The Privateers* (London, 1975), 2.

[27]Kendall, *Private Men-of-War*, 6. The original Cinq Ports consisted of five Kentish ports: Hastings, Romney, Hythe, Dover, and Sandwich. The towns of Winchelsea and Rye were added later.

[28]Kendall, *Private Men-of-War*, 4. See also Twiss, *Black Book*, I, 33-173.

[29]Roscoe, *Prize Court*, 9.

avoided an explicit definition of the law to allow their privateers and the Royal Navy the widest possible latitude.[30]

The Role of the Admiral

The king's inability to police his seas (or his ships) to the satisfaction of the medieval carrying trade led him to borrow the Mediterranean concept of an admiral, a Latinization of the Arabic amir-al-baba, commander of the sea. When Norman crusaders captured the Saracen Kingdom of Sicily in the mid-eleventh century, they adopted "emir," the Arabic term for the local governors. In Palermo, the emirs commanded the fleet of war vessels. The title was transcribed in Latin as "ammiratus" and eventually, admiral.[31] By 1246 the title of admiral was used in Venice, Genoa, Sicily, and France. It is not recorded in England until 1296 when an admiral is mentioned as a person authorized by the king to enforce the customary law of the sea.[32] As Cheyette points out, however, the first English admirals seem to have held the title in the absence of any particular jurisdiction, so that the "office of admiral may thus be the rarest bird in the medieval administrative bestiary: one that was created in theory before it was instituted in practice."[33]

Appointed for the fleets of the North, South and West (of the Thames), the first admirals were selected at the king's pleasure, generally for a year. In 1360, the king appointed Sir John Beauchamp the first high admiral of England. To finance the dignity and importance of the office, the king ceded a portion of the crown's rights of prize to the admiral in perpetuity.[34] The regional admirals reported to the high admiral who possessed "a clearly recognized judicial authority" in the person of a deputy with power to hold pleas on matters of prize. According to Donald A. Petrie, in the fourteenth century, the admiral's duties increased to include hearing and adjudicating three categories of maritime claims: criminal cases, suits between private parties (instance jurisdiction), and public cases.[35]

During the reign of Edward III (1327-1377), a victory over the French at Sluys in 1340 established English claims to sovereignty over the seas. It also reinforced the admiral's newly acquired civil jurisdiction over "torts, offenses on the high seas and in ports within the ebb and flow of the tide, as well as over matters of prize and contracts

---

[30]Tracy, *Attack on Trade*, 13. Hugo Grotius (1583-1645) and John Selden (1584-1654) laid the legal and philosophical foundations for later work on the international law of the sea, including prize.

[31]Donald A. Petrie, "Forbidden Prizes," *American Neptune*, LIV (1994), 171.

[32]D.G.L. Fraser, "The Origin and Functions of the Court of Vice-Admiralty in Halifax, 1749-1759," *Nova Scotia Historical Society*, XXXIII (1961), 57. According to Hattendorf *et al.*, eds., *British Naval Documents*, 33, the admiral's role had more to do with assembling the fleet than leading it.

[33]Cheyette, "Sovereign and Pirates," *Speculum*, XLV (1970), 50.

[34]H.C. Rothery, *Prize Droits* (London, 1915), 12-13.

[35]Petrie, "Forbidden Prizes," *Am. Nep.*, LIV (1994), 171.

within the Laws of Oleron."[36] His responsibility for the security of maritime commerce paralleled the jurisdiction of local magistrates on land, making him the king's "sheriff and justice on the coasts ... and below the first bridges on tidal rivers and creeks."[37] By the late fourteenth century, with a jurisdiction firmly identified and a deputy-admiral familiar with civil procedure to assist him, the admiral assumed the role of "guardian of public and private rights at sea and in ports, and was, either alone or in association with other officers and persons, constantly commissioned by the Crown to investigate, report on and redress maritime grievances."[38]

Although the admiral's supervision of letters of marque was crucial to the smooth conduct of international trade and diplomacy, the majority of his business focused on domestic maritime jurisdiction. Early admiralty suits were preoccupied with wreck, droits, loss, or salvage, and other mercantile business for which the admiral was entitled to certain emoluments, often half the value of the item before the court. Inevitably, it was not long before the admiral's new jurisdiction interfered with local seaport courts, some of which claimed to hold ancient rights in the form of charters from the crown, or express grants of admiralty jurisdiction. The ancient jurisdiction of a court of admiralty or of vice-admiralty over crimes committed on the high seas was later withdrawn, because the civil procedural law applying in such a court provided neither for the examination of witnesses in open court nor for trial by jury.[39] Since the value of perquisites at stake could be considerable, neither side was willing to renounce its rights. The opening salvo was fired in the reign of Richard II (1377-1399) when two statutes passed in 1389 and 1391 attempted to restrict the admirals' courts to matters occurring only on the high seas, and to deny them power over maritime contracts or pleas that had been entered into on land.[40] Thus began a struggle for jurisdictional supremacy that lasted nearly as long as the admiralty court itself.

The realization that navies required administration and financial management began the transition from the Tudor "Navy Royal" to the Royal Navy of the nineteenth century. The mid-sixteenth century saw the creation of the Council for Marine Causes comprising a vice-admiral, a surveyor, a master of naval ordnance, and a treasurer appointed by royal patent. The position of controller general of victuals was added in 1550. The role of the deputy or vice-admiral was more that of the admiral's legal

---

[36] Lord and Sprague, *Cases*, 2.

[37] Helen Crump, *Colonial Admiralty Jurisdiction in the Seventeenth Century* (New York, 1931), 5.

[38] Roscoe, *Prize Court*, 4.

[39] Marsden, *Laws and Customs*, II, xix, xx. Among the coastal towns claiming exemption from admiralty jurisdiction, Marsden lists Newcastle, Tynemouth, Rochester, Colchester, Southampton, and Bristol, the latter being exempted as early as 1403. Arthur J. Stone, "The Admiralty Court in Colonial Nova Scotia," *Dalhousie Law Journal*, XVII (1994), 366.

[40] F.L. Wiswall, Jr., *The Development of Admiralty Jurisdiction and Practice since 1800* (London, 1970), 4.

representative in court. The vice-admiral was usually trained in civil law so that he could adjudicate prize matters, leaving the admiral free to manage the affairs of the fleet.[41]

The Development of Prize Law

The one jurisdictional area over which there seems to have been little dispute was that of piracy and prize, especially during wartime. Although fourteenth-century England still lacked a navy, there was a tradition of coastal towns or noblemen fitting out ships of war for public service in the pay of the king, under the admiral's command. For example, in return for supplying the king with fifty-seven ships per year, the Cinq Ports enjoyed special rights and privileges from the crown. There were also occasions when wealthy individuals furnished a ship at their own expense. Not only did admirals police the proper use of letters of marque issued by the crown to avenge piracy, they also decided what constituted legal prize and monitored wartime seizures with a close eye to their perquisites. The Black Book of Admiralty, an early fifteenth-century handbook of admiralty practice, states that when prizes were taken by a privately-owned ship in the pay of the king, the king and the owners each received one-fourth the value. The remaining half was shared among the captors (the ship's crew worked for varying amounts), with the admiral receiving one or two shares of each prize, depending on whether he was present at the time of capture. Needless to say, "prizes were rigidly controlled by the admiralty and no prize taken by a member of the admiral's fleet could remove it from the fleet on pain of a fine double the value of the prize."[42] The shifting state of peace and war in late medieval Europe so narrowed the distinction between legitimate prize and piratical spoil that deciding the numerous cases before the admiralty court could not help but stimulate the growth of prize jurisdiction. Unfortunately, chronic piracy, lack of formal procedure, and the failure of the courts to satisfy many foreign complaints or resolve local disputes in a disinterested manner undermined the validity of these early judicial efforts.[43]

Under the Tudors, the creation of a Royal Navy, manned and equipped at the crown's expense, and the gradual enforcement of law at sea helped regulate maritime commerce. Meanwhile, several administrative changes accelerated the establishment of prize law. In 1540, the Navy Board was created to assume responsibility for such civil and administrative duties of the Admiralty as conditions of seamen and equipping the fleet. This left the High Court of Admiralty in sole charge of legal and judicial questions concerning policy and prize. Thereafter, "it proceeded summarily and efficiently to apply

---

[41]Hattendorf *et al.*, eds., *British Naval Documents*, 91. In 1546, the vice-admiral's salary was nearly £280 per month, while a mariner's monthly pay in the same period was 5s. See also Lord and Sprague, *Cases*, 2. Also Roscoe, *Prize Court*, 7, cites Marsden, *Select Pleas*, I, xlii.

[42]Rothery, *Droits*, 14. While the navy had always been obliged to share a portion of its prize money with the crown and the admiral, medieval merchants who funded their own ships were originally entitled to the full value of their prizes. In the sixteenth century, the Lord High Admiral received a perquisite of one-tenth of all prizes whether naval or privateer captures. By 1708, the admiral had renounced his tenth in order to encourage prizemaking. Twiss, *Black Book*, I, 21. Runyan, "Rolls," *AJLH*, XIX (1975), 104. See 6 Ann, c.37.

[43]Roscoe, *Prize Court*, 10. Marsden, *Laws and Customs*, 1, 118.

sea law and customs to maritime and commercial disputes that common law had no machinery or jurisprudence to deal with."[44]

In time of war, by virtue of a royal proclamation or prize act, the admiralty court was granted jurisdiction over prize. This power enabled the prize court to apply the international law of nations to the property of foreign sovereigns ordinarily exempt from the rest of admiralty or English law. While developing procedures to administer increasingly complex prize regulations and international treaties, the courts were constantly struggling to remain impartial. Unlike the other courts of the realm, the prize courts had always been closely associated with the crown, possibly because their existence was so closely tied to the royal prerogatives of war and prize. Whatever the reason, the international implications of prize decisions meant that the executive was sometimes tempted to try to influence the court's judgements on the basis of political rather than judicial considerations. It is to the credit of the practitioners that they withstood this pressure and adopted "plain modes of discovering truth and of bringing to a hearing maritime cases in which British and foreign subjects are equally interested."[45]

By the time of Elizabeth I (1558-1603), private armed ships sailing under letters of marque had become legally recognized vessels of war, and hundreds of them prowled the seas searching for Spanish ships. Not coincidentally perhaps, Elizabethan England was also characterized by an enormous increase in the number of pirates, many of the latter being interchangeable with the former. So many officials, customs officers, magistrates, jurors, and local folk were either participants in, or beneficiaries of, piratical activities that it was almost impossible for the Admiralty to get a case to court. Even the queen is said to have instructed her vice-admirals at least to "avoid the appearance of conniving at piracy."[46] Despite attempts at legal safeguards, the queen's decision to furnish sea rovers like Drake and Raleigh with letters of marque turned privateering into a national industry. If, as K.R. Andrews suggests, virtually every English voyage to the West Indies between 1588 and 1595 was a privateering venture, it is little wonder that Elizabeth's "plunder for pay" scheme created more conflicts than it resolved.[47]

In 1585 England once more summoned the services of "the merchauntes, owners of shippes and others, whose goods have been arrested in Spayne, and have licence from the Lorde Admirall to repayre unto the seas, according to a commission granted from Her Majestye in that behaulfe."[48] To exercise more control, the privateer articles of that war required that proof of loss on behalf of the captured ship was to be made in the admiralty court. Another demanded that captors post a bond to bring their

---

[44]Lord and Sprague, *Cases*, 3. Also Joseph D. Doty, *The British Admiralty Board as a Factor in Colonial Administration, 1689-1763* (Philadelphia, 1930), 14.

[45]Roscoe, *Prize Court*, 41-43, 68.

[46]Neville Williams, *Sea Dogs* (London, 1975), 149.

[47]K.R. Andrews, ed., *English Privateering Voyages to the West Indies, 1588-1595*, (Cambridge, 1959), 8. Instructions of 1591. See also Kendall, *Private Men-of-War*, 14.

[48]Kendall, *Private Men-of-War*, 236.

prizes back to England for adjudication. They were also forbidden to tamper with the cargo, a process known as "breaking bulk." These were the first of many such instructions issued for every war, including the Napoleonic wars, which sought to curb the worst excesses of privateers by making them conform to the law of nations. A few years later, privateers were obliged to bring back at least one member of the captured crew to answer questions concerning the capture.[49] That abuses continued to occur is illustrated by the fact that a bond for good behaviour in Elizabethan times could be up to £1,000, an enormous sum for the period.[50] In fact, it was not until 1666 that a law was passed forbidding English privateers from killing or maiming captive crews in cold blood![51]

Fortunately, Sir Julius Caesar's appointment as judge of the High Court of Admiralty in 1583 led to the removal, and occasional hanging, of the most corrupt court officials. Similarly, the development of a cadre of admiralty lawyers helped control the most outrageous acts of piracy and led to the recognition of the admiralty's jurisdiction over marine causes of a criminal and commercial nature during peace, as well as its wartime role as the court for prize. Although David Starkey contends that enforcing the law of the sea regarding piracy at this time owed more to the balance of power in Europe than impartial justice, by the end of Elizabeth's reign the admiralty court was acknowledged as "the sole tribunal of first instance for the trial of the legality of captures made at sea."[52] From 1520 to 1648, the expansion of royal powers at the expense of Parliament led to a growing rift between practitioners in the king's civil law courts such as admiralty, chivalry, and ecclesaistical courts, and the courts of common law. Jurisdictional tussles with common law proponents continued to challenge the legitimacy of the admiralty court at home, but by the sixteenth century it had attained international status abroad. According to Roscoe, in 1544 members of the admiralty court were involved in a question of prize law arising from the war between the emperor of Germany and France. He does not explain why they were consulted concerning a Dutch recapture of a French prize originally from Ragusa carrying Venctian goods, but he notes the ruling that the ship was not lawful prize to the Dutch.[53]

Lawful Prize

Having traced the origin and halting early development of prize law as a function of an expanding admiralty jurisdiction, it is appropriate to examine the legal character of the process. As has been noted, the procedure for administering prize law was by tribunal

---

[49] Andrews, ed., *Privateering Voyages*, 8.

[50] Marsden, *Laws and Customs*, I, xviii. In 1571, John Hawkins was ordered "doe not robb, spoile, molest ne evill entreate, anye of her Majestie's subjects."

[51] Pares, *Colonial Blockade*, 53.

[52] David Starkey, "Pirates and Markets," *Research in Maritime History*, VII (1994), 59-80. Marsden, *Laws and Customs*, I, xxx.

[53] Roscoe, *Prize Court*, 13.

before a judge. Admiralty process was unique within English law in that the legal action was commenced against the ship itself *(in rem)* rather than the owner. While the legal complexities of this concept continue to attract scholars, "by the eighteenth century the idea is dominant that the proper basis of action in Admiralty is the ship's liability."[54] As far as prize cases were concerned, since it was unlikely that the owner would be aboard at the time of capture, securing the ship and cargo was far simpler and more cost-effective. Without a defendant in the case (the ship) to interrogate, the ship's papers, cargo documents such as bills of lading, and sworn affidavits by crew members aboard both the captor and the prize formed the basis for judgement.[55] Marsden maintained that "the law of nations requires good faith; therefore every ship must be provided with complete and genuine papers, and the master at least should be privy to the truth of the transaction."[56] Therefore, the facts of a prize case should be obtainable from documentary evidence alone. So seriously was this regulation taken that, as Marsden concludes, if papers were falsified or missing or the master "grossly prevaricate," the law of nations allowed for the owner of the ship to lose his claim for court costs or even his ship, depending on the degree of misbehaviour and the pertinent treaties. Because there were no juries, the judge's deliberations were generally brief, and the prize was either restored to its owners or condemned as "good and lawful" within a matter of weeks. Timing was particularly important when the cargoes at stake were perishable and risked damage or total loss by being detained for any length of time. The efficiency and expediency of prize court judgements made them popular with both privateers and merchants whose wartime interests centred more on serving themselves than their country.

From the first, those who objected to the decisions of the prize court could launch an appeal to the king in chancery. Until 1625, the king delegated members of his Privy Council to review each case.[57] After 1625, the privy councillors comprising this body were officially constituted as the Lords Commissioners of Appeals in Prize Causes. Owners, captors, or other claimants wishing to appeal were required to post a bond of several hundred pounds for the prosecution of their appeal within a specified length of time. If the appeal were successful against him, the captor paid; if not, the claimant footed the bill. As the rules governing prize became more precise and the courts better organized, there were fewer grounds for appeal.[58]

---

[54]P.M. North, *Cheshire's Private International Law* (London, 1974), 84. M.J. Pritchard and D.C.E. Yale, eds., *Hale and Fleetwood on Admiralty Jurisdiction* (London, 1993), xxxviii-xlvii, present several possibilities for the derivation of *in rem* action from Roman law to a process common in the middle ages. They refer to the "ambivalent character" of the process even before the sixteenth century and discuss it in light of both Roman law and later developments.

[55]Roscoe, *Prize Court*, 68.

[56]Marsden, *Laws and Customs*, II, 351.

[57]Ibid., 85-86. Roscoe notes that 1595 was the earliest date he found for a published judgement by delegates in a prize appeal. Colombos, *Law of Prize*, 17, quotes Rymer's *Foedera*, XIX, 7, for this information.

[58]Although appeals to the High Court of Admiralty prior to the War of 1812 were not reviewed, of the over 700 cases determined in the vice-admiralty court in Halifax between 1812 and 1815, only forty-five decisions (less than seven percent) were appealed.

The last significant obstacle to prize jurisdiction emerged from within the legal profession itself. Over the years, although admiralty courts had gradually achieved judicial independence and international credibility on issues of maritime law, they had occasionally transgressed into areas of common law jurisdiction where responsibilities overlapped. During the sixteenth century the courts of common law tried to block actions being heard in admiralty court and vice-versa by means of writs of prohibition.[59] These writs not only halted an admiralty process, they disqualified the admiralty court from dealing with it. The conflict, as described by M.J. Pritchard and D.E.C. Yale was "a contest between the authority conferred by royal patent (admiralty) and the authority of statute" to which common law judges laid claim.[60] Hostility escalated with the appointment of Sir Edward Coke (1552-1634) as chief justice of Common Pleas in 1606. Coke, who "hated Admiralty and every other jurisdiction that was not the common law"[61] insisted that the admiralty court had no jurisdiction where common law had a remedy. During his years in office, he attempted to halt dozens of admiralty proceedings that threatened to adjudicate matters above the high water mark, including reprisal and prize. Eventually, the more lucrative private suits of instance jurisdiction were largely withdrawn from the admiralty bench and bar.[62] Coke was removed from the bench in 1613, possibly as a result of his intransigence, but prohibitions continued to reduce the overall jurisdiction of the admiralty court in everything but prize. Fortunately for the civilians, the numerous maritime wars of the eighteenth century assured them a flourishing business in prize cases.[63]

While admiralty jurisdiction was fighting for its life, prize law underwent several important refinements during the political turmoil of the Commonwealth and after the Restoration of Charles II. By this time, letters of reprisal were issued only after a declaration of war. At the beginning of the Commonwealth (1649-1660), the Prize Act of 1649 simplified prize judgements considerably by recording them in plain English instead of bad Latin.[64] Meanwhile, new regulations streamlined the taking of inventories and handling prize as well as examining the captured crew. The office of the Lord High Admiral was abolished during the Commonwealth, and although later restored, it never again attained its former power.[65] The proceeds from prizes, which had previously been shared among captors, owners, and crown in varying proportions; were now to be shared equally between the captors and the common treasury "to raise a fund for wounded

---

[59]Marsden, *Laws and Customs*, I, 359.

[60]M.J. Pritchard and D.E.C. Yale, *Hale and Fleetwood*, 1.

[61]Senior, *History of Maritime Law*, 271.

[62]Petrie, "Forbidden Prizes," *Am. Nep.*, LIV (1994), 171.

[63]Marsden, *Laws and Customs*, II, 359. See also *Select Pleas*, II, lxxix.

[64]Roscoe, *Prize Court*, 28.

[65]Lord and Sprague, *Cases*, 4.

officers and other charitable purposes, rewards, etc."[66] To illustrate the relative value of maritime prize under consideration, during the Civil War and tensions with the Dutch Republic, the newly created collectors of prize goods are said to have dealt with £181,715. 2. 9 worth of property between April 1649 and September 1650.[67] It is no wonder that control of prize jurisdiction was somewhat of a prize in itself.

The Restoration of Charles II (1660-1685) and the outbreak of yet another war against the Dutch in 1665 prompted the appointment of Sir Leoline Jenkins to compile a report for the guidance of the prize court that outlined the method for conducting a prize suit and the proper procedures concerning capture, claims, and appeals. It even proposed that the court should sit twice weekly, or more often if necessary, to ensure the rapid disposal of prize cases.[68] Since Elizabethan times, letters of marque had allowed merchant crews engaged on a regular trading venture to obtain a licence to cover them in case a prize-making opportunity arose. Meanwhile, the conventional private ship of war continued to carry a large crew working for shares, extra armament, and increasingly specific instructions for cruising against the enemies of the crown. Jenkins, a judge of the High Court of Admiralty (1668-1685), first coined the term "privateer" to refer to the latter ships outfitted strictly for raiding.[69] His decisions laid down some basic principles of prize law including the right of neutrals to trade with the enemy unless they attempted to break a blockade or carry contraband, arguing that "a friend's ship could not be confiscated because it carried enemy goods; but that an enemy ship made enemy goods," and insisting that a privateer, even though he exceeded his commission, was not a pirate and should be disciplined by his own country.[70] His extensive knowledge of international law and the fairness of his judgements earned Jenkins an international reputation, and his decisions were used as precedents "by those who presided in seats of foreign juridicatures."[71]

Refining the Rules

As the practice of privateering evolved from a simple expedient for destroying enemy commerce at no cost to the crown, to a legally constituted, often extremely lucrative

---

[66] Rothery, *Droits*, 16. According to Tracy, *Attack on Trade*, 16, the 1708 prize act (6 Anne, c. 27) required all prizes to be condemned in the High Court of Admiralty and the value of the prize deposited in a "Prize Fund." Half of this amount was paid to the Treasurer of Admiralty to support seamen's charities.

[67] Roscoe, *Prize Court*, 33. During the so-called Second Anglo-Dutch War (1665-1667) Dutch losses are estimated at 1000 to 1700 vessels. R. Davis, cited in J.R. Bruijn, "Dutch Privateering during the Second and Third Anglo-Dutch Wars," *Course et piraterie: Études présentées à la Commission Internationale d'Histoire Maritime à l'occasion de son XVe colloque international pendant le XIVe Congrès International des Sciences historiques* (San Francisco, 1975), I, 79.

[68] Roscoe, *Prize Court*, 38.

[69] See K.R. Andrews, *Elizabethan Privateering: English Privateering During the Spanish War, 1585-1603* (Cambridge, 1964). Garitee, *Private Navy*, 6.

[70] Sir William Holdsworth, *A History of English Law* (1938; reprint, London, 1966), XII, 654-656.

[71] William Senior, "The Judges of the High Court of Admiralty," *Mariner's Mirror*, XIII (1927), 343.

enterprise, the maritime law that governed the ownership and awarding of prize became increasingly complex. From 1692 on, prize acts either accompanied, or shortly followed, the declaration of almost every war.[72] Naval prize consisted of all ships and vessels, armed or merchant, belonging or adhering to the enemy taken at sea, in enemy territory, or ports of the United Kingdom, including contraband of war.[73] During the reign of Charles II a distinction was drawn between what constituted legal prize to privateers and what were considered rights or Droits of Admiralty and of the crown. Following a declaration of war, naval ships could make prize based on their general commission, but privateers had to wait until the king proclaimed a prize act authorizing letters of marque and reprisal. Any property seized in port or at sea before the official declaration of war reverted to the crown. Droits of the crown also included joint captures by combined army and navy forces, and all captures by privateers before the issue of a prize proclamation. Droits reverting to the Admiralty included captures made by non-commissioned vessels such as packet boats or customs vessels (before 1801) or by privateers whose letters of marque were not valid against the nation whose ship they seized. Although privateers were not entitled to captures made in port during hostilities (these too became Droits of Admiralty), if they gave information leading to seizure by an authorized official, they occasionally received a reward.[74]

Meanwhile, the crown's traditional right to a share in all prize was gradually reduced and part of it transferred to the office of the lord high admiral to enhance his consequence, not to mention his income. The Privateers Act of 1693 eliminated the admiral's tenth and gave privateers the full value of their prizes. In 1707 the lord high admiral surrendered his tenth to the crown. Under 6 Anne, c. 37, 1708, the crown renounced its share in the first of a series of important prize acts, that gave both naval and privateer captors full statutory right to their prizes. Lydon claims that the abolition of the Royal Droit increased privateer profits by 30 percent,[75] although it probably did more to encourage naval enlistment than prompt investment in privateers. Entitlement to the full value of prize was an enormous incentive for naval officers who stood to gain the most from such legislation. An admiral actively engaged at sea was almost guaranteed a modest fortune from the war of 1739-1748 onwards.[76] Renewed in an Act of 1740, the Prize Acts of 1744 and 1756, and the Privateers Act of 1759, this provision for full prize had the added advantage of reducing the crown's influence in the matter of prize. It "deprived the Crown of any right to control the seizures by administrative order and

---

[72]Kendall, *Private Men-of-War*, 69.

[73]Rothery, *Droits*, 12.

[74]Ibid., 108.

[75]Lydon, *Pirates*, 58. J.S. Bromley, "Prize Office and Prize Agency at Portsmouth, 1689-1748," in *Corsairs and Navies, 1660-1760* (London, 1987), 464. Bromley also notes that this statute replaced the traditional bonuses of gunnage and tunnage with the more profitable incentive of head money.

[76]Julian Gwyn, *The Enterprising Admiral: The Personal Fortune of Admiral Sir Peter Warren* (Montreal, 1974), 15, calculates Admiral Sir Peter Warren's earnings for the period 1739-1748 at £127,405. Prior to the reforms of 1707, the navy had to share title to its prizes with the crown. Although the amount gradually diminished over time, the royal share ranged from one-half to one-tenth of the prize.

of any influence with the captors where justice and diplomacy required the prize to be released."[77] As Swanson suggests, the imposition of these new regulations on colonial privateering activities signalled both the increasing political strength of privateer interests and parliament's growing desire to exert some control over them.[78] As both factions became aware of the economic potential of privateering throughout the eighteenth century, tensions between colonial and imperial ambitions mounted.

One of the thorniest problems confronting prize courts had always been whether the ownership of the vessel or the cargo should determine lawful prize. Generally, from the mid-sixteenth century on, English courts followed the longstanding French rule of "robe d'ennemi" under which enemy goods carried in the holds of friends' ships were condemned along with the ship.[79] According to Marsden, the 1753 Report of Law Officers clarified the status of captured goods once and for all. In a memorandum to King George II, William Murray, Lord Mansfield (1705-1793), and three colleagues summarized the principles of proceeding in prize cases. They declared that, according to the law of nations, enemy goods on a friend's ship are lawful prize, while a friend's goods captured aboard an enemy ship, excepting contraband of war, must be restored. Contraband comprised anything that might be of service to an enemy's forces and included weapons, ships' stores, and even copper sheeting for the hulls of ships. Any property that could not be proven to be neutral was presumed to belong to the enemy.[80] With court procedures and questions of ownership firmly established, the role of the courts in administering prize law finally achieved its modern form.

Colonial Vice-Admiralty Courts

England's colonial expansion was a significant feature of the seventeenth and eighteenth centuries. Originally created to monitor fishing rights, colonial vice-admiralty courts were also supposed to protect the colonies from attack by sea, visit foreign ships entering harbour, safeguard the colonial company's monopoly on trade, and seize any interloping vessels.[81] Since pirates quickly followed in the wake of colonial merchantmen, it was not long before colonial vice-admiralty courts had to decide cases of spoil. In 1688 an Act for the More Effective Suppression of Piracy empowered colonial admiralty courts to try piracy cases within the colonies. It also permitted commanders of naval expeditions against pirates to exercise vice-admiralty jurisdiction aboard ship, thus providing a

---

[77]Pares, *Colonial Blockade*, 66. Tracy, *Attack on Trade*, 16 and Swanson, *Predators and Prizes*, 34-35, mention the reoccurrenceof the full-prize provision through several acts.

[78]Swanson, *Predators and Prizes*, 48. Tracy, *Attack on Trade*, 19, claims that attacks on trade during the five wars waged between 1702 and 1783 saw privateers account for forty percent of the prizes, half of them during the American Revolutionary War. Both Swanson and David J. Starkey, *British Privateering*, argue that privateering expanded throughout the century.

[79]Marsden, *Select Pleas*, II, xviii. Tracy, *Attack on Trade*, 69, claims France abandoned the doctrine of "robe" in the seventeenth century. The king's instructions to warships in 1681, 1692, and 1704 ignored existing treaties and reverted to the doctrine of "robe."

[80]Marsden, *Laws and Customs*, II, 350, 352.

[81]Helen J. Crump, *Colonial Admiralty Jurisdiction in the Seventeenth Century* (London, 1931), 59.

financial incentive for the navy to pursue pirates.[82] As Lord and Sprague point out, at the very time that Judge Coke was working on behalf of the common law to curtail admiralty courts in England, the Board of Trade and Plantations was furnishing colonial courts with all the jurisdiction claimed by the English court of admiralty at the time of its broadest prerogative.[83]

The creation of vice-admiralty courts, as they were known, was crucial to the consolidation and extension of imperial power overseas. They served to enforce trade and revenue laws and provided a legal outlet for the on-the-spot resolution of maritime conflict. Usually a vice-admiralty court was included in a colonial charter.[84] Jamaica boasted the first vice-admiralty court with full prize jurisdiction in 1658, followed by Barbados a few years later. Within twenty-five years there were courts in Virginia; Boston, Massachusetts; New York City (including New Jersey); and Philadelphia, Pennsylvania.

The need for maritime justice often preceded the courts. In the early years of the seasonal fishery in Newfoundland, the inevitable maritime conflicts over seamen's wages, rights of shippers, collision, and colonial trade laws were settled in a rather ingenious fashion by the authority of the "fishing admiral." As fishing vessels arrived for the season, the master of the first ship became the "fishing admiral," the second was known as vice-admiral, and the third master to arrive was the rear-admiral. This system worked well enough until the settlement of Newfoundland brought fishermen into conflict with colonists over their use of the woods and shore. In 1615, John Mason was appointed governor of Guy's Plantation, as Newfoundland was called. He carried with him a commission from the High Court of Admiralty to set up the first vice-admiralty court, which sat in the community of Trinity Bay for the three months.[85]

In the small, but strategically important colony of Nova Scotia, the first duly commissioned year-round vice-admiralty court was established at Annapolis in 1720. According to British High Court of Admiralty records, Annapolis' first vice-admiralty court judge was Daniel Henry, followed by John Bradstreet (1729) and Edward How (1737). Unfortunately, Arthur Stone's careful research failed to find the records of this, or any other Atlantic provincial vice-admiralty courts existing before the court was re-established at Halifax in 1749. Responsible for both instance and prizes cases, courts of vice-admiralty were opened in 1787 for New Brunswick, while a few years later, similar courts were created for the islands of Saint John (Prince Edward Island) and Cape

---

[82] Robert C. Ritchie, *Captain Kidd and the War against the Pirates* (Cambridge, Mass., 1986), 127-159. Seven naval warrant officers sitting as a court could hold a trial for piracy, and the ships and captured goods were treated as prize. The Offenses at Sea Act of 1806 (46 Geo. 3, c.72) subsequently extended British colonial court jurisdiction to all offenses committed at sea.

[83] Lord and Sprague, *Cases*, 4.

[84] Doty, *Admiralty Board*, 20.

[85] Crump, *Colonial Admiralty*, 28.

Breton. These courts were essential to avoid the cost in time and possible damage to cargo entailed in prosecuting prize cases back in England.[86]

By commissioning colonial governors as vice-admirals, the crown provided the mechanism for adjudicating admiralty cases, including prize, in their home ports.[87] Not only were colonial privateers encouraged by the speedy justice of their prize courts, but local merchants and investors appreciated the efficiency of trial by tribunal and the convenience of having captured cargoes on hand to sell the minute they were condemned. Once the fees and procedures of the various courts had been regulated, the jurisdiction of vice-admiralty courts in the colonies covered "all manner of maritime contracts and agreements, felonies within the jurisdiction and treasure trove, anchorages, salvages and collisions."[88]

The "stormy and troubled" relationship between the admiralty courts and the common law courts that characterized Judge Edward Coke's career found a parallel in America.[89] In discussing how some corporate or proprietary colonies balked at the imposition of English laws and objected to the absence of a jury in admiralty causes, Crump suggests that many seventeenth-century religious immigrants to America had good reason to distrust the prerogative and chancery courts of England where no juries were used. In addition, vice-admiralty courts could and periodically did impose unpopular trade acts from England. Although some early colonists resented this aspect of the courts and tried to incorporate them into the colonial government, the courts persisted. "They had been hindered, their officers harassed and as far as possible the colonists had avoided using them but no sure way had been found whereby their powers could be legally nullified."[90]

Early opposition to colonial courts within America was matched by a similar distrust within admiralty court ranks. In 1718, Sir Henry Penrice, judge of the High Court of Admiralty (1715-1751), cautioned the Admiralty against allowing vice-admiralty courts in the plantations "since it is much to be feared that they are not well versed in the Law of Nations and treaties between us and other states; and it is well known that they do not proceed in that regular manner as is practised in His Majesty's High Court

---

[86]Stone, "Admiralty Court," *DLJ*, XVII (1994), 364-365. Stone points out Fraser's inaccuracy in claiming that the first vice-admiralty court was set up in Halifax in 1749. This, in fact, was the second such court. In ten years of operation after 1749, the Halifax vice-admiralty court heard 137 cases, forty-six of those related to prize.

[87]Marcus Rediker, *Between the Devil and the Deep Blue Sea: Merchant Seamen, Pirates, and the Anglo-American Maritime World, 1700-1750* (Cambridge, 1987), 317-319. According to Stewart, *Reports*, 407, the regional vice-admiralty courts had fallen into disuse in England by the end of the eighteenth century. During the War of 1812, the High Court of Admiralty had sole jurisdiction for British Admiralty cases.

[88]Fraser, "Origin and Function," *NSHS*, XXXIII (1961), 63.

[89]Ubbelohde, *Vice-Admiralty Courts*, 19. Stone, "Admiralty Court," *DLJ*, XVII (1994), 375, refers to a 1761 petition to Chancery for a writ of prohibition against the Nova Scotia vice-admiralty court, but it concerned the court's jurisdiction in a breach of revenue laws rather than prize.

[90]Crump, *Colonial Admiralty*, 128, 31.

of Admiralty."[91] Despite Penrice's fears, both Parliament and the English High Court ruled that colonial prizes were the sole jurisdiction of vice-admiralty courts.

Vice-admiralty courts quickly established themselves as part of the legal machinery of eighteenth-century British North America. In 1708 the English parliament legalized the trying of cases in vice-admiralty courts and outlined procedures for adjudication and appeals. Since many privateers complained about the fees entailed in prize judgements, estimated at 60 percent of the total value, the eighteenth century saw the abolition of the Royal Droit or one-third share owed to the king or colonial governor.[92] To make privateering more attractive and generate more business for the vice-admiralty courts, the prize act of 1740 accompanying the outbreak of King George's War set court fees at £10 for a vessel under 100 tons and £15 for a larger one, although according to Swanson, this limit was frequently ignored.[93] By this time, rival American admiralty jurisdictions were actively competing for business. Among the most enthusiastic privateers were those from Rhode Island, who entered the fray early and captured numerous valuable prizes. Adjudicating prizes entailed a variety of court costs and it would appear that customers shopped around for the best rates. In defense of his court's fees, Massachusetts Judge Robert Auchmuty placed an ad in the *Boston Gazette* of 2 June 1740 that proclaimed:

> Whereas it is insinuated (without any colour of truth) in order to discourage the bringing in prizes into the Court of Vice-Admiralty for the provinces of the Massachusetts-Bay, New Hampshire, and the colony of Rhode Island and Providence Plantations in New England: that the fees of that court for condemnation were excessive, and more than in other courts of vice-admiralty in His Majesty's dominions. These are therefore to advertise the publick that the fees of that court in such cases are considerably less than in any other of His Majesty's Plantations, and always were so intended.[94]

Colonial prize courts became part of North American warfare because they fulfilled an economic need by condemning prizes and dealing expeditiously with commercial disputes. Throughout the eighteenth century, England's numerous wars afforded colonial privateers ample opportunity to make use of their prize courts. The frequent condemnation of extremely valuable prizes captured the imagination of the

---

[91] J. Franklin Jameson, ed., *Privateering and Piracy in the Colonial Period Illustrative Documents* (1923; reprint New York, 1970), 313. Sir Henry Penrice to Josiah Burchett, Secretary of the Admiralty, 29 Nov. 1718.

[92] Lydon, *Pirates*, 57-58.

[93] Swanson, *Predators and Prizes*, 46. Although Swanson was referring to the eighteenth century, sample court fees in Table 3.1 reveal the £15 ceiling was no longer enforced by 1812.

[94] Howard M. Chapin, *Privateering in King George's War, 1739-1748* (Providence, R.I., 1928), 25. Swanson, *Predators and Prizes*, 44. Lydon, *Pirates*, 122. In discussing court fees, Lydon suggests that court costs still represented 2.5-3.5 percent of the prize value but could rise to twenty-eight percent on appeal. This would explain the rivalry among various admiralty jurisdictions.

American public and assured the future of the vice-admiralty courts for the next one hundred years.

United States Admiralty Courts

Even after the political rupture of the American Revolution, both American and English prize courts continued to function in virtually the same manner. In 1775, the American Continental Congress issued a series of prize regulations based on the existing English model except for a brief experiment to try prize cases using juries. This attempt proved unworkable chiefly because the complexities of international law were beyond the knowledge of the average jury.[95] In 1776, the first American reference to the question of neutral goods on neutral ships (an issue that became extremely significant in Anglo-American maritime relations) appeared in a treaty plan presented to the king of France.[96]

As a neutral nation with a large economic stake in maritime trade, the United States wanted to ensure that neutral vessels remained free to navigate the high seas as long as they carried no contraband or enemy troops. Carleton Savage suggests that American maritime policy was taken from one of the treaties of Utrecht between Great Britain and France because the United States wanted its position on neutral trade to become part of the law of nations.[97]

After the American Revolution, each of the thirteen states boasted its own vice-admiralty court. The legal foundation for federal prize law is found in Article III of the Constitution, which vested the judicial power of the United States in the Supreme Court and other inferior courts. Section II of the article extended these judicial powers to all cases of admiralty and maritime jurisdiction.[98] Sir James Marriott, England's judge of the High Court of Admiralty (1778-1798), condemned the American Constitution as having "a wildness in this law that marks strongly the real character of the Americans; it is perfectly savage."[99] Unmoved by his criticism, the Supreme Court proclaimed the international status of American prize law with a 1795 decision that stated: "a decree in a court of admiralty in a prize case, binds all the world."[100]

Despite their brief history, the vice-admiralty courts of the United States rapidly established themselves as part of the American legal system and played an important role in the War of 1812. The war, in fact, provided American vice-admiralty courts with

---

[95] Carl Ubbelohde, *The Vice-Admiralty Courts and the American Revolution* (Chapel Hill, N.C., 1960), 21.

[96] Carleton Savage, *Policy of the United States toward Maritime Commerce in War* (Washington, D.C., 1934), 2. For the text of Article 26, see 133. "And it is hereby stipulated that free Ships shall also give a Freedom to Goods."

[97] Savage, *Maritime Commerce*, 3.

[98] McFee, *Law of the Sea*, 157. The American Constitution of 1787 gave Congress exclusive power to regulate prize and gave the federal judiciary the sole power to sit as admiralty courts. British cases were treated as precedents for American prize cases. Petrie, "Forbidden Prizes," *Am. Nep.*, LIV (1993), 171. (The United States Constitution, Article 3, Section 2).

[99] Roscoe, *Prize Court*, 57.

[100] Lord and Sprague, *Cases*, 9.

numerous opportunities for applying the international law of prize to both naval and privateer captures. In the case of *The Nereid*, the United States Supreme Court articulated its position on the issue of neutral rights once and for all. "The rule that the goods of an enemy found in the vessel of a friend are prize of war and that the goods of a friend found in the vessel of an enemy are to be restored is believed to be a part of the law of nations as generally, perhaps universally, acknowledged."[101]

In British North America by the end of the eighteenth century, and virtually until the procedural changes of the First World War, English prize courts were the arbiters of all property captured at sea. The great eighteenth-century English jurist, Lord Mansfield, defined their jurisdiction:

> The end of a prize court is to suspend the property till condemnation, to punish every sort of misbehaviour in the captors, to restore instantly, if upon the most summary examination there don't appear a sufficient ground; to condemn finally, if the goods really are prize, giving everybody a fair opportunity to be heard.[102]

As Britain and America headed into the nineteenth century, the English prize court had achieved international recognition as "a storehouse of rules of international law ...embedded in judicial precedents."[103] It had secured independent jurisdiction over all property seized at sea, and gradually earned respect both at home and abroad for its fair decisions. With prize proclamations automatically accompanying every declaration of war, and standard instructions regulating privateers and the taking of prize, maritime law and order was firmly established during war. The appointment of Thomas Scott (later Lord Stowell) as judge of the High Court of Admiralty (1798-1820) and his subsequent publication of his decisions created a reservoir of judicial precedents for the court and made its work accessible to a wider audience.[104] In his discussion of the function of admiralty in 1789, Scott distinguished between its role in instance and in prize: "The former proceeds originally by arrest, in order to compel bail to be given to submit to its jurisdiction: but that is not done in the Prize Court, whose jurisdiction is founded on a higher authority than the mere consent of the parties: it is founded on the right to enforce the law of nations." While admiralty exerted its authority by means of holding the ship, prize courts extended that jurisdiction over persons obtaining possession of the proceeds of a prize. Referring to the admiralty's longstanding authority over prize, Scott suggested that the new prize acts, dating from 1707 (6 Anne, c. 13), "were drawn up principally for the direction of the Vice-Admiralty Courts, to which a jurisdiction over questions of prize was thereby for the first time given." The inclusion of procedural instructions in

---

[101]Savage, *Maritime Commerce*, 288.

[102]Stewart, *Reports*, 319. Although Great Britain's signature of the Declaration of Paris officially ended privateering in 1856, the British admiralty courts continued to adjudicate naval prize during the First World War.

[103]Roscoe, *Prize Court*, 53.

[104]Ibid., 55.

subsequent prize acts indicate that Parliament felt the colonial vice-admiralty courts would benefit from ongoing direction.[105]

With France and Great Britain at war in Europe, the United States envisioned enormous gains in the exercise of her traditionally neutral trade. A pre-war flurry of embargoes and trade restrictions played havoc with American plans and insulted her newfound nationalism. As naval recruiters and would-be privateers looked on expectantly, preparations for war accelerated on both sides of the Atlantic. With a long history of practice behind them and a growing list of precedents to draw on, the vice-admiralty courts in Atlantic Canada and America were well prepared for war. The next chapter examines the procedures developed by the vice-admiralty courts and traces the sequence of legal actions they established for taking a prize from arrest through adjudication to the final sentence.

Figure 3: Seal of the High Court of Admiralty.

[105]Pritchard and Yale, eds., *Hale and Fleetwood*, lxiv-lxv, discuss Scott's judgement in *Smart v. Wolff* in 1789.

Chapter 3
Prizemaking and the Vice-Admiralty Court at Halifax

By 1812, the Halifax Court of Vice-Admiralty had had over half a century to refine its procedures for adjudicating prize. The American Revolution and sporadic war with France provided the court with dozens of precedents for the administration of prize law against goods or vessels captured from the enemy or forfeited by neutrals for breach of the international law of nations. The role of the Halifax vice-admiralty court was crucial in a legal and economic sense. Regulating vice-admiralty court procedures was a series of documents including petitions, allegations, and affidavits that generated the evidence the court needed to condemn or restore a prize. The court, its judge, and officers had to be both honest and competent since their decisions were so closely tied to the economic success or failure of prizemaking. While captors occasionally complained about the cost of adjudication, there were no accusations of illegality, nor did anyone attribute court registrar Richard Uniacke's great wealth to more than the energetic pursuit of legitimate fees. In comparison, there are numerous criticisms surrounding the often unscrupulous activities of prize agents. Although appeals from prize judgements did occur, Judge Alexander Croke rarely had a decision overturned by the High Court of Admiralty. The vice-admiralty court was a key participant in prizemaking in Atlantic Canada during the War of 1812. By highlighting the key practitioners, reviewing court procedures, and examining the cost of vice-admiralty activities, this chapter confirms that the adjudication of prize was both legitimate and lucrative.

Although not totally extant, the Vice-Admiralty Court Series of prize files held in the Public Archives of Canada contains a wealth of information concerning the proceedings, testimonies, court costs, accounts, and sales of over 600 vessels seized as prize by British naval vessels and privateers from New Brunswick and Nova Scotia between 1812 and 1815. By analyzing these records, it is possible to derive a sequence for the proceedings of the court, determine the impact of various court costs, and understand why certain verdicts were appealed and what considerations influenced the court's decisions.

While the mechanics of prizemaking by privateers and naval vessels will be examined in later chapters, it is important to recognize that the act of capture was but the first step in a complex legal process, which by 1812, had become "as formalized as a quadrille."[1] By law, captors were obliged to send their prizes to their home port for adjudication. As well as being the home port for the Royal Navy in North America, Halifax, Nova Scotia, served as a base for numerous privateers. Prizes taken into other ports were often transported to Halifax along with their papers so that their captors could take advantage of the larger, more lucrative Halifax market for foodstuffs or luxury goods.

---

[1]Melvin H. Jackson, *Privateers in Charleston, 1793-1796* (Washington, D.C., 1969), vi.

Arrival in port initiated a series of events that could take from three weeks to several years to resolve. Each step required legal documentation with its attendant fee eating into the captor's profits while enriching the custom house and the courts. As historian H.C. Timewell suggests, "The seizure of a prize became much of a gamble because of high legal costs, delays in the Prize Courts, litigation between partners and other claimants, together with the cost of maintaining a prize in port while awaiting adjudication."[2] Despite the odds, the prizemakers must have considered the risk worth taking or their vessels would never have left port.

The Prelude

As Great Britain and the United States faced off in a war that few supported and many circumvented, the court of vice-admiralty stood by to deal with the inevitable maritime conflict. From the court's re-establishment in Halifax in 1749, the lieutenant governor, as vice-admiral, received nominal jurisdiction over such issues as maritime contracts and agreements, felonies within this jurisdiction, treasure trove, anchorage, salvage, and collisions at sea. Unlike its parent admiralty court in England, the colonial vice-admiralty court was also obliged to preside over the enforcement of numerous Trade and Navigation Acts, much to the disgust of many colonists. The court's chief value to the colonial economy, however, was as a prize court in time of war. During the first decade of its existence, the Halifax vice-admiralty court heard 137 cases, 46 of which involved prizes.[3]

In 1749, under Judge Edward How, the Halifax vice-admiralty court received rather broad powers to hold courts throughout the province, compel witnesses to testify, and within the province, "to fine, convict, punish, chastise, and reform and imprison" anyone violating the law and jurisdiction of the admiralty court. The actual work of Judge How's court consisted of ordinary civil or "instance" jurisdiction over general maritime issues, concurrent jurisdiction with common law courts over breaches of Imperial trade or revenue laws, and special wartime jurisdiction over prize. In the mid-eighteenth century, the province of Nova Scotia or Acadia included Cape Breton Island, the Island of Saint John (Prince Edward Island), Quebec (until 1764), and New Brunswick (until 1784). A court of vice-admiralty was established in Saint John in 1787. Judge How managed his territory with the help of a registrar or scribe and his deputies: a marshal and "serjent" of mace to take custody of property arrested by the court, sell it, and execute court decrees and sentences; a crier; and a doorkeeper. The advocate general of the court, also called the procurator general, represented the crown's special interests, specifically in prize and revenue cases. Although the Halifax Court of Vice-

---

[2]H.C. Timewell, "Guernsey Privateers," *Mariner's Mirror*, LVI (1970), 213.

[3]D.G.L. Fraser, "The Court of Vice-Admiralty in Halifax, 1749-1759," *Nova Scotia Historical Society*, XXXIII (1961), 69, 80. The first case extant for Halifax involved a sailor's wages, which the court ordered paid. Lionel H. Laing, "Nova Scotia's Admiralty Court as a Problem of Colonial Administration," *Canadian Historical Review*, XVI (1935), 152. The judges of the Nova Scotia vice-admiralty court up to the War of 1812 were Edward How (1749), Benjamin Green (1749-1753), John Collier (1753-1769), Richard Bulkley (1769-1799), James Brenton (1799-1800), and Dr. Alexander Croke (1801-1815).

Admiralty eventually adopted the English tradition of proctors and advocates with separate court duties, as Arthur Stone points out, this specialization was slow to develop, and provincial lawyers acted as either.[4]

According to Carl Ubbelohde, colonial vice-admiralty courts functioned on three levels. Locally, they decided disputes arising between merchants and seamen; as agents of imperial policy after 1696, the courts were empowered to serve as tribunals for prosecution of the British Navigation Acts. When war came, the courts took on an international dimension as arbiters of the law of nations concerning prize.[5]

By 1763, the end of the Seven Years' War, Britain revised her Navigation Acts to rationalize her expanded imperial trading network. Through their dubious involvement in enforcing these Acts, vice-admiralty courts became firmly identified with Britain's imperial system. To guarantee British access to colonial goods not produced in England, and perhaps, to control American competition, Britain restricted the export of such colonial products as sugar, rice, tobacco, molasses, cotton, furs, and naval stores to certain English ports. Not only did this not endear the Board of Trade and Plantations to the mercantile community of North America, it also perverted vice-admiralty courts "to a use not countenanced in the parent court and one which was certain to arouse hatred and animosity."[6]

Growing unrest in the American colonies and frequent transgressions against the Navigation Acts prompted the British Board of Trade to streamline the vice-admiralty court system in North America. At that time, Halifax boasted one of eleven vice-admiralty courts in the New World. As patronage appointments by the lieutenant governors, the judges of these courts derived a certain prestige and influence from their position, although their incomes were fixed by colonial statute and based on set fees augmented by a percentage of the value of goods they condemned. Unfortunately, while this may have reduced the cost to the Board of Trade, the percentage system tended to encourage judges to let self-interest temper their judgement.

In October 1764, the Board of Trade selected Halifax as the site of a single "supercourt" for all British North America. Dr. William Spry was appointed commissary deputy and surrogate judge over a territory that stretched from Newfoundland to Florida. Spry's powers ran concurrently with those of the existing colonial admiralty courts but

---

[4]Arthur J. Stone, "The Admiralty Court," *Dalhousie Law Journal*, XVII (1994), 366, 369. Stone cites the duties of the Halifax Court of Vice-Admiralty from the High Court of Admiralty commission for Judge How. In *David Copperfield*, Steerforth describes a proctor as "a sort of monkish attorney" and advocates as "men who have taken a doctor's degree at college," noting that both get "very comfortable fees." Charles Dickens, *David Copperfield* (1850; reprint, New York, n.d.), 335-336.

[5]Carl Ubbelohde, *The Vice-Admiralty Courts and the American Revolution* (Chapel Hill, N.C., 1960), 12. The colonial vice-admiralty courts enforced the Navigation Acts until the acts were repealed in 1849.

[6]V.T. Harlow, *The Founding of the Second British Empire, 1763-1793* (London, 1952), I, 159. See also Marcus Rediker, *Between the Devil and the Deep Blue Sea: Merchant Seamen, Pirates, and the Anglo-American Maritime World* (Cambridge, 1987), 316. Laing, "Admiralty Court," *CHR*, XVI (1935), 152, feels that the jurisdiction of vice-admiralty courts in administering the Navigation Acts was "unwarrantable" and possibly contributed to the American Revolution.

without power to hear appeals from them.[7] His annual salary was £800 regardless of the number of cases heard, and the court sat the first and third Wednesdays of each month. American merchants, who had always preferred the faster, simpler deliberations of the vice-admiralty court process, objected to taking their cases to Halifax and boycotted the new court. The last straw came in 1765 with the imposition of Stamp Act duties on legal documents, which further added to the cost of obtaining a judgement in Judge Spry's court. Business in Spry's new court fell off badly by 1766, leading him to complain, "the employment I have had here in my court has been too inconsiderable and trifling to be communicated."[8] Spry left Nova Scotia shortly thereafter to become governor of the Barbados.

As early as May 15, 1760, the *Boston Gazette* carried an article entitled "Instructions from the Town of Boston to their Representatives," which claimed, "the American courts of admiralty seem to be forming by degrees into a system that is to overturn our constitution and to deprive us entirely of our best inheritance, the law of the land." In September 1768, Britain finally bowed to American pressure by issuing four commissions for vice-admiralty court judges in Halifax, Boston, Philadelphia, and Charleston with annual salaries of £600 and a percentage of court fees. Nevertheless, increasingly rebellious Americans continued to reject the courts along with other British institutions. While the Halifax court is rumoured to have yielded enough income by October 1770 to pay Spry's successor's salary for two years, the Boston court earned a mere £95 in forfeitures, and the judge's salary had to be paid from the naval stores fund. According to Ubbelohde, only the Halifax court continued to perform its vice-admiralty court functions during the American Revolution, although several states experimented with existing courts and such ideas as trying prize cases before a jury.[9]

France's declaration of war against Great Britain in 1793 prompted Nova Scotians to apply for some twenty letters of marque. Much of the privateering experience acquired against France in this period by men like Simeon Perkins, Joseph Freeman, Joseph Barss, and Enos Collins was turned to good use against the United States in 1812. Hostile naval activity against France increased both the workload and the revenues of the Halifax court. Between 1797 and 1803, the court heard over 200 cases.[10] By then, the controlled number of vice-admiralty courts, their extended jurisdiction, higher salaries, and greater social consequence made colonial courts attractive to qualified civil lawyers

---

[7]Laing, "Admiralty Court," *CHR*, XVI (1935), 158.

[8]Ubbelohde, *Vice-Admiralty Courts*, 56.

[9]Laing, "Admiralty Court," 155, quotes the Boston paper. Ubbelohde, *Vice-Admiralty Courts*, 193.

[10]Charles Bruce Fergusson, ed., *The Diary of Simeon Perkins, 1797-1803* (Toronto, 1967), I, liv. In 1803, two new vice-admiralty courts were instituted in Malta and Bahamas/Bermuda. See James Stewart, *Reports of cases argued and determined in the Court of Vice-Admiralty at Halifax, in Nova Scotia from the commencement of the war, in 1803, to the end of the year 1813, in the time of Alexander Croke LLD., Judge of that Court* (Halifax, N.S., 1813), viii.

such as Judge (later Sir) Alexander Croke.[11] In 1801, Croke chose the severe yet healthy air of Halifax over the luxurious but hazardous climate of the West Indies and served as judge of the vice-admiralty court for the next fourteen years.

Figure 4: Sir Alexander Croke, portrait by Robert Field.

Source: National Gallery of Canada.

The Practitioners

i) Sir Alexander Croke

Admired by his registrar, James Stewart, who dutifully recorded 600 pages of Croke's judgements, Dr. Croke seems to have been well respected for his legal knowledge and universally despised for everything else he did. Described by one Nova

[11]Stewart, *Reports*, v. The salary of the judge was set at £2,000 per year with up to an additional £2,000 per year in fees and perquisites.

Scotia historian as "brilliant, cynical and grasping,"[12] Croke's difficult personality soon offended virtually every level of society, eventually making him "the most disliked man in Halifax."[13] Extremely conservative by training and inclination, Croke was a staunch Anglican and a strong opponent of democratic government of any sort. At the same time, he fancied himself a poet and satirist and wrote poems deriding the foibles of his own social class with, as one biographer put it, "more bad temper than wit."[14] One such poem, entitled *Inquisition*, circulated through Halifax drawing rooms in 1808. Its thinly disguised characters created indignation and anger and further alienated Croke from his peers.

About the same time, the newly-appointed lieutenant governor, Sir George Prevost, was sent to Martinique to quell a rebellion. Croke, as a senior member of the Legislative Council, took over as lieutenant governor and president of the legislature. Convinced that he could spend provincial monies more judiciously that the legislators, Croke took the unprecedented step of withholding the president's token assent to the province's appropriations bill. This refusal left Nova Scotia unable to use the taxes it collected to pay for road repair, salaries, or even to buy arms in the event of war. An outraged legislative committee condemned Croke's actions as "extraordinary, undignified and an abuse of power."[15] Immediately upon Prevost's return, the bill was passed. In a dispatch from Prevost to Lord Castlereagh in August 1809, Prevost refered to Croke's demand for half his salary as well as any fees and emoluments Prevost earned as military commander in Martinique. He argued that if Croke's petition were granted, Prevost would receive nothing at all for his service in Martinique.[16]

Amazingly enough, in August 1811, when Prevost became commander-in-chief of Lower Canada, Croke once again assumed control. This time he was only in charge for six months, and the legislature was not in session during that period. Croke once more applied for half of Prevost's salary including emoluments for the period. In writing to Under Secretary of State Sir Robert Peel in January 1812 regarding Croke's petition, Prevost's successor, Lieutenant Governor Sir John Coape Sherbrooke, hoped that the request would not be granted because "the Commander-in-Chief's share of the seizure of a cargo of flour made during the short administration of Dr. Croke will exceed five hundred pounds."[17] Croke's request was indeed denied.

---

[12]T.H. Raddall, *Halifax, Warden of the North* (1971; reprint, Toronto, 1980), 133.

[13]Hon. John Doull, *Sketches of Attorney Generals of Nova Scotia, 1750-1926* (Halifax, N.S., 1964), 61.

[14]Hon. Adam G. Archibald, "Sir Alexander Croke," *Nova Scotia Historical Society*, xxx (1880), 120.

[15]Ibid., 122.

[16]Ells, Margaret, ed., *A Calendar of Official Correspondence and Legislative Papers, Nova Scotia, 1802-1815* (Halifax, N.S., 1936), 188, Sherbrooke to Sec. of State, 19 Aug. 1809, [Vol. 58, doc. 90].

[17]Ibid., Sherbrooke to Under-Sec. Peel, 14 Jan. 1811, 240, [Vol. 59, doc. 26].

Upon his retirement in 1814 from a province that was only too glad to see him go, Croke was rewarded with a knighthood and an annual pension of £1,000. Although Croke never achieved his original goal of "precedence above all magistrates, or officers of government whose jurisdiction and offices are merely confined to Nova Scotia," Croke certainly left his mark on the Nova Scotia Vice-Admiralty Court.[18]

ii) Richard John Uniacke

One of the most successful members of Croke's court was Richard John Uniacke, who represented the crown as advocate general of the vice-admiralty court, and subsequently served the province of Nova Scotia as attorney general for over thirty years. A man of "great natural eloquence, talent and industry,"[19] the Irish-born Uniacke came to Nova Scotia as a young man of twenty. After a brief flirtation with the American Revolutionary cause, necessitating a hasty flight back home, Uniacke returned to Nova Scotia in 1783 as solicitor general. But his real ambition was the position of attorney general. In this he was constantly thwarted by Samuel Sampson Blowers, the Speaker of the House in the provincial Legislative Assembly, who was first appointed attorney-general in 1784. Perhaps as a palliative, Uniacke was made advocate general of the vice-admiralty court, "an office that would be instrumental in making his fortune."[20] Along with the fees it entailed, Uniacke's position brought him into contact with some of Nova Scotia's most prominent merchants, such as Simeon Perkins, whose privateers supplied numerous prizes for Croke's court to adjudicate. Noting the money to be made, Uniacke was not above a little speculative investment in privateers himself. In 1799, Uniacke finally obtained his appointment as attorney general. Despite being an officer of the crown, by 1800 the energetic Uniacke also ran the largest private legal practice in the province. His public duties included Speaker of the House, member of the Legislative Assembly, and governor of King's College. In 1805 he published *Statutes at Large*, a compendium of all legislation passed in Nova Scotia from 1758 to 1804.

During the War of 1812, Uniacke used the substantial fees he amassed as an official of the vice-admiralty court to achieve the social status to which he aspired. Various sources place his earnings at £50,000 during the course of the war.[21] His lucrative income as advocate general of the vice-admiralty court enabled him to finance a several-thousand acre estate, Mt. Uniacke, between 1813 and 1815. Described by one of his early political opponents as "a great lubber insolent Irish rebel," in Cuthbertson's opinion, "no one gained a greater mastery over the complex and bewildering laws of trade and navigation." Unlike Sir Alexander Croke, Uniacke is remembered as

---

[18]Laing, "Admiralty Court," *CHR*, XVI (1935), 159, quotes a letter from Croke to Hobart, 28 Jan. 1802, (PRO C.O. 217/77) arguing for a higher rank for the judge of the court of vice-admiralty.

[19]Doull, *Attorney Generals*, 29.

[20]Brian Cuthbertson, *The Old Attorney General* (Halifax, N.S., 1980), 16.

[21]Peter Waite, Sandra Oxner, Thomas Barnes, eds., *Law in a Colonial Society: The Nova Scotia Experience* (Toronto, 1984), 127.

"unquestionably the most influential Nova Scotian in the first quarter of the nineteenth century."[22]

The Problem

The activation of a vice-admiralty court as a prize court required a declaration of war usually followed by a prize act. Once Britain was at war, the Lords Commissioners of Admiralty were commissioned under the Great Seal to authorize the seizure and detention of enemy vessels and the judgement of such prizes before the High Court of Admiralty in London, or in colonial vice-admiralty courts. By this commission, the Admiralty issued a warrant ordering courts such as the one at Halifax to proceed against captured enemy vessels according to the international law of prize. From 1708 on, virtually every British declaration of war had been accompanied by a prize act ordering general reprisals against the enemy.[23] The Prize Act of 1809 (49 George III) enacted against France and other enemies of the crown remained in effect until 1812.

One of the anomalies of the War of 1812 was Britain's delay in responding to America's June 16 declaration of war with one of her own. This left Nova Scotia Lieutenant Governor Sir John Coape Sherbrooke in an awkward position. While Britain urged him to avoid hostilities, those merchants whose ships had fallen prey to American privateers besieged him, as head of the vice-admiralty court, for letters of marque.

Sherbrooke's solution was to issue general commissions based on the Prince Regent's order-in-council of 31 July 1812. This urged the detention of American vessels except those with licences, those released from Embargo, or those vessels still continuing their original voyage. Although restraint, not condemnation, was the purpose of the order, Sherbrooke used it to justify his authority to issue letters of marque to several privateer vessels between June and October.

The absence of an official declaration of war left the privateers, despite their commissions, in a legal limbo and embroiled them in court battles that outlasted the war. In 1818 Charles Uniacke articulated the crux of the argument against Sherbrooke's commissions: "Until the court receives authority to act through the regular and legal channel, it cannot undertake to administer the laws as applicable to prize, and to settle the conflicting issues of nations."[24] Although Canadian-based privateers captured American and foreign prizes almost immediately, Judge Croke usually disallowed these early captures or condemned them as droits of admiralty since they were seized by unauthorized vessels in the absence of a legal state of war. Naval captures, on the other

---

[22]Cuthbertson, *Attorney General*, 52, v.

[23]E.S. Roscoe, *Reports of Prize Cases determined in the High Court of Admiralty before the Lords High Commissioners of Appeals in Prize Causes and before the Judicial Committee of the Privy Council from 1745 to 1859* (London, 1905), I, vii. An exception occurred in June 1739 when Britain issued letters of marque against Spain but did not declare war until October. A new prize act was not enacted until 1740.

[24]Beamish Murdoch, *Epitome of the Laws of Nova Scotia* (Halifax, N.S., 1833), IV, 110. Judgement of C. Uniacke Esq., Vice-Admiralty Court at Halifax, case of the *Nabby*. Charles Uniacke was the son of R.J. Uniacke and succeeded Sir Alexander Croke as judge of the court of vice-admiralty in 1815.

hand, were acts of national self-defence, even without a declared war, and the vice-admiralty court usually upheld such prizes.

The Process

With a well-established vice-admiralty court manned by skilled practitioners, the privateers and Royal Navy vessels operating out of Atlantic Canada had the benefit of a finely-tuned legal mechanism to help them transform captures into cash. No prize was guaranteed, however, and even when a captor overcame the many maritime hazards threatening his prize, he still had to run the legal gauntlet of petitions, claims, affidavits, and appeals that could siphon his potential profits into the coffers of the court.

i) Prize Master's Affidavit

Legal action on a prize could not begin until the prize master of the captured vessel swore an affidavit of papers before the local registrar of the vice-admiralty court or his deputy. This affidavit confirmed details of the capture and furnished the names of both captor and prize, latitude when captured, closest landmark (if known), time of day, and identified any allied ships in sight at the time of capture. Since the visible presence of another ship, and its implied threat, might influence a vessel's decision to surrender, this information was essential for determining claims of joint capture. The affidavit also identified the prize's port of origin, its destination, and cargo based on the captured ship's papers. So important were the ship's papers to the final judgement that any vessel carrying false documents or concealing or destroying papers before capture was automatically liable for condemnation.[25] The prize master's affidavit listed the documents captured with the ship and usually concluded with a sworn statement that all papers were numbered and deposited in the court registry without alteration. The cost of "filing and entering affidavit of prize master and filing and numbering exhibits" varied from 15 s. (*Anna*) to £1 (*Protectress*) up to £11.18.0 (*Resolution*). All fees were paid to the court registrar.[26]

ii) Petitions

Once the ship's papers were registered, the captor's agents or owners petitioned the court to issue several standard court documents. A review of documents filed in the Halifax Court of Vice-Admiralty over the course of the war reveals that as the court process became better established, hand-written documents gave way to printed forms where court officials simply filled in the blanks. Some of these forms appeared at one stage of the war only to fall out of use later on. This could represent evolving court practice, or indicate the inability of a busy court to keep up with its paperwork.

---

[25]R.G. Marsden, ed., *Documents Relating to Laws and Customs of the Sea* (London, 1915), II, 353. Regulations for Adjudication, 1665. See also chapter 2.

[26]PAC, RG 8, IV, Vol. 116, *Anna*, Affidavit of George Brown (HMS *Acasta*), 19 July 1813; Vol. 118, *Protectress*, Affidavit of George Henry Ayton (HMS *Victorious*), 8 July 1813; HMS *Majestic* captured *Resolution* 25 Sept. 1813 but it took until Oct. 1815 to settle court costs of £366.

Whatever the reason, three types of petitions – for warrant for custody, for a monition, and for an examination – left a somewhat sporadic trail through the prize files.

Petitions for warrant, for example, requesting the judge to issue a warrant for the marshal of the vice-admiralty court to take the vessel and goods into custody appear in certain cases during 1813 but drop off in 1814. Since the legal process could not begin until the captured ship and its papers were officially handed over anyway, an official petition for such a warrant was probably unnecessary – except for the court fees it generated.

The marshal and the collector of customs for the port of Halifax were jointly responsible for the security of captured vessels and cargoes pending adjudication. Depending on the length of time a vessel was held in custody, the fees earned by these two worthies could be considerable. The marshal's standard fee was 7s.6d. per day, while the collector earned about half that amount. Thus, for *Howe*, the custody fees for 153 days in port totalled £57.7.6.[27] Custody costs for *Mary*, recaptured by HMS *Wasp* in 1814, represented only £1.2.6 out of £41.14.2 court costs and the case was concluded in three weeks.[28] One of the longest cases involved the schooner *Penelope* and a cargo of thirteen tierces of coffee captured by the New Brunswick privateer *General Smyth* in August 1812. It took two years to condemn this prize to the crown *jurae coronae* and award the cargo to the captors. In recognition of the lengthy detention, the court halved the custody fees, but even then, once £163.10.10 custody fees and other court costs were deducted from the profit of £338.10.11½ from the sale of the coffee, the captors were left with less than £70.[29]

Although incomplete, the Accounts and Records file of prizes reveal four ships held in custody for 298 days and thirty-five more held for over 200 days.[30] Many of these vessels were prizes taken between June and October 1812, when Great Britain was trying to avoid outright confrontation with the United States by delaying a declaration of war. The lag in processing these provincial prizes might have been due to their dubious legal status.

Custody fees were based on the length of detention, extra security requirements such as watchmen, or other court-ordered services. In the case of recaptured British vessels, which were worth less to the captors, prize acts generally waived the payment of court costs to encourage the recovery of captured vessels and cargoes.[31] After 1740 the vice-admiralty court could no longer condemn recaptured vessels to the captors, but had to return them to their owners. Salvage awards could be no higher than half the

---

[27]P.A.C., RG 8, IV, Vol. 132, *Howe*, recaptured by HMS *Plumper*, 5 Sept. 1812. Captor awarded salvage of 1/8 of the appraised value of £500 or £62.10.

[28]PAC, RG 8, IV, Vol. 136, *Mary*, captured 6 Oct. and condemned 1 Nov. 1814.

[29]PAC, RG 8, IV, Vol. 92, *Penelope*, Record of Sales, 25 May 1815.

[30]PAC, RG 8, IV, Vol. 129, Accounts 9-11.

[31]Swanson, *Predators and Prizes*, 44, indicates that by the Prize Act of 1740, captors of recaptured vessels were not obliged to pay court costs.

value of the vessel, and the amount of salvage depended on the length of time a vessel lay in enemy hands. According to James Lydon, a recaptured prize was only worth half the appraised value after it had been in enemy hands at least four days. The purpose of this clause was to ensure that privateers did not allow a vessel to be taken as prize in order to recapture it immediately for salvage.[32] The Prize Act of 1805 extended to 1813 reiterated the requirement to restore captured vessels to their former owners upon payment of salvage. By the War of 1812, however, naval recaptors received one-eighth of the appraised value of the prize and privateers received one-sixth.[33]

In his examination of New York privateering in the eighteenth century, Lydon suggests that the average cost of a basic condemnation was approximately ten percent of the value of the prize. Because not enough values are known for vessels condemned in the Halifax vice-admiralty court, it was difficult to make a comparison. A survey of prize data for the War of 1812, however, revealed a twelve percent ratio of court costs to the total cost of condemnation. Table 3.1 lists costs for custody and court fees for eight captures and ten recaptures selected at random from among the Accounts and Record files.[34] Court costs range from five percent to more than 100 percent of the cost of custody. In the case of salvage, although fees show a similar variation, court costs average out to ten percent of the value of the salvage award.

Nearly eighty percent of the 1812 cases contain a document called petition for monition, while almost none appears in files after 1813. This petition requested the judge to issue the usual monition for the prize. It noted the name of the prize, the captor, and affirmed that the papers were deposited in the registry. Since a monition was issued for every prize and the number of that monition was written on every prize document related to the case, it appears that the petition for monition was eventually considered redundant to the legal process.

The last petition, another document that appears only rarely, requested the judge to issue a commission authorizing a "fit and proper person" to examine at least one member of the captured crew according to a series of thirty-four standard questions known as the standing interrogatories. Appendix 2 lists the standard questions posed to one or more crewmembers or passengers.

iii) Monition

Whether a prize file contained any or all of the above petitions, at least seventy-five percent contain a monition issued the same day or soon after the petition for monition. The vice-admiralty court judge issued monitions in the name of the king and ordered or "admonished" anyone with a claim to the prize, "tackle, apparel and furniture and the goods, wares and merchandise laded therein" to be "monished, cited and called to judgement" twenty days after entering port and posting the monition, or the next court day, at 11 a.m. At that time, claimants were required to show "in due form of law" why

---

[32]James G. Lydon, *Pirates, Privateers and Profits* (Upper Saddle River, N.J., 1970),113.

[33]45 Geo. III, c. 72, VII. An exception to the rule was if the recaptured vessel had been used by His Majesty's enemies as a ship of war. In such a case, it could be adjudged lawful prize.

[34]PAC, RG 8, IV, Vol. 129, Accounts 9-11.

the prize should not be pronounced as enemy goods and declared "good and lawful prize" to the captor. Most monitions bear a hand-written note by the deputy-marshal certifying the date that the monition was executed. Captured vessels anchored in port had a copy of this monition nailed to the mast. The collector of customs took charge of cargoes seized from vessels that had been released, abandoned, or destroyed and posted the monitions publicly on the custom house door.

Table 3.1
Court costs as a percentage of total custody costs and salvage awards.
Court decisions indicate either R (restored) or C (condemned).

Date	Vessel	Decision	Court Cost	Custody	%
18-07-12	*Actress*	*Jurae Coronae*	£ 24. 8. 4	£ 103. 9. 7	25%
21-08-14	*Albion*	R (salvage) £ 631 (9%)	£ 70. 3. 3	£ 426.10. 5	11.5%
11-10-13	*Charlotte*	R (salvage) £ 773 (33%)	£ 29. 1.10	£ 180.12. 8	11%
31-08-13	*Divina Pastora*	R (appeal)	£ 30. 9. 0	£ 218.	9%
27-08-13	*Euphemia*	R (ship) C (cargo)	£ 57. 5. 0	£ 310. 4. 2	20%
28-04-13	*Henry*	R (licence)	£ 26. 1. 8	£ 51. 0.10	50%
24-08-14	*Landrail*	R (salvage) £ 130 (10%)	£ 14. 5. 8	£ 14. 3. 6	100%
26-03-15	*Louisa*	R (salvage) £ 340 (13%)	£ 48. . 4	£ 480	10%
16-06-13	*Loyal Sam*	R (salvage) £ 1,662 (1.5%)	£ 27.18. 4	£ 130	20%
04-05-14	*Maria Francisco*	R (salvage) £ 270 (13%)	£ 38.13.10	£ 253. 6. 1	15%
21-04-14	*New Zealander*	R (salvage) £ 851 (11%)	£ 95. 9.10	£ 713. 5. 8	15%
04-12-13	*Policy*	R (salvage) £ 1,044 (3%)	£ 34	£ 331	17%
18-06-13	*Protectress*	C (R-appeal)	£ 26. 1. 8	£ 500	5%
07-09-13	*Resolution*	C	£ 39.13.	£ 247	16%
26-06-13	*Santiago*	R	£ 46.11. 8	£ 551. . 3	8%
15-07-12	*Start*	JC	£ 26. 1. 8	£ 427	6%
29-05-14	*Success*	R (salvage) £ 371 (9%)	£ 36.16. 4	£ 118.14. 6	30%
21-07-14	*Tyger*	R (salvage) £ 1,137 (4%)	£ 49. 5	£ 202.12. 1	20%
AVGE		(10%)			12%

Once a monition was posted, it was the master's duty to register a protest or claim immediately and advise his owners. He then had to retain the services of a trial lawyer or proctor to enter a claim for the vessel in vice-admiralty court along with an affidavit as to the rightful ownership of the vessel and cargo. A bond or security for the claim was also deposited with the court registrar. According to Dr. Croke, any delay in the process after the prescribed twenty days "is the fault of the suitors themselves, for each party has the power of compelling his adversary to proceed to trial under pain of making compensation for the delay."[35] Unfortunately, there seems to have been a number of exceptions to this rule.

iv) Allegations

With the court duly petitioned, the prize papers registered with the court, and claimants advised of their opportunity to make their case, vice-admiralty court proceedings moved into the courtroom. The key document on which the crown's case rested was the allegation in a prize cause, or libel, which was submitted by the advocate and procurator general on behalf of the king or his regent. This document first established grounds for condemnation based on the general reprisals issued against American vessels, goods, and citizens in the 13 October order-in-council and reaffirmed the right of the vice-admiralty court to hear prize cases "according to the Courts of Admiralty and the Law of Nations." It listed the vessel type, name, and master of the prize, the date captured, and the type, name, and master of the captor. The allegation confirmed that the prize was enemy-owned and liable to condemnation. It finally alleged that all premises upon which the cause was based were true, public, and notorious and urged the court to condemn accordingly.

Other allegations could accompany the libel for prize. For example, prior to the October order-in-council, the agents for admiralty could submit a document known as an allegation for condemnation as a droit of admiralty. This applied to prizes taken by unauthorized captors.[36] Many privateer cases in the early months of the war contain such a claim by the agents for admiralty in Halifax, Samuel Hood George, Edward Brabizon, and Brenton Haliburton. The basis for their authority was a document dated 22 June 1812, passed by the receiver general of rights and perquisites of admiralty. As duly appointed agents in maritime places within admiralty jurisdiction, these men were entitled to collect dues legally adjudged to belong to the office of the lord high admiral. Although the court condemned some fifty-six vessels as droits of admiralty, most were returned to their captors on appeal. In the case of the *Liverpool Packet*, seventeen prizes worth £21,875 seized in 1812 and condemned as droits of admiralty were eventually returned to the captor after a two-year High Court Appeal process.[37]

---

[35]Stewart, *Reports*, 589.

[36]PAC, RG 8, IV, Vol. 124, *Lydia*, captured 24 Oct. 1812 by the New Brunswick privateer, *General Smyth*.

[37]PAC, RG 8, IV, Vol. 128, Accounts and Records, 11 Nov. 1814, Prince Regent's Warrant.

v) Standing Interrogatories

With or without a petition to examine, the court next undertook to question one or more representatives from the captured crew. Although ships' masters were most commonly interviewed, mates, seamen, passengers, supercargoes, cooks, and coopers all appeared as deponents. In cases of abandoned or released vessels where no crew member was available for questioning, a member of the prize crew usually provided the deposition to the best of his ability. Foreign crewmen, unable to make their depositions in English, were provided with a translator at the captor's expense. The registrar's fee for an examination under the standing interrogatories was £1.3.4 according to *Minerva*'s bill.[38]

Because vice-admiralty court proceedings were not held before a jury, the judge required an examination that was both thorough and searching to ensure that he had enough facts on which to base his decision.[39] The captors, however, chose which crew members to carry back to testify. Of 512 examinations on file, 217 (44%) were masters, 107 (20%) were seamen, 82 (16%) were mates, and 106 (20%) were cooks, cabin boys, passengers, carpenters, stewards, or pilots. While the master or supercargo tended to be the best informed regarding the ship's papers and licences or other extenuating circumstances regarding the vessel or its cargo, this knowledge did not always work to the captors' advantage. The documents contain several references to masters being sent off to distant ports aboard cartels or set down on remote coastal locations to prevent them from reaching Halifax and being examined by the vice-admiralty court. Instead, the prize crew carried back an illiterate seaman or cook in the hope that his ignorance of administrative details would result in a favourable judgement for the captors.[40]

vi) Disposition

Based on the allegation in a prize cause, the prize master's affidavit, and the examination of one or more crew, the vice-admiralty court judge had enough information to be able to condemn or acquit. If doubts remained, claimants could furnish further proof by means of petitions and affidavits from interested parties or their agents on both sides. Naturally, the more valuable the vessel and/or cargo, the more legal effort was exerted to convince the court. One of the most common petitions was issued from the advocate general to the judge requesting a commission to order the marshal to unload all or part of the prize cargo. The petition to unlade was usually a bid to preserve the cargo

---

[38] Of 664 cases on file, 452 or seventy percent had at least one and as many as seven crew members examined. Occasionally no crew were available, as in PAC, RG 8. IV, Vol. 84, *Fair Play* – crew deserted with papers and Vol. 87, *Jefferson* – master and crew allowed on shore near George's Island by HMS *Bream*. Translation costs are noted in PAC, RG 8, IV, Vol. 91, *Minerva* captured by *Matilda*, 5 Aug. 1813.

[39] J. Franklin Jameson, ed., *Privateering and Piracy in the Colonial Period: Illustrative Documents* (1923; reprint, New York, 1970), 525.

[40] PAC, RG 8, IV, Vol. 78, *Calson*, Examination of Ebenzer Webber, seaman, 16 July 1813; Vol. 109, *Mary*, Examination of Samuel Corson, cook, 21 Jan. 1814.

from being damaged by weather, leakage, or theft while under adjudication.[41] Occasionally, a petition for sale accompanied the petition to unlade. This addressed the problem of delayed judgement putting perishable cargoes such as corn or flour at risk. In such a case, both captor and claimant stood to lose if the cargo were destroyed or damaged. By selling the cargo at auction for current market value, and depositing the money with the registrar until the case was decided, the cargo retained its value for the eventual owner. Not only did this practice work to everyone's advantage, it also assured merchants in ports such as Halifax, Saint John, and Liverpool, access to cargoes of food and manufactured goods that were generally in short supply due to wartime restrictions. Merchants could purchase scarce commodities at prize auctions for reasonable prices, and then take advantage of a seller's market for the goods. In this way, those who invested in privateers could realize immediate profits from sales while waiting for the final disposal of the prize.

The court responded to such petitions with appropriate commissions for unlivery and sale. By these instruments, the judge of the vice-admiralty court, on behalf of the king, ordered the marshal to sell the ship and cargo at auction to the highest bidder "after giving due notice thereof in a public newspaper for at least fourteen days."[42] A review of the accounts of sale transmitted to the judge reveals that many successful bidders were often the same merchants who had interest in the privateers that had captured the prize. Thus the profits were kept within a small mercantile community and usually reinvested in the pursuit of more prizes.

Recaptures

To encourage both naval and privateer crews to recapture their own or allied vessels from the enemy, the courts awarded captors a percentage of such prize as salvage. As a further incentive, recaptors were not obliged to pay court costs, which, as Table 3.1 indicates, could be expensive. Under the prize act in force in 1813, naval crews received one-eighth, while privateers earned one-sixth of the appraised value of the ship and cargo. Although recaptures were worth less as prizes, they were often easier to seize, and at least for the navy, a possible source of men. According to Beamish Murdoch, return of recaptured allied vessels and goods relied on the rule of reciprocity. Goods belonging to an ally were restored if the law and practice of the ally would have restored British goods under the same circumstances.[43] The act exempted former British vessels that had been converted to enemy warships or privateers. In such cases, the court condemned the vessel, and the captors received full value for the prize. Usually British or neutral vessels retaken from American privateer prize crews were returned to their

---

[41]PAC, RG 8, IV, Vol. 133, *Policy* captured by HMS *Loire* and *Ramilies*, 4 Dec. 1813.

[42]PAC, RG 8, IV, Vol. 73, *Anson*, Decree of Delivery, 27 Nov. 1813. For the brig *Sibae*, Vol. 96, the cost of a notice and a crier was £1.2.6.

[43]Murdoch, *Epitome*, 112. Appendix 1 notes 137 recaptures of which less than a dozen were condemned or otherwise not restored to their owners on payment of salvage.

owners upon payment of salvage to the recaptors. Finally, the registrar received a poundage fee of 3 s. per pound.

In most cases, vessel and weather-permitting, captains were anxious to continue their original voyage. Rather than awaiting a court decision and risking the loss or spoilage of their cargoes, many captains petitioned the court for an appraisal.[44] Once the value of the ship and cargo was assessed, the captain could put up security or bail for the salvage and court costs with the registrar and continue his voyage.

Appraisers were allotted a couple of days to inspect the vessel and its cargo to assess the salvage value. Occasionally, they had to petition for permission to unload because the hull could not be appraised without emptying the vessel. Once the cargo was removed, many captains decided not to bother reloading, but sold the cargo, and the ship, even if it looked more cost-effective for the owners.

When the judge of the vice-admiralty court issued a commission to appraise, the marshal named two or three merchants as appraisers. Where specialized cargoes such as ship stores, iron, or possible war materials were involved, a local shipwright or blacksmith might be added to the appraisers to contribute his specialized skills. It is interesting to note that the same people appear regularly as appraisers earning 3s. each time for their service. Since many of these same men were also investors in privateers, it leads one to speculate whether these men were chosen for their expertise, their friendship with the marshal, or their interest in gaining first-hand knowledge of the cargoes coming up for sale.[45]

The decision of the vice-admiralty court judge could take several forms. There was a certificate of condemnation that certified that the captured vessel was condemned to the captor as "good and lawful prize," or to the king *jurae coronae*. There could be a decree of delivery that ordered the registrar to deliver the prize, duly condemned to the captor for sale. As previously noted, recaptures received a decree of salvage against the prize, her captain, and/or other claimants. This meant the vessel was condemned in salvage, and the owner was usually ordered to pay costs incurred by both sides.

Vessels that were not adjudged as prize were restored to their owners by means of a decree of restitution where costs were assigned and agreed to by both captors and claimants. Captors of *Middlesex*, which was found to have a valid licence and restored, had to pay costs for both sides plus the king's advocate's fees totalling £52.11.10. The privateer captors of *George Washington* were lucky enough to escape with no court costs at all when the ship was restored. Even the judge gave up his fees! On the other hand, the court was outraged when HMS *Alphea*, while serving as a cartel ship under a flag of truce, captured *Zodiac*. Not only was the capture illegal, but the captain ignored Admiral Herbert Sawyer's orders to restore the vessel immediately. Three months later, the ship was badly damaged by an inexperienced prize crew driving it on the rocks en route from Liverpool to Halifax. Judge Croke rebuked *Alphea*'s captain for his

---

[44]PAC, RG 8, IV, Vol. 132, *Aeolus*, retaken by HMS *La Hogue*, 28 Apr. 1813.

[45]Appendix 7 identifies various merchants who acted as appraisers for the court.

negligence, and vindicated British honour by ordering him to pay all court costs as well as full compensation for damages, expenses, and demurrage.[46]

Decrees of restitution were also issued for vessels registered to Spanish, Swedish, and Portuguese owners, or those of other neutral nations. Since many appeals seem to involve foreign-owned vessels, it would appear that the colonial vice-admiralty court regarded neutral ownership somewhat less rigorously than the High Court of Admiralty.

Most case files consulted contain a copy of the court's definitive sentence or final decree. In this document, the vice-admiralty court judge, after "first calling upon the name of Christ, and having God alone before our eyes," pronounced sentence upon the vessel.

Appeals

Those captors or prize owners who were dissatisfied with the verdict of the vice-admiralty court had fourteen days to enter an appeal to the High Court of Admiralty in London. To discourage vexatious appeals, the court demanded that the appellant post a bond to prosecute an appeal, which required a deposit of £150 to £300 depending on the size of the vessel. All pertinent court documents had to be copied (for a fee) and sent to England to await the attention of the Lords Commissioners of Appeal in Prize Causes.[47] Appellants also had to employ an English lawyer or proctor to act for them and apply to the English Appeal Court Registry for an inhibition. The appellant, the judge, the registrar, and the opposing party were all served with the inhibition, which took approximately nine months to obtain. In a letter to Lord Castlereagh on 15 January 1814, D. Rehausen, the Swedish minister of state, complained about the expense incurred by his countrymen whose vessels had been seized by colonial privateers and naval vessels despite their neutral status. Even if they were restored on appeal, he objected, there was still considerable loss of capital and insurance rates of twenty to twenty-five percent.[48]

Since they could be lengthy, not to mention expensive, appeals were only launched when a prize of considerable value was at stake or the appellant had a very strong case.[49] Although the outcome of many appeals is not known, the few appeals

---

[46]PAC, RG 8, IV, Vol. 84, *Middlesex*, captured by *Liverpool Packet*, 8 Sept. 1812; Vol. 85, *George Washington*, captured by *Retaliation*, 3 May 1813; Vol. 76, *Zodiac*, captured by HMS *Alphea*, 6 Aug. 1812.

[47]This was a body of privy councillors especially commissioned after 1708 for the purpose of trying prize appeals. Jameson, ed., *Privateering*, xii.

[48]Stewart, *Reports*, Addenda, 1.

[49]According to Carl E. Swanson, *Predators and Prizes: American Privateering and Imperial Warfare, 1739-1748* (Columbia, S.C., 1991), 37, if the Privy Council upheld the verdict of the vice-admiralty court, the appellant had to pay treble the costs! In over 600 cases reviewed, less than seven percent, or only forty-five appeals are registered. Of these, the appeal was withdrawn in four cases (retraxit), the appellant failed to provide the necessary information and the appeal was denied in nine cases, and in two cases, the appeal was deserted. The decision of the Halifax court was overturned on appeal in at least

found indicate a relatively low success rate. Appellants who persevered must have felt the risk was worth it.

Prize Agency

Because of the mobile nature of naval service, men and ships were often either decommissioned or stationed thousands of miles away by the time the vice-admiralty court passed judgement on their prizes. To safeguard their interests and collect any prize money or salvage awards due, captains, officers, and crews appointed prize agents (sometimes the same one, sometimes different ones) to sell prizes on their behalf and manage their money until they could collect it. As Tony Gutridge's study of prize agency suggests, this work attracted the more opportunistic clerks and officials in the Navy Office, dockyard officials, and ships' pursers. There were few controls on the activities of prize agents, at least in the early years, and the profession "had a terrible reputation for dishonesty and sharp practice, often well deserved."[50]

Overcharging for services was one of the most common abuses, followed by fraud. After 1805, to prevent agents charging for services that were not rendered by bona fide employees, only those actually discharging agency duties were entitled to the standard commission of five percent on the net value of the sales of ship and cargo. Unscrupulous agents also delayed payment of prize money, often for years. The rules were full of loopholes, and even the threat of £500 fines for misbehaviour weighed lightly against the potential profits to be made from withholding payment to gain the interest on prize money held in trust or to use it for personal investments. Sometimes agents paid out shares promptly to the captain and officers, so that they would be less inclined to protest when the men went unpaid for months. Additional regulations imposed in 1809 required navy prize agents to take out licences, established a register of prizes and captors, and created the post of inspector of prize accounts, which speeded up the distribution of prize money to within a year. After that, anyone wishing to become a prize agent had to post a £5,000 bond as proof of good faith.

With a clientele that was frequently out of sight, if not mind, prize agents engaged in a very competitive profession. English firms already administering their naval clients' financial and legal needs teamed up with partners at outports and overseas centres and with useful contacts within the navy to expand their client base. Appendix 6 lists the agents for various Royal Navy vessels stationed in British North America throughout the war and the dates they were appointed. Three-quarters of the vessels had agents in either England or the colonies or both.

George Redmond Hulbert, one of the most prominent agents, was a former navy purser and flag secretary to Sir John Borlase Warren in 1807 and again in 1812. With representatives in England and Bermuda, Hulbert shared their commissions or brokerage fees from every sale. Gutridge suggests that by the time Vice-Admiral

---

seventeen cases (about two percent of the total cases).

[50]Tony Gutridge, "Aspects of Naval Prize Agency," *Mariner's Mirror*, DXXX (1994), 46. For a discussion of attempts to reform the Prize Office in the seventeeth century, see J.S. Bromley "Prize Office and Prize Agency at Portsmouth, 1689-1713," *Corsairs and Navies, 1660-1760* (London, 1987).

Alexander Cochrane replaced Warren in 1814, Hulbert returned to England probably £30,000-£40,000 richer.[51]

Appendix 7 identifies twenty Halifax merchants and two from Saint John, New Brunswick, who served as prize agents for either privateers or naval vessels. John Dougan, agent to the commissioners for American Crown Droits in 1812, as well as a bondsman for the unsuccessful 1814 privateer *Sherbrooke*, boasts the largest number of naval clients, thirty-four, followed closely by Hulbert, agent for twenty-four vessels. Aside from those individuals serving only a few ships, the remaining prize agency business was largely distributed among William Balhetchet, James Fraser, Thomas Heavyside, Charles Martyr, and the firm of Hartshorne and Boggs. Prize agency must have been reasonably lucrative since many of these names reappear as purchasers for prize cargoes at auctions or as participants in other aspects of maritime commerce during the war.

Not to be outdone, the Admiralty also appointed its own "officers and agents duly authorized to recover, seize, collect and take, the rights and perquisites of Admiralty." Halifax natives Samuel Hood George, Edward Brabazon Brenton, and Brenton Haliburton were appointed 22 June 1812 to serve as agents for the Admiralty. Many vice-admiralty court cases for vessels captured before the declaration of general reprisals contain allegations from the agents of admiralty claiming these prizes as droits of admiralty. Unfortunately, most were declared droits of the crown instead, and the agents did not make the commissions they anticipated.[52]

Among the documents relating to *New Zealander*, one of several British whale ships taken by USS *Essex* and recaptured by HMS *Belvidera* on 21 April 1814, there is a petition from one of the Halifax-based agents for the Admiralty. On behalf of the Treasurers of Greenwich Hospital, Brenton Haliburton asked the court to distribute £ 840.15.8 in salvage "as soon as it becomes payable." This money was paid to Hartshorne and Boggs as agents of *Belvidera*. Although the ship had since returned to England to be paid off, Hartshorne refused to forward the money to James Sykes, their prize agent in London. Hartshorne and Boggs' reply acknowledged receipt of Captain Byron's direction to forward the prize money and agreed to proceed with the court's directions regarding disbursement, which they received on 7 December 1814.[53]

Usually, it was the captor's agent, with an eye to his commission, who petitioned the court to sell cargoes that were valuable or vulnerable. Similarly, it was often the agent who applied for a commission to appraise a vessel to expedite the issue of salvage. As agent for HMS *Emulous* in July 1812, Lawrence Hartshorne, Jr., asked for a four-month extension of credit on £3,544.7.11 from the date of sale of the cargo from the brig *Illuminator*, for the benefit of all involved "given the present state of the market in Halifax." Concern for his clients' interests also prompted Thomas Heavyside, agent for HMS *Shannon*, to petition the court to unload the provisions and stores aboard USS *Chesapeake* to prevent plundering by souvenir hunters. He maintained that some "in

[51]Gutridge, "Naval Prize Agency," 48.

[52]PAC, RG 8, IV, Vol. 119, *Economy*, Allegation of Agents of Admiralty, 26 Jan. 1813.

[53]PAC, RG 8, IV, Vol. 136, *New Zealander*, Petition of Brenton Haliburton, Nov. 1814.

the hurry and bustle on board said ship continue to take articles of value without being observed."[54]

From the timing of notices posted by various agents in the *Nova Scotia Royal Gazette*, it would appear that the process of legal condemnation and sale took an average of four to five months. In November 1812, Hartshorne and Boggs placed a notice in the paper advising all those aboard HMS *Colibri* at the capture of *Fanny* and *Mariner* in July that shares would be distributed at the company's counting house. In March 1813, a similar notice asked claimants to appear for the distribution of shares of the proceeds from the brig *Thorn* captured in October 1812. This prize had to be shared among the officers and crew of HMS *Nymph, Tenedos, Shannon*, and *Curlew*, all of which were in company at the time. According to the prize act, money obtained from the sale of prizes and not claimed after due notice, should be transferred to the Treasurer of Greenwich Hospital in England to be invested in public securities for the benefit of the captors. Agents in New Brunswick and Nova Scotia were naturally more concerned with interest-earning opportunities a bit closer to home.

From time to time, agents found themselves opposing each other in court. Andrew Wright, agent for HMS *Spartan*, petitioned the court in a joint capture in November 1813 when the agents for HMS *Statira* and *Martin* refused to pay. His client claimed a share in the schooner *Belle*, but because Captain Brenton had refused to man a number of prizes, and apparently had written a letter relinquishing his right to share in *Belle* and three others, agents Thomas Godfrey (*Statira*) and William Ayre (*Martin*) both objected to the petition.[55]

Although Gutridge maintains that it was not uncommon for agents to fall into bankruptcy taking their clients' prize money with them, Canadian-based agents did not abuse the system unduly. They did, however, use the system to their best advantage. Because of the number of vessels and shares involved, an agent's work was often very complicated. Canny prize agents, such as John Dougan and James Fraser, Halifax agents for a number of the vessels involved in the Chesapeake blockade, capitalized on the lengthy delays by the courts, the irregular movement of naval vessels, and poor transatlantic communication to put off payment as long as legally possible. For example, in June 1813, HMS *Dover* and the blockading squadron recaptured the schooner *Harriet*. A year and a half later, the court received a petition for monition against Fraser because three of the captors, HMS *Marlborough, Mohawk*, and *Barossa* had left the station, and their prize money remained unclaimed. Richard Uniacke, H.M. advocate and proctor, presented a second petition on behalf of Greenwich Hospital. Fraser responded that he would pay the shares for *Marlborough* and *Mohawk* as soon as he knew how many men were involved in each ship. Meanwhile, John Dougan, agent for *Barossa*, wanted his ship's share paid directly to him instead of Greenwich. Although willing to pay whomever the court decided, Fraser explained that since the ship was burnt after the cargo was *removed, and no one from the captured ship was present, it took a long time to resolve

[54]PAC, RG 8, IV, Vol. 124, *Illuminator*, Affidavit of Agents for Captors, 21 Nov. 1812; Vol. 79, *Shannon*, Petition for Unlivery, 9 June 1813.

[55]PAC, RG 8, IV, Vol. 178. *Belle*, Petition of Thomas Godfrey and William Ayre and Petition of Andrew Wright, both 19 Nov. 1813.

the case. The cargo of oil, sealskins, and fish was finally condemned in November and sold for £2,082.15.6. Fraser promised that once he obtained a proper crewlist, he would pay out the prize money. As for Dougan, Fraser suggested he should pay costs for bothering the court. Dougan maintained that he notified George R. Hulbert months earlier regarding *Barossa*'s crew. Moreover, since *Barossa* was likely to stop at Halifax en route to the West Indies, if Dougan had the prize money, he could pay it directly to *Barossa* and thus save the men the deductions that would result if Greenwich Hospital handed over the shares.[56] Both the court and the agents knew that those who benefitted most from such consideration were the agents themselves.

Prize agents were also involved in the payment of salvage money awarded for recaptures. In the 28 July 1813 edition of the *Nova Scotia Royal Gazette*, John Fraser notified officers and crew of HMS *Borer* that salvage would be paid for the schooner *Lark* and its cargo on board *Borer* in three days. Shares not claimed would be recalled at Fraser's counting house every Thursday and Saturday for three months thereafter according to law.[57]

Within the small mercantile community of Nova Scotia, it was inevitable that commercial rivalries would take on a personal edge. In the case of the *Santa Cecilia*, captured by HMS *Wasp*, 14 September 1813, Richard Tremaine, agent for the owners, accused John Dougan and John Barnett, agents for *Wasp*, and Garret Miller, appraiser, of "improper conduct." In a petition dated 12 January 1814, Tremaine claimed the agents were negligent in allowing Miller to appraise the vessel at a reduced value in order to buy it himself. Tremaine demanded that the agents for *Wasp* take an oath that the ship and cargo would be sold for the interest of the captors, or at least, at public auction. Since the court had already issued a decree of delivery on bail for the ship and cargo on 31 December 1813, even under the circumstances, they could not set aside that decree.[58]

The Cost of Justice

Negotiating the legal shoals of prizemaking could be nearly as treacherous as navigating at sea. The most cost-effective cases were the simple ones that required no additional proofs, proceeded without extra claims, and generated no appeals. Expenses also varied according to which port a prize was taken. According to Table 3.2, Halifax was the most expensive port, but this may also reflect the fact that many vessels carried into Halifax were disputed or complicated captures to begin with and necessitated additional paperwork and delays on the part of the vice-admiralty court.

---

[56]PAC, RG 8, IV, Vol.86, various monitions and petitions from 25 Oct. to 17 Nov. 1814.

[57]*Nova Scotia Royal Gazette*, 28 July 1813, 3.

[58]PAC, RG 8, IV, Vol. 96, *Wasp*, Petition of R. Tremaine, 12 Jan. 1814, and Affidavit of R. Tremaine, 18 Feb. 1814. Tremaine appraised fourteen vessels during the war.

Table 3.2
Comparison of Court Costs for Different Provincial Ports

Town	No. of Captures	No. with Costs	Average Cost
Halifax, N.S.	519	327	£230.5
Liverpool, N.S.	92	47	£ 87.
Saint John, N.B.	58	46	£ 88.
Annapolis, N.S.	12	12	£ 46.
Shelburne, N.S.	10	9	£ 113.
Yarmouth, N.S.	10	6	£ 62.
Windsor, N.S.	3	3	£ 42.

For those who used the system, however, as well as for those who administered it, the procedures were clearly understood and overall, the odds lay with the prizemaker. Relying on experience gained in the American Revolution and the wars with France, the officers of the Halifax Court of Vice-Admiralty adjudicated most cases that appeared before them with competence and dispatch. Even though Judge Croke may not have been personally popular, the Lords Commissioners of Appeals only rarely overturned his legal decisions.

Although the fees levied by the vice-admiralty court occasioned a great deal of complaint from colonial inhabitants, the wealth that flowed into provincial coffers from the condemnation of prizes counterbalanced heavy wartime losses suffered by the fishing industry, as well as by those whose property was captured at sea, who were impressed, or who lost money to American competitors.[59] As the volume of court business ebbed and flowed throughout the war, the procedures for determining prize remained firmly in place. Secure in the knowledge that their efforts, if properly directed, had a much better than even chance of success, the owners, investors, and privateersmen of Nova Scotia and New Brunswick eagerly put to sea in search of prize. Chapter 4 examines their role as prizemakers.

[59] Laing, "Admiralty Court," 161.

Chapter 4
Public Service, Private Profits

For the maritime merchants of early nineteenth-century British North America, the prospect of war did not bode well for business. Years of embargoes and trade restrictions had already deprived ship owners and merchants of commercial opportunities on both sides of the border. Meanwhile, conflict in Europe interrupted their regular trade with such neutral nations as Spain, Portugal, and Sweden. War with the United States meant closure of neighbouring markets and risk of capture by American naval vessels and privateers. It posed a serious economic threat to the hundreds of small coastal traders from New Brunswick and Nova Scotia who plied the Eastern seaboard.

The Napoleonic Wars forced the Royal Navy to concentrate most of its strength in Europe, leaving trade along the coast of the Maritime provinces virtually undefended. By the time the United States declared war against Britain in June 1812, only a few naval vessels patrolled the Atlantic station. The navy's North Atlantic fleet, except for one ship-of-the-line, was still in Bermuda.[1] Many Nova Scotians remembered the Revolutionary War when American forces briefly occupied Liverpool, or recalled paying a ransom to keep Lunenburg from being burnt.[2] Anxious to avoid similar attacks on their unprotected shores by swarms of American privateers and a small but determined American navy, Atlantic Canada turned to privateering to defend its shipping. In the thirty months of war, hundreds of merchants and seamen pledged their money, their freedom, and even their lives to take part in the business of privateering fully realizing that success as a privateer could be as elusive as the prizes they sought.

In examining the impact of privateering on the War of 1812, this chapter addresses several aspects of private armed warfare as they applied to the provinces of New Brunswick and Nova Scotia. While not as strategically important as the Royal Navy, privateering profoundly affected the economic and social life of communities such as Liverpool, which invested heavily in ships, crews, and supplies. In the wartime economy of Atlantic Canada, privateering offered a potentially profitable, albeit transitory, outlet for merchant capital. Smaller in size and fewer in number than their American counterparts, provincial privateers nevertheless averaged nearly the same number of prizes per vessel. They worked carefully within the legal and administrative framework of privateering to ensure as many prizes as possible were upheld in court.

While prize cargoes and vessels were generally handled with care by their captors, prisoners of war were not always so well treated. The policies of both Great Britain and the United States officially subscribed to humane treatment "conformable to the usage and practice of the most civilized nations during war," but often political and economic pressures

[1]The fleet wintered in Bermuda from November to July. Walter Ronald Copp, "Military Activities in Nova Scotia During the War of 1812," *Collections of the Nova Scotia Historical Society* (1938), XXIV, 59.

[2]John Leefe, "A Bluenose Privateer of 1812," *Nova Scotia Historical Quarterly*, III (1973), 5.

worked against the best intentions of administrators.[3] Motivated by a mixture of public spirit and private enterprise, Canadian-based privateers enhanced local prosperity while chipping way at American trade. Without achieving great wealth or major victories, the privateers of New Brunswick and Nova Scotia provided a major incentive for peace.

The Atlantic Privateers

Within weeks of the declaration of war, merchants in American ports along the East Coast rushed to commission virtually anything afloat. Shipyards bristled with new craft on the stocks. The first American privateer, the 30-ton *Fame*, was commissioned 1 July 1812.[4] During the course of the war, over 500 American letters of marque followed in its wake. While most were sloops and schooners of several hundred tons, capable of transatlantic cruises, some were no more than open fishing boats. When a tiny 10-ton privateer put into Salem with three English prizes, *Niles Weekly Register* announced, "It will not much amaze us, bye and bye, if these people go out to fight the enemy in washing tubs."[5]

Although equally keen to begin making prizes, privateers from New Brunswick and Nova Scotia needed a British declaration of war to enable the Admiralty to issue letters of marque. Lieutenant Governor Sherbrooke's decision to sign commissions under his own authority, in anticipation of war, meant that the *Liverpool Packet*, the only successful privateer commissioned before 13 October 1812, had to fight for its prizes twice – once at sea and later, in the courts. Similarly, in the fall of 1812, New Brunswick Lieutenant Governor Symth's decision to issue letters of marque to *General Smyth* and the 70-gun sloop *Brunswicker* earned him heavy censure from the Foreign Office.[6]

Between July 1812 and January 1815, some forty-seven private armed vessels obtained letters of marque signed by the lieutenant governors of New Brunswick or Nova Scotia. Colonial governors administered the crown's regulations concerning who received commissions and under what conditions. They were encouraged to issue letters of marque in time of war "to suitable persons under adequate safeguards," and few were ever refused.[7] Although letters of marque were in the name of a single ship, they automatically extended to cover any prizes captured by that vessel, so that if a prize took a prize in turn, the capture was legal. By the War of 1812, British vessels were forbidden to carry commissions from neutral nations or to harry neutral trade without good reason.

---

[3]Allan Rosas, *Legal Status of Prisoners of War* (Helsinki, 1976), 67. Rosas refers to article 1 of a cartel agreement between Great Britain and the United States in 1813.

[4]Samuel Eliot Morison, *The Maritime History of Massachusetts, 1783-1860* (1921; reprint, Boston, 1961), 200.

[5]*Niles Weekly Register*, 26 Sept. 1812.

[6]W.S. MacNutt, *New Brunswick, A History: 1784-1867* (Toronto, 1963), 156. The *Brunswicker* was the former *Commodore Barry*, an American revenue cutter condemned by the Halifax Vice-Admiralty Court in August 1812. According to C.H.J. Snider, *Under the Red Jack* (Toronto, 1927), 225, *General Smyth* brought in four prizes worth £7,000 in ten weeks.

[7]J. Franklin Jameson, ed., *Privateering and Piracy in the Colonial Period, Illustrative Documents* (1923; reprint, New York, 1970), x.

Prizes had to be brought into a "convenient" port for judgement, which tended to be the privateer's home port. If this proved impossible, the closest allied port was acceptable; for example, Britain's colonial courts of vice-admiralty in Jamaica or Bermuda were entitled to condemn prizes captured by British privateers.[8]

Of Nova Scotia's private armed vessels, the first, and the largest, was the 623-ton letter of marque *Caledonia*, commissioned 17 July 1812. While *Caledonia* does not appear to have ever captured a prize, the *Liverpool Packet*, the province's second privateer, more than made up for this failure with at least fifty prizes to its credit and countless others chased, lost, or let go. More successful than any sister ships, the *Liverpool Packet* represented the exception rather than the rule. Stories of the *Liverpool Packet*'s valuable prizes and fortunate crew fired the enthusiasm of would-be privateers from Halifax to Saint John.

Figure 5: *Liverpool Packet*, ca 1815.

Source: Courtesy W. Wood Collection.

[8]James G. Lydon, *Pirates, Privateers, Profits* (Upper Saddle River, N.J., 1970), 67. Godfrey Lushington, *A Manual of Prize Law* (London, 1866), 13-14.

The odds against a successful capture were so high during the period, that the arrival in port of one ship in three was considered a good average.[9] Storms, navigation hazards, and accidents took their toll. American privateers or naval vessels often recaptured prize crews sailing home. Finally, after 1813, the few commissioned vessels from Atlantic Canada had to compete with nearly 100 prize-hungry Royal Navy vessels which out-weighed, out-manned, and out-gunned the provincial privateers. If the 200 letter of marque prizes that actually reached port and court in Atlantic Canada represent only one-third of the total privateering effort, the American coastal trade was fortunate that there were not more provincial privateers.

The Nature of Privateering

Whether driven by patriotism or profit, privateering was a major component of the Atlantic coastal economy. Entrepreneurs and merchant shipowners found an outlet for investment capital that would otherwise have lain idle, experienced seamen found employment, shore-based industries such as shipbuilding, ropemaking, and chandlery prospered, and the courts and auctions provided work for an array of clerks, prize agents, lawyers, and notaries. While some condemned privateering as little better than piracy, others appreciated the economic alternative it offered. Thomas Jefferson put the role of the privateer into perspective:

> One man fights for wages paid him by the government, or a patriotic zeal for the defence of his country; another, duly authorized, and giving the proper pledges for his good conduct, undertakes to pay himself at the expense of the foe and serve his country as effectually as the former, and the government drawing all its supplies from the people is, in reality, as much affected by the losses of one as the other, the efficacity of its measures depending upon the energies and resources of the whole.[10]

Commerce raiding was, in fact, the merchant's way of waging war.

Despite the privateers' role as an auxiliary naval force, the Royal Navy remained prejudiced against them as rivals for the same ships, men, and prizes. They jealously guarded their official status by ensuring that no one would confuse a privateer with a ship of His Majesty's Navy. Beginning with the war with Spain in 1739, letter of marque vessels were forbidden to wear any jack, pendant, or ensign worn by the British Navy. Instead, along with defining the colours appropriate to merchant ships, the articles of 1740 required that privateers "wear a red jack with the Union Jack described in the canton at the upper corner thereof near the staff."[11] Fortunately for the Atlantic privateers, international law did not require them to fly their own colours until preparing

---

[9]Snider, *Red Jack*, 112.

[10]George Coggleshall, *The American Privateers* (New York, 1861), xliv.

[11]R.G. Marsden, ed., *Documents relating to Laws and Customs of the Sea* (London, 1915), II, 428.

to open fire. Usually, the distinctive red jack on their bowsprit was not apparent to their intended victims until it was too late.

Although they resented the free-ranging privateers, the navy recognized that their random cruising patterns made private armed vessels ideal intelligence gatherers. Accordingly, letters of marque obliged captains to keep an exact journal of their cruises, list where and when prizes were seized and their value, make note of American strength and ship movements, and transmit this, and any other information regarding the "design of the enemy," to the Admiralty. Documents seized with the schooner *Mary* of Bath contained such naval intelligence. A crudely written note from a crewman aboard the privateer, *Sir John Sherbrooke,* advised Admiral Warren "Nave in Boston Presedent Congres rede for sea & the Rat r f sea."[12]

While all privateers had to carry letters of marque, not all letter of marque vessels were privateers. They shared the same legal status, but were distinguished by their intent. Armed with a letter of marque, a captain had two choices. He could undertake a regular trading voyage, hire extra hands, and use his commission when, and if, a likely prize crossed his bow. Or he could abandon all pretence to trade, take on extra guns and shot, empty his hold of cargo, hire a large crew to work for shares, and try his luck on a two-or three-month cruise as a privateer. The cost of outfitting a privateer depended on how much time and money owners and backers were willing to invest. Since a letter of marque could virtually be had for the asking, many saw it as a cheap, easily-obtainable means of supplementing shipping income at a time when there were few entrepreneurial alternatives.

Strategically, privateering provided Canada's coastal inhabitants with a measure of security and defence that, at least for the first part of the war, was unavailable from either the Royal Navy or local military forces. Richard Pares downplays the defensive value of American privateers in the mid-eighteenth century, because, although they engaged enemy privateers and recaptured merchant vessels, they did not deliberately search out warships. Carl Swanson disputes this argument for the 1740s, while Richard E. Winslow, III, maintains that "without the presence of the American privateers in the Revolutionary War and the War of 1812, the United States would never have been able to hold off the British Navy." Walter Copp considers that Atlantic Canada's privateers were more important to the safety of the Maritimes than the militia.[13] Whatever the defensive impact of privateers on maritime strategy, the psychological value of seeing privateers sail their prizes into port no doubt contributed greatly to local morale.

A Dicey Business

Naval historians, such as Alfred Thayer Mahan, have felt that privateering had more to do with gold than glory. Mahan believed it was of "the nature of a commercial project

---

[12]PAC, RG 8, IV, Vol. 90, *Mary*, 23 Mar. 1813.

[13]Richard Pares, *Colonial Blockade and Neutral Rights, 1739-1763* (Oxford, 1938), 25. See Carl E. Swanson, *Predators and Prizes: American Privateering and Imperial Warfare, 1739-1748* (Columbia, S.C., 1991), 219. Richard E. Winslow, III, *"Wealth and Honour": Portsmouth During the Golden Age of Privateering, 1775-1815* (Portsmouth, N.H., 1988), 240. Walter Ronald Copp, *W.R. Copp Family Papers*, (PANS, MG 1, Vol. 233), 34.

or speculation conducted by commercial men upon mercantile calculation and profit."[14] Certainly, the privateering activities of New Brunswick and Nova Scotia fit this description. Most merchants, seamen, and investors in Atlantic Canada came from small shipbuilding communities like Liverpool and Lunenburg, or from larger commercial ports like Halifax and Saint John. Each ship was privately owned (by one or more people) and secured by local bondsmen. Financing for the vessels came from families whose sons served as crew and captains aboard each others' ships, and married into each others' families.

While major investors in privateering like Enos Collins, a Liverpool native living in Halifax, and the Barss and Freeman families of Liverpool, Nova Scotia, turned the war to their advantage, many others were left empty-handed. Although no articles of agreement have been found for provincial crews, it is likely that they followed standard mercantile practice. According to Clement Crowell, vessels built and purchased by groups usually divided the cost into sixty-four shares and split the profits on a per-share basis after the voyage. This enabled merchants to invest small amounts of money in a larger number of vessels, thereby reducing their risk. The prize record of commissioned vessels from New Brunswick and Nova Scotia reveals that fifteen, or 33 percent of them, took no prizes at all. These ships, as well as ten vessels that only took one prize apiece, were most likely letters of marque, rather than serious privateers. Thus, for at least half of the commissioned ships in British North America between 1812 and 1815, there was little or no profit in privateering.[15] Whether investors' expectations were low or their motives were not purely financial, lack of success did not discourage ongoing support of privateering ventures throughout the war.

The economic effect of privateer activity on the small, southern Nova Scotia shipbuilding community of Yarmouth presents a good example of the mixed returns from privateering investments. Several of the forty-five vessels built at Yarmouth between 1812 and 1815 sailed under letters of marque. During the course of the war, American cruisers captured nine Yarmouth vessels. Similarly, two local privateers, *Fly* and *Broke*, brought nine American coastal vessels into Yarmouth harbour in July and August 1813. Although most of the prizes were ten to fifteen years old, their cargoes of lumber, firewood, furniture, foodstuffs, and naval stores were worth enough to compensate for the community's losses.[16]

What prompted otherwise practical merchants, seafarers, grocers, and bankers to participate in the "dicey business of privateering?"[17] Mahan contends that participants chose privateering by default: "When their regular avenues of commerce were closed by

---

[14]Alfred Thayer Mahan, *Sea Power in its Relation to War of 1812* (Boston, 1905), I, 396.

[15]Clement Crowell, *Novascotiaman* (Halifax, N.S., 1979), 4. See Appendix 3, Letter of Marque Vessels, New Brunswick and Nova Scotia. The ten vessels without any recorded prizes were: *Caledonian, Union, Sir John Sherbrooke, Bunker Hill, Star, Brunswicker, Herald, Edward, Eleanor, Intrepid, Sherbrooke, Ann, Snapdragon, Thinks-I-To-Myself*, and *Saucy Sixteen*.

[16]Crowell, *Novascotiaman*, 4. The nine prizes brought into Yarmouth were *Randolph, Polly, Rebecca, Friendship, John and Merriam, Samuel, Freeport, Dolphin*, and *Diamond*. The Yarmouth militia took a tenth vessel, the American privateer *Fame*, on 14 Dec. 1814.

[17]Marcus Rediker, *Between the Devil and the Deep Blue Sea: Merchant Seamen, Pirates and the Anglo-American Maritime World, 1700-1750*, (Cambridge, 1987), 61.

war, shipping and seamen were driven to privateering to earn any return at all."[18] In fact, the obvious eagerness with which both sides sought letters of marque points to a much more positive attitude towards prizemaking. In Appendix 4, the names of owners, investors, captains, and prize masters appear in several categories, often illustrating a progression from prize master to owner as profits were reinvested in new privateering ventures. Jerome Garitee's suggestion that between 1812 and 1815 privateering was a perfect complement and the principal outlet for Baltimore's commercial money and aggressive commercial spirit could apply equally to any of New Brunswick or Nova Scotia's privateering communities.[19]

The Liverpool Experience

The community of Liverpool, Nova Scotia, home of Atlantic Canada's most famous privateer, the *Liverpool Packet*, provides a glimpse into privateering society. Situated some seventy miles south of Halifax, Liverpool was a bustling port with "a reputation of being a rather raunchy and licentious place in the late eighteenth century."[20] Between 1760 and 1820, Liverpool's population burgeoned from 800 to 4,000 inhabitants. The proximity of Liverpool to Eastport, Maine, and the longstanding trade between the two ports, legal and otherwise, persisted throughout the war. Privateering simply added a new dimension to existing commercial relationships.

A tightly-knit merchant elite dominated Liverpool's economic life. Men like Enos Collins, Joseph Freeman, and James Barss "had their teeth sharpened by a long period of incessant sea warfare in which many of them had participated as owners if not operators of privateers."[21] Liverpool merchants eagerly invested not only their expertise but their money in privateers, accounting for fifteen of the twenty-seven commissioned vessels registered in Nova Scotia.[22] On 18 August 1812, a former slave tender, known as the *Black Joke*, received its first letter of marque as the *Liverpool Packet*. Bought for £420 at a prize auction in 1811, the vessel was originally operated as a mail and cargo packet by Enos Collins, his brother-in-law Benjamin Knaut, and the brothers James and John Barss, all ex-privateers and shipmates from Liverpool.

After July 1812, under successive captains John Freeman, Joseph Barss, and Lewis Knaut, the sleek, swift schooner was transformed from packet to predator, quickly earning a reputation as "the evil genius" of the American coasting trade. In the first six

---

[18]Mahan, *War of 1812*, 407.

[19]Jerome R. Garitee, *The Republic's Private Navy: The American Privateering Business as Practiced by Baltimore during the War of 1812* (Middletown, Conn., 19877), xvi. Garitee suggests that a single share in a Baltimore privateer cost $1,000 to $4,000 with active investors spending @$40,000. His estimates have over ten percent of Baltimoreans involved in privateering. See, 37.

[20]C.G. Hartlin, "From a Torrent to a Trickle - Liverpool, Nova Scotia," in James H. Morison and James Moreira, eds., *Tempered by Rum*, (Halifax, 1988), 64.

[21]Ibid., 64. Enos Collins' diverse mercantile interests eventually drew him to Halifax, but he continued to invest in Liverpool-owned privateers throughout the war.

[22]See Appendix 4. Owners and investors from Liverpool participated in fifty-five percent of Nova Scotian privateering enterprises and over one third of all privateering in Atlantic Canada.

months of the war, the *Liverpool Packet* carried home prize after prize, generating outraged editorials in the American press. In twenty days, this "insignificant fishing schooner," had captured eight or nine sail, worth $70-90,000, owned almost exclusively by Boston merchants. In December alone, thirteen hundred barrels of flour, nine thousand bushels of corn, and sixty bushels of oats were diverted from Boston to Nova Scotia.[23] So serious was the threat posed by the *Liverpool Packet* that the mere rumour that the *Liverpool Packet* lay off their coast was enough to drive all the vessels sailing out of Holmes Hole one morning back into port.[24] There is no doubt that the privateer hit New England merchants where it hurt. In the winter of 1812, the American House of Representatives debated the possibility of cutting a canal through Cape Cod as a less costly alternative to losses through commerce raiding!

Captured in June 1813 by the privateer *Thomas* of Portsmouth, New Hampshire, the *Liverpool Packet* took on a new name, *Young Teazer's Ghost,* and cruised briefly but unsuccessfully as an American letter of marque. Captain John Perkins bought the vessel next and sailed it as the *Portsmouth Packet* until HMS *Fantom* captured it in October 1813. Enos Collins bought his former vessel at auction once again and the *Liverpool Packet* was soon at sea taking American prizes under Captain Caleb Seely. At least seventeen prizes marked the second half of the *Packet*'s career, several of them very valuable.[25] Janet Mullins sums up the vessel's career: "This coaster carried fifty prizes before the Court of Vice-Admiralty, revolutionized traffic along the Atlantic seaboard, started the project of the Cape Cod Canal by her destructiveness, was captured by the Americans, recaptured by the English and continued her successful career as a privateer to the end of the war."[26]

The case of the Swedish schooner *Falun* illustrates the magnitude of privateering enterprise in Liverpool. The *Liverpool Packet* and *Retaliation* captured *Falun* in January 1814, despite its status as a neutral vessel, and carried it into Liverpool. While awaiting adjudication, thieves broke into *Falun* and further damaged the already-plundered cargo of dry goods. Acting on behalf of the schooner's owners, prize agent William King Reynolds of Halifax petitioned the vice-admiralty court to order the vessel removed to Halifax to ensure disinterested parties evaluated the loss. He argued, "Your petitioner has been informed and verily believes that most of the respectable people in Liverpool are interested in the privateers *Liverpool Packet* and *Retaliation*, and tho [sic]

---

[23]Leefe, "Bluenose Privateer," *NSHQ* (1973), III, 11. The 1 Jan. 1813 issue of the Boston *Messenger* carried the story of the *Packet*'s early success while the *American Shipping Intelligence* of May 1813 gave the *Liverpool Packet* the "evil genius" title. See Mullins, *Liverpool Privateering*, 49-51. Cargoes are found in PAC, RG 8, IV, Vol. 73, *Fenelon*; Vol. 75, *Polly*; Vol. 76, *Two Friends, Columbia,* and *Three Friends*; Vol. 82, *Dove*; and Vol. 97, *Susan*.

[24]Leefe, "Bluenose Privateer," *NSHQ* (1973) III, 14. Leefe quotes a statement by Captain Windsor of Holmes Hole, Massachusetts, from an article in the New York *Commercial Advertiser*, 15 Mar. 1813.

[25]*HMS Nymph* captured *Thomas* 30 June 1813. As the privateer *Wolverine, Thomas* sailed out of Liverpool, N.S., with twelve prizes to her credit. Appendix 1 lists all the prizes the *Liverpool Packet* brought in to the vice-admiralty court during the war, while Appendix 3 indicates the prize totals under each of the vessel's four letters of marque. Captain Seely's letter of marque was issued the end of November 1813.

[26]Mullins, *Liverpool Privateering*, 25, 43, 59, 145.

they are in the opinion of your petitioner honest men, yet he most humbly conceives that they may be prejudiced by their interest."[27]

As a one-time bondsman for *Retaliation* and a part-owner of the Halifax privateer *Retrieve*, Reynolds himself may not have been completely disinterested. In fact, he was likely afraid that Liverpool's smaller market would mean the ship and cargo would "not sell for anything like their real value." Enos Collins and Joseph Allison, Halifax merchants and co-owners of the two privateers, were willing to compensate *Falun*'s owners for any theft, but were not obliged to ensure the owners the highest appraisal value for their cargo – especially if Collins and Allison wished to bid on it themselves! They countered that the distance between Liverpool and Halifax was insignificant and they could prove that "there are a great many persons of the first respectability in that place totally disinterested." In the end, two merchants recommended by Collins and Allison and supervised by Reynolds surveyed the damage and appraised the loss at £2,050.16.3½ Nova Scotia currency. On 22 April, the vice-admiralty court recognized *Falun*'s licence, restored it to the owners, and ordered the captors to pay all costs and to make good all damages occasioned by plunder or losses.[28]

Of the thirty-three Liverpool-based owners and investors identified in Appendix 4, nine participated in two or more privateering ventures, with five men investing in four or more cruises. In Garitee's study of Baltimore privateers of the same period, the degree of commitment is gauged by the frequency of investment, rather than the amount risked. Marginal investors in Baltimore backed one voyage, while active investors sponsored four or more.[29] In terms of frequency, no other centre in the Atlantic provinces supported as many privateering ventures with so many investors as Liverpool. In fact, Nova Scotia's major multiple investor in privateering was Enos Collins whose part-ownership of the *Liverpool Packet* contributed to his subsequent wealth.[30]

In Canada's maritime provinces, privateering had been a family business from the mid-eighteenth century. Simeon Perkins and William Freeman built Liverpool's first privateer, the *Lucy* in 1780. In 1799, the crew of the *Charles Mary Wentworth*, co-owned by Perkins and his neighbour, Snow Parker, included two young men from Liverpool who were soon to leave their mark on the history of Canadian privateering - Enos Collins and Benjamin Knaut. By 1800, Perkins, Parker, Collins, and others had shares in three more privateers.[31] Over the next few years, these men established the reputations, not to mention the fortunes, that enabled them to play a significant role in Nova Scotia's privateering activities in the War of 1812.

---

[27]PAC, RG 8, IV, Vol. 105, *Falun*, Affidavit from William K. Reynolds, 1 Apr. 1814. Other documents cited include a petition from Enos Collins and Joseph Allison, 3 May 1814, and the monition for *Falun*, 4 Mar. 1814.

[28]Ibid., Vol. 105, *Falun*.

[29]Appendix 4 lists seventeen names as well as sixteen unidentified Liverpool investors in the *Saucy Sixteen*, some of whom may have overlapped with the first group. Garitee, *Private Navy*, 33.

[30]Peggy Anderson, "Enos Collins 1774-1871," *Canadian Arts and Antiques Review* (1981), III, 29.

[31]Leefe, *Atlantic Privateers*, 18, 22. Mullins, *Liverpool Privateering*, 14. Fergusson, Charles Bruce, ed., *The Diary of Simeon Perkins, 1797-1803* (Toronto, 1967), xlvii. The privateers were the *Duke of Kent, Rover*, and *Nymph*.

Figure 6: Joseph Barss, portrait by unknown artist.

Source: Queen's Country Museum, Liverpool, N.S.

A profile of Liverpool's privateers reveals a closely-linked mercantile society bound by family and financial ties, and sharing similar religious, political, and economic points of view. For many of the original Liverpool families like the Barss, privateering was a natural occupation. A son of Snow Parker married a daughter of Joseph Barss; two of Enos Collins' sisters wed privateersmen. One became Mrs. Benjamin Knaut, and the other married Caleb Seely, a master of the *Liverpool Packet*. One of Enos Collins' brothers, Freeman, married the sister of John, James, and Joseph Barss, all of whom owned shares in the *Liverpool Packet*. Privateers *Thorn, Wolverine*, and *Rolla* were also part of the Joseph Barss and Company fleet. The Barss and Freeman families were related by marriage to the prominent De Wolf family, whose members owned shares in both *Retaliation* and *Rolla*. Benjamin Ellenwood, prize master and captain of *Retaliation* and *Shannon*, was related to the Freeman family through his mother.

The close business and personal relationships between owners, investors, and crew are evident in the overlapping roles these men played in each others' ventures. John Freeman and John Morine worked as prize masters aboard *Sir John Sherbrooke, Retaliation,* and *Wolverine*. Isaiah Barss served on the *Liverpool Packet, Wolverine, Rolla,* and *Minerva*. Siphorous Cole escorted prizes for the *Liverpool Packet, Wolverine*, and *Rover*. Privateers not only worked on each others' vessels, they bought each others' homes. For example, in 1816, Caleb Seely purchased Simeon Perkins' house from his widow, while Perkins' son John occupied a house formerly owned by the Freemans. When Enos Collins moved to Halifax, he lived in a house built by John Moody with whom he shared the first bond for the *Liverpool Packet*. The movement of officers and crews between vessels and their changing roles within the privateering enterprise indicate that cooperation rather than competition was the key to success in a privateering community like Liverpool.[32]

Privateering was clearly considered a respectable activity since it attracted such distinguished entrepreneurs as Simeon Perkins, Enos Collins, and Samuel Cunard, all of whom owed their subsequent political or commercial success to their investments in privateering. John Barss, for example, capped a privateering career with a seat Nova Scotia's Legislative Assembly from 1813-1820 and 1826-1830. John Freeman served in the Assembly for twenty-five years.

Along with his partner, Joseph Allison, Enos Collins purchased American prize ships and cargoes at auction for bargain prices and resold them at a profit. After the war, Collins consolidated his fortune through banking and other investments. Reputed to be the richest man in Canada, Collins died peacefully at age ninety-seven, leaving an estate worth between six and nine million dollars. Samuel Cunard's shipping fortune is likewise attributed to the judicious purchase of several prize vessels, which earned him a reputation for good judgement and sound business practice among his peers. As bondsman for *Dart, Ann*, and *Snapdragon*, Cunard's "reliability in large and important transactions ... quickly placed the firm in the front rank of the numerous enterprising

---

[32] *Dictionary of Canadian Biography*, s.v. "Barss, John." Fergusson, *Diary of Simeon Perkins*, III, xvi, 13, 18, 40, 197, 308; Janet E. Mullins, *Some Liverpool Chronicles* (Liverpool, N.S., 1980), 39.

concerns of the day." Eventually, both Collins and Cunard were associated in the Halifax Banking Company, founded in 1825, and known locally as Collins Bank.[33]

It is difficult to compare the impact of privateering activities on Atlantic Canada and the United States, since the population of New Brunswick and Nova Scotia was approximately one-tenth of New England. Certainly the employment of some 1200-1500 seamen in the private armed vessels commissioned in Atlantic Canada had a major effect on the maritime economy. Within four months of the U.S. declaration of war, Salem and Baltimore boasted forty letter of marque vessels each, and New York City had raised fifty cruisers, representing perhaps twice the manpower of the Canadian provinces from three American cities.[34]

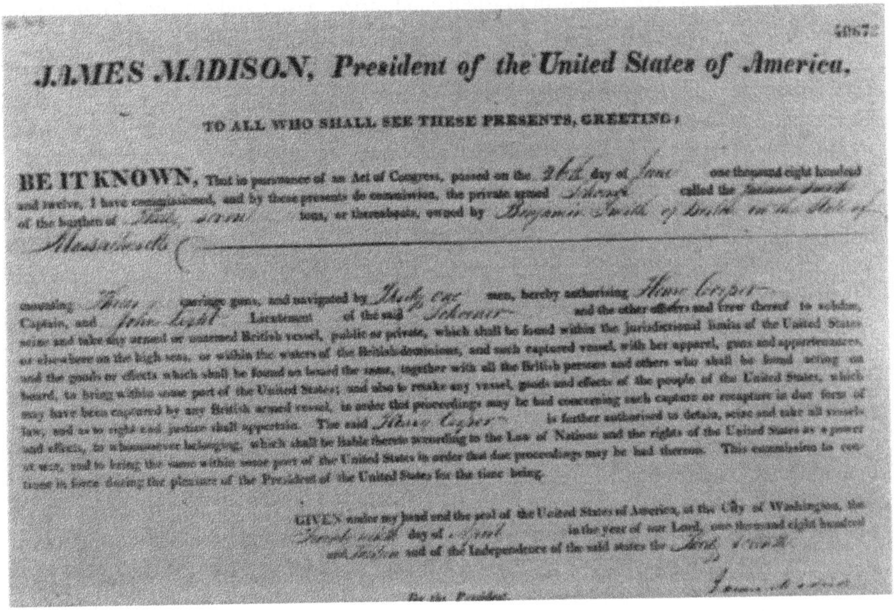

JAMES MADISON, President of the United States of America.

TO ALL WHO SHALL SEE THESE PRESENTS, GREETING:

BE IT KNOWN, That in pursuance of an Act of Congress, passed on the [illegible] day of [illegible] one thousand eight hundred and twelve, I have commissioned, and by these presents do commission, the private armed [illegible] called the [illegible] of the burthen of [illegible] tons, or thereabouts, owned by [illegible]

mounting [illegible] carriage guns, and navigated by [illegible] men, hereby authorizing [illegible] Captain, and [illegible] Lieutenant of the said [illegible] and the other officers and crew thereof to subdue, seize and take any armed or unarmed British vessel, public or private, which shall be found within the jurisdictional limits of the United States or elsewhere on the high seas, or within the waters of the British dominions, and such captured vessel, with her apparel, guns and appurtenances, and the goods or effects which shall be found on board the same, together with all the British persons and others who shall be found acting on board, to bring within some port of the United States; and also to retake any vessel, goods and effects of the people of the United States, which may have been captured by any British armed vessel, in order that proceedings may be had concerning such capture or recapture in due form of law, and as to right and justice shall appertain. The said [illegible] is further authorised to detain, seize and take all vessels and effects, to whomsoever belonging, which shall be liable thereto according to the Law of Nations and the rights of the United States as a power at war, and to bring the same within some port of the United States in order that due proceedings may be had thereon. This commission to continue in force during the pleasure of the President of the United States for the time being.

GIVEN under my hand and the seal of the United States of America, at the City of Washington, the [illegible] day of [illegible] in the year of our Lord, one thousand eight hundred and [illegible] and of the Independence of the said states the [illegible]

By the President

Figure 7: Letter of Marque for the American privateer *Juliana Smith*.

Although American privateers outnumbered their provincial counterparts by more than ten to one, incomplete data concerning tonnages for both American and Canadian privateers makes it difficult to compare their relative sizes although American vessels tended to be larger. Table 4.1 compares data from fifty-nine letters of marque

---

[33] A. Martin Payne, "Life of Sir Samuel Cunard," *Collections of the Nova Scotia Historical Society* (Halifax, 1918) XIX, 76. Collins Bank eventually became the Bank of Nova Scotia.

[34] Mullins, *Liverpool Privateering*, 24. The population of Atlantic Canada at the time was probably no more than 10,000 people.

from captured American vessels, Garitee's data for known Baltimore vessels, and tonnage data for Canadian-based letters-of-marque in Appendix 3.[35]

While private armed vessels from the Atlantic provinces were predominantly under 100 tons, Table 4.1 suggests that the majority of American privateers were in the 100-200 ton range or above. Larger American privateer vessels, more heavily manned and armed, pursued Britain's lucrative seaborne commerce in Europe and the Caribbean. Given their proximity to their own coast at the time of capture, it is likely that the captured American privateers found in Appendix 1 represented the smaller end of the privateer scale. Fortunately for Atlantic Canada, many of the over 500 American vessels eventually commissioned during the war cruised distant coastlines as far away as the Pacific in search of richly laden prizes. This left the American coast to their Canadian cousins who were content to stalk smaller, less well-defended prey closer to home.

Table 4.1
Comparative Tonnages for Private Armed Vessels from Baltimore, Captured American Privateers in Appendix 1, and Atlantic Privateers in Appendix 3.

Tonnage	Baltimore	US Gen	Atlantic
0 - 100 t.	8 (6%)	12 (20%)	19 (52%)
100 - 150 t.	26 (21%)	8 (13%)	5 (15%)
150 - 200 t.	22 (18%)	11 (18%)	4 (12%)
Total Privs	122	59	33
% < 200 t.	56 (45%)	31 (52%)	28 (84%)

Readying for Sea

The decision to trade or cruise influenced the choice of vessel. For the privateers of Atlantic Canada, a swift, manoeuvrable schooner of one hundred tons or less proved the most popular. Such vessels had to be strong enough to carry a heavy press of sail and withstand the recoil of a light battery. Because they were outfitted for only two to three months of cruising, storage capacity was less critical. Like their American counterparts, the Nova Scotia privateers preferred the all-round sailing qualities of the two-masted topsail schooner described by historian Howard Chapelle as "stiff" and "weatherly."[36] Table 4.1 compares the success rates for each vessel type and illustrates the predominance of small, fast schooners in the provincial prize stakes.

American privateers showed a similar preference for schooners. Mahan cites an 1853 study by Lieutenant George F. Emmons that broke down the 526 American privateers into 364 schooners (70%), sixty-seven brigantine/brigs (12%), thirty-five sloops (6%), twenty-six ships (5%) and thirty-four others (7%). Despite differences in size and number, capture rates of and by American and Atlantic Canadian privateers

[35]Garitee, *Private Navy*, 113.

[36]Howard I. Chapelle, *The History of American Sailing Ships* (1956; reprint, New York, 1982), 132-133.

were quite similar during the war. Mahan's figures indicate 108 or twenty-eight percent of American privateers were lost or captured. This compares very closely to the ten or twenty-one percent of the forty-seven provincial privateers lost. While captures account for a certain percentage of lost potential, many privateers were simply unsuccessful. Mahan estimates that less than half of the American letter-of-marque vessels captured any prizes. He calculated that 207 or thirty-nine percent of U.S. privateers accounted for 1344 prizes, an average of 6.5 prizes apiece. Applying the same criteria to New Brunswick and Nova Scotia, thirty-seven private armed vessels or eighty percent of all letters of marque took 228 prizes, an average of six captures per vessel. Although their performances were nearly identical, the smaller provincial fleet and fewer valuable prizes overall meant that the Canadian-based privateers earned less than the Americans.[37]

Table 4.2

Distribution of Provincial Privateer Vessel Types and their Prizes

Priv. Type	Number	% of Total	Prizes	% of Prizes
schooner	26	53	182	80
sloop	6	13	21	9
brigantine/brig	6	15	18	8
ship	2	4	0	0
others[a]	4	11	5	3
unknown	3	4	2	
Totals	47	100	228	100

[a] includes jebacco boats, cutters, and a lugger.

The list of letter of marque vessels in Appendix 3 indicates the variety of vessel-types comprising the Atlantic provinces' private armed fleet, including two ships and six brigantines. Five smaller sloop-rigged privateers, most of them from New Brunswick, did not enjoy the success of their larger comrades; eleven of their fourteen prizes fell to one vessel, the *Dart*. Of the larger privateers, only the crew of the 273-ton brigantine *Sir John Sherbrooke* (the former American privateer, *Thorn*) distinguished themselves with eighteen captures. Despite its success, the first *Sir John Sherbrooke* was too expensive to operate as a privateer and was sold before the end of 1813 as a freighter trading to Europe and the West Indies.[38]

---

[37]Emmons' figures are cited in Mahan, *War of 1812*, II, 242-243. Mahan cites them to argue that the U.S. Navy outperformed letter-of-marque vessels. Chapelle, *American Sailing Ships*, 133, suggests that the problem of obtaining enough men to sail a large vessel governed the size of privateers. Garitee, *Private Navy*, 113, refers to a State Department regulation which prohibited commissions for vessels with less than twenty crew "because such vessels were often smugglers."

[38]Mullins, *Liverpool Chronicles*, 21. The American privateer *Saucy Jack* eventually chased *Sir John Sherbrooke* into Rockaway, New Jersey, in 1814. It was beached and burnt when the American prize crew failed to get through the British blockade.

Like the *Sherbrooke*, few Atlantic privateers were purpose-built. A steady supply of captured American vessels, already adapted for privateering, meant that it was quicker and more efficient to buy privateers at auction and put them to immediate use against their former countrymen than to build one. Not only did American-built vessels sail well, their familiar shape and rig deceived would-be prizes and enabled privateers like *Retaliation* and *Wolverine* to approach their victims more closely before the alarm was raised. In the cat-and-mouse game of privateering, the more closely one resembled the enemy the better. Affidavits from captured crews attest to the frequent confusion of colonial privateers for American cruisers, and captains hiding or destroying their licences to avoid being captured by their compatriots. Alex Newcombe, master of the schooner *Joanna*, held off producing his import licence from John Moody and Company of Halifax until he was sure that *Dart* really was a British privateer. Unfortunately, when he rowed over to show his licence, Captain John Harris retorted that "he did not care for it, that it was worth nothing and that he would take all vessels worth sending in and told this deponent if he did not pull away from the privateer he would sink the boat in which he was and positively refused to give him a passage in either of the said vessels."[39] In this case, Harris' judgement was correct, and the prize was condemned to the *Dart*. The highly successful Captain Joseph Barss of the *Liverpool Packet* often camouflaged his own identity and that of his crew and ship to catch the unwary.[40]

Depending on the initial cost of the privateer and its state of seaworthiness, getting to sea could mean an investment of several thousand pounds. The purchase of additional guns and ordnance, extra masts, sails, and rigging (to cope with the inevitable wear and tear), and provisions for up to one hundred men for two to six months added to the overall cost of a privateering expedition. Perhaps in an attempt to save money, *Dart's* owners petitioned Lieutenant Governor Sherbrooke to replace defective guns captured aboard the vessel with ordnance borrowed from New Brunswick.[41] Garitee's study of Baltimore privateers of the period suggests the average cost of outfitting a cruising vessel was $25,000 or approximately £5,000.[42] Given the smaller scale of Atlantic Canadian operations, the overall cost of a privateer may not have been as high, but to the participants, the relative investment in guns, ships, and crews was probably significant.

i) Affidavit of Sureties

The roles and responsibilities of each participant in a privateering venture, from the owners to the cabin boy, were clearly defined. Before they petitioned the lieutenant

---

[39]PAC, RG 8, IV, Vol. 88, *Joanna*, Examination of Alex Newcombe, master, 8 July 1813.

[40]Mullins, *Liverpool Privateering*, 48.

[41]*NS Leg. Papers*, Petition of Robert Shives, James Hay, Jr., and J.T. Hanford (the owners of *Dart*) to Sherbrooke, 5 May 1813, [Vol. 226, doc. 67].

[42]Garitee, *Private Navy*, 111. On 24 Oct. 1812, the Deputy Paymaster General's Office issued a notice that £1 notes would be received at and issued from the Pay Office at the rate of $4 each. *NS Royal Gazette*, 4 Nov. 1812, 3. In referring to costs of licensed goods, Herbert Heaton calculates cargoes worth £1,000 British currency at "nearly $20,000." Herbert Heaton, "The Erosion of Economic Warfare," Bradford Perkins, ed., *The Causes of the War of 1812* (New York, 1962), 45. Over the course of the war, a rough estimate of £1 to $5 U.S. currency is probably accurate.

governor for a letter of marque, the owners were obliged to post a bond for the vessel's good behaviour. The amount pledged varied with the size of the ship: £1,500 for a vessel with up to 150 crew, £3,000 for a larger one. Most Atlantic privateers were bonded for the sum of £1,500, although a few smaller bonds for £750 are noted in Appendix 4.[43] The bond seems to have been shared by at least two guarantors, sometimes, but not necessarily, the vessel's owners. Since each bondsman signed an affidavit of sureties confirming that he was worth more than the amount of his bond over and above his just debts, it made good business sense to share the liabilities as well as the profits. Presumably, the reason merchants such as Enos Collins, Samuel Cunard, William K. Reynolds, and John Moody invested in numerous privateers was to spread out their capital and reduce the risks involved.

ii) Articles of Agreement

Although no articles were found for provincial privateers, the general similarity in their maritime practices suggests that the articles of agreement found aboard American privateers such as *Friendship* or *Buckskin* reflected comparable regulations. Most seamen were accustomed to signing a standard ship's articles document that accompanied every commercial voyage. A comparison between articles of agreement for the schooner *Lark*, of Yarmouth, Nova Scotia, and the Salem privateer *Buckskin* revealed several similarities. Although *Lark*'s four-man crew earned monthly wages and *Buckskin*'s crew of twenty worked for shares, both crews had to pledge to do their duty, obey their officers, remain with the ship for the duration of the voyage, and safeguard the cargo. *Lark*'s agreement also demanded that the men avoid "immorality and vice of all kinds." As privateers, *Buckskin*'s crew agreed to additional articles concerning incentives, compensation for injuries or death, punishment for desertion or misbehaviour, and distribution of prize money. Various articles defined the division of prize money between the owners and the ships' company, specified the captain's right to cabin stores and furniture of any prizes, and reserved five shares for the captain to distribute to deserving crew members as he saw fit. Shares could be lost for cowardice, insubordination, disobedience, or drunkenness in action. Crews could not strike male prisoners or treat female prisoners rudely. There was a bonus of $20 for the first to sight a prize worth $100 per share, and an extra half share for the first man on the enemy's deck if orders were given for boarding. Prize money owing to anyone killed in action went to his legal representatives for the use of his widow, children, or elderly parents. Anyone losing an eye or a joint received $50 while the loss of an arm or leg meant $300 from the gross sum of prize. In the neighbourly society of privateering, it is not surprising that every effort was made to provide for the families of privateers killed or wounded by accident or in action.[44]

---

[43]Walter Minchinton and David Starkey, "Characteristics of Privateers Operating from the British Isles Against America, 1777-1783" in Timothy J. Runyan, ed., *Ships, Seafaring, and Society: Essays in Maritime History* (Detroit, 1987), 253. Article 3 of the American Act concerning Letters of Marque, Prizes and Prize Goods of 26 June 1812 required that the owners and commander of the vessel give bond "with at least two responsible sureties, not interested in such vessel" for $5,000 if the crew is up to 150 men, and $10,000 for a larger crew.

[44]PAC, RG 8, IV, Vol. 133, *Lark* and Vol. 120, *Buckskin*.

The vessel's owners bore the cost of equipping and victualling a privateer on the understanding that they would receive a percentage, usually half, of the net profits from a cruise. To ensure that the question of shares and any other regulations governing the voyage were fully understood, the owners, officers, and crewmen signed a contract known as the articles of agreement. Before the privateer left port, the articles were read aloud, and each man signed or made his mark, legally binding himself for the cruise in return for a certain number of shares. What motivated privateersmen was the expectation of a valuable prize. Given the average wage of $15-30 per month for a crewman aboard a coastal trader of the period, it would take only a few small prizes to match or exceed that figure. Captain Thomas Freeman's share as prize master of *Columbia*, captured by *Liverpool Packet* in December 1812, was £530. Few crews, however, were as lucky as *Dart*'s, who were said to have earned the astronomical sum of $500 each from their first cruise.[45]

Each crew member, according to his rank, was entitled to a specified number of shares, whether he remained on the vessel or left in mid-cruise to sail home a prize. According to Crane and Cranwell, the captain of an American privateer received twenty shares, the first mate fifteen, the second officer twelve shares, and so on down to the cabin boy.[46]

iii) The Ship's Company

Within the close-knit privateer communities of New Brunswick and Nova Scotia, assembling a crew was usually not a problem. Relying on the reputation of the ship and captain, most vessels quickly obtained a full complement of men. Seamen trained on trading voyages along the New England coast knew where the shoals and narrows lay and were well aware of secluded bays and harbours where a ship might safely lie in wait for a likely prize. From the statements of captured crews, it appears that the Nova Scotians' favourite cruising ground curved around Cape Cod and Martha's Vineyard, where main coastal shipping lanes intersected trans-Atlantic trade routes. Certainly, captains such as *Liverpool Packet*'s Joseph Barss and *Sir John Sherbrooke*'s Joseph Freeman had a sixth sense where prizes were concerned. Their natural flair for being in the right place at the right time was "supplemented by an intimate knowledge born of experience, of the trade routes and the seasonal variations of commerce and the ways of the merchant captains both in convoy and proceeding independently."[47] Knowing one's prey was but one asset. From the set of a sail against the horizon captains had to judge whether a vessel was worth hailing, weigh the risks involved in chasing an unknown stranger (which could turn out to be heavily armed), and assess which vessels were likely to be condemned as prize. Chapin's contention that a successful privateer

---

[45] According to Garitee, by the seventeenth century, the English government required articles of agreement between owners and crews. Garitee, *Private Navy*, 7, 132-133, 139-140. Garitee's suggested wages are consistent with the information found in crew lists aboard American prizes. *Lark*'s mate, John Parry, earned £5 per month and seamen William Bridges and Frederick Ferris earned £5 and £4.10 respectively. PAC, RG8, IV, Vol. 133, *Lark*. Mullins, *Liverpool Privateering*, 26 and Snider, *Red Jack*, 11.

[46] W.B. Crane and J.P. Cranwell, *Men of Marque* (New York, 1940), 21.

[47] C.S. Forester, *The Naval War of 1812* (London, 1957), 77.

captain had to be well versed in law and diplomacy as well as in seamanship, navigation, and sea fighting is borne out in the record of Atlantic Canada's privateer captains.[48]

Second to the captain in importance were the prize masters. Usually junior officers, equivalent to a third or fourth mate, prize masters had to be both responsible men and capable sailors because of their dual role as captor and prize court witness.[49] Unlike regular crew members, the two or three prize masters attached to each privateer usually performed no shipboard duties. Their responsibility was to sail their unfamiliar prizes safely to port with as few hands as possible. Although they received extra shares for their expertise, their role was not an easy one. Garitee's list of an American prize master's duties includes resisting attackers, evading the blockading squadron, and using commercial expertise to select the most appropriate port for his prize cargo. Crane and Cranwell sympathize with the prize master who was "forced to operate most of his prizes with barely hands enough to work the vessel; he frequently had a hold full of prisoners who were always waiting for a chance to retake their ship; and he had to be constantly on the watch for enemy cruisers and privateers."[50] Putting into Shelburne harbour in a fog, the American prize master of *Ceres* did not realize his mistake until hailed by a naval vessel. With great presence of mind, he presented the vessel's original documents and was permitted to sail away. Less fortunate was the prize master aboard *Jane*, prize to the *Liverpool Packet*. In the confusion ensuing after the mate navigating the vessel was knocked overboard by the mainsail, *Jane*'s American captain armed himself and forced the prize crew to sail the vessel to Boston.[51]

Prizes were also vulnerable to recapture by naval vessels or enemy privateers. After firing five shots to pull the sloop *Packet* over, *Fly* was forced to give it up to the Salem privateer *Fame* two days later. En route to Machias, *Matilda* recaptured the prize and sent it into Digby, Nova Scotia. The same month, the Swedish brig *Christiana* was seized by *Retrieve*, retaken by the American privateer *Teazer* a few miles off Halifax, and eventually recaptured by HMS *Borer* and *Wasp* a week later.[52] Clearly, the prizemaster's job was not always smooth sailing. Having obtained a commission, a vessel, a captain, and a crew, all the owners and investors of a privateer adventure required was a fair wind and a few plump prizes.

---

[48]Howard Chapin, *Privateering in King George's War, 1739-1748*, (Providence, R.I., 1928), 11.

[49]Lydon, *Pirates*, 216.

[50]Garitee, *Private Navy*, 138, suggests that American privateers carried from four to eight prize masters depending on the size of the vessel, and presumably, the optimism of the owners. Letters of Agreement from various prize files indicate that prize masters, because of their special duties, were entitled to more shares than regular crewmembers. Crane and Cranwell, *Men of Marque*, 290.

[51]Ibid., 278. Leefe, "Bluenose Privateer," *NSHQ* (1973), III, 8.

[52]PAC, RG 8, IV, Vol. 92, *Fame*, Examination of Moses Rivers, 24 June 1813; Vol. 80, *Christiana*, Examination of Charles Fenly, master, 18 June 1813.

Privateer Perquisites

While they tended to avoid violence, Atlantic Canada's privateers were not above helping themselves to items aboard their prizes. Foodstores, liquor, clothing, or personal items belonging to their victims were perceived as their due. On the other hand, breaking bulk, or looting a prize cargo, was scrupulously avoided. Not only did the vice-admiralty court frown on such illegal behaviour, but the collector of customs took any reduction in his five percent duties on captured goods very seriously indeed.

In over 200 cases, there is only one serious claim against a privateer for breaking bulk. The mate of the Swedish vessel *Falun*, jointly captured by the *Liverpool Packet* and *Retaliation*, accused *Retaliation*'s prize master, Henry Fader, of allowing his crew to break into the cargo of dry goods and fill their jackets so full "that they appeared almost as big as a hogshead with their coats buttoned round them!" When he protested, the mate was told "that if he did not hold his tongue he [the prize master] would put him in irons, calling him a damn rascal and many other opprobrious terms."[53] After a number of petitions, affidavits, claims, and appraisals, the court restored *Falun* and ordered the captors to compensate the owners for over £2,000 lost through damage and plunder. It was a lesson neither privateer cared to repeat.

Article XV of the royal instructions to privateers forbade captors from touching goods under $600 belonging to any female captured, but left the return of property under $300 to the discretion of the captain or officers. Always gentlemen it seems, privateers on both sides were very careful not to upset the few female passengers they encountered. An analysis of responses to question eighteen of the standing interrogatories regarding any loss incurred as a result of the capture, reveals a number of thefts of either clothing or money. For example, the mate of the brig *Richmond* accused captain Benjamin Ellenwood of *Retaliation* of taking his quadrant, quarter wages, and two chests. The previously-mentioned mate of Falun claimed that the *Retaliation*'s prize crew stole three shirts, four cravats, two waistcoats, and one pair of pantaloons from him. The master of the same ship lost seven fine linen shirts, eleven handkerchiefs, seven pairs of stockings, a pair of pantaloons, a vest, his violin, and two music books, and was threatened with a beating if he did not give up his watch. The *Liverpool Packet* relieved *Union*'s master of a few clothes, a razor, and $90.[54]

If personal losses were the exception, ships' stores were frequently plundered. Since rations were closely calculated aboard most privateers, many captors took the opportunity to replenish their stocks at the expense of their prizes. The *Liverpool Packet* was accused of taking small amounts of flour and rice from *Janus* and *Polly* and refurbishing their galley with a box of crockery from among the fifty crates of china captured aboard *Anson*.[55]

---

[53] PAC, RG 8, IV, Vol. 105, *Falun*, Examination of William Cross, mate, 7 Mar. 1814.

[54] PAC, RG 8, IV, Vol. 95, *Richmond*, Examination of Winslow Thomas, mate, 1 June 1813; Vol. 76, *Union*, Examination of Joseph Hall, master, Oct. 1812.

[55] PAC, RG 8, IV, Vol. 87, *Janus*, Examination of John Mowat, mariner, 4 July 1814; Vol. 75, *Polly*, Examination of Abraham Williston, master, 7 Nov. 1813; Vol. 73, *Anson*, Examination of John Smith, master, 9 Nov. 1812.

Liquor was a popular perquisite as victorious privateers doubtless toasted prizes *Mary*, *Betsey*, and *Experiment* with a barrel or two of their own gin! The crew of the *Liverpool Packet* liberated a puncheon of rum from *Adventure*'s hold and stole all seventeen cases of noyeau liqueur from the supercargo aboard *Falun*.[56] Another *Liverpool Packet* prize crew drank *Factor*'s wine "daily and as often as they saw fit ... from the casks on board which they appeared to drink as freely as water."[57] Occasionally, privateers treated themselves to sweeter rewards such as sugar, molasses, syrup, and chocolate. Other items taken included cheese, lemons, coffee, and even a pot of tamarinds belonging to the master of *Minerva*.[58]

Atlantic Canada's privateering depredations were not extensive. The thought of investors forfeiting a £1,500 bond for good behaviour or the fear of losing their prize, fines, or imprisonment might have deterred them. Or perhaps the men of New Brunswick and Nova Scotia were simply typical of their fraternity. As Crane and Cranwell suggest, "the majority of the men who sailed in private armed vessels, whether French, English or American, behaved themselves with all the honesty consistent with the proper conduct of a well-regulated war."[59]

Generous Warfare

Privateering afforded participants an opportunity to use their expertise or their capital to pursue private profit in the line of public duty. Few failed to appreciate the value of serving their country while filling their pockets at the enemy's expense. The practical merchants who invested their capital "were far more horrified by red ink than by blood"[60] and tried to keep risk at a minimum. Bearing this in mind, it is not surprising that the sea actions of New Brunswick and Nova Scotia privateers were less than heroic. Few shots were fired – in anger or otherwise – and less than a handful of people lost their lives in battle.[61]

Although some vessels tried to evade capture or put up a fight, bluff and bravado were usually enough to carry the prize. H.C. Timewell's study of Guernsey privateers describes prizemaking. "The technique of capturing a prize was to avoid doing much damage to the victim and rely upon a show of force to cause the enemy to strike. A few shots across the bow were usually sufficient and an engagement rarely lasted for

---

[56] PAC, RG 8, IV, Vol. 90, *Mary*, Examination of Henry Williams, passenger, 23 Aug. 1813; Vol. 101, *Adventure*, Examination of John Martin, master, 5 July 1814; Vol. 78, *Betsey*, Examination of William W. Eddy, cook, 8 Apr. 1813; Vol. 114, *Experiment*, Examination of Simeon Gardiner, passenger, 14 Feb. 1815; Vol. 106, *Gustava*, Examination of George Mackay, supercargo, 31 Jan. 1814.

[57] PAC, RG 8, IV, Vol. 122, *Factor*, Examination of Samuel Low, master, 28 Sept. 1812.

[58] PAC, RG 8, IV, Vol. 91, *Minerva*, Examination of John Scott, master, 18 Sept. 1813.

[59] Crane and Cranwell, *Men of Marque*, 17.

[60] Melvin H. Jackson, *Privateers in Charleston, 1793-1796* (Washington, D.C., 1969), vi.

[61] Mullins, *Liverpool Privateering*, 68.

more than thirty minutes.[62] *Eunice*'s crew "tried pretty hard to get away," and *Comet* led *Rolla* on a nine-hour chase before being taken, but many prizes seized by the Atlantic privateers were either unarmed, unmanned, or at anchor when taken, thus further reducing the captors' risks. The basically non-violent character of North American privateering owed more to common sense than to lack of courage. Combat inevitably damaged either the privateer or the prize; injuries reduced and demoralized a crew; and repairs meant delays and missed prize opportunities. The challenge of trying to seize as many ships as possible while risking the least possible danger afforded colonial seamen plenty of "scope for initiative and ingenuity as well as for courage and endurance."[63]

Despite their efforts, privateers faced risks. For example, when shots were exchanged during the joint capture of the 260-ton ship *Loyal Sam* by the privateers *Sir John Sherbrooke* and *Matilda* of 273 tons and 50 tons, respectively, either good luck or poor marksmanship prevented anyone from being killed.[64] In June 1813, *Fly*'s captain, Enoch Stanwood, became one of the first Canadian privateersmen killed in action, when American militia forces near Machias attacked the privateer and the three prizes it was escorting. In January 1815, during the final months of the war, Siphorous Cole, lieutenant aboard *Rover* and prizemaster of the sloop *Betsey*, died in a vain attempt to defend his prize from recapture by the Saybrooke, Connecticut, volunteers.[65]

Given the individualistic nature of privateering, the adventurous personalities involved, and the temptation to interpret rules more liberally once out of sight of land, it is surprising that so few abuses occurred. Although there were some legal safeguards in place, for example, an act of 1798 prohibiting the embezzlement of property on prizes, as Pares explains "the civil responsibility of privateers and their owners for damages was even less clearly defined than the control which the Government exercised over them."[66] Snider proudly maintains that, unlike their American cousins, no provincial privateer was ever responsible for any instance of cruelty, of personal robbery, of insult to women, or of wanton slaughter. Mullins praises the gentlemanly behaviour of the captain of the famous *Liverpool Packet*. "Of the hundred or more vessels overhauled in his nine months of privateering not one, as far as minute scrutiny of all known records show, registered a complaint of cruelty or outrage against Joseph Barss."[67] Even *Niles Weekly Register*, which regularly berated the Royal Navy for plundering, cruelty, and malicious damage to American property, seldom rebuked the Canadian privateers.

Although the governor of Bermuda endorsed Americans, saying "Yankees fight well and are gentlemen in their mode of warfare," some American privateers proved to

---

[62]H.C. Timewell, "Guernsey Privateers," *Mariner's Mirror*, (1970), LVI, 205.

[63]Forester, *Naval War of 1812*, 74.

[64]PAC, RG 8, IV, Vol. 105, *Eunice*, Examination of John Hill, acting mate, 22 June 1814; Vol. 114, *Comet*, Examination of David Dewoll, seaman, 25 Feb. 1815; Vol. 132, *Loyal Sam*, Allegation of Henry Wells, passenger, 12 July 1813.

[65]*NS Royal Gazette*, 30 June 1813. Mullins, *Liverpool Privateering*, 39.

[66]Pares, *Colonial Blockade*, 15, 50.

[67]Snider, *Red Jack*, 5. Mullins, *Liverpool Privateering*, 53.

be less scrupulous. Despite the fact that American commissions restricted privateer activities to the high seas (at least no closer to land than the low water mark), there were several instances of privateers attacking isolated coastal communities around Digby and Yarmouth.[68] A letter from Lieutenant Governor Sherbrooke to Lord Bathurst in November 1812 documents at least one case of murder. A crewmember of the Boston privateer *Wily Reynard* robbed and murdered Francis Clements, an unarmed elderly Nova Scotian living on a small island. Sir John assured Lord Bathurst that his men had subsequently captured and jailed privateer Lieutenant Thomas Swaine for the crime.[69]

The treatment of passengers and crews captured by privateers was usually good and occasionally generous, especially in the early days of the war. The *Times* of London, on 11 September 1812, reprinted a complimentary passage from a Boston newspaper stating that "the port of Halifax is crowded with prizes; yet they are generously treated, for the captors give up all the adventures and the baggage; and none but valuable vessels are sent in; coasting vessels not molested as yet."[70] Similarly, Mrs. Elizabeth Bell of Nova Scotia, whose passage aboard the schooner *Ann* was disrupted by the privateer *Dolphin* and rerouted to Salem in August 1812, publicly thanked her captors in the pages of *Niles Weekly Register* for the kind treatment she received: "Mrs. Elizabeth Bell ... begs leave to acknowledge with much gratitude, the gentlemanly and humane treatment of the captain, and prize master of the *Dolphin*, in returning to her 900 dollars together with all her personal effects."[71]

Prisoners of War

A constant threat to privateers on both sides was not just capture, but captivity. In a wartime situation where manpower was scarce, the loss of experienced sailors not only hampered war efforts but also affected morale. *Niles Weekly Register*, for example, reported the dismal state of more than 1,200 American prisoners confined in a two-storey former barracks and nearby hulk at Melville Island near Halifax. Not only were these brave American tars doomed to breathe their last in pestilential conditions, but "to heighten the poignancy of their reflection" Niles accuses the British agent for prisoners, Andrew Miller, of telling them "to die and be damned - the King has 130 acres of land to bury them."[72] Such newspaper stories trumpeting the ill treatment of prisoners stirred up patriotic emotions and made the return of prisoners a political, as well as economic, priority.

---

[68]The comments by Bermuda's Lieutenant Governor, Major General George Horsford, date from the early months of the war, Horsman, *War of 1812*, 59. Barry J. Lohnes, "British Naval Problems at Halifax During the War of 1812," *Mariner's Mirror*, LIX, (1973), 323.

[69]*NS State Papers*, Sherbrooke to Bathurst, [No. 61], 132. The attack occurred 9 Oct. 1812 and two days later, HMS *Shannon* escorted *Wily Reynard* to Halifax as a prize.

[70]*Times*, 11 Sept. 1812.

[71]*Niles Weekly Register*, 8 Aug. 1812.

[72]*Niles Weekly Register*, 20 Nov. 1813.

The spectacular destruction of the American privateer *Young Teazer* in June 1813 illustrates how serious the threat of capture could be. When the British seized the successful New York-registered privateer *Teazer* in 1812, its owners promptly decided to build a larger, faster vessel to avenge their loss. Designed for maximum effect, *Young Teazer* mounted a carved alligator with gaping jaws at its bow. Aboard the 124-ton, all-black schooner, Captain William B. Dobson's crew included one of the original *Teazer*'s first lieutenants, and a possible deserter from the Royal Navy, named Johnson.[73] If captured aboard an armed American vessel, deserters faced the death penalty for treason, not just imprisonment like their American shipmates. On 27 June 1813, HMS *La Hogue* chased *Young Teazer* into Mahone Bay, Nova Scotia. Captain Dobson tried to escape his pursuers in the fog and fading daylight, but as the fog lifted, *La Hogue*'s boats closed in. At that point *Young Teazer*'s carpenter, Elijah Gunnison, claimed he saw Johnson heading below decks with a lit stick from the galley. Gunnison's undated account from the Liverpool *Advance* describes his coming to in the middle of a mess of floating wreckage and helping haul some of the survivors into a boat "half blind, scorched, blackened, deafened, half stunned with shattered limbs and missing fingers but alive". The *Nova Scotia Royal Gazette* carried the same story on 30 June 1813. "It is supposed," the *Gazette* speculated, "that the *Teazer* was blown up intentionally by some of the crew - the explosion was great and destructive, out of 36 men which were then on board 8 only were saved, including this deponent."[74] The Americans rowed the boat to Amholtz Island where they surrendered to Martin Rafuse who delivered them to Lunenburg. Ironically, the same issue of the *Gazette* records the capture of *Liverpool Packet* by the privateer *Thomas* of Portsmouth, New Hampshire.

A series of meticulous instructions regulated the administration of prisoners, detailing who were entitled to parole, where they were to be detained, and how much each prisoner cost. Management of the prisoner of war population was extremely important given the thousands of prisoners involved. P.K. Crimmin calculates that by 1812 there were 52,649 French prisoners of war in Britain, as well as hundreds of prisoners from Denmark, Norway, the Netherlands, Spain, Germany, Italy, and Greece. Ira Dye's study of War of 1812 prisoners claims that 14,000 American sailors, or roughly fourteen percent of a potential 100,000- man sea force, spent at least part of the war as prisoners. This figure seems unusually high, since it is double the estimated 6,000-7,000 prisoners Crimmin suggested in a similar study. It is likely her figures include the nearly 2,500 Americans serving in the Royal Navy at the outbreak of war who gave themselves up rather than fight against their countrymen.[75] Dye estimates that while these surrendered men were the largest single group of prisoners in the first year of the war, by October 1814, they represented only fifteen percent of prisoners of war.

---

[73]Dobson reappears again in July 1813 as the captain of *Young Teazer's Ghost*, one of several privateer incarnations of the *Liverpool Packet* during its American captivity. Winslow, *Wealth and Honour*, 170.

[74]*NS Royal Gazette*, 30 June, 1813, 3. PANS, MG 100, Vol. 210, /6 - *Advance* article, n.d. Two of the crew were buried in Chester, Nova Scotia. Dwight Tanner, "Young Teazer, The Making of a Myth," *Nova Scotia History Quarterly* (1976), VI, 407-410.

[75]P.K. Crimmin, "The Impact of the Exchange of Prisoners of War on the Defense of Shipping in the Americas, 1812-1814," Clarke Reynolds, ed., *Global Crossroads and the American Seas* (Missoula, Mont., 1988), 151.

In contrast to the thousands of captured American seamen, including privateers, surrendered prisoners were not eligible for exchange until the end of the war. Many of these captives languished in colonial prison depots or hulks in Halifax, Quebec City, Bridgetown (Barbados), Kingston (Jamaica), and New Providence Island (Nassau), or in British prisons near Bristol or Dartmoor.[76]

Figures for British prisoners of war are inaccurate, partly because the United States lacked Great Britain's efficient administrative structure developed during the war with France, and partly because many American captors found keeping prisoners on board until they could be imprisoned or exchanged too expensive or inconvenient. This was the case when the privateer *Alexander* captured the British vessel *Dart*. The officers and crew, "being desirous of speedily returning to our several homes," gave their parole to Captain Benjamin Crowninshield that, as soon as they reached a British port, they would obtain leave and "cause to be sent to Boston, or some port in the United States of America, as many American citizens who are prisoners of war, as we are in number, and of equal rank, and will cause them to be delivered to the Marshal or proper officer."[77] P.K. Crimmin estimates the volume of prisoners as 2,650 seamen from 1,300 British vessels.[78] Haphazard American control over prisoner transfers and exchanges enabled many British captives to escape their captors. Some who could not beat the Americans joined them. Colonel Thomas Barclay, Britain's agent for prisoners in America, suspected that two-thirds of British prisoners captured in raids along the Chesapeake Bay in 1813 deserted to the Americans within three months.[79] Thanks to Barclay's efforts to ensure proper rations and other necessities, British seamen were relatively well-accommodated as they awaited exchange in cities such as Salem; Schenectedy, New York; Providence, Rhode Island; Wilmington, Delaware; Annapolis; Savannah; and New Orleans.

America's government-appointed agents for prisoners were less sympathetic. In October 1812, the United States government commissioned John Mitchell, former consul to Santiago de Cuba, as agent for the exchange of the American prisoners of war held on Melville Island, about a half-hour walk from Halifax. As the number of often-unruly prisoners increased, so did the British officials' concern for their safety and management. Instead of lobbying against overcrowding and illness on behalf of his unfortunate countrymen, Mitchell supposedly used his contacts with prisoners of war on parole in Halifax to pass on information regarding ship movements to the American government. Officials held him responsible for the capture of up to ten licensed vessels

---

[76] Ira Dye, "American Prisoners of War, 1812-15," Timothy J. Runyan, ed., *Ships, Seafaring and Society: Essays in Maritime History* (Detroit, Mich., 1987), 293, 302. Dye uses an 1818 study that calculated six sailors per 100 tons of training vessel and eight per 100 tons of fishing vessel.

[77] PAC, RG8, IV, Vol 77, *Alexander*, Parole of crew, 6 Apr. 1813.

[78] Crimmin, "Impact," 148.

[79] Ibid., 150. Barclay, a former British consul in New York, was appointed in Dec. 1812.

en route from Halifax to American ports.[80] Britain's decision to close the overcrowded Melville Island depot in 1814 and transfer the prisoners to Dartmoor, neatly resolved both Mitchell's espionage and the need to enlarge prison facilities.

Unfortunately for American prisoners of war held in Britain, the United States appointed Reuben Beasley, the overworked American consul in London, to take care of their affairs. Cool and detached by nature, Beasley rarely replied to prisoners' requests for help and, Dye notes, made only two prison visits throughout the war.[81] This convinced prisoners Beasley did not care for them, yet he thoroughly investigated accusations that British surgeons from HMS *Pelican* neglected wounded American sailors aboard the *Argus* after its capture. Beasley's report to Secretary of the Navy Jones reveals both concern and relief that *Argus*' surgeon, Mr. Inderwick, had paid "the most prompt and particular attention ... to the wounded under the most difficult circumstances."[82] Unaware that Beasley's efforts on their behalf were constantly frustrated by the Transport Office bureaucracy, imprisoned Americans assumed that their agent disliked them and returned the sentiment with general hatred.[83]

The policies governing prisoner of war treatment reflected efforts on the part of both sides to control costs while bowing to the political necessity of maintaining "a public posture of humane treatment." While the Lords Commissioners of the Admiralty were responsible for British policy concerning prisoners, the daily conduct of prisoner affairs fell to the Transport Office under the Commissioners of the Transport Board. Their objective was to deny the United States access to its captured seamen for as long as possible. The Board strongly encouraged non-naval American prisoners to enter the Royal Navy or the merchant fleet and returned all recaptured British naval personnel to service immediately. Dye commends the Transport Office bureaucrats for administering their duties strictly but fairly, and often with considerable forbearance.[84]

Until mid-1813 British prisoners of war in America were the responsibility of Secretary of State James Monroe. General John Mason's appointment as Commissary General for Prisoners of War transferred the administration of prisoners' affairs to the department of the secretary of war. Americans generally had better luck than the British in convincing their prisoners to change sides. Their official policy made exchanging

---

[80]Charles Bruce Fergusson, "The Establishment of the Consulate of the United States of America in Halifax," *NSHQ*, (1973), III, 62. Mitchell's instructions from Secretary of the navy Alexander Hamilton are found in William S. Dudley, ed., *The Naval War of 1812, A Documentary History*, I, 227-228, hereafter referred to as *Naval Docs*. Early in the war, Colonel Barclay was ordered to move into the interior of the country. When they discovered Mitchell's spying, the Lords of the Admiralty instructed Lieutenant Governor Sherbrooke to move Mr. Mitchell inland as well. *NS Leg. Papers*, 29 Jan. 1814, 309, [Vol. 62, doc. 107].

[81]Ibid., 300.

[82]Dudley, ed., *Naval Docs.*, II, 275.

[83]Dye, *Argus*, 296.

[84]Dye, "Prisoners of War," 299. From 1806 until its demise in 1817,the Transport Board assumed responsibility for all captured seamen. See P.K. Crimmin, The Prisoner of War Registers, 1793-1815: A Possible Archival Source for Maritime History," *Mariner's Mirror* (1994), LXXX, 469.

British captives for Americans held in Canada and the West Indies its first priority; those in British prisons came later.[85]

Prisoners were either officers or other ranks. In return for their promise not to escape, officers were generally granted parole under lightly supervised conditions in specified parole towns in England, or in Halifax or Saint John in the Atlantic provinces. The other ranks, including many American privateers, were not given parole, but sent to prison depots or prison ships, known as hulks. Civilian dependants and non-combatants were usually given parole and exchanged as quickly as possible.[86]

In theory, the Admiralty regarded the crew of private armed vessels as subject to the same rules of prisoner exchange as captured naval crews – except privateers had a lower rate of exchange. For example, according to Great Britain's sliding scale, an admiral could be exchanged for sixty seamen, the captain of a man-of-war for fifteen, but a privateer captain was worth only three men.[87] As prisoners of war, the privateer officers received the same courtesy as naval officers, and were allowed to move freely within a town while on parole. C.J.H. Snider claims that "the sojourn of captured American commanders in Halifax or Saint John was often short and seldom severe. Some came there again and again, being promptly paroled, exchanged and recaptured."[88]

Ex-privateer George Coggleshall's study of United States privateers counters Snider by contrasting the harsh way Britain treated American prisoners of war with the kindness British captives received from the Americans. The Admiralty, he claimed, had ordered British crews to take all charts, books, and nautical instruments off a prize. Supporting him are numerous responses to the standing interrogatories that list personal losses of such equipment as a spyglass, quadrant, charts, and instruments.[89] Captives, including captains, mates, supercargoes, and crews were all sent to prison or "stowed away in filthy prison ships" with no opportunity for parole or liberty except in cases where powerful influence was exerted. American captors, claimed Coggleshall, held all property sacred and allowed prisoners out on their parole of honour. In fact, "the seamen were so well fed and amply provided for, that in very many instances they left the county with great reluctance, when exchanged."[90] Unfortunately for Captain Joseph Barss of the *Liverpool Packet*, his custody in Portsmouth, New Hampshire, was neither brief nor benevolent. His captors treated him harshly, keeping him confined in irons. On 14 July 1813, Enos Collins and Joseph Allison wrote to Lieutenant Governor Sherbrooke asking

---

[85]Ibid., 296.

[86]Crimmin, "Impact," 148.

[87]Ibid., 148.

[88]Snider, *Red Jack*, 42.

[89]PAC,RG 8, IV, Vol. 121, *Enterprize*, Examination of Freeman Bourne, master, 15 July 1812; Vol. 121, *Dolphin*, Examination of William Dyer, master, 15 Sept. 1812; Vol. 73, *Aristomenes*, Examination of Rufus Fanning, mate, 1 Sept. 1812; Vol. 92, *Porcupine*, Examination of William Austin, first lieutenant, 23 June 1813.

[90]Coggleshall, *American Privateers*, 341-342.

him to intervene to secure Barss' release.[91] According to Janet Mullins, Sherbrooke finally obtained Barss' exchange but the terms of his parole were so strict that he was unable to return to privateering.[92] Richard Winslow, III, offers an entirely different scenario. He cites a public notice by the Marshal of New Hampshire District in the Portsmouth *Gazette* of 19 July 1814. It offered a fifty-dollar reward to anyone apprehending Joseph Barss, Jr., "formerly commander of the British privateer *Liverpool Packet*," and returning him to the keeper of the jail at Portsmouth. The notice mentions Barss "had for a long time been in close confinement, as a hostage for Captain Nichols, and on the 27th of April last admitted to his parole."[93] Whether he was exchanged or escaped, Barss showed no desire to risk capture a second time.

Cartel

At the beginning of the war Britain and the United States followed what had been the standard international practice of cartel, or prisoner exchange by sea. As defined by the *English Reports*:

> Cartel is a mode of intercourse between hostile nations, invented for the purpose of alleviating, in some degree, the calamities of war, by restoring to their liberty those individuals who may happen to have fallen into a state of captivity. It is for the mutual exchange of prisoners of war; and, therefore properly speaking, it can have a place between belligerents only.[94]

By this practical and mutually beneficial means, a privateer chose one or two crew representatives from the captured vessel to swear affidavits for the court, and allowed the rest of the crew and passengers to sail to the nearest safe port aboard a less valuable vessel. Once commissioned as a cartel, a vessel was protected from further capture on the journey to and from the designated port. Any wilful damage to a cartel ship required complete restitution in value and damages on the part of the offender.[95] Before leaving their ship, the privateer prisoners gave their parole, promising not to take up arms against the captor's nation until they were exchanged.

The cartel system spared privateers the necessity of reducing their own crews to sail home old, leaky, or sluggish prizes. It also freed them from housing and feeding

---

[91] *NS Leg. Papers*, 14 July 1813, 293. Petition of Enos Collins and Joseph Allison to Sherbrooke [Vol. 226, doc. 88]. Leefe, "Bluenose Privateer," 17, suggests that Captain Barss' harsh treatment was retribution for similar hardships inflicted on Captain Nicholls of the Newburyport privateer *Decatur*.

[92] Mullins, *Liverpool Privateering*, 53.

[93] Winslow, *Wealth and Honour*, 170.

[94] *English Reports*, CLXV, Ecclesiastical, Admiralty and Probate and Divorce V, (Edinburgh, 1923), 1232.

[95] John Colombos, *A Treatise on the Law of Prize* (London, 1949), 168, cites Lord Stowell's decision on the cartel *The Actaeon* (1815), in which he ordered that the vessel's owner "must be put as nearly as possible in the same state as he was before the deprivation of his property took place."

merchant traders or even potentially dangerous privateer prisoners for the duration of a cruise, especially since the personalities that made men good privateers, often made them "disorderly and violent prisoners when captured."[96] A neutral or unwanted vessel could carry captive crews to a nearby port where the local agent for prisoners would monitor their activities as they awaited exchange. The disadvantage in the system for Great Britain was that cartels were off-limits to the Royal Navy hunting for prizes to recapture or sailors to impress. Moreover, the generally haphazard way privateers accounted for prisoners enabled many captives to escape without being recorded for exchange purposes, thus defeating the whole purpose of the system. As a result, the Lords Commissioners of the Admiralty refused to ratify cartel agreements with the United States after November 1812.[97] Although privateers continued to release captured crews aboard vessels called cartels throughout the remainder of the war, they were not recognized as official prisoner exchanges.

Prize and Reprise

The profitability of privateering is a nettlesome issue, but several scholars have determined that private armed warships did earn profits. In his study of New York City privateering, for example, James Lydon reported that Manhattan predators realized profits of 140 percent during King George's War and the French and Indian War.[98] Similarly, in his study of British colonial privateering in the 1740s, Carl Swanson estimated that colonial private men-of-war earned an annual rate of return of more than 130 percent for capturing a prize of average value.[99] David J. Starkey's survey of eighteenth-century British privateering concludes that, despite the risks to their lives and fortunes, privateering presented seafarers and shipowners with a "fleeting and extraordinary opportunity for profit."[100] Financial success was not limited to the earlier conflicts. Patrick Crowhurst's study of French privateering from 1793 to 1815 indicates that although privateering in the Napoleonic Wars was not as profitable as in the earlier period, profits could be made if a corsair captured at least one richly laden ship, brought it safely to his home port, took it quickly to court, and drew up his accounts accurately so as to avoid counter charges and legal expenses.[101] Richard Winslow, III, sums up the case for privateering in Portsmouth, New Hampshire, as "a losing proposition"

---

[96]Crimmin "Impact," 151.

[97]Donald Petrie, "The Ransoming of Eliza Swan," *American Neptune* (1993) LIII, 13-15.

[98]Lydon, *Pirates*, 253.

[99]Carl E. Swanson, *Predators and Prizes: American Privateering and Imperial Warfare, 1739-1748* (Columbia, S.C., 1991), 218.

[100]David J. Starkey, *British Privateering Enterprise in the Eighteenth Century* (Exeter, 1990), 282.

[101]Patrick Crowhurst, *The French War on Trade: Privateering 1793-1815* (Brookfield, Conn., 1989), 170.

during the war of 1812. For entrepreneurs facing no other alternatives to legitimate trade, however, it was "the only game to play."[102]

For privateering to remain economically viable, commissioned vessels had to maintain a steady stream of prizes and cargoes that brought their captors a satisfactory return on investment. A review of over two hundred privateer prizes brought before the Vice-Admiralty Court of Halifax indicates that all but nine were original captures. Although recaptures were generally easy prey, since most were undermanned by prize crews unfamiliar with either the vessel or the route, they were also worth less to the captor than a regular prize.[103]

In the New England coastal waters cruised by New Brunswick and Nova Scotia privateers, most potential recaptures were likely to be British-owned vessels that the vice-admiralty court inevitably returned to their original owners, leaving the privateer crew to share a mere one-sixth of the appraised value of ship and cargo. Only the heavily laden *Loyal Sam* jointly retaken by *Sir John Sherbrooke* and *Matilda* in June 1813 justified its recapture with a handsome salvage award of £1,662. For most vessels, the average salvage allowed was under £200, although when *Sir John Sherbrooke* brought in *Paragon, General Hodgson*, and *San Gabriel* on 19 May 1813, the crew earned £556 in salvage for one day's work.[104]

While not legally exempt from capture under English law, boats engaged in coastal fisheries had been granted immunity from very early times. In several High Court of Admiralty decisions, Lord Stowell supported the freedom of French fishing boats on the grounds of "mutual accommodation between neighbouring countries and of tenderness to a poor and industrious order of people."[105] Although American privateers seemed to capture few fishing vessels, this was largely because they had their sights set on richer prizes with marketable cargoes. They felt "there was little sport and little profit in running down small and smelly fishermen from Canadian ports."[106] The Halifax Court of Vice-Admiralty, on the other hand, did not share this sympathy for American fishing vessels and regularly condemned them as prize. For Atlantic Canada's privateers, American fishing vessels were ideal prey. Usually under 100 tons, unarmed, lightly crewed, and disinclined to fight for their cargo, most fishing vessels saw no point in trying to escape and were sitting at anchor when they were taken. Although by no means lucrative, the seizure of fishing vessels enabled New Brunswick and Nova Scotia privateers to strike a blow against American commerce at virtually no risk to themselves

---

[102]Winslow, *Wealth and Honour*, 240.

[103]The amount of salvage money was legislated by the prize act in effect during the war. See chapter 3.

[104]PAC, RG 8, IV, Vol. 133, *Loyal Sam*; Vol. 92, *Paragon*; Vol. 132, *General Hodgson*; Vol. 96, *San Gabriel*.

[105]John Colombos, *A Treatise on the Law of Prize* (London, 1949), 161, cites orders from Henry IV to his admirals in 1403 and 1406 in Rymer's *Foedera*, VIII, 336,451 as well as an 1801 British order regarding the seizure of French boats.

[106]Crane and Cranwell, *Men of Marque*, 67.

and still earn a few pounds for their effort. The willingness of the court to condemn these prizes no doubt encouraged the practice.[107]

Privateers from New Brunswick and Nova Scotia seized vessels of all sizes but, as Table 4.3 illustrates, the majority of prizes throughout the war were under 100 tons, which reflects both the relatively small size of the privateer vessels and the cautious mien of their crews that naturally prompted them to prey on vessels their own size.

If tonnage captured represents one side of the equation, the volume of shipping available to draw from represents the other. Thus, while the percentage of prize vessels under 100 tons rose twenty percent between 1813 and 1814, the overall volume of tonnage captured was cut in half. Pushing its blockade northwards, the Royal Navy bottled up more and more of the trade along the Eastern Seaboard, until not only the size, but the quality, of prizes deteriorated. The Atlantic privateers were driven to capturing fishing boats for lack of any other prey.

Table 4.3

Prize Tonnages Captured by Nova Scotia and New Brunswick Privateers.[108]

Year	Under 100 T	100-200 Tons	200 + Tons	Tons ?	Total
1812	16 (64%)	6 (24%)	3 (12%)		2,295
1813	78 (65%)	27 (25%)	4 (5.5%)	4	9,965
1814	50 (85%)	7 (11%)		3	3,344
1815	5 (86%)	1 (14%)			465
Total	149	41	7	7	16,069

Not unexpectedly, prizemaking ventures conducted by New Brunswick and Nova Scotia privateers followed a seasonal pattern. In January and February, few merchant vessels, except the lost or most desperate, willingly risked their cargoes and lives against a howling North Atlantic gale, so privateers rarely ventured out of port until spring. The loss of the privateer *Rolla* with all hands in a January gale in 1815 left many widows and orphans in Liverpool as a testimony to the dire consequences of winter cruising.

Due to the delay in obtaining letters of marque at the beginning of the war, one-third of the twenty-five prizes taken by Atlantic Canada's privateers in 1812 were made in December. In 1813, March, July, and August were the busiest months for the provincial privateers with eighteen, twenty-one and nineteen prizes sent in respectively. In 1814, prize numbers fell more than fifty percent, but over half the privateer captures were made between June and September. In January and February 1815, privateers accounted for only six prizes. While prize figures varied with the seasons, they also reflected the volume of seaborne traffic accessible to privateers throughout the war. The large number of prizes made in the first half of 1813 dropped off sharply by September,

---

[107]According to Appendix 1, nineteen out of twenty American vessels described as "fishing" at the time of capture were condemned to their captors as "good and lawful prize."

[108]Based on figures from Appendix 1.

indicating a decline in shipping, probably due to the tightening of the Royal Navy's close blockade. Table 4.4 reveals the seasonal variations in prizemaking.

Denied their regular commercial outlets, merchants, investors, ship owners, and seafarers turned to the familiar practice of privateering to compensate for lost trade. By nature conservative and cautious, New Brunswick and Nova Scotia merchants and backers weighed the risks inherent in privateering very carefully. They calculated the prospect of combat, recapture, and captivity against the opportunities for prize money and adventure, and despite the odds, privateering remained a popular activity. Even though Snider argues that a fast-sailing vessel of good capacity could have made more money in trade after 1813, investment in privateering continued throughout the war; one vessel, *Dove* even obtained a letter of marque in January 1815.[109]

Table 4.4
Atlantic Canadian Privateer Captures by Month.[110]

Month	1812	1813	1814	1815	Total
January		8	4		12
February				2	2
March	18				18
April	15				15
May	7	5			12
June	10	10			20
July	21	8			29
August	2	19	7		28
September	3	6	8		17
October	7	1	2		10
November	5	4	6		15
December	8	12	5		25
	25	**113**	**59**	**6**	**203**

By spreading the risks and rewards of privateering across a business community linked by close personal, political and economic ties, at least half the participants profited enough to justify their investment. The lucky ones, like Thomas Freeman, made up for twenty years of seafaring in just two weeks of cruising aboard *Retaliation*.[111] According to James Lydon, the average profit realized through privateering was 140 per cent, although a large proportion of privateers made no money at all. Lydon's calculations are based on the assessed value of the prize, divided by one-third less ten per cent.[112]

---

[109]Snider, *Red Jack*, 144.

[110]Compiled from data in Appendix 1.

[111]Leefe, *Atlantic Privateers*, Introduction.

[112]Lydon, *Pirates, Privateers, and Profits*, 253.

Legitimized by a letter of marque and subject to the regulations of the Vice-Admiralty Court, the privateers of Atlantic Canada waged a modestly successful private war against American commerce between 1812 and 1815. Those unlucky enough to spend time in enemy hands realized how precarious their status was as privateers. Their prizes, while rarely spectacular, maintained a steady pressure against enemy shipping and contributed to a growing disenchantment with the war. Although aggravating and costly to its victims, commerce raiding alone could not inflict the kind of economic damage to American shipping that the Royal Navy's close blockade of American ports did after 1813. Chapter 5 examines the role of naval prize making in the War of 1812.

Chapter 5
On His Majesty's Service

The Royal Navy that contemplated the War of 1812 in North America was a far cry from Britain's once-potent instrument of imperial supremacy. Dazzled by Nelson's glorious victory at Trafalgar, British politicians failed to see the navy's inability to close the ever-widening cracks in the colonial system. In British North America, years of Admiralty neglect compounded by a serious shortage of manpower and a dearth of naval supplies in the Halifax Dockyard, thwarted the efforts of successive admirals on the Atlantic station to remedy the situation.

This chapter will discuss how, despite its many weaknesses, the Royal Navy played a pivotal role in both beginning and ending the War of 1812. The navy's policy of impressment helped draw America into the war and served as a constant irritant throughout the hostilities. Naval morale suffered when the United States Navy's unexpectedly strong performance forced the Admiralty to abandon traditional fleet actions for a tedious blockade of American ports interrupted by disastrous individual ship duels. Fortunately, prize money and financial incentives such as salvage, head money, ransom, and joint capture ensured that naval crews maintained their commitment to capturing American and foreign prizes.

Prior to 1812, Royal Navy forces were concentrated in Europe, leaving only a few ships to protect Britain's far-flung colonies. Lack of a strong naval presence at the start of the war encouraged and emboldened American privateers for the first few months and caused inhabitants of New Brunswick and Nova Scotia to fear for their security. Mediocre commanders matched the shrunken state of the squadron almost throughout the war. Within weeks of the American declaration of war, Admiral Sir John Borlase Warren replaced the weak and indecisive Vice-Admiral Herbert Sawyer. An Admiral of the White, Warren was a successful squadron commander but he lacked experience with larger forces and was "not more than a competent strategist."[1] Yet his new command of the combined Atlantic and West Indies stations stretched from Newfoundland to the Caribbean.

Striving to make do with a fleet that was undermanned, ill-supplied, and in disrepair, Sawyer was incapable of pressing any advantage his ships obtained in the first year of the war, contenting himself with "sportive thrusts" against the American coast.[2] Fortunately, Britain's defeat of Napoleon in Europe freed up nearly seventy vessels and over a thousand men and put an end to Sawyer's inconclusive manoeuvring in North America. Peace with France, followed by the appointment of Vice-Admiral Sir

---

[1]Barry J. Lohnes, "British Naval Problems at Halifax During the War of 1812," *Mariner's Mirror*, (1973), LIX, 317.

[2]George F.G. Stanley, *The War of 1812: Land Operations* (Toronto, 1983), 338.

Alexander Cochrane to succeed Warren in August 1814, finally provided the fleet with some decisive leadership and helped draw the conflict to a close.[3]

The Atlantic Squadron

At peak pre-war complement in 1810, only a handful of Royal Navy vessels patrolled the Atlantic coast, convoying merchant vessels, protecting the Newfoundland fishery, and offering a limited defence against enemy cruisers. This force consisted of the admiral's flagship HMS *Africa*, a 64-gun ship of the line, a few frigates (32-44 guns), and some twenty smaller vessels.[4]

When Vice-Admiral Sawyer's fleet sailed to Bermuda for the winter in November 1811, only HMS *Atalante* (18) and the apparently unseaworthy *Aeolus* (32) were left to guard Halifax. On 22 April 1812, Nova Scotia Lieutenant Governor Sir John Coape Sherbrooke wrote Lord Liverpool, British Secretary of State, bemoaning the dilapidated state of his province's fortifications and complaining that only *Atalante* defended Halifax. Sherbrooke hoped that in the event of war with America, a system of defence would be developed to allow enough vessels on the station "to protect the coast from insult and the trade from molestation." Instead, Sherbrooke's worst fears were realized, and by 1812 "the Halifax squadron reached a state of incapacity which seldom has been equalled in the history of the Empire."[5]

The Royal Navy's Atlantic fleet returned to Halifax in June 1812, four days after the United States declared war. Ordered to sail well off the American coast, Admiral Sawyer was unaware of the situation for several days. On 24 June, HMS *Belvidera* (36) carried home the first naval prize of the War of 1812, the 238-ton brig *Malcolm*. Between then and Britain's official declaration of war on 13 October, naval crews captured 114 prizes, sixty-eight of which were condemned to the crown *jurae coronae* instead of to their captors. Another thirty-six naval recaptures were restored to their owners on payment of salvage to the recaptors. Compared to the privateers' sixth, naval salvage awards were only an eighth of the appraised value of the ship and cargo, and usually had to be shared among a larger crew and the admiral. Rich prizes were

---

[3]Herbert Sawyer, Vice-Admiral of the Blue, commanded the Atlantic squadron from 1810 to Aug. 1812. Vice-Admiral Warren (1753-1822) succeeded Sawyer, who was replaced by Vice-Admiral Cochrane (1758-1832) in 1814. In terms of precedence, the Admiral of the Fleet was the senior officer, followed by the Admirals of the Red, White, and Blue respectively. The system of squadronal colours was abolished in 1864.

[4]William S. Dudley, ed., *The Naval War of 1812, A Documentary History* (Washington, D.C., 1985), I, 83, hereafter called *Naval Docs*. At the outbreak of war the U.S. Navy had sixteen ships in commission (excluding gunboats) while Great Britain had HMS *Africa* and two dozen smaller vessels stretched from Halifax to Bermuda.

[5]Margaret Ells, ed., *A Calendar of Official Correspondence and Legislative Papers, Nova Scotia, 1802-1815* (Halifax, N.S., 1936) Sherbrooke to Sec. of State, 22 Apr. 1812, [Vol. 59, doc. 37], 255. Reginald Horsman, *The War of 1812*, 56, identifies the main British ships off the American coast as *Acasta* (40), *Guerriere* (38), *Belvidera* (36), *Shannon* (36), *Aeolus* (32), *Southampton* (32), and *Minerva* (32). Lohnes, "Naval Problems," 317, describes conditions in Halifax.

rare, with most recaptures amounting to less than £200. In fact, during the war, only twenty-two naval salvage awards exceeded £1,000. Denied full value for such prizes yet obliged to rescue all captured British vessels, whatever their worth, the navy's morale plummeted. No wonder, when Admiral Warren arrived in Halifax to take up his new duties, he found his staff "dispersed, reduced and disheartened."[6]

Within a month of assuming command, Admiral Warren lost four ships of the Atlantic squadron and *Barbadoes* (28) of the Leeward Island squadron to wreck or capture. With *Guerriere* (38), *Laura* (8), *Emulous* (18), and *Chubb* (4) out of action and four ships destined for England and Brazil, Warren's force was in "a very reduced state." By January 1813 he had to solicit reinforcements from the secretary of the Admiralty. Reluctantly, they agreed to furnish him with four ships of the line and enough frigates and sloops to enable him "to strike some decisive blow," but after that, the vessels had to be sent back their respective posts![7] As their confidence in Warren waned, the Admiralty decided to return to a divided command in North America. In early 1813, Warren assumed responsibility for the North American Station, and Admirals Sir Alexander Cochrane, Philip Durham and William Brown took over the West Indies, the Windward Islands, and the Leewards respectively.

In November 1813, *Niles Weekly Register* reported that, according to the latest accounts from Halifax, the Royal Navy's forces comprised 106 vessels of war carrying 3,139 guns. Ranged against this "pretty handsome armament" was the American naval fleet, excluding vessels on the Great Lakes, consisting of eight or nine frigates of thirty-two to forty-four guns and ten or eleven smaller vessels. Although the Admiralty had first scorned America's small but agile frigates as "terrible non-descripts," by late 1813 several British ships of the line, including some that had served under Nelson, had been cut down to frigate size to counter the efforts of USS *President*, *Constitution*, and *United States*. The tiny American Navy had earned Britain's grudging respect, as Niles boasted, making "more noise and exciting more apprehension to the British than all the other navies of the world."[8] Given the Royal Navy's crippling weakness in both supply and command, these fears were well founded.

The American Navy

The development of the American navy had been a subject of often heated debate from the earliest days of the United States. Although President George Washington authorized the construction of six frigates in 1793, only three were actually completed before

---

[6]Naval prizes are listed in Appendix 1. Chapter 3 deals with salvage awards. Provincial Bounty for Seamen, *Nova Scotia Royal Gazette*, 26 Aug. 1812. Proclamation by Admiral Warren, 9 Oct. 1812; also 14 Oct. 1812. Lohnes, "Naval Problems," 320.

[7]Dudley, ed., *Naval Docs*, I, 508-509, Warren to Secretary of the Admiralty John W. Croker, 5 Oct. 1812; and II, 1992, 17, Croker to Warren, 10 Feb. 1813. John Wilson Croker was the secretary of the Admiralty from 1809 to 1819. The four 74-gun ships were HMS *La Hogue*, *Valiant*, *Sceptre*, and *Plantagenet*.

[8]*Niles Weekly Register*, 20 Nov. 1813 and 18 Dec. 1813. E.S. Maclay, *A History of the American Privateers* (New York, 1899), xix.

economic and political turmoil at home and peace with North Africa in 1795 caused a national re-examination of the naval issue.[9] Craig L. Symond's study of America's early naval policy suggests that most politicians did not question the existence of a navy, but rather its purpose and cost. Navalists, or the pro-naval faction, were "concerned with image, honour, prestige and diplomatic clout" which a national navy would entail. The anti-navalist vision, held by Thomas Jefferson among others, cast the navy in a defensive rather than offensive role. While Jefferson supported the use of American naval power against pirates, he felt it should not present a larger burden than the disease it was designed to cure.[10]

Elected president in 1801, Jefferson wanted to ensure that America's naval policy would raise no alarm in Britain. He felt the creation of a purely defensive force composed of small, cheap, quickly deployed gunboats suitable for protecting American ports and harbours would not give the Royal Navy an excuse to build up arms against the United States. As historian Gene Smith suggests, while Jefferson's gunboats reflected naval policy in a narrow sense, in a more comprehensive way, "they were a political-military program upholding broader government decisions." The *Chesapeake* incident marked a steady deterioration in Anglo-American relations to the point where anti-navalists argued in 1809 that "the long-run advantages of a navy outweighed the uncertain possibility of provoking a war."[11] Politicians from all parties and factions debated the issue for months until, in January 1810, Congress voted to fit out four frigates, *John Adams*, *United States*, *Essex* and *President*, that were most nearly ready for sea. While the Royal Navy lacked leadership and supplies at the outset of the war, the fledgling U.S. Navy was in even worse shape. Paul Hamilton, secretary of the navy from 1809 to 1812, was a South Carolina rice planter with absolutely no maritime experience and a reputed over-fondness for drink. Luckily for the United States, William Jones, a Philadelphia merchant, succeeded Hamilton at the end of 1812. Jones' seafaring background included a stint as a privateer during the Revolutionary War.[12] This change of leadership, coupled with a small, keen cadre of naval commanders, gave the United States Navy an unexpected but welcome fighting edge.

At the outset of the war, American maritime strategy eschewed a large sea-going navy in favour of Thomas Jefferson's gun-boat system. According to George F.G. Stanley, Jefferson assumed any war between Great Britain and the United States would

---

[9]The completed frigates were *Constitution*, *Constellation*, and *United States*.

[10]Craig L. Symonds, *Navalists and Antinavalists: The Naval Policy Debate in the United States, 1785-1827* (Newark, N.J., 1980), 12-15.

[11]Gene A. Smith, *"For the Purposes of Defense": The Politics of the Jeffersonian Gunboat Program* (Newark, N.J., 1995), 125. Symonds, *Navalists and Antinavalists*, 13.

[12]Lohnes, "Naval Problems," 330, refers to Hamilton's alcoholism in a footnote. Christopher McKee, *A Gentlemanly and Honourable Profession: The Creation of the U.S. Naval Officer Corps, 1794-1815* (Annapolis, Md., 1991), 9-11, attributes Hamilton's failure to his poor administrative skills rather than a drinking problem. R.G. Albion, *Makers of Naval Policy, 1798-1947* (Annapolis, Md., 1980), 47-48. Unlike the Royal Navy, many American naval officers gained their early experience as privateers. Maclay, *American Privateers*, vii.

take the form of blockade and raid with Britain doing the blockading and America the raiding. Such strategy eliminated the need for expensive battleships in favour of fast "hit and run" vessels and privateers financed by private interests at no cost to the Treasury. Jefferson's narrow focus, combined with the traditional anti-navalism of inland states, ran counter to popular support for the navy. Stanley concludes that what really put an end to agitation for an expanded United States Navy was the discovery "that war was much more expensive than members of Congress thought it should be."[13] Compared to Britain's 74-gun ships-of-the-line capable of multi-ship fleet actions, gunboats were small vessels (40-80 feet long and 15-20 feet across), variously rigged, with one or two masts. A gunboat carried a crew of twenty, one or two long cannon and a couple of smaller guns suitable for coastal and riverine defence. Unlike a sloop of war provisioned for four months, and worth up to $75,000, a gunboat could be launched for a few thousand dollars.[14] In the summer of 1812, some two hundred of these undeniably cheap but "miserable vessels ... lay about in harbours in various conditions of uselessness." This contemporary analysis of the American navy recommended that it either be enlarged or laid by. "It is too small as an instrument to chastize England, or to afford our coasts and commerce any valuable protection against her. The arming of merchantmen meets our peculiar approbation."[15]

Six months later, when the House Naval Affairs Committee sought ways to correct mismanagement in the naval establishment, it criticized gunboats for not justifying their considerable cost. In his January 1813 response to the chairman of that committee, Lieutenant Charles Morris of the Washington Navy Yard suggested the sole use for gunboats was in harbour stations at point blank range when they were protected by land batteries, or behind a shoal and beyond enemy grapeshot. They were not even useful as training vessels.[16]

Opposed by only seven frigates, described as "eggshells armed with hammers," and a dozen or so sloops, the British felt they had little to fear from the Americans. In fact, an article from the *London Evening Star* in mid-December 1812, claimed that Britain's maritime superiority was "part of the law of nations." Preoccupied with protecting its own shipping and merely harassing American trade, Britain allowed America to seize the initiative. Of what possible threat was the United States Navy, "a piece of striped bunting flying at the mast-head of a few fir-built frigates, manned by a

---

[13]Stanley, *Land Operations*, 43, 45.

[14]Dudley, *Naval Docs.*, II, 45, Sec. of the Navy Jones to Senator Samuel Smith, 22 Feb. 1813, regarding the cost of a sloop of war as one-third of a frigate. Smith, *Purposes of Defense*, 16, compares the $302,700 construction cost of the U.S. frigate *Constitution* to $12,000 for a two-cannon gunboat. Annual maintenance costs for the same gunboat were $11,000 versus $ 113,600 for the frigate.

[15]James Barnes, *Naval Actions in the War of 1812* (New York, 1896), 10. *Niles Weekly Register*, 7 Dec. 1811. In a later issue, 13 Nov. 1813, Niles reported that the American navy's gunboats were to be laid up. Those unfit for service would be sold, and others distributed in the harbours of the maritime frontier.

[16]Dudley, ed., *Naval Docs.*, II, 23. Lieutenant Charles Morris to Congressman Langdon Cheves [Chairman, Naval Affairs Committee], 9 Jan. 1813.

handful of bastards and outlaws?"[17] Cockiness turned to shock, however, when Captain David Porter's 32-gun frigate *Essex* met HM Sloop *Alert* (16) on 13 August 1812. Within eight minutes, superior American gunnery and shiphandling had disabled the smaller foe and evened the score for the loss of the U.S. Brig *Nautilus* a month before.[18]

A week later, the embarrassing loss of the more evenly matched HMS *Guerriere* (38) to the 44-gun frigate USS *Constitution* further shook British confidence and loosed a storm of editorial comment on both sides of the Atlantic. That the undermanned *Guerriere* was returning to Britain to have its rotten masts replaced was irrelevant. As far as the propaganda war was concerned, Americans had passed their first test of seamanship and naval mettle with flying colours.[19]

Surprised and delighted by their early victories, American naval captains, like Commodores John Rodgers and Stephen Decatur, looked forward to matching wits and weapons with the no-longer invincible Royal Navy. As the London *Times* reported, Rodgers' ship, USS *President*, brazenly carried two flags into action - one proclaiming "no impressment" and the other boasting "This is the haughty President, how do you like her?"[20] Rodgers and Decatur were, in fact, among a handful of U.S. naval captains who earned over $10,000 in prize money as a result of their efforts in the War of 1812.[21] Secretary of the Navy Jones, however, feared that the imminent arrival of more British naval vessels, the blockade of America's coast, and increased activity by the Atlantic privateers posed too great a threat to his small navy. Accordingly, on 22 February 1813 he ordered naval commanders to cruise singly to avoid the possibility of a fleet action, since "our great inferiority in naval strength does not permit us to meet them on this ground without hazarding the precious germ of our national glory."[22]

Meanwhile, faced with a lack of resources, the unexpected prowess of its American opponents and the public outrage each loss generated, the Admiralty issued secret instructions to all its station commanders ordering frigate captains to avoid single-ship combat. A captain should first try to retreat, but "if he finds that he has the

---

[17]John K. Mahon, *The War of 1812* (Gainesville, Fla., 1972), 8, cites C.S. Forester's description. The "singular article" from the *London Evening Star* appears in *Niles Weekly Register*, 26 Dec. 1812.

[18]Dudley, ed., *Naval Docs.*, I, 443. Captain David Porter to Sec. of the Navy Hamilton, U.S. Frigate *Essex*, 3 Sept. 1812.

[19]*Niles Weekly Register*, 12 Sept. 1813, called the capture "one of the most splendid achievements in maritime history." On 21 Nov. 1812, Secretary Hamilton recommended that *Constitution*'s crew receive $100,000 in lieu of prize money for their great gallantry, skill, and sacrifice. Dudley, ed., *Naval Docs.*, I, 578.

[20]*Times*, 16 Aug. 1813.

[21]McKee, *Honourable Profession*, 494, Table 33, credits Decatur with earnings of $30,099 and Rodgers with $19,743.

[22]Dudley, ed., *Naval Docs.*, II, 48. Circular from Secretary of the Navy to Commanders now in port refitting. Jones was secretary of the navy from 19 Jan. 1813 to 1 Dec. 1814. McKee, *Honourable Profession*, 11.

advantage in sailing, he should endeavour to manoeuvre, and keep company with her, without coming to action, in the hope of falling in with some other of His Majesty's ships with whose assistance the enemy might be attacked with a reasonable hope of success."[23] With the American navy avoiding fleet actions, and the British navy discouraging single-ship engagements, offensive naval strategy was at a stalemate. Ironically, the situation reduced both navies to the same style of guerre de course as privateers.[24]

Unsurprisingly, bigger ships caught larger prey. E.B. Potter's study of sea power found that in the twenty-five engagements between British and American naval vessels, the score was twelve to thirteen for the United States with the victories generally falling to the ship with the heaviest firepower.[25] For the benefit of its readers, *Niles Weekly Register* kept a regular tally. In November 1813 the U.S. Navy lost 141 guns to capture and eighteen to wreck compared with British losses of 455 guns captured and 338 wrecked.[26] Although these figures actually represent a proportionately greater loss of American naval strength as compared to British, publication in such a fashion boosted American morale at a time when there were few victories to report.

As Britain's blockade gradually closed off southern Atlantic ports and crept northward from the Chesapeake, the U.S. navy's effectiveness declined proportionately. The strength of British ordnance, numbers, and experience began to take its toll. In 1812, the Royal Navy captured three American naval vessels, *Nautilus, Wasp*, and *Vixen*, and the revenue schooner *James Madison*. *Viper, Chesapeake*, and *Asp* plus Gunboat No. 121 fell in 1813; and *Essex, Frolic, Rattlesnake*, and *Siren* followed in 1814. Outnumbered and outgunned, American naval vessels were finally driven from the sea.[27]

In November 1812, the *Nova Scotia Royal Gazette* reprinted a letter Commodore Rodgers published in Boston. It listed the vessels destroyed in his previous five-month cruise and noted 216 prisoners sent to England on parole. Rodgers modestly concluded: "During my cruise, although I have not added any additional lustre to the character of our little navy, I have nevertheless rendered essential service to my country, I hope, by harassing the enemy's commerce, and employing to his disadvantage more

---

[23]Dudley, ed., *Naval Docs.*, II, 183. Croker to Station Commanders in Chief, 10 July 1813.

[24]Alfred Thayer Mahan, *The Influence of Sea Power upon History, 1660-1783*, (1890; reprint, London, 1965), 540. According to Mahan, commerce destruction relied on dispersion of the fleet, while naval warfare demanded that vessels be concentrated in one area. See also Major James Ripley Jacobs and Glen Tucker, *The War of 1812 - A Compact History* (New York, 1969), 15.

[25]E.B. Potter, ed., *Sea Power - A Naval History* (New York, 1960), 223.

[26]*Niles Weekly Register*, 20 Nov. 1813. The loss of 800 guns amounted to twenty-five percent of the 3,139 guns said to belong to British ships of war, compared to American losses that probably accounted for more than thirty percent of the total U.S. armament.

[27]See Appendix 1.

than a dozen times the force of a single frigate.[28] Although Rodgers was still able to wreak a certain amount of havoc against British shipping while cruising off South America, his was really the only significant American naval presence throughout 1814. As young naval historian Theodore Roosevelt proudly proclaimed, while the United States navy had little *material* effect on Great Britain, thanks to American skill and spirit, the navy found "a way to do more damage than we received in a naval contest with England."[29] Given time, opportunity, and more commanders of Rodgers' calibre, the young, feisty American navy might well have challenged Britain's dispirited fleet to a fight to the finish.

British Naval Problems at Sea and Ashore

During the War of 1812 in Atlantic Canada, competition between the navy and privateers for ships, sailors, and prizes was grounded in real need, at least on the navy's side. Hard pressed to protect English trade and navigation on both sides of the Atlantic, the Admiralty could only spare a handful of ships for North America. To compensate for this lack of vessels, the navy frequently commissioned prizes for its own use. In 1812, the Royal Navy turned the ship *Magnet* into a prison hulk. Two American privateers, *Curlew* and *Rapid*, served as fleet tenders, and USS *Nautilus* took the place, and the name, of HMS *Emulous* (wrecked in August 1812). Even though reinforcements eventually arrived from England, the navy continued use the prize courts as a source of vessels throughout the war.[30]

Recommissioning American prizes was not only more expedient and less expensive than building naval vessels, there was also an unexpected tactical advantage. On observing a vessel with a distinctive American rig, American privateers had to decide whether to ignore it as a fellow countryman, or attack it on the chance it had fallen into British hands. Historian Howard Chapelle suggests this happened in January 1813 when the privateer *Anaconda* fired on the American naval schooner *Commodore Hull*. "The employment of American-built schooners in the British navy and the lack of recognition

---

[28] *NS Royal Gazette*, 3 Nov. 1812. HMS *Endymion* finally captured Rodgers in Jan. 1815. List of U.S. naval captures in Otto Von Pivka, *Navies of the Napoleonic Era* (London, 1980), 265. A measure of the quality of these vessels was the re-assignment of six of them to the Royal Navy.

[29] Theodore Roosevelt, *The Naval War of 1812* (1882; reprint, Annapolis Md., 1987), 404. Roosevelt mentions the development of new American technology such as Robert Fulton's submarine and advances in torpedoes and iron-clads at the end of the war, which might have enabled American naval vessels to penetrate the British blockade and even the odds on the open sea.

[30] See Appendix 1. Other prizes taken into the navy were *USS Chesapeake, Arab, Erie, Lynx*, and *Racer* in 1813, and *Nighthawk, Rattlesnake, Brizi*, and *Three Friends* in 1814.

signals between government and privateer vessels were probably the cause of this serious mistake."[31]

Not only was the squadron short of vessels, but as Lohnes points out, lack of dockyard supplies and qualified shipwrights meant that losses or damage to existing vessels could have serious repercussions. When the *New Emulous*(14) accidentally fired on HMS *Chubb* in August 1812, the latter was laid up for the entire war. Similarly in November 1813, when "one of the most violent hurricanes ever known here" cast a number of naval vessels ashore at Halifax, His Majesty's fleet received a crippling setback. Warren related the details of the damage to the Admiralty and pledged "every possible endeavour to have them repaired, with every dispatch which the strength of this yard and their own means admit of."[32] In fact, *Fantome* (18), *Manly* (12), *Arab* (18), and *Thistle* (12) were out of service for the rest of the war. Other ships did not see action for many months, further reducing the fleet's effectiveness.

If sound fighting ships were in short supply on the Atlantic station, so too were provisions for His Majesty's forces at home and abroad. By the third week in August, the Admiralty had issued 180 licences to American, Swedish, Portuguese, and Spanish vessels, mainly to transport flour for Wellington's troops in Spain.[33] As early as 10 October 1812, Richard Uniacke petitioned the vice-admiralty court on behalf of Admiral Warren for immediate procurement of several prize cargoes. He requested *Patriot*'s cargo of 1300 barrels of flour, peas, and beans lest "the measures of His Majesty's government may be much embarrassed and retarded." Similarly, the navy needed the several thousand pounds of flour and other provisions aboard *Sally Ann* because Warren had to supply 9,000 men in Bermuda and complained that he could not buy flour, peas, and beans in any part of British North America.[34]

Food shortages and difficulty in supplying vessels on blockade duty along the American coast persisted throughout the war. On 18 October 1813 Lieutenant Governor Sherbrooke alerted Lord Bathurst to a serious shortage of onions for the navy. This might explain why, when HMS *Acasta* captured the vessel *Stephanie* on 16 July 1814, the captor ignored 320 barrels of flour and twenty-six kilograms of hog's lard but took off most of 1600 ropes of onions.[35] *Niles Weekly Register* recounts numerous instances of

---

[31]Howard Chapelle, *The History of American Sailing Ships* (1935; reprint, New York, 1982), 190. According to Dudley, ed., *Naval Docs.*, II, 31-34, *Anaconda*'s first lieutenant mistook *Commodore Hull* for the "greatly feared *Liverpool Packet*" and opened fire, wounding an officer and two crewmen. A court martial acquitted him because *Commodore Hull*'s crew wore fur caps like those popular in Halifax, and this provided a reasonable doubt about the schooner's nationality.

[32]Lohnes, "Naval Problems," 322; Dudley, ed., *Naval Docs.*, Warren to Croker, Halifax, 13 Nov. 1813, II, 284.

[33]Mahon, *War of 1812*, 55.

[34]PAC, RG 8, IV, Vol. 116, *Patriot*, Petition of H.M. Advocate for cargo for H.M. Service, 10 Oct. 1812; Vol. 118, *Sally Ann*, Petition of Uniacke, 10 Oct. 1812.

[35]*NS Leg. Papers*, Sherbrooke to Bathurst, 18 Oct. 1813, [Vol. 111, doc. 17]. PAC, RG 8, IV, Vol. 112, *Stephanie*, Examination of Francis W. Raymond, master, 25 July 1814.

British sailors foraging ashore for food. On one occasion, boats from the Chesapeake squadron under "that ruffian" Rear Admiral Cockburn were accused of attacking the Cape Henry lighthouse, "sacking" the keeper's pantry and lighthouse, and "capturing" hams, minced pies, and sausages. In November, Niles accused three boats from the Chesapeake squadron of raiding a house belonging to C.J. Drury, driving the family away, and stealing a barrel of herrings, the cloth he had on his loom, his cabbage, his only milch cow, and a well-grown yearling. Then, when the man's daughter moved toward the shore to look for her brother, one of the Englishmen actually fired at her but missed.[36]

Of course the navy did not always steal for its supper. Many captains scrupulously paid for food or water they obtained, whether their vendors were willing or not. In April 1813, HMS *Shannon* and *Tenedos* halted a fishing schooner from Beverly, Massachusetts. The naval vessels not only paid the Americans "top market prices" for their cargo of fish, but gave them a keg of "good Jamaican rum" to help them swallow their loss.[37] Other "depraved" American suppliers, much to Niles' disgust, openly traded with the enemy. One such was the owner of a sloop from Stonington, Connecticut, who pulled alongside HMS *Superb* with a deckload of cattle for sale in August 1814. *Niles Weekly Register* singled out Block Island, off the Rhode Island coast, at the mouth of Long Island Sound, as "the rendezvous of the enemy, and the place where they obtain supplies of provisions and water." Such trade was not limited to the New England area. An American War Department secret agent operating in North Carolina reputedly discovered that a certain customs agent cleared vessels for Baltimore with cargoes of shingles "when it was 'well known' that they carried livestock and that they returned too quickly to have made the voyage to Baltimore."[38] Supplying blockade vessels was an ongoing logistical problem for the Royal Navy, which relied heavily on the resourcefulness of its own men and the enterprise of the enemy.

Serious weaknesses handicapped the Admiralty at every turn. Yet the navy was expected to overcome these odds and bring the war to a speedy conclusion. In America, Niles' newspaper condemned the British for using excessive force to capture American vessels, behaviour he called "Nelsonizing the Main." Meanwhile, English papers rebuked the navy for not doing enough! The *London Pilot* of 20 March 1813 complained about the navy's apparent lack of retaliation against America for the loss of nearly 500 British vessels in the first seven months of the war. "They insult and laugh at our want of enterprise and vigour ... and come and go as they please ... they advance to the very chops of the channel ... nothing chases, nothing intercepts, nothing engages them but to yield them triumph."[39]

---

[36]*Niles Weekly Register*, 20 Feb. 1813 and 27 Nov. 1813.

[37]Ralph Eastman, *Some Famous Privateers of New England* (Boston, 1928), 43.

[38]*Niles Weekly Register*, 13 Aug. 1814 and 19 Nov. 1814. Sarah McCulloh Lemmon, "Dissent in North Carolina during the War of 1812," *North Carolina Historical Review*, XLIX, (1972), 108. Lemmon quotes from Letter Book 19, 416-417 of William Hawkins, governor of North Carolina, 1811-1814.

[39]*Niles Weekly Register*, 27 Feb. 1813 and 8 May 1813.

Figure 8: HMS *Shannon* leading USS *Chesapeake* into Halifax Harbour.

Source: Courtesy Maritime Museum of the Atlantic.

Aware of the navy's shortcomings and sceptical of its ability to protect their shores, both New Brunswick and Nova Scotia commissioned private armed vessels for provincial service. In petitioning the vice-admiralty court for delivery of the captured privateer *Gleaner* to Nova Scotia, Richard Uniacke, His Majesty's advocate, argued that the coasts "are now infested on all sides by a great number of privateers that have already almost brought the coasting trade and commerce of this province to a stand in consequence of the daily captures made by said privateers."[40] Whether they were intended to replace or reinforce the navy, Nova Scotia's *Gleaner* and New Brunswick's *Brunswicker* and *Hunter* served their provinces with varying degrees of success. Fortunately for the citizens of New Brunswick and Nova Scotia, both the numbers and the effectiveness of the Royal Navy improved during the course of the war.

Manpower Shortages

Manning Royal Navy ships had always been problematic, but was resolved in part by resorting to press-gangs and harsh discipline to keep the vessels afloat. Crew requirements were heavy; a 1st rate ship of the line carrying 100 guns required a crew of 850-

---

[40]PAC, RG 8, IV, Vol. 123, *Gleaner*, Petition of H.M. Advocate for Delivery, 7 Aug. 1812. *HMS Colibri* captured *Gleaner* of Kennebunkport, Me., 23 July 1812.

875 men, a second rate (90-98 guns) needed 100 fewer men, and so on down to a sixth rate (20-30 guns) manned by 160-200 men.[41] Securing crewmen for these and all the other sloops, schooners, transports, and armed vessels necessary to conduct a naval war on two fronts haunted the Royal Navy throughout the war. Illness, injury, loss at sea, and battle casualties, coupled with desertions, meant that the recruiter's job was never-ending. Although the navy was legally allowed to exercise the power of impressment "over all persons of a seafaring character, whether employed on the sea or on navigable rivers" there were a number of exemptions at various times. In 1708, under 6 Ann, c. 37, seamen serving aboard English merchant ships and privateers "employed in any part of America" were specifically exempted from impressment. For all other English territories, the Exemption from Impressment Act of 1739 gave exemption from impressment only to foreigners serving on all British merchantmen and privateers. The Prize Act of 1740 did not mention the previous exemptions but did not repeal them either. This led to some confusion over impressment in later wars and rather liberal interpretations by the Royal Navy in the War of 1812. The navy justified its policy of impressment by claiming that since the sea was common to all nations, Britain shared a common jurisdiction for reclaiming its "vagrant seamen." While this excuse may have applied to stopping American vessels, it is difficult to imagine how Captain Scott of HMS *Centurion* explained pressing a Swedish seaman, who could not even speak English, from the captured vessel *Dalkarlen*![42]

Numerous memoirs of the Napoleonic era feature American sailors impressed to serve aboard British naval vessels under dreadful conditions. One such account by Connecticut-born James Durand describes his virtual abduction from a vessel in Plymouth harbour while awaiting a voyage back to the United States. On the night of 19 October 1809, he was dragged out of bed by men from HMS *Narcissus* and reluctantly embarked on a six-year career in the British navy as a gunner, musician, and sailor. As he lamented, "had I known my destiny that night, I would have instantly committed the horrid crime of self-murder." Sharing the living and fighting conditions of his English shipmates, Durand was wounded in action, defrauded of his wages, denied shore leave for three years, and finally, released from his "detestable bondage" in September 1815 with neither wages nor pension to show for his service.[43]

---

[41]Von Pivka, *Napoleonic Navies*, 161.

[42]Viscount Hailsham, ed., *Halsbury's Laws of England being a Complete Statement of the Whole Law of England*, XXVIII (London, 1938), 562. The section on impressment indicates that the original idea of impressment did not involve physical compulsion. Press money, or the "King's shilling" was given to anyone voluntarily joining the army or the navy. "Seafaring character" meant that ship's carpenters could be pressed but not shipwrights. Among those listed as exempt from the press under various statutes were saltwater ferrymen, gentlemen yachtsmen, the Greenland trade, fishermen, the sugar trade, insurance offices' watermen, and the coal trade. Alfred Thayer Mahan, *Sea Power in its Relation to the War of 1812* (Boston, 1905), I, 3. PAC, RG 8, IV, Vol. 103, *Dalkarlen*, Petition of Johan Magnus Berg, master, 16 Dec. 1814.

[43]James Durand, *An Able Seaman of 1812* (1820; reprint, New Haven, Conn., 1926) HMS *Narcissus* was a 32-gun, fifth rate ship of the line.

A similar account by Elias Hutchins, published in 1853, traced the Royal Navy career of an American sailor from his impressment in 1803 to his release in 1815. Hutchins summed up his career as a pressed sailor: "After serving in the English Navy 12 years, and enduring a thousand indescribable hardships, I was released in a foreign land without one farthing in my pocket, and thus left to beg my way from Portsmouth to London." While doubtless written and published for financial as well as patriotic reasons, and exaggerated in parts, these stories provide a glimpse of life in the Royal Navy from a common sailor's point of view. They reveal the harsh conditions shared by all who served below decks, whatever their country of birth.[44]

Compared to the relatively free and easy life of privateering, life aboard a naval vessel must have seemed grim and oppressive. Although scholars like N.A.M. Rodger have helped revise the "floating hell" stereotypes of naval service, life aboard a king's ship antelopestill featured "overcrowding, poor food, poor pay, and a harsh rough life with a fair chance of death by violence in one way or another."[45] Not only were many seamen reluctant to join the navy, but once war was declared, naval crewmen deserted in vast numbers. For example, three marines and nine seamen fled HMS *Albion* while anchored in Tarpaulin Cove, Martha's Vineyard, in late 1813. Despite Captain Devonshire's threat to destroy all the houses on the island unless the men were given up, the deserters escaped. Mahon estimates that British naval desertions in North America averaged 2,500 per year. If Admiralty estimates are correct, some 20,000 British seamen sailed aboard American vessels in 1812. In his study of the Admiralty, Stanley Bonnet calculates that between 1811 and 1813, naval press-gangs seized 29,405 men. During the same period, 27,300 men deserted. Deducting the 3,000 men who participated in the press, Bonnet arrives at a net loss in manpower over the period.[46]

Naval recruitment in British North America was an even greater challenge than in England. From 1811 on, Admirals Sawyer and Warren wrote numerous letters to the Admiralty pleading for more men. In August 1812, Lieutenant Governor Sherbrooke offered a provincial bounty of five guineas to be paid immediately to any able seaman volunteering to serve on the king's ships on the Atlantic Station. He cannot have had much success since Admiral Warren issued a proclamation six weeks later offering "Free pardon and forgiveness" on behalf of the Prince Regent to anyone willing to give himself up and declare his state of error. At least two men, Philip Cottenburg and Thomas Fleet of Halifax, entered the Royal Navy service to avoid sentencing. In general, however, such magnanimity failed to persuade either those "seduced to serve" on American ships,

---

[44]William Bryant, *The Old Sailor: A Thrilling Narrative of the Life and Adventures of Elias Hutchins, during 40 Years on the Ocean - Related by Himself* (1853; reprint, Cape Porpoise, Maine, 1973.)

[45]N.A.M.Rodger, *Wooden World: An Anatomy of the Georgian Navy* (Annapolis, Md., 1986), 60-68. Rodger qualifies the hardships of eighteenth-century naval life in terms of what a sailor's had been prior to entering the navy. H.E. Pullen, *The Shannon and the Chesapeake* (Toronto, 1970), 2.

[46]Stanley Bonnet, *The Price of Admiralty* (London, 1968), 16; Pullen, *Shannon and Chesapeake*, 3. American figures for impressment were much higher, see chapter 3. *Niles Weekly Register*, 8 Jan. 1814, 316; Mahon, *War of 1812*, 7.

or Royal Navy deserters "forced to serve against their native country" to fight under British colours.[47]

When a Royal Navy ship was unable to achieve a full complement, the admiral could issue a warrant for impressment in the province. The naval commander in chief then applied to the governor and council for permission to land a press-gang, usually twenty-four hours before sailing.[48] Unfortunately for the British navy, Nova Scotians strenuously objected to the press. When HMS *Thetis* pressed "two industrious young men," Edward McCray and Matthew Allen of Pictou, Nova Scotia in 1809, Robert Pagan petitioned the legislature on their behalf. Within a week, the house asked the governor for their relief since their pressing was "highly illegal, unconstitutional, and oppressive," as well as being detrimental to the province. They complained about the economic and social upheaval impressment caused "many young men natives of the province and not subject to impressment, [who] have been alarmed least they should have the same fate and frequently have fled from their home and occupation on that account."[49]

In May 1813 William Sabatier of the Nova Scotia Committee on Trade reminded Lieutenant Governor Sherbrooke that both the king's Instructions and Admiral Warren's orders expressly forbade impressment on shore. In July, Sherbrooke advised Lord Bathurst that he had received a memorial from persons interested in the trade, fisheries, and agriculture of the province asking for more protection of trade. They demanded that the Admiralty enforce existing regulations against impressing British seamen outward bound, foreign seamen in the merchant service and fishermen and landsmen belonging to the province.[50] The same summer, Halifax merchant Richard Tremaine initiated a public disturbance when he interfered with a naval captain's attempt to press a "deserter." Tremaine wrote to Sherbrooke on 30 July 1813, "Your Excellency will at once see the difficulty a Magistrate has to perform his duty if sailors arm'd with clubs are allowed to range the streets of Halifax, take hold of whom they please, call them deserters, and at once take upon them to beat those or others who interfere without control." Sherbrooke finally wrote Rear-Admiral Griffith a week later that His Majesty's service would "be much benefited by the entire discontinuance of impressment" in Halifax for the remainder of the war.[51]

---

[47]Provincial Bounty for Seamen, *NS Royal Gazette*, 26 Aug. 1812. Proclamation by Admiral Warren, 9 Oct. 1812; *NS Leg. Papers*, 271, Deputy Provincial Sec. to the Sheriff of Halifax County, 4 Nov. 1812, [Vol. 140, 437].

[48]Pullen, *Shannon and Chesapeake*, 2.

[49]Beamish Murdoch, *A History of Nova-Scotia or Acadie* (Halifax, N.S., 1867), III, 299. See also *NS Leg. Papers*, [Assembly Papers, Vol. 16], 195-197.

[50]*NS Leg. Papers*, Sherbrooke to Bathurst, 4 July 1813, [Vol. 59, doc. 27].

[51]*NS Leg. Papers*, 289, William Sabatier to Sherbrooke, 25 May 1813, [Vol. 226, doc. 74], 294; Richard Tremain to Sherbrooke, 30 July 1813, [Vol. 226, doc. 90], 296; Sherbrooke to Rear-Admiral Griffith, 7 Aug. 1813, [Vol. 111], 31-34.

Instead of the press, resourceful captains used everything from financial incentives to emotional appeals to lure men into the service. Captain John Pascos of HMS *Tartarus* placed the following advertisement in Halifax's *Acadian Recorder* on 16 February 1813:

NOW OR NEVER

> All able bodied SEAMEN and sturdy LANDSMEN, willing to serve His Majesty, and enrich themselves, are invited forthwith to enter for His Majesty's ship TARTARUS, captain John Pascos, fitting with all expedition to take more American Indianmen : she will be ready for sea in a few days. Those fond of pumping and hard work had better not apply – the TARTARUS is as tight as a bottle; sails like a witch – scuds like a Mudian, and lays to like a gannet – has one deck to sleep under and another to dine on – dry hammocks, regular meals, and plenty of grog – the main brace always spliced when it rains or blows hard – a few months more cruising, just to enable her brave crew to get Yankee dollars enough to make them marry their sweethearts, buy farms and live snug during the peace that is now close aboard of us.

HIS MAJESTY'S AND PROVINCIAL BOUNTIES	
Able Seaman	£ 10.05.0
Ordinary	2.10.0
Landsmen	1.10.0[52]

Although there is no indication of Captain Pascos' success, it is obvious that, at least in Halifax, an appeal to self-interest carried more weight than a patriotic call to arms for king and country.

In spite of the rivalry between the navy and privateers, the Royal Navy rarely tried to press men off Atlantic letters of marque. By the summer of 1814, however, the navy's need for men reached crisis proportions and several provincial privateers ended up as naval crews. *Crown* lost two men early in July 1814, *Rolla* had five men impressed on 18 July, and *Lively* lost two more less than a week later. On occasion, the navy's frustration with their private armed colleagues boiled over into hostility. Admiral Hotham, commander of the British blockading squadron in the Chesapeake, pressed six of *Union*'s crew, joint prize to the *Liverpool Packet* and *Rolla*, and then threatened to burn the *Liverpool Packet* if he caught it west of Cape Cod again![53]

---

[52] *Acadian Recorder*, 16 Feb. 1813, quoted in J.S. Martell, "Halifax During and After the War of 1812," *Dalhousie Review* (1943), XXIII, 290-291.

[53] Lohnes, "Naval Problems," 333, footnote 94. W.R. Copp, PANS, MG 100, Vol. 233, Family Papers.

Even at full complement, the calibre of Royal Navy crews and captains in North America was often dubious. Lohnes suggests that the numerous shipwrecks that plagued the navy in the first few months of the war owed as much to inept and inexperienced crews as to the weather. Typical was the unlucky HMS *Emulous* (18), wrecked off Halifax, replaced, and within a few weeks, responsible for the near destruction of one of its sister ships. Other disasters included the loss of HMS *Barbados* (28) in September 1812 with several of its convoy and £60,000 for the Halifax Dockyard payroll. In December, HMS *Plumper* (12) went down with £70,000 in specie aboard.[54]

When ignorance or incompetence shared the deck with greed, the results could be disastrous. On 1 August 1812, HMS *Alphea* (10), sailing as a mail packet under a flag of truce, illegally seized the unsuspecting *Zodiac*. To compound the error, *Alphea*'s inexperienced prize crew ran the ship aground on Ragged Reef off Shelburne, Nova Scotia, and just barely limped into Liverpool. Once the master and captain went ashore, the crew proceeded to get drunk and abandon the pumps until there was five feet of water in the hold. *Zodiac*'s damaged cargo of rice and seven hundred barrels of flour were removed to a nearby warehouse, which subsequently collapsed, destroying what was left of the cargo. In his judgement, Sir Alexander Croke berated Lieutenant Jones for such reckless misuse of a flag of truce and issued an unprecedented order for the captors to pay all costs, damages, and expenses incurred.[55]

Naval Prize and the Profit Motive

Unlike privateers, who had to petition for a letter of marque to capture enemy vessels once war was declared, the Royal Navy was automatically on alert. Captains were entitled to use their powers of visit, search, and detention against merchant vessels of any nationality in any waters except those within three miles of a neutral state. Long-established regulations stipulated that officers must exercise good judgement concerning visits and treat all vessels and crews with strict propriety. Even Mahan, while defending the navy's right of search, took care to specify that such powers should only be used to determine the nationality of the vessel and the character of the voyage, and not for impressment.[56]

Although any enemy vessel could be brought to in time of war, British naval captains did not detain neutral merchantmen without a good cause, such as evading a visit, resisting search, or carrying false papers. They also halted anyone suspected of carrying contraband, breaching blockade, or trading with the enemy. Naval vessels contravening international law, the Naval Prize Act, or any other Admiralty orders or

---

[54]Lohnes, "Naval Problems," 322.

[55]PAC, RG 8, IV, Vol. 76, *Alphea*, Affidavit of George Brown, first mate, 24 Oct. 1812. This is the only instance in the court records reviewed that a captor was assigned all costs.

[56]Mahan, *War of 1812*, I, 8.

instructions jeopardized the condemnation of a prize.[57] Only when he had conducted a proper visit and search, and if he found evidence of wrongdoing admissible in a prize court, could an officer detain a vessel. Vice-admiralty court documents record several instances where one naval officer permitted a vessel to proceed only to have another ship's captain seize the prize and gain a condemnation. The possibility of prize money had to be weighed against potential court costs – but to many, the risk was worth it.

Under the British system, the burden of proof on seizure fell to the vessel's owner, not the Royal Navy. Caffrey calculates that the cost of hearings dismissed early through lack of proof amounted to $2,000-$3,000 and as much as $5,000 for a full term case. This cost American ship owners millions of dollars each year and resulted in frequent lawsuits against their would-be captors. For this reason, confirming the nationality of the vessel and cargo before making prize was of prime importance.

During the War of 1812, it was relatively easy to change or neutralize the nationality of a vessel for the purpose of evading capture or prosecution in a prize court. For example, a ship with American registration on the outward voyage to Saint Bartholomew could easily return as a neutral Swedish vessel following a fraudulent transfer of ownership. Another ploy was to hire a captain of the appropriate nationality and make sure the crew rehearsed a common story in advance. If everyone replied to the standing interrogatories in the same way, it was very difficult for the vice-admiralty court to disprove the nationality of a prize. As Patrick Crowhurst suggests, "naval captains, faced by a lack of concrete evidence, seldom wished to present a weak case to a sceptical Admiralty court and face a counter charge for damages from the nominal owner if they failed to prove their case."[58]

Prize money served the Royal Navy in several ways. Officially awarded "for the better and more effective encouragement of the sea service,"[59] prize money also raised morale aboard ship, controlled disgruntled sailors, and united officers and crews in a common cause. A typical prize was the Baltimore letter-of-marque schooner *Daedalus*, captured by HMS *Nieman* off the Delaware Capes on 18 September 1814. When asked how he expected to run a cargo of Haitian coffee past the blockade into New York harbour, seaman Samuel Parish confidently testified "from superior sailing!"[60] As Parish and many others learned, underestimating the navy's seamanship and its abiding interest in prize money could be costly.

---

[57]Godfrey Lushington, *A Manual of Prize Law* (London, 1866), ix-xviii, 1-12. Sir William Scott's judgements frequently relied on Vattel (1714-1767) as an authority in interpreting the law of nations concerning search. According to Vattel, "a deliberate and continued resistance of search on the part of a neutral vessel to a lawful cruiser, is followed by the legal consequences of confiscation." Joseph Chitty, ed., Emerich de Vattel, *The Law of Nations or Principles of the Law of Nations Applied to the Conduct of Affairs of Nations and Sovereigns*, (Philadelphia, 1857).

[58]Kate Caffrey, *The Lion and the Union: The Anglo-American War 1812-1815* (London, 1978), 63. Patrick Crowhurst, *The French War on Trade: Privateering 1793-1815* (Brookfield, Conn., 1989), 35.

[59]Bonnet, *Price of Admiralty*, 29.

[60]PAC, RG 8, IV, Vol. 103, *Daedalus*, Examination of Samuel Parish, seaman, 24 Sept. 1814.

i) Head Money

If prize money were not sufficient incentive, an act of parliament in 1740 entitled naval officers and crews head money, or a bounty paid on each captured seaman. Monies for this grant came from public funds and represented a fixed amount – usually £5 per man.[61] Legal historian E.S. Roscoe suggests that parliament intended head money "to compensate officers and men for the low rate of pay in the Royal Navy and to stimulate them to greater exertions in time of war."[62] Petitions, such as one to Judge Croke by the captain of HMS *Antelope*, indicate that the navy certainly felt head money was worth fighting for. Captain Carpenter claimed that, because his vessel was within a "short gunshot" of HMS *Newcastle* (60) when she captured the American privateer brig *Ida* on 9 August 1814, he was entitled to head money plus a share of the hull. A further petition on behalf of *Antelope*'s captain, officers, and crew claimed head money according to the Prize Act.[63]

The United States also used the incentive of head money to encourage American prizemakers. The bounty offered for prisoners was set by act of Congress and raised from $20 per prisoner in 1812, to $25 in 1813, until it reached $100 per head in 1814.[64] Given the negligible ship traffic in or out of American ports by 1814, it is unlikely many navy or privateer crews took advantage of the higher bounties.

ii) Ransom

Ransom, once a legitimate source of wartime seafaring income, was forbidden to British vessels after 1782. In 1805, under 45 Geo. III, c.72, naval vessels were liable for a £500 penalty and privateers risked losing their letter of marque for accepting ransoms.[65] Nevertheless, during the War of 1812, there are several references to British captains ransoming American vessels and vice versa. The first reference occurs in July 1812, although it was more like a toll than ransom. Niles claims that HMS *Plumper* removed over $10,000 in specie from three American vessels and then allowed them to proceed. That the practice probably continued throughout the war is indicated by Lohnes' account of HMS *Nymph* ransoming ten American ships for $7000 between 11 June and 8 July 1814 without reporting it to the authorities.[66]

---

[61]Roscoe, *Prize Cases*, II, 201. Beginning with 6 Ann, c. 37, the award of £5 head money remained constant in prize acts up to and including the War of 1812.

[62]E.S. Roscoe, *A History of the English Prize Court* (London, 1924), 82.

[63]PAC, RG 8, IV, Vol. 108, *Antelope*, Petition of Captain, officers and crew, 7 Sept. 1814. The prize act was 53 Geo. III, c. 63.

[64]Garitee, *Private Navy*, 168.

[65]Allan Rosas, *The Legal Status of Prisoners of War* (Helsinki, n.d.), 53-54, discusses changing attitudes toward the payment of ransom in the seventeenth and eighteenth centuries. He credits the philosophies of the Enlightenment and the French Revolution for improved international understanding of prisoners of war.

[66]*Niles Weekly Register*, 25 July 1812. Lohnes, "Naval Problems," 325.

For a captain on blockade duty, such as HMS *Statira*'s Hazard Stackpole, it was almost impossible to leave his post or reduce his forces by manning a prize back to Halifax. At the end of May 1813, his ship captured the sloop *Plough Boy* bound from Delaware to Philadelphia. Fearing the arrival of a squadron of enemy frigates and reluctant to send in a prize whose hull was in poor condition, Stackpole was about to order the vessel destroyed. When the master offered $1,000 for the vessel, however, and promised to return home without completing his journey, Stackpole accepted. A month later, for similar reasons, he agreed to ransom the American brig *Fanny* for $2,000. The vice-admiralty court upheld his decision, calling it an extraordinary case of moral necessity.[67]

Where his own men were concerned, Stackpole was not so understanding. On 18 June, he ordered one of his junior officers, Edward Brenton, to man twelve prizes into Halifax. Brenton refused, preferring a court martial for disobeying orders to risking the safety of his ships, the honour of his flag, or his own reputation for "the private emolument of individuals."[68]

In November 1813, Captain Joseph Hayes of HMS *Majestic* hit upon the novel idea of ransoming three small vessels recently captured off Provincetown, Maine, for fresh water. Reinforcing his offer with a threat to destroy every house in town; Hayes soon received 202 puncheons of water. Niles does not indicate whether these supplies were ever paid for by HMS *Nymph* as Hayes had promised.[69]

In August 1814, the Nova Scotia privateer *Lively* captured a Boston-owned schooner. In response to a question regarding previous captures, the *Dove*'s cook admitted that HMS *Nimrod* had taken them prize three weeks earlier, "let them go on paying six hundred dollars ransom money," but kept their papers. There is no reference to what became of the ransom money.

American naval vessels were not restrained from accepting ransom. Niles describes the early success of USS *Essex* at the end of July 1812. En route to Baltimore, *Essex* cut out a vessel carrying 150 much-needed soldiers from a convoy of British transports and ransomed the men for a bill of exchange worth $14,000 on a London bank. Donald Petrie recounts the case of the Scottish whaling ship *Eliza Swan* taken by Commodore John Rodgers (USS *President*) on 24 July 1813. With too many prisoners to feed already, and a long homeward voyage ahead of him, Rodgers struck a deal with Captain Young to ransom the prize for £ 5,000. In such instances, the captured captain or his agent agreed to cease hostilities against the enemy in return for the captor renouncing his right to destroy the vessel. Both sides signed bills of exchange, binding the captured vessel's owners to pay the pre-arranged ransom upon presentation of the bill of exchange. The captain himself usually signed an additional bond, personally

---

[67]PAC, RG 8, IV, Vol. 92, *Plough Boy*, Affidavit of Lieutenant Charles Samuel White, HMS *Statira*, 31 July 1813. James Stewart, ed., *Reports of cases argued and determined in the Court of Vice-Admiralty at Halifax, in Nova Scotia from the commencement of the war, in 1803, to the end of the year 1813, in the time of Alexander Croke LLD., Judge of that Court* (Halifax, N.S., 1813), 554.

[68]PAC, RG 8, IV, Vol. 78. *Belle*. Captain Edward P. Brenton to Captain Stackpole, 18 June 1813.

[69]*Niles Weekly Register*, 11 Sept. 1813.

guaranteeing payment of the bill should the owners renege. The ransom document also served as a safe-conduct agreement by allowing the prize a set amount of time to sail to a designated port over a specified route, while protecting it from subsequent capture by American privateers or naval vessels.[70]

American merchants were quick to take advantage of the possibilities arising from the use of ransom. In April 1813, the privateer *Retaliation* seized the American brig *Richmond*, despite *Richmond*'s licence from the governor of New Brunswick. Owner Ethel Olmstead of Eastport, Maine, asked Messrs. John and Michael Tobin of Saint John to ensure that Captain Thomas received a certificate to make it appear the brig was ransomed before condemnation.[71] Proof of ransom would help him conceal his English identity from his neighbours, while possession of a British licence would make them suspicious. By denying naval ships access to this problematic but expedient tool, Britain forced the navy to rely more heavily on prize money and resort to various stratagems to gain as much of it as possible.

iii) Joint Capture

When pickings were slim, ships fought for their prizes in court instead of at sea, by claiming joint capture. Under international law, the ship to which a prize struck its flag was deemed the captor. Joint capture could be claimed on the grounds of cooperation, for example, being near enough at the time of capture to intimidate the prize into surrendering. The vessel, however, physically had to assist in the capture to earn a share of the head money. Joint claims could also be based on association, such as being part of a blockading force, cruising in company, or being one of several vessels chasing another under orders from a senior commander. Since, in the eyes of the court, "the actual captor is the favourite of the law," anyone desiring to dispute another's capture had to provide strong evidence.[72]

HMS *Statira*'s agent successfully claimed that because the vessel was part of the blockade, the crew were entitled to share in the prize money from the capture of *Flight* by HMS *Spartan* and the Chesapeake Squadron, even though *Statira* was on patrol in the upper part of the bay at the time the prize was made. The same association argument, however, failed for the storeship HMS *Abundance* seeking a share of *Ulysses*, prize to HMS *Majestic* and *Ring Dove*.[73]

On another occasion, the officers and crew of HMS *Albion* claimed the right to share *Chili*'s prize money, because Admiral Cockburn awarded their captain an equal

---

[70] *Niles Weekly Register*, 1 Aug. 1812. Petrie, "Eliza Swan," 103.

[71] PAC,RG 8, IV, Vol.95, *Richmond*, Ethel Olmstead to John and Michael Tobin, Apr. 1813.

[72] *English Reports*, CLXV, Ecclesiastical, Admiralty and Probate and Divorce V (Edinburgh, 1923), 1343. Lushington, *Prize Law*, 68.

[73] PAC, RG 8, IV, Vol. 84, *Flight*, Petition for joint capture by Thomas Jeffrey, purser, *Statira*, 5 Oct. 1813. Claim granted 16 Oct. 1813; Vol. 98, *Ulysses*, Petition of Josiah Oake, master, HM Storeship *Abundance*, 23 Aug. 1813 and Response to Petition, 10 Nov. 1813. Petition for joint capture and subsequent appeal denied.

share with *Nimrod*'s captain. Arguing on behalf of *Nimrod*'s crew, Richard Uniacke claimed that the capture took place late at night after a long chase, when *Albion* was probably thirty miles away, and it was too dark for the prize to see anything, even if *Albion* had been nearby. Furthermore, *Nimrod*'s crew refused to give up their rights to the prize and to be bound by any private agreements between captains.[74]

Captain Nathaniel Mitchell, commander of HMS *Nimrod* (18) was not above resorting to outright duplicity to avoid sharing his prize money with a larger colleague. In December 1813, after boarding the *Sparkler*, he assured HMS *Armide* (38), in sight at the time, that they were not going to make prize. When *Armide* later discovered that *Nimrod* had laid claim to the vessel, the case went to court, and *Armide* was duly awarded joint capture. Reluctant to make *Nimrod* pay court costs for the much larger vessel, the judge ordered each of them to pay their own costs but chastised *Nimrod*'s captain for his behaviour.[75]

Privateers were also liable to claims of joint capture by aggressive naval captains. In July 1813, HMS *Atalante* petitioned the vice-admiralty court against the Halifax privateer *Crown* for joint capture of *Sibae*. *Crown*'s crew swore that they had sighted the ship before dawn but waited until 7:00 a.m. when they could see that the prize was worth taking. Within two hours the capture and transfer of papers were complete. *Atalante*'s crew, who reached the vessels about noon, maintained that they heard the *Crown*'s men say the capture occurred between 9 and 10:00 a.m. At issue was when the actual capture had occurred, and whether *Atalante* could have been in sight at the time, and thereby contributed to the capture by its presence. The testimony of John Adams, master of *Crown*, described his objections to Captain Hickey's highhanded behaviour. Not only did Hickey call him an "insolent fellow" and threaten impressment, *Atalante*'s surgeon even examined Adams to determine whether his wounds from previous battles in His Majesty's navy really rendered him unfit for service. Disappointed, Hickey pressed two of Adams' best prize men. Short-handed, Adams had to put into Shelburne for more men at which point three more of his crew deserted for fear of impressment. Adams hastily put to sea without sufficient crew only to fall prey to an American privateer. Despite *Atalante*'s bullying tactics, the ship was awarded a £4,909 share of *Sibae*.[76]

Gentlemen and Jack Tars

Forced by circumstances to fight a frequently frustrating and often unprofitable defensive war at sea, naval crews treated their American opponents well or ill depending on the personalities of the captains or prize masters involved. Although *Niles Weekly Register* delighted in recounting every real and rumoured instance of naval bullying, there were many occasions when Royal Navy captains showed genuine concern for their captives.

---

[74]PAC, RG 8, IV, Vol. 79, *Chili*, Responsive Allegation by R. Uniacke for *Nimrod*'s crew, 30 Sept. 1814. Petition for joint claim rejected 15 Oct. 1814.

[75]*English Reports*, 1341.

[76]RG 8, IV, Vol. 96, *Sibae*, Response of John Adams, captain, 25 Aug. 1813.

The "petty plundering" of the New Point Comfort lighthouse by vessels of the Chesapeake blockade was countered by Lt. Gibson of HMS *Alban* giving *Betsy* back to its captain as an "act of charity." HMS *Dover*'s cruel prize master may have abused Roscio's master "by severe language and threats" and hit his boy for no reason, but a gentlemen like Sir George Collins, captain of HMS *Leander*, recommended that *Victory* be restored to its owners because the captain helped Collins when his ship was in trouble among the Nantucket shoals.[77]

Like their privateer colleagues, the navy frequently supplied their galley, wardrobes, and quarter decks with items seized from captured vessels. Captured crewmen testified to removing ships stores, such as bread, flour, sugar, tea, cheese, crackers, meat, fruit, rum, and wine. Certainly, it would be hard to fault HMS *Maidstone*'s prize master for broaching a cask of *Stockholm*'s rum without the master's consent for the comfort of his prize crew who had endured wet, rainy weather to take the vessel. While many affidavits, especially in the early months of the war, refer to small thefts of clothing by naval crews, Gundon Waterman, mate of *Union*, claimed to have lost a great part of his "linnen and wearing apparel worth $120" following capture by HMS *New Emulous* in 1812. Stranger still, M. Garesche, supercargo of *Amanda* claimed to have lost a trunk containing all of his and his wife's clothing, while David Chadwick, master of *Sally*, lost a feather bed! Various affidavits list quadrants, books, charts, watches, eye glasses, and mate John Bock's pair of silver mounted pistols as stolen or missing. There are also, however, references to captains promising to return stolen articles or punishing their men for such behaviour. One prize captain confined the prize crew who plundered part of *Aristomenes*' cargo and "took bad care of the ship". The prize master of *Charles Fawcett* stopped his men from plundering their prize the first day aboard, while Captain Stackpole had two of his men flogged for stealing cheese from the master's cabin aboard *Sally Ann*.[78]

In terms of behaviour toward their captives, there was little difference between the actions of the navy and those of the privateers. From time to time, the navy tried to harness privateer energies for the service of the king through intelligence gathering and the purchase of captured cargoes. Nevertheless, relations between the two remained wary, perhaps because of philosophical rather than professional differences. Kendall believes that " the Navy never quite approved of privateering, complaining among other things, that it was a mercenary institution which demoralized seamen by substituting greed for patriotism."[79]

---

[77]*Niles Weekly Register*, 15 Jan. 1814. PAC, RG 8, IV, Vol. 101, *Betsy*, Affidavit of Robert Gibson, master, 22 Sept. 1814; Vol. 95, *Roscio*, Examination of Fructuoso Jose Carvao, master, 29 July 1813; Vol. 113, *Victory*, Agreement to Return, 22 Aug. 1814.

[78]PAC, RG 8, IV, Vol. 75, *Stockholm*, Examination of Lazaire Chapelain, master, 16 Sept. 1812; Vol. 76, *Union*, Examination of Gundon Waterman, mate, 5 Sept. 1812; Vol. 73, *Amanda*, Examination of M. Garesche, supercargo, 20 Apr. 1813; Vol. 96, *Sally*, Examination of David Chadwick, master, 28 Oct. 1813; Vol. 122, *Friendship*, Examination of John Bock, mate, 2 Oct. 1812; Vol. 73, *Aristomenes*, Examination of Joseph Brewster, master, 1 Sept. 1812; Vol. 73, *Charles Fawcett*, Examination of John Colburn, master, 18 Sept. 1812; Vol. 118, *Sally Ann*, Examination of Park Allyn, mate, 24 Sept. 1812.

[79]Charles Wye Kendall, *Private Men-of-War* (London, 1931), 1.

Unlike privateers who chose their targets from the point of view of profit, the Royal Navy had to defend British shipping and further His Majesty's strategic and political objectives by hailing all enemy or neutral vessels. Although the navy captured more and larger ships than the Atlantic privateers, the struggle to reconcile duty with profit probably added to the navy's frustration, especially in the early months of the conflict, when many prizes slipped away as droits, and others saw what little value they had dwindle away in court costs.

Evaluating Naval Prize

Of nearly 700 prize cases adjudicated in the Halifax Court of Vice-Admiralty, naval captures represent 487 or roughly seventy percent of the total. This figure does not include those vessels destroyed at sea, ransomed, recaptured, or sent into American ports as cartels. Despite dividing the rewards among a much larger crew, the volume of naval captures was high, and the potential for extremely valuable prizes higher still.

Because naval vessels were entitled to make prize immediately upon the American declaration of war, the record of naval captures for 1812 is far higher than for privateers. In 1812, naval vessels seized 118 prizes, over four times the prizes and eight times the tonnage captured by privateers. Nearly half of all naval prizes in 1812 exceeded 200 tons, while the rest were evenly distributed between those over and under 100 tons. In 1813, naval prizes outnumbered those of privateers by nearly two to one, but outweighed them by three to one. Roughly one-quarter of these prizes were 200 tons or more. By 1814, thanks largely to the successful maintenance of the blockade, both the number and size of potential American prizes declined.

Table 5.1
Naval Captures by Month.

Month	1812	1813	1814	1815	Total
January		0	0	3	3
February		1	1	2	4
March		8	6	3	17
April		29	6		35
May		28	20		48
June	2	32	16		50
July	40	35	29		104
August	45	23	23		91
September	19	22	22		63
October	10	16	11		37
November	0	9	8		17
December	2	13	3		18
Total	118	216	145	8	487

Throughout the war, July and August were the Navy's busiest months for prizemaking, as the heaviest sea traffic and the best sailing weather facilitated captures. By comparison, cold weather and seasonal storms in January, February, March, November, and December kept both predators and prey off the seas. While naval captures followed a seasonal pattern similar to privateers', the navy did not have the same freedom to cruise in search of prizes. Instead, most naval vessels were confined to blockade duty, especially in 1814, and had to be content with seizing ships that tried to escape their net either entering or leaving American harbours. Table 5.1 illustrates how much the seasons, or the weather, affected the success of the Royal Navy throughout the war.

The arrival of Vice-Admiral Sir Alexander Cochrane to succeed Warren in the summer of 1814, coincided with a joint land-sea offensive under Lieutenant Governor Sherbrooke that attacked Washington and Baltimore and seized the coast of Maine from Eastport to Castine at the mouth of the Penobscot River. That year, the navy captured nearly three times as many prizes as privateers but five times the tonnage, although prize levels fell dramatically by thirty to forty percent for both privateers and naval vessels. Between January and March 1815, only fifteen prizes were seized in all, but the eight Royal Navy captures outweighed the privateer captures two to one. The differences in size and firepower between the American and British navies make it difficult to compare their prizemaking efforts, but calculating the average number of prizes per vessel is quite interesting. Jacobs claims that twenty-two American warships claimed 165 British vessels, an average of 7.5 captures apiece. On the other hand, from the captures listed in Appendix 1, it appears that roughly 100 British navy vessels captured 475 prizes – not all of them American. The Americans thus seem to be twice as successful as the British. Table 5.2 offers a survey of prize tonnages similar to that developed for privateers to illustrate the superiority of the Royal Navy effort.

Table 5.2
Prize Tonnages Captured by the Royal Navy

Year	Under 100T	100-200T	200+ T	? T	Total
1812	28 (24.3%)	23 (20%)	42 (36.5%)	22 (20%)	15,614
1813	69 (31.8%)	60 (27.6%)	45 (20.7%)	43 (19.8%)	26,913
1814	45 (29.8%)	36 (23.8%)	33 (21.8%)	37 (25%)	16,481
1815	1 (12.5%)	4 (50%)	2 (25%)	1 (12.5%)	1,093
	143	123	122	103	50,100

Compared to the privateer prizes, the Royal Navy prizes outweighed the privateer prizes nearly four to one overall. As with privateers, the largest number of prizes were made in 1813, nearly double those taken in either 1812 or 1814. The dramatic decline in prizes made in 1814 shows the effect of the naval blockade on the fortunes of the British predators, as well as their American and neutral prizes. Even in the first few months of 1815, the majority of prizes were on the small side.

While Admiral Lord Nelson deemed privateers no better than pirates, he was certainly committed to earning prize money for his efforts.[80] In fact, many naval

[80]Nelson complained to his wife on 6 Nov. 1795, "I hope the cargo will be a prize and would do very well did we not share with all the squadron ... my share will not be much; fifty pounds perhaps instead of £700 but I cannot help it." G.P.B. Naish, (ed.) *Nelson's Letters to his Wife and other Documents:*

officers depended on prize money to supplement their meagre wages. The breakdown of shares aboard naval vessels was generally in eighths. As described by N.A.M. Rodger, the commander in chief received one eighth, the commander got one-quarter (plus the flag officer's eighth if the ship were under private orders), an eighth to the master and lieutenants, another to warrant sea officers, another to inferior and petty officers, and the remaining quarter to private men, seamen, and marines.[81] The *Nova Scotia Royal Gazette* published the following division of shares among the officers and crew of HMS *Bacchante* (38) from the capture of the privateer *Macdonough* on 1 November 1814.

Flag proportions		£ 93.15. 5½
1st class	commander	£ 87.10.11
2nd class	master	£ 28. 2. 7½
3rd class	lieutenants	£ 12.15. 9
4th class	warrant officers	£ 5. 6.11½
5th class	inferior officers	£ 3. 6. 9
6th class	gun crew	£ 1. 1. 4½
7th class	seamen, marines	£ 1. 2. 3
8th class	boys	£ .11.11½[82]

Unfortunately for the men of HMS *Bacchante*, the privateer carried no freight, making it less valuable than a richly loaded cargo ship. HMS *Dragon* recaptured *Vestal*, 247 tons, for Buenos Aires in September 1814. The prize cargo of tallow, horse hair and horse, ox, and deer hides sold at auction for £13,483 despite water damage. Shared among the crew, the salvage amounted to £2,449.[83] At least a third of the navy's prizes in 1814 were well-laden vessels over 100 tons recaptured from American prize crews. America's loss was the Royal Navy's gain.

Prevented from engaging in either fleet actions or single ship combat, naval commanders in both the U.S. and British navies were forced to conduct a hit-and-run style of warfare better suited to privateers. While naval vessels, owing to their numbers and size, were more successful than privateers in harassing American trade, they too were eventually reduced to pulling up small fry of little prize value. With outgoing trade at a standstill, and incoming prize cargoes snatched out of their grasp, American merchants felt the blockade's squeeze from two sides. Chapter 6 discusses the economic effects of prizemaking by both the Royal Navy and privateers.

1785-1831 (London, 1958), 225.

[81]Rodger, *Wooden World*, 129.

[82]*NS Royal Gazette*, 5 Apr. 1815. Rates are roughly approximate for the various categories of crew members aboard a naval ship.

[83]PAC, RG 8, IV, Vol.137, *Vestal*, Settlement of Salvage, 30 Dec. 1814; Sales, Jan. 1815.

Chapter 6
The Fortunes of War

Obscure and inconsequential in terms of political or strategic achievements, the War of 1812 made its major impact on the pockets of merchants, tradespeople, and consumers. Ship losses, declining trade, and rising prices affected every aspect of American and British life. For the first time, a small but feisty American navy challenged British naval dominance with seafaring and sea-fighting skills that rivalled Great Britain's. The Royal Navy's gradual blockade of American shipping, a rigorous convoying policy, and skyrocketing marine insurance rates raised commercial risk to unacceptable heights. Once the United States and Great Britain realized that the cost of continuing the war outweighed any possible gains, either economic or political, both sides agreed to peace. Economic pressure – not decisive military or fleet actions – finally brought the war to an end.

In 1812, neither nation could afford all-out war. British troops in Spain, and later in North America, depended on American foodstuffs that were transported to them legally under licence or covertly out of blockaded ports. Despised by privateers and navies on both sides, the licensed trade was a necessary evil that kept markets open and generated profits to help defray the cost of the war. In fact, the intent of nineteenth-century commercial warfare was not to destroy an enemy's trade completely, but rather to drain its wealth by halting its exports and forcing it to purchase one's own.[1] British merchant interests, harassed by hundreds of enthusiastic American privateers, continually lobbied the Admiralty for better convoy protection. The Royal Navy found itself torn between a "political" obligation to protect trade and the strategic naval demands of war at sea.

Commercial Warfare

In June 1812, American headlines trumpeted the cause of free trade as a reason for declaring war. The United States was not attempting to usurp Britain's role as a mercantilist nation by acquiring new markets, but rather to ensure America's continued access to European markets as a neutral nation. As both sides soon discovered, the price of free trade was not cheap. Historian Stanley Bonnet calculates America's war cost at least 1,877 lives and $13 million. Britain, too, paid dearly for antagonizing the United States to the point of war. Jerome Garitee calculates that Britain lost an average of thirty-three vessels per month throughout the war, worth $40 million, or three times the value of American losses. In two and a half years of fighting, the United States' accumulated a war debt of $105 million. Britain's national debt, swollen by ten years of war in Europe prior to the War of 1812, rose from £451.7 million in 1800 to £840.5 million in

[1] Michael J. Crawford, "The Navy's Campaign against the Licensed Trade in the War of 1812," *American Neptune* (1986), XLVI, 171, quotes a letter written by Thomas Jefferson in Jan. 1813 in H.A. Washington, ed., *The Writings of Thomas Jefferson*, VI, 93.

1814. By any standard economic indicators such as import and export trade figures, currency stability, food prices, wages, rents, insurance rates, transportation costs, or customs fees, the war played havoc with the economies of both Great Britain and the United States.[2]

On the other hand, the maritime merchants of New Brunswick and Nova Scotia found a number of ways to turn the war to their advantage. Prize ships and cargoes swelled revenue receipts in every Atlantic port, and naval spending between 1805 and 1815 pumped some £2.9 million into the Nova Scotia economy alone.[3] Revenue receipts for the port of Halifax, representing income derived from maritime traffic, trebled from £31,041 in 1812 to £93,759 by 1814, and then fell to £60,758 in 1815.[4] Provincial vessels eagerly replaced their American competitors in the West Indies trade, as ambitious merchants like Enos Collins and Samuel Cunard manoeuvred to carve out a permanent niche for themselves. Their success in the West Indian re-export trade was at the expense of various American states that watched receipts plummet from $15.6 million in 1805 to $5.9 million in 1811 and finally, to $302,781 in 1813.[5]

Blatantly anxious to consolidate their profits, the Halifax Committee of Trade petitioned Lord Bathurst to protect the morals of the Caribbean colonies, and coincidentally their trade, from the fatal effects of contact with the United States because "the sentiments, habits and manners, both political and moral of the lower order of the Americans are dangerous and contaminating to a very great degree!"[6] Unfortunately for the Atlantic provinces, the limited markets of British North America were no match for the vast American hinterland that reopened to British trade after the war. The economic depression that engulfed Atlantic Canada after 1815 could properly be considered a cost of war. Despite his concern for the fortifications of Atlantic Canada, Lieutenant Governor Sherbrooke was convinced that war with the United States was likely to involve more commercial than military conflict. In November 1812 he confided to Lord Bathurst that trade, not territory, appeared to be America's main objective. Attacks on seagoing commerce pointed to American strategy that would concentrate on preventing British provisions from reaching New Brunswick and Nova Scotia while ensuring that provincial shipments of British manufactures did not enter the United States.[7]

---

[2]Stanley Bonnet, *The Price of Admiralty* (London, 1968.), 27. Jerome R. Garitee, *The Republic's Private Navy: The American Privateering Business as Practiced by Baltimore during the War of 1812* (Middletown, Conn., 1977), 244. John K. Mahon, *The War of 1812* (Gainesville, Fla., 1972), 385, claims that the U.S. war debt was paid off in twenty years.

[3]Julian Gwyn, "Rum, Sugar, and Molasses," in James H. Morrison and James Moreira, eds., *Tempered by Rum* (Halifax, N.S., 1988), 114, bases his income figure of £2.9 million on price hikes of beef to 300% over pre-war costs and wage increases in Halifax of up to 150%.

[4]Copp, "Nova Scotian Trade," in K.G. Rawlyk, ed., *Historical Essays on the Atlantic Provinces* (Toronto, 1967), 88.

[5]Alfred Thayer Mahan, *Sea Power in its Relations to the War of 1812* (Boston, 1905), II, 181.

[6]Ells, Margaret, ed., *A Calendar of Official Correspondence and Legislative Papers, Nova Scotia, 1802-15* (Halifax, N.S., 1936), 300. Draft memorial to Earl Bathurst from the Halifax Committee of Trade, 8 Oct. 1813, [Vol. 304, doc. 2, no. 66].

[7]Ibid., 271, Sherbrooke to Bathurst, 6 Nov. 1812, [Vol. 59, doc. 79].

Whether America needed British goods as badly as Britain needed American markets remains debatable. Certainly, the interdependence of their trade meant that when ship traffic decreased both economies suffered. The estimated volume of British shipping destroyed or captured during the War of 1812 ranges between 1,500 to 2,500 vessels depending on the source. Historian Edgar Maclay claimed that twenty-three American naval vessels and 517 privateers captured 1,554 British prizes worth $45,500,000. On 19 March 1813, the London *Times* declared that Americans had taken 513 British vessels in just eight months between 4 August 1812 and 9 March 1813, although seventy-five had been recaptured.[8] In December 1814, Lloyd's insurance underwriters advised the British House of Commons that from the start of the war to date, Americans had captured 1,175 British vessels, of which 373 or approximately one-third, had been recaptured or given up.[9] Paul Kennedy relies on contemporary lists to suggest that Britain's enemies captured almost 11,000 British merchant vessels between 1793 and 1815. Although this is a truly staggering number, Patrick Crowhurst suggests that it represented only 2.5 percent of the total tonnage of Britain's vast commercial fleet.[10] Fear of capture restricted shipping and reduced Britain's income from customs duties and taxes. British expenditures in 1813 exceeded £111 million as compared to tax revenues of £73 million. War with Napoleon, exacerbated by the loss of profits from £12 million worth of trade per year with the United States, elevated Britain's public debt to new heights. British imports from the United States dropped from £11,846,513 in 1807 to £1,841,253 in 1811, declining even further after 1812.[11] A corresponding decrease in America's export trade caused similar financial difficulties for the U.S. Treasury.

The Toll on America

Even before the war, the American merchant fleet had suffered casualties at the hands of various European powers. According to one estimate, by 1810 the British had seized nearly 1,000 American ships, France had taken 500, and a further 300 had fallen to Danish, Neapolitan, Spanish and Dutch flags. Between 1812 and 1815 Britain captured

---

[8]E.S. Maclay, *A History of American Privateers*, (New York, 1899), viii, calculates that the American navy seized 254 British vessels worth $6.6 million as compared to 1,300 prizes worth $39 million taken by U.S. privateers. London *Times*, 19 Mar. 1813.

[9]Godfrey Hodgson, *Lloyd's of London* (London, 1986), 47-58 provides a brief history of Lloyd's from its beginning as a coffee house in London's business district in 1687. Following a move to the banking area on Lombard Street in 1694, Lloyd's became a gathering place for maritime investors and an auction room, especially for the sale of prize goods captured during the war with France and Spain between 1698-1712. After fifty years of uncontrolled growth, the more serious underwriters split off from the coffee house gamblers to form the new Lloyd's in 1769. Relocated in their new quarters above the Royal Exchange in 1771, Lloyd's grew from the original seventy-nine investors to nearly 2,000 members in 1814.

[10]Paul M. Kennedy, *The Rise and Fall of British Naval Mastery* (London, 1976), 140-141. *Niles Weekly Register*, 13 Aug. 1815 and 6 Jan. 1816, estimates British losses, including Newfoundland fishing vessels and West Indian craft at 1,300 to 2,500 sail. Garitee, *Private Navy*, 243, also uses Niles' figures. Reginald Horsman, *The War of 1812* (London, 1969), 152, suggests that Britain lost twenty-five vessels per month versus Garitee's average of one British vessel per day. Patrick Crowhurst, *The French War on Trade: Privateering 1793-1815* (Brookfield, Conn., 1989), 31, feels that the estimate of 11,000 captures is "probably erroneous."

[11]Mahon, *The War of 1812*, 95. According to H.C. Allen, *The Anglo-American Relationship Since 1783* (London, 1959), 57, peacetime exports rose again in 1815 to £13,255,374 per year.

another 500 American sail. The economic noose finally tightened when the Royal Navy began blockading the American coast, completely disrupting maritime trade. Given the smaller size of the United States merchant marine, the loss of 2,500 American ships over ten years was proportionately more damaging than the rough toll of 10,000 British vessels lost over the same period. Naval captures during the war reflect a similar discrepancy in the size of the two fleets. The Royal Navy may have lost more vessels overall, but this amounted to less than one percent of the total number of warships. The smaller United States Navy, on the other hand, lost more than twenty percent of its men-of-war.[12]

Captures at sea, however crippling, did not undermine American trade as significantly as the demoralising and debilitating blockade that drove the war right onto American shores. American letter of marque vessels that successfully evaded British cruisers on the way to sea faced a gauntlet of privateers and Royal Navy blockade vessels on their return. By June 1813, John Price of Wells, Massachusetts, fretted about the impact of the blockade. "When it will end God only knows," he wrote to his brother, " but if not shortly, the difficulties we shall have to encounter will become insupportable ... provisions of every kind are remarkably scarce and dear."[13] Many American merchants and investors, who outfitted privateers, donated vessels to block harbours, enlisted in their local militias, and bought canons to defend their towns, were more motivated by economic self-interest than patriotism. They felt that winning was the only way to end the war and get back to trade. To that end, in June 1813 Secretary of the Navy William Jones urged Lieutenant William Henry Allen of the USS *Argus* to hit Great Britain where it hurt, "by annoying and destroying his commerce, fisheries and coasting trade." Jones' plan came to naught when Britain's twin measures of blockade and convoy began to bear fruit in 1813.[14]

Ship captures packed a psychological as well as an economic punch. Fear of attack by provincial privateers like the *Liverpool Packet* compelled many New Englanders to reorganize their transportation routes. While the risk of capture had to be weighed against the high cost of insurance, the additional factor of rising prices due to trade disruption and shortages began to feature in the economic equation. Shipping, despite being faster and cheaper, became increasingly risky. As insurance and prices climbed higher, some merchants began to consider whether they could improve their profits by exchanging wind for wagon power.

---

[12] C.S. Forester, *The Naval War of 1812* (London, 1957), 120, claims that Americans losses kept pace with Britain's but because of their smaller fleet, their loss was more significant. In terms of pre-war American losses, Kate Caffrey, *The Lion and the Union: The Anglo-American War, 1812-1815* (London, 1978), 51, suggests that 468 American vessels were seized by the French navy between 1807 and 1812 while, according to James Monroe, prior to 1812 the British seized an American ship every two days, although they were often released. Gomer Williams, *History of the Liverpool Privateers* (London, 1897), 431. George Coggleshall, *The American Privateers* (New York, 1861), 394, claims that in three years of war, Great Britain lost some 2,000 ships including merchantmen and warships. This includes 1,800 sail said to have been burnt, sunk or destroyed plus vessels captured on the Great Lakes and others not worth mentioning. E.B. Potter, ed., *Sea Power - A Naval History* (New York, 1960), 212.

[13] PAC, RG8, IV, Vol. 78, *Calson*, John Price, Wells, Mass., to his brother in the West Indies, 20 June 1813.

[14] Donald Petrie, "Forbidden Prizes," *American Neptune* (1994), LIV, 166. Potter, ed., *Sea Power*, 208, 214, insists that the blockade inflicted 100 times more loss than the American navy could.

Unfortunately, cargoes that would have filled the hold of an average-sized coasting vessel, crewed by two or three men, required a dozen wagons and many more wagoneers. Simply hiring enough wagons to handle the volume of American shipping by land posed a major problem. Moreover, given the disreputable condition of the roads and turnpikes in most parts of the eastern seaboard, and the higher cost of labour, land hauling took ten times longer and cost one hundred times more than travel by sea. Not only did it take forty-six days in good weather to haul supplies from Charleston to Philadelphia, but the transportation charges were four times the cost of producing the goods. That merchants even considered this expensive "mud clipper" trade illustrates the desperate situation created by the blockade.[15]

Higher prices, fewer available goods, gluts in one place, shortages in another, and unstable markets everywhere affected every level of society. A cost comparison of basic foodstuffs like flour and sugar in blockaded versus non-blockaded ports confirms the increasing pressure on the American economy. Early in the war, when the risk of capture was relatively slight, flour cost $4.50 per barrel in Richmond, Virginia, and $6.50 in Baltimore. In Boston, where twenty-seven vessels destined for that port were captured in 1812, flour hit $12 per barrel. By January 1813 flour prices in Norfolk had reached a ten-year high of $10.50 cash per barrel. The next year the price of sugar felt the impact of the blockade. Before the blockade was extended sugar cost $9.00 per hundredweight in New Orleans and $18.75 in Boston. Afterwards, sugar prices in New York were $21.50 per hundredweight, a dollar higher in Philadelphia, and $26.50 in Baltimore, nearly triple that of New Orleans.[16]

At the end of August 1813, readers of *Niles Weekly Register* saw how dramatically prices fluctuated between Boston, New York, Philadelphia, and Baltimore for commodities such as flour, sugar, and rice. Philadelphians had to pay $12 for the same hundredweight of rice that cost Bostonians $9. A barrel of superfine flour ranged from a low of $6 in Baltimore to $11.87 or nearly double that in Boston. As early as June 1813 superfine flour prices reached $58 per barrel! A hundredweight of brown sugar cost $26.50 in Baltimore but only $18.75 in Boston. Fortunately for Halifax, so much muscovado sugar was captured aboard American prizes in 1813 and 1814 that sugar prices remained relatively low. In mid-September 1813, *Niles Weekly Register* condemned the great speculation in coffee, sugar, and tea in Boston, New York, Philadelphia, and Baltimore where forty to fifty million pounds of coffee were on hand. The writer congratulated Baltimoreans for doing without or using substitutes, instead of paying inflated prices of up to thirty-eight cents for a pound of coffee, $3-$4 per pound

---

[15]C.H.J. Snider, *Under the Red Jack* (Toronto, 1927), 3. Major James Ripley Jacobs and Glenn Tucker, *The War of 1812 - A Compact History* (New York, 1969), 158. See also Morrison and Moreira, eds., *Tempered by Rum*, 213. John Armstrong, "The Significance of Coastal Shipping in British Domestic Transport, 1550-1830," *International Journal of Maritime History*, III (1991), 70-76, claims that English coasters were more economical than road transportation even during war due to lower labour costs per ton, free wind power versus expensive horse feed, the possibility of earning extra money by carrying passengers by sea, and lower wartime insurance of 2s.3d. to 4s.3d./cwt by ship as opposed to 16s./cwt by road. Forester, *Naval War*, 21. *Niles Weekly Register*, 6 Mar. 1813, puts the cost of a coasting licence from North Carolina to Boston at $300.

[16]In 1812 only four ships for Baltimore were taken and none of the six from various ports destined for Virginia were headed to Richmond. See Mahan, *War of 1812*, I, 297, 184, 206 and Gwyn "Rum, Sugar, and Molasses," in Morison and Moreira, eds., *Tempered*, 12, for prices of various commodities. PAC, RG8, IV, Vol. 188, *Protectress*, Letter to James Eames, Lisbon, 23 Jan. 1813.

for tea, and $40 per hundredweight for sugar. When the news of peace reached New York in 1815, sugar prices apparently dropped from $26 to $12.50 per hundredweight.[17]

Years of war with France had driven the British economy into a serious slump even before 1812, resulting in widespread unemployment and severe depression, both at home and in Atlantic Canada.[18] This factor, combined with unexpectedly formidable attacks by American privateers and naval vessels early in the war, might have forced Great Britain to come to terms with the United States much earlier. Napoleon's defeat in Russia in late 1812, however, relieved some of the pressure on Britain to negotiate peace with the United States and enabled the Admiralty to devote more resources to a commercial blockade of the American coast.

Strict and Rigorous Blockade

On 27 November 1812, Great Britain implemented "the most systematic, regularized and extensive form of commerce destruction known to war." Frustrated in its desire to meet the American navy head on and settle the War of 1812 in one conclusive fleet action, the British navy was forced to resort to the slow, inglorious tourniquet of close blockade.[19]

For a blockade to be recognized as "close and effective," as specified under the Declaration of Armed Neutrality of 1780, it had to constitute an actual physical barrier to entry into a port.[20] America's 2,000 miles of coastline and thousands of bays, river mouths, and harbours made this a difficult assignment. Lacking the men and ships to enforce a blockade of the entire coast at once, Admiral Warren opted for a gradual extension of British control.

His strategy relied on the northern states' generally lukewarm attitude toward the war, and the continued willingness of many American merchants to participate in the licensed trade. By sparing New England from the initial impact of the blockade, Admiral Warren hoped to keep the inhabitants noncommittal for as long as possible. When southern democrats complained that Boston has escaped the British blockade that had been extended to all American ports south of Connecticut, the *Nova Scotia Royal Gazette* reprinted one New Englander's response. The author advised the southern "meddlers" not to trouble themselves further on their account since "Boston-folks have no notion of

---

[17]Maclay, *American Privateers*, xv. *Niles Weekly Register*, 18 Sept. 1813, and 8 Jan. 1814.

[18]Both Potter, ed., *Sea Power*, 209, and Kennedy, *Great Powers*, 129, refer to the weakened state of the British economy on the eve of war. According to Thomas Raddall, *Halifax, Warden of the North* (Toronto, 1971), 143, Halifax was also in serious trouble prior to the outbreak of war. He points out that in the year ending Feb. 1811, one in four inhabitants of Halifax, or roughly 2,500 people, subsisted on fuel and food distributed by the Society for the Relief of the Poor.

[19]Mahan, *War of 1812*, I, 286. Mahan points out that blockade is not necessarily a military operation. Because it restricts the activities of neutrals as well as the enemy, its impact tends to be more commercial than strategic.

[20]D.P. O'Connell, *The Influence of Law on Sea Power* (Manchester, 1975), 20, suggests that because poorly enforced eighteenth-century blockades tended to alienate both enemy and neutral alike, the Declaration of Armed Neutrality resolved the issue by defining what constituted a blockade under international law. Not only did a blockade have to be "real" and effective, but which ports were under blockade had to be advertised through notices in the papers or printed proclamations. On several occasions, captured crews claimed they did not know their destination was under blockade.

Blockades any more than they have of Embargoes, Non-Intercourse and War."[21] Warren's gamble paid off for both sides. Not only did he achieve his strategic objective, but Massachusetts banks saw their deposits quadruple from $2.67 million in 1810 to $8.8 million in 1814. Supplies of specie also increased from $1.56 million to $6.39 million in the same period.[22]

The blockade of the Chesapeake Bay area began in late December 1812. British strategy focused on crippling American trade where it would have the most immediate effect – in the grain-growing hinterland serving the major cities of Philadelphia, Baltimore, and Washington. By February Admiral Warren was ready to launch amphibious raids in the bay "to frighten American politicians into withdrawing troops from the Canadian border to defend the rich and vulnerable plantations of the Chesapeake" not to mention Washington itself. Rear-Admiral George Cockburn aboard HMS *Marlborough* (74) commanded the squadron while Sir Thomas Sidney Beckwith led an expeditionary force of 2,400 Royal Marines. Within weeks, raiding parties and naval vessels seriously disrupted trade by seizing shipping up and down the James, York, Rapahannock, and Potomac rivers. Merchants and citizens suddenly felt the pinch, as trade plummeted and insurance rates and commodity prices steadily rose.[23]

By March 1813 Warren pushed the blockade southward from Rhode Island to the Mississippi River. Viscount Melville privately reminded him: "We do not intend this as a mere *paper* blockade, but as a complete stop to all trade and intercourse by sea with those ports as far as the wind and weather, and the continual presence of a sufficient armed force, will permit and ensure."[24] U.S. commerce was swiftly rerouted south. Although roughly one-third of pre-war American domestic exports had come from the southern states, by 1813 this figure had risen considerably. Trade gains in North and South Carolina, however, were offset by declines in New England where domestic exports fell from twenty percent of the national total to ten percent in the first year of the war.[25] In March alone, five small vessels destined for New York, and one from New Jersey fell prey to naval capture or privateers. This represented a loss of 400 tons of shipping, plus cargoes of fish, rum, sugar, china, iron, ashes, brimstone, plaster, candles, chocolate, and cordwood. The failure of these goods to reach market denied supplies to consumers and inflicted financial hardship on their owners. The presence of British reconnaissance vessels off Ocracoke, North Carolina, and the reported capture of a sloop by HMS *Highflyer*, a former American privateer, greatly alarmed the

---

[21]*NS Royal Gazette*, 2 June 1813.

[22]Mahan, *War of 1812*, I, 297.

[23]William S. Dudley, ed., *The Naval War of 1812, A Documentary History* (Washington, D.C., 1985), I, 309, hereafter called *Naval Docs*. Rear-Admiral Cockburn was ordered from Cadiz in Dec. 1812 to reinforce Admiral Warren with four ships of the line and several smaller vessels. He eventually became Warren's second-in-command. Mahan, *War of 1812*, I, 411, points out that when Warren announced that no more licences would be granted for the transport of flour, Baltimore flour prices fell $2 per barrel.

[24]Dudley, ed., *Naval Docs.*, II, 78. Viscount Melville to Admiral Warren, 26 Mar. 1813. An order followed a few days later for a rigorous blockade of the ports and harbours of New York, Charleston, Port Royal, Savannah, and of the Mississippi River.

[25]Mahan, *War of 1812*, II, 179.

inhabitants of the Carolinas. In a letter captured aboard the brig *Orion* in May 1813 Gordon Mumford of Charleston confirmed that the blockade had "greatly shackled commerce and now that of our port of Charleston and Savannah will give it the last blow."[26]

Many British naval officers found blockade duty distasteful. One naval captain, touched by the cruel efficiency of the blockade, returned a captured vessel because it belonged to an old man with eight children who had lost $20,000 worth of shipping in two years. When Admiral Warren returned to Halifax and Admiral Cockburn sailed to Bermuda in September 1813, Captain Robert Barrie of HMS *Dragon* was left to hold the Chesapeake with a skeleton force of one ship of the line, two frigates, and a few smaller vessels. He complained in a letter to his mother "this blockading affair is a sad disappointment to me who expected a cruize off New York for the winter."[27]

Despite remaining relatively porous throughout 1813, the blockade was the centrepiece of Britain's overall military strategy in North America. In October 1813 the London *Times* commended Admiral Warren's activities in the Chesapeake, including the capture of Kent Island for keeping all the southern states on the alert and serving as a powerful diversion for British troops in Canada.[28] With so much coastline to patrol, it was unrealistic to expect the Royal Navy to be everywhere at once, or to assume that American blockade runners would not take advantage of this fact. In May 1813 Captain Thomas Capel of HMS *La Hogue* advised Warren "with great mortification" that two U.S. frigates, *President* and *Congress*, slipped by his forces in the fog.[29]

James Monroe, American secretary of state and later president, contended that if Britain could not maintain the close and rigorous blockade prescribed by international law, "it formed no lawful obstacle to neutral and friendly vessels desiring to visit and trade with the United States."[30] President Madison substantiated this argument with a message issued on 19 September 1814 that acknowledged Britain's naval presence but countered that "our private cruisers also have not ceased to annoy his commerce, and to bring their rich prizes into our ports, contributing thus, with other proofs, to demonstrate the incompetency and illegality of a blockade, the proclamation of which is made the pretext for vexing and discouraging the commerce of neutral powers with the United States."[31] It is unlikely, however, that Madison's statement did much to allay the fears of those who saw the results of the blockade on their tables and in their pockets. Nor did

---

[26]P.A.C., RG 8, IV, Vol. 92, *Orion*, Gordon Mumford (owner) to a Spanish colleague, 11 May 1813. Referenceto Ocracoke in Dudley, ed., *Naval Docs.*, II, 151.

[27]Mahon, *War of 1812*, 249. Also, Captain Robert Barrie to Mrs. George Clayton, 4 Sept. 1813, in Dudley, ed., *Naval Docs.*, II, 384.

[28]*Times*, 12 Oct. 1813.

[29]Dudley, ed., *Naval Docs.*, II, 105-106, Capel's account of the escape of USS *President* is in a letter to Admiral Warren, 11 May 1813.

[30]Carleton Savage, *Policy of the United States toward Maritime Commerce in War* (Washington, D.C., 1934), 9. Monroe's statement was made the end of June 1814.

[31]*Niles Weekly Register*, 24 Sept. 1814.

it help the twenty or so ships from Amsterdam, Lisbon, Malaga, Calcutta, South America, and the West Indies that were seized or recaptured by blockading vessels between July 1814 and February 1815. In pronouncing them "good and lawful prize," the Halifax Vice-Admiralty Court proved that the blockade was not only legal, but becoming increasingly vexatious.

The activities of British blockading vessels reflected the personalities of their commanders. Vice-Admiral Cochrane, who relieved Warren in April 1814, disliked Americans intensely. In his opinion, Americans "like spaniels ... must be treated with great severity before you can even make them tractable." Not surprisingly, Cochrane was hated and despised for the activities of his men. In contrast, in 1814 the citizens of Eastport, Maine, publicly thanked Captain Thomas Hardy for the "liberal and honourable conduct" shown by army and navy forces under his command.[32]

Unlike privateers, who were forbidden incursions on land, the Chesapeake blockaders were under no such restraint.[33] In fact, Admiral Cockburn's crews "descended on farms and plantations, carried off food and other property – some of which was paid for – encouraged slaves to run away, and generally made nuisances of themselves." The loss of some 3,600 slaves, who were encouraged to seek refuge in New Brunswick and Nova Scotia between 1812 and 1815, caused serious financial problems for their owners both during and after the war. Writing from St. Mary's, Maryland, to a friend near Washington, an unidentified American worried about "the most terrible evil ... the defection of negroes, which is extending to a ruinous and most alarming extent."[34]

Transplanted slaves also faced considerable economic hardship upon their arrival in Atlantic Canada. Although free, many black newcomers lacked both capital and skills to establish themselves in their new land. When 1,700 released slaves arrived aboard British ships from the southern United States in 1814, agriculture was the only pursuit available to them. Needless to say, they experienced the same problems as their white neighbours trying to farm inferior and rocky soil. In October 1814, the deputy provincial secretary of Nova Scotia advised the Commissioners of the Poor that the lieutenant governor had granted their petition on behalf of destitute blacks allowing them soldiers' rations from the king's stores and admission of the neediest to the poor house. Several days later, Sherbrooke issued a proclamation prepared by Vice-Admiral Cochrane regarding the provision of food and shelter for destitute Negro families who had arrived in the province from the United States during the war. He also promised Cochrane to do everything in his power to aid the distressed refugees. In fact, the British

---

[32]Caffrey, *Lion and Union*, quotes Cochrane, 257. GeorgeF.G. Stanley, *The War of 1812 - Land Operations* (Toronto, 1983), 369, mentions Captain Hardy.

[33]W.R. Copp "Military Activities in Nova Scotia During the War of 1812," *Collections of the Nova Scotia Historical Society* (1938), XXIV, 64, indicates that American privateers were not permitted attacks on land, but this instruction was not sticdy obeyed. The *Halifax Gazette* of 23 June 1813 recorded an American privateer raid on the inhabitants of Beaver Harbour, N.B. Crewmen from the privateer whale boat *Weazel* of Castine, Maine, plundered several inhabitants of their clothes and belongings before being chased off.

[34]W.B. Crane and J.P. Cranwell, *Men of Marque* (New York, 1940), 26, discuss the Royal Navy's activities in the Chesapeake. *NS Royal Gazette*, 8 Dec. 1813. Reprinted from a New York paper of 16 Nov., the letter (dated 6 Nov. 1813) notes 100 to 200 Negroes joining the British fleet in the previous week.

government offered to relocate any black families who wished to go to Trinidad. Fearing what they thought would be a return to slavery, most blacks opted to remain in the unfamiliar northern climate. Eventually, black communities grew up at Hammond's Plains, Preston and areas outside Halifax. They also shared the growing pains associated with the Atlantic provinces' post-war depression.[35]

On 16 November 1813, Admiral Warren proclaimed the entire American coast under blockade. Within months it was so effective that all the principal ships of the U.S. Navy, except for *Constitution*, were securely bottled up in port, and twenty-nine American blockade runners had been captured. By year-end citizens of New York City actually feared a direct invasion. Meanwhile, American merchant traffic had dwindled to eleven percent of what it had been in 1811.[36] As a weapon of economic warfare, Britain's blockade succeeded so well that on 4 April 1813 the Russian minister advised Admiral Warren that he would be willing to negotiate an armistice between the two combatants, but nothing would occur unless Britain raised the blockade "since the latter does them more harm than all the hostilities!"[37]

Britain's order-in-council extending the blockade resulted in political and economic repercussions throughout the affected states, yet a surprising number of American coaster crews claimed to know nothing about it. Affidavits by several captured crewmen examined by the Halifax Vice-Admiralty Court indicate no knowledge that their port of destination was under blockade. Since New York papers did not publish the proclamation of 20 March 1813 until 6 May, it is possible that John Jubin, master of the brig *Orion*, captured 16 May by HMS *La Hogue*, might not have heard that New York was blockaded. Luckily, Jubin had a licence to carry his cargo of flour and Indian meal to Lisbon, and his vessel was restored. Among the documents captured aboard *Hoppet* on 25 October 1813 was an affidavit from eighteen New York merchants. They testified that none of them would have hesitated to send out a licensed or neutral vessel on or after 16 May since "licensed American and neutral vessels have almost daily arrived here from foreign ports, which, after having been boarded and examined by the ships of war of His Britannic Majesty cruising off Sandy Hook, had been suffered to enter this port." They claimed that neither Spanish, Swedish, nor Portuguese consuls or government officials had received any notification of the blockade of New York and were of the "full and entire conviction of the non-existence of any actual blockade." Antoine Beaupin, master of *Republican*, contested his capture by HMS *Nimrod* on 11 July 1813 based on a story that appeared in Boston's *Daily Advertiser* on 2 July. If, Beaupin argued, the

[35]Mahon, *War of 1812*, 314. W.S. MacNutt, *The Atlantic Provinces: The Emergence of Colonial Society, 1712-1857* (Toronto, 1968), 158. J.W. Lawrence, *Foot-Prints; or, Incidents in Early History of New Brunswick* (Saint John, N.B., 1883), 96, refers to a group of 371 of these former slaves who travelled from Halifax to Saint John, N.B., to found the community of Loch Lomond. *NS Leg. Papers*, 326, Deputy Prov. Sec. (H.H. Cogswell) to J.G. Pyke, James Foreman and Crofton Uniacke, Commissioners of the Poor, 3 Oct. 1814, [Vol. 141, 27]. The correspondencebetween Cochrane and Sherbrooke is in Vol. 111, 97-103.

[36]Robert Greenhalgh Albion, *Makers of Naval Policy 1798-1947* (Annapolis, Md., 1980), 186, discusses reactions in New York. According to Potter, ed., *Sea Power*, 213, American commerce in 1812 was sixty-five percent of 1811, most of it under licence. In 1813, the blockade was extended and trade fell to forty-five percent of 1811. With total blockade in effect in 1814, trade was down to eleven percent of the 1811 figure. In his introduction, Garitee, *Private Navy*, xvi, refers to the success of the blockade.

[37]Mahan, *War of 1812*, II, 177.

article indicated that HMS *Protectress* turned a Spanish brig away from Boston, which was under blockade, and ordered it back to New York, it meant that New York was not yet blockaded. As evidence to the contrary, vice-admiralty court registrar Charles Morris submitted a list of four vessels, including Jubin's, captured by the blockading squadron in May. Although Beaupin appealed the court's decision to England, *Republican* was finally condemned in 1816.[38]

Compulsory Convoy

As the blockade applied steady pressure to American commerce on their very doorstep, convoying denied prizes to the few American privateers and naval vessels not yet confined to port. Dating back to the Middle Ages, convoying is mentioned in Letters Patent issued by Edward III. On 3 January 1338, Genoese galleys hired to scour the seas off Scotland for enemies were ordered "to convoy and protect ships of our kingdom voyaging to Scotland or into northern waters with victuals and supplies for our people there."[39]

Convoying was a necessary but usually thankless duty for the navy. The independent nature of merchant captains meant that they frequently disregarded the convoy leader's instructions and them blamed him for any mishaps they suffered! Following war with Spain in 1741 the Admiralty ruefully acknowledged "nothing is more frequent than that the complaints of the commanders of convoys of the obstinacy or folly of several masters of merchant ships, who refuse to obey their signals or directions for the better keeping company together; but disregarding all order or government, desert their convoys from impatience of getting sooner into port; by which means and sometime by separations in fogs or bad weather, many have fallen into the enemy's hands."[40]

In 1772 the Admiralty attempted to regularize convoy administration and curb the main areas of abuse through a series of eleven instructions for convoy commanders. The first obliged commanders to provide each merchant ship master with a book of printed instructions containing the private signals and other appropriate directions and to date and sign the books and distribute them at no charge. The Admiralty received a copy of the list of ships in each convoy. No commander or member of any ship could receive money or gratification for their services. Naval commanders were forbidden to chase out of sight of the convoy and ordered to be vigilant always and help any master in trouble. If anyone disobeyed the regulations or behaved negligently so as to delay the convoy, the commander was to take note of it and advise the Admiralty as soon as possible. Additional instructions required commanders to carry a toplight at night and specified who could wear lights and make or repeat signals in a large convoy.

---

[38] PAC, RG8, IV, Vol. 92, *Orion*, Gordon Mumford, owner, 11 May 1813; Vol. 86, *Hoppet*, Affidavit, 1813; Vol. 94, *Republican*, newspaper clipping from the Boston *Daily Advertiser*, 2 July 1813, from William Ayre, late secretary to Vice-Admiral Sawyer.

[39] John B. Hattendorf, R.J.B. Knight, A.W.H. Pearsall, N.A.M. Rodger, and G. Till, eds., *British Naval Documents 1204-1960* (Washington, D.C., 1993), 21, Letters patent, Edward III, 3 Jan. 1338.

[40] Ibid., 369, Admiralty document, 19 Feb. 1741.

When several different convoys sailed in company, the oldest commander became the senior officer "to preserve order and good government" within the convoy. Commanders of different convoys were instructed to sail together like divisions of a fleet and to follow certain rules when separating. Convoy commanders were also under orders to take in any ships of His Majesty's allies or friends they might encounter.[41] The explicitness of these instructions reveals that, even after centuries of practice, convoying remained an uneasy marriage of mercantile and naval interests.

By 1808, all provincial shipping had to abide by the Compulsory Convoy Act and by the next year six annual convoys regularly left Halifax for England and Europe between April and November. Between December and May similar convoys left England for the Mediterranean, South America, and the East and West Indies. As of 31 July 1812, all shipping from Great Britain to North America or the West Indies was ordered to proceed under convoy. Two weeks later Lieutenant Governor Sherbrooke issued a proclamation prohibiting all vessels from leaving Nova Scotia except in convoy, and the Act was rigidly enforced throughout the war. British owners were legally obliged to travel in convoy and pay a convoy duty for the protection it entailed. As an incentive, failure to comply invalidated their insurance.

Even neutral vessels sought the safety of convoys. *Mary*, a small Swedish-registered schooner recaptured en route from Cape Henry, Haiti, to Boston, was delayed when the Admiral on the Jamaica Station failed to provide convoy for them, "contrary to his promise." The owners of *Mary* and its sister ships finally had to let the vessels depart alone "to save double insurance," but as London investor Hercules Sharpe was warned, his vessel stood a poor chance of reaching the United Kingdom because of the large number of "Yankee privateers" out and in the passages around Cape Henry. The ever-present threat of American and French privateers and naval vessels persuaded almost all but the most foolhardy or desperate to seek safety in numbers.[42]

One of the problems with convoying was that there were always more vessels in a convoy than a few Royal Navy escorts, called "bulldogs," could protect. After a few days at sea, the slower, less seaworthy, or more heavily laden vessels began to fall behind, often losing contact when fog or foul weather intervened. Convoys were most vulnerable at the end of their voyage. As they neared port, participants often felt secure enough to disperse and sail for home on their own. To curb this practice, Britain imposed heavy fines for leaving a convoy. Regular convoy departure schedules were common knowledge, often published by obliging newspapers such as the London *Times,* which proudly announced that 2,000 recruits and 1,000 tons of military stores and clothing "would be embarked with the utmost expedition and ... proceed under convoy of the

[41]Ibid., 369, Instructions to Commanders of Convoys, 1772.

[42]MacNutt, *Atlantic*, 130. Mahan, *War of 1812*, I, 388, mentions that the 31 July date coincided with Britain's peace with Sweden and Russia. The one exception to the convoy rule was a class of vessels Garitee, *Private Navy*, 148, refers to as "running ships" that were allowed to sail unescorted. Only very large and powerful privateers dared tackle these large, heavily-armed and manned vessels with valuable cargoes. According to Crowhurst, *War on Trade*, 55, French privateers also took advantage of convoy gathering points such as the Isle of Wight where outgoing shipping was relatively well protected but became vulnerable to French corsairs on the return journey. PAC, RG8, IV, Vol. 135, *Mary*, George Krochmann to Hercules Sharpe, 31 July 1813.

Liffey, for the Chesapeake.[43] In June 1813, concern for convoy safety prompted William Sabatier to address a petition to Lieutenant Governor Sherbrooke on behalf of the Halifax Committee of Trade. "The Committee, Sir, are of opinion, that it is not good policy to give public notice, in the manner of the present instance, of the sailing of convoys or to fix upon the time too long beforehand."[44] Like the submarine wolf-packs of a century later, American privateers often worked in pairs, shadowing a convoy for days. At the first opportunity one privateer would decoy the nearest man-of-war while the other slipped in and cut out one or more prizes. Then they would exchange roles, waiting for darkness to cover their approach.[45]

Convoys out of Halifax, while generally successful in deterring enemy attacks, deprived Admiral Warren of the use of at least one ship of the line, one or two frigates and a couple of sloops for the duration of the voyage. This meant he was constantly beseeching the Lords of the Admiralty for replacement vessels to combat the swarms of American privateers harassing Atlantic Canada's maritime trade. In February 1813, John Croker, first secretary of the Admiralty, admonished Warren for his demands when he already had more vessels under his command than the small American navy would seem to warrant. He accused Warren of either exaggerating the numbers of privateers, or leaving the principal American ports so poorly guarded that ships were able to escape the blockade unmolested! As far as threats to trade were concerned, Croker reiterated the Admiralty's direction "that no merchant vessels should be permitted to sail without convoy and that frequent and regular protection should be afforded between the different ports of your command."[46] At the same time, however, the Admiralty expected Warren to achieve his strategic objectives of eliminating the American navy and neutralizing the privateer threat.

Warren's dilemma reflected that of the Admiralty. Besieged by the commercial lobby, the British government tried to maintain business confidence by protecting commerce, while the navy viewed this duty as subsidiary to its principal task of sweeping American naval vessels from the sea. The Admiralty accused Warren of not only failing to prevent American naval vessels from putting to sea, but of neglecting to advise their lordships about the enemy's movements, or for that matter his own, in time for the Admiralty to react. Annoyed by the need to send heavy convoys to North America, Croker rebuked Warren for obliging the Admiralty "to employ six or seven sail of the line and as many frigates and sloops, independent of your command, in guarding against the possible attempts of the enemy."[47]

Wind and weather often combined with man-made problems to thwart the convoy premise of safety in company. The ship *Mary*, from Greenock to Quebec, left Cork in convoy with HMS *Leander* and *Hamadryad* but lost them in fog. The American

---

[43]*Times*, Portsmouth, 15 Aug. 1814.

[44]*NS Leg Papers*, William Sabatier to Sherbrooke, 24 June 1813, [Vol. 226, doc. 75].

[45]Garitee, *Private Navy*, xvi.

[46]Dudley, ed., *Naval Docs.*, II, 18, First Secretary of the Admiralty, John W. Croker to Admiral Warren, 10 Feb. 1813.

[47]Mahan, *War of 1812*, I, 403, also cites letters from Croker to Warren on 9 Jan. and 20 Mar. 1813.

privateer *Diomede* plucked the ship off Newfoundland on May 21 but, luckily for the owners, HMS *Martin* recaptured *Mary* on 1 June 1814. HMS *Atalante*'s six-ship convoy left Spithead on 9 November 1812 but only one reached Halifax: American privateers took two transports, one was lost in a snowstorm in the Bay of Fundy, one put back to England, one ended up in the Barbados, and the last one finally reached Halifax in February. Of these, the loss of military supplies such as forty pieces of battering cannon, a large quantity of Congreve rockets, 2,000 barrels of gunpowder, muskets, cordage, and other warehouse stores aboard the transport ship *Lady Johnston* was probably the most serious. Similarly, when the *Madison* privateer plucked government transport No. 50 out of a convoy from Halifax to St. John and took it into Gloucester, Maine, the British lost 100 casks of gunpowder, 880 uniforms for the 104th regiment, cloth for officers' uniforms, and ten casks of wine as well as drums, trumpets, and other regimental accoutrements, which together with the ship, brought the captors $50,000. Such losses, whether reported in the British or American press, highlighted the weaknesses of the convoy system and the vulnerability of British shipping to both natural and human hazards.[48]

Exceptions to the convoy rule were rare. The occasional merchantman, unable or unwilling to pay the war-heightened cost of insurance, risked sailing unaccompanied in the hope that false colours and a fast ship would help evade capture. British Post Office packets, at approximately 200 tons, well-crewed, and heavily gunned, relied on their reputations as fierce fighters to protect them. Nevertheless, determined attacks by the U.S. Navy brought in eighteen of the twenty-two mail packets captured during the War of 1812, while American privateers accounted for three.[49] By keeping shipping together, the convoy system reduced the number of targets available and made prizes so hard to find that marauding American naval vessels or privateers cruising the shipping channels after 1814 found the pickings very slim indeed.[50]

Maritime Risk: Insuring and Securing Trade

The success of prize-hungry naval and privateer vessels on both sides of the Atlantic Ocean can be gauged by insurance rates. Well established in the marine insurance field by 1800, Lloyd's of London underwriters had developed a constitution or Trust Deed in 1811 to regularize the writing of shipping policies and to ensure that its members had enough capital to cover wartime losses. Throughout the war, Lloyd's members worked with the Admiralty organizing convoys and exchanging shipping intelligence. As the number of claims increased, premiums hit unheard-of levels, adding to the already heavy cost of maritime trade. Entries in Lloyd's shipping books tracked both the landings and the losses of marine traffic while newspapers, such as the *Liverpool Mercury*, published

---

[48] P.A.C., RG8, IV, Vol. 136, *Mary*, Examination of Archibald Moore, master, 2 July 1814.

[49] Howard Robinson, *Carrying British Mails Overseas* (London, 1964), 314. Ten of the twenty-two captured packet crews were later rewarded for bravery in resisting capture. Robinson states that twenty-five seamen were killed and 115 wounded aboard British mail packets during the war.

[50] *Times*, 24 Mar. 1813. Coggleshall, *American Privateers*, 38. Mail packet crews described by Crane and Cranwell, *Men of Marque*, 98 and Mahan, *War of 1812*, II, 130.

the score. Impudent attacks by American privateers right off the coast of Great Britain raised the cost of insuring a voyage across the Irish Channel to thirteen guineas per £100. This, the *Naval Chronicle* exclaimed, "was three times higher than it was when we were at war with all of Europe!"[51] So dangerous was the trip to Halifax that insurance, if it could be obtained, ranged from thirty guineas per £100 or thirty-three percent over the standard premium.[52] Similarly, in the United States, insurance costs reflected the growing probability of capture as the British blockade tightened its grip along the American coast. Before Boston was blockaded, the cost of marine insurance from Boston to New York or to Eastport, Maine, was roughly seven to ten percent of the value of the ship. Charges increased to ten percent for Philadelphia and twelve to fifteen percent from Boston to the Chesapeake. Ships sailing to Savannah paid twenty-two to twenty-five percent insurance while premiums from Boston to New Orleans reached thirty percent. Foreign shipment to France, America's only European market, carried a premium of thirty to fifty percent. Six months later, 200 vessels sat idle in Boston harbour and insurance costs climbed to fifty percent. By the end of 1814, insurance in the city cost as much as seventy-five percent of a ship's value.[53]

Judging from the large number of negative or "unknown" answers to the Standing Interrogatory question concerning whether a vessel and/or its cargo were insured, it appears that the majority of owners may have decided to forego insurance and accept the risk. A few American investors, like Henry Didier, Jr., insisted that all cargoes be shipped in first rate Baltimore schooners, which were insurable because of their great speed.[54] Only a handful of American or foreign prizes seem to have been even partly insured. Of 144 vessels captured in 1812, only eighteen respondents replied that their vessels and/or cargoes carried any insurance. *Maria*, a Spanish prize taken 13 July 1812, was insured at five percent while *Ceres'* licence from Liverpool to Boston paid insurance at only 2½ percent. By mid-October when the New Brunswick privateer *General Smyth* seized *Reward* en route to Lisbon, the prize was partly insured at twenty percent.[55]

In 1813, 268 vessels were seized, but there are only twenty-five recorded statements indicating insurance. The letter of marque *Volant*, from Bayonne to Boston, carried partial insurance at twenty-five percent, but *Amanda*'s supercargo, M. Garesche,

---

[51] Hodgson, *Lloyd's*, 47-58. Lloyd's underwriters also supported the shipping industry by contributing to the Shipping Fund for widows and orphans of sailors as well as subscribing to various funds to celebrate famous naval victories. Donald P. Hickey, *The War of 1812 - A Forgotten Conflict* (Urbana, Ill., 1989), 218, quotes the *Naval Chronicle*, July to Dec. 1814, 244.

[52] *English Reports*, CLXV, Ecclesiastical, Admiralty and Probate and Divorce V, (Edinburgh, 1923), 1172-1187, Letter from R.G. Van Polanen, New York, 20 Aug. 1809 to His Excellency the Minister of Marine and Colonies, Amsterdam. The letter discusses the cost of insuring cargoes of coffee and sugar at the usual rate of ten percent.

[53] *Niles Weekly Register* published insurance rates from Halifax to London and Castine (20%) along with a list of fifty-two Royal Navy vessels lost or captured since the outbreak of war on 31 Dec. 1814. Donald Macintyre, *The Privateers* (London, 1975), 171-172, quotes the *Liverpool Mercury* of 7 May 1813. Mahan, *War of 1812*, II, 182. Snider, *Red Jack*, 3, mentions the cost of insurance to New Orleans as an indication of the impact of Atlantic Canada's privateers. Hickey, *Forgotten Conflict*, 230.

[54] Garitee, *Private Navy*, 116.

[55] PAC, RG 8. IV, Vol. 125, *Maria*, Examination of Jabez Norton, master, 20 July 1812; Vol. 73, *Ceres*, Examination of Seth Webber, master, 3 Sept. 1812; Vol. 118, *Reward*, Examination of Amos Hill, master, 5 Nov. 1812.

refused to pay the forty percent premium demanded for a voyage from France to Philadelphia. The *Liverpool Packet* from Lisbon was insured at Boston against all but British capture, but the cargo of salt, fruit, and dry goods was insured in London. To protect his exotic cargo of camphor, sugar, coffee, nutmeg, and "dragons blood" from Batavia to Providence, Rhode Island, the owner of *Hope* insured himself for £60,000, but the amount of the premium is not mentioned.[56]

Of the 214 prizes taken in 1814, only twenty-one deponents confirmed some type of insurance. These include *Eliza*, from New York to Eastport, partly insured by a Boston firm at thirty-three percent; *San Joaquin*, from Cuba to Newport, Rhode Island, whose insurance did not apply against British cruisers; and *Favorite* from Calcutta to New South Wales whose cargo of wheat and rice was insured, but not the vessel. Other non-insured cargoes included *Charles*' hold full of fish, oil, and lumber, taken en route from New Brunswick to Barbados, and 100 chests of tea from Bahia to New Haven, Connecticut, aboard *Conde dos Arcos*. Only two examinations from among the fifteen prizes seized in 1815 revealed a knowledge of insurance.[57] Several respondents mentioned being insured at Lloyd's or in London, two at Boston, one at New York, and one in Calcutta, but the sample is far too small to offer any real perspective on the wartime insurance industry. Lack of documentation also makes it difficult to determine the relationship between insurance rates and a merchant's decision to ship or not. Certainly, the high cost of insuring a vessel and/or its cargo would have to be weighed against the risk of loss entailed by capture and any potential profits to be made.

In Atlantic Canada insurance premiums did not rise as dramatically because several companies usually shared the cost of insurance that might cost eight percent on seventy-five percent of the vessel's value in the year it was insured. Nova Scotia vessels paid about eleven percent per year with a return of three percent if there were no losses during the period of insurance.[58]

By 1814, the combined tactics of blockade and convoy brought American trade to its knees. An unidentified Baltimorean confessed to readers of the *Nova Scotia Royal Gazette* of 19 May 1813: "Our situation is more distressing than pride and obstinacy will permit most to allow, and many dare to complain of. Exactly that of a besieged city is our condition. Nothing doing, all business at a stand, nothing talked of but the enemy and the war. What an enormous tax upon us is the war! The price of every thing almost doubled, and our supplies by water totally cut off! If no change takes place in a few months the middling classes of society must leave the place, and go where they can get employ and support their families."[59] As prices for staple commodities such as flour and

---

[56]PAC, RG 8, IV, Vol. Vol. 99, *Volant*, Examination of Nathan Perley, master, 5 Apr. 1813; Vol. 73, *Amanda*, Examination of M. Garesche, supercargo, 20 Apr. 1813; Vol. 89, *Liverpool Packet*, Examination of Samuel Nickels, master, 8 July 1813; Vol. 86, *Hope*, Examination of Jeremiah Jordan, master, 11 Aug. 1813. Dragon's blood was a type of tree gum from Sumatra.

[57]PAC, RG8, IV, Vol. 108, *San Joaquin*, Examination of Domingo Riverol, supercargo, 7 May 1814; Vol. 104, *Eliza*, Examination of Abraham Merrit, master, 11 July 1814; Vol. 102, *Conde dos Arcos*, Examination of Theophilo di Mello, master, 1 Sept. 1814; Vol. 135, *Favorite*, Examination of Robert Fielder, chief mate, 9 Sept. 1814; Vol. 135, *Charles*, Examination of John Everett, master, 19 Nov. 1814.

[58]Clement W. Crowell, *Novascotiamen* (Halifax, N.S., 1973), 376.

[59]*NS Royal Gazette*, 19 May 1813.

sugar reached new heights, once-prosperous communities suffered shortages and individuals faced great hardship. The few privateersmen still on the prowl found the oceans nearly empty of prey. On 17 June 1814 the secretary of the navy told Commodore Isaac Hull, director of the Portsmouth Naval Yard, that he could spare no men to protect the yard, and it was better to burn the ships on the stocks than "defend them at an expense far transcending their value."[60] Unable to protect its ships on land or at sea, America's war effort crumbled along with the economy.

Economic Impact

Britain's blockade strategy had a powerful, albeit temporary, effect on American commerce. Captured vessels, if condemned, represented the double loss of both cargo and ship to the owners. Even owners whose vessels were eventually released were deprived of time, possible market opportunities, and the use of their vessels and crew while awaiting the vice-admiralty court's verdict. Table 6.1 compares the economic damage caused by naval and privater vessels in terms of tonnage captured.

Prizemaking also had an emotional impact in terms of the distress it caused businesses, individuals and communities. Vincent Nolte of Vincent Nolte & Company, New Orleans, confided his fears to Alexander Baring, Baring Brothers and Co., London on 6 April 1813. The war entailed, he complained, "very heavy sacrifices on our part and bears so hard on all classes of citizens." Not only was communication severed between New Orleans and the Atlantic states, but only two foreign vessels had arrived in the past nine months. With no reasonable expectation of peace for at least two or three years, Nolte suggested that Baring charter a couple of neutral Swedish vessels in England and send them over in ballast. They could clear out cargoes of cotton for Cadiz, Lisbon, or Gothenburg and return to England under the protection of a licence.[61]

In December 1813, only five of forty-four American vessels in Boston cleared from that port, but in March 1815, less than a month after news of peace reached Boston, 144 vessels sailed out, all but twenty-six to foreign destinations.Once relieved of the crushing weight of the blockade, American shipping virtually exploded back to life. Such increased traffic accounted for a dramatic rise in port receipts, and even the number of fishing licences issued rose from 16,453 in 1814 to 48,147 in 1816![62]

At the uneven mercy of the blockading squadron, several communities on Cape Cod chose to pay what amounted to tribute to avoid both bombardment and plundering by the Royal Navy. The peaceable Quaker community of Nantucket Island found the threat of starvation so serious by August 1814 that they were compelled to declare neutrality to get food through the blockade. The affidavit of Jared Gardner, a passenger

---

[60]Gardner Weld Allen, ed., *The Papers of Isaac Hull* (Boston, 1929), 35.

[61]PAC, RG 8, IV, Vol 118, *Pilgrim*. Vincent Nolte to Alexander Baring, 6 Apr. 1813. Baring (later Lord Ashburton) was a banker and financier closely connected to the United States through business and marriage. In 1808 he authored *An Inquiry into the Causes and Consequences of the Orders in Council: and an Examination of the Conduct of Great Britain towards the Neutral Commerce of America*. See Vincent Harlow and Frederick Madden, *British Colonial Developments 1774-1834, Select Documents* (Oxford, 1953), 283.

[62]Mahan, *War of 1812*, II, 181-206.

aboard the Nantucket sloop *Fame*, captured 23 July 1814 by HMS (*Spencer*, *Nymph*, and *Leander* reveals the extent of the island's deprivation. Gardner states that the Washington Benevolent Society of Nantucket appointed him and Captain Timothy Folger to draw their "calamitous and distressed" situation to Admiral Milne's attention and ask for his humane consideration in allowing them to carry a cargo of 138 barrels of beef and pork and forty-six small kegs of butter to their desperate neighbours.

Gardner's community of 750 were mostly defenceless inhabitants opposed "to the present unnatural, unnecessary and destructive war." Earning their livelihood from whaling, Nantucketeers did not produce enough cattle, wood, or grain to sustain themselves when the blockade destroyed their former trade with Boston. *Fame* had sailed under a flag of truce to Milne and had been assured that their coastal vessels would not be molested as long as they were carrying provisions for their own consumption. Unfortunately for Gardner, although HMS *Nymph* was willing to let them proceed, Captain Paggett of *Spencer* insisted that his orders were to bring in every ship he met regardless of whether it might be condemned as prize or not. Although *Fame* was finally restored to its owners, it spent over a month in detention, and the owners had to pay costs of £255. A petition for unlivery and sale on 24 August reveals that Captain Folger had to sell part of his hard won cargo to pay his costs.

Philosophically opposed to war in the first place, Nantucket's hard-pressed Quaker population had little difficulty deciding between starvation and neutrality. In exchange for permission to import provisions, fuel, and fish from nearby ports, the islanders surrendered their public stores, agreed to supply British warships, and ceased paying taxes to the United States. In return, Admiral Cochrane worked for the release of all Nantucket prisoners of war, although the conflict ended before he could achieve this end.[63]

Individuals were also forced to bear the burden of the blockade. After a hard winter in Newport, Rhode Island, Phoebe Hammond's doctor ordered her not to eat Indian corn if she wanted to regain her health. Driven by "sickness and the greatest necessity," Phoebe reluctantly begged her "coussen Champlin," a New York merchant, for a little tea, coffee, sugar "or anything you have in your family to eat or drink ... This horrid war has thrown my children all out of business that I have none to help me neither sailor nor 'mechnick' can get a days work to do." Sadly, on 1 April 1813, the Nova Scotia privateer *Sir John Sherbrooke* seized the sloop *Fame* carrying Phoebe's letter and her plea for help remained unanswered.[64]

By the time the War of 1812 ground to a halt, trade had ceased to be either free or active. Attacks on shipping drove prices up and exports and imports down. Prohibitive insurance rates and uncontrolled prices caused severe personal and commercial hardships. The British blockade of the American coast soon countered the early damage American privateers inflicted on British trade and the small but amazingly proficient United States Navy. The movement of American maritime traffic ground to a halt. Simultaneously,

[63]Hickey, *Forgotten Conflict*, 215. Cochrane's interest in Nantucket prisoners of war seems a bit out of place, given his attitude described above. It may reflect, however, his approval of the "sensible" behaviour of the Nantucket community. Samuel Eliot Morison, *The Maritime History of Massachusetts, 1783-1860* (Boston, 1921), 208. PAC, RG 8 IV, Vol. 105, *Fame*, Examination of Jared Gardner, passenger.

[64]PAC, RG 8, IV, Vol. 84, *Fame*, Phoebe Hammond to Mr. John Champlin, Mar. 1813.

Britain's strict enforcement of the convoy system deprived the few American vessels able to get to sea of likely prizes.

Outside of a few dramatic naval and military actions, the commercial cut and thrust of capture, blockade, and convoy characterized the War of 1812. A few brilliant victories by individual U.S. naval vessels could not overcome the sheer weight of metal the Royal Navy could bring to bear. Despite their initial success, American privateers gradually lost their incentive to take prizes, as the risk of capture increased and the size and value of their prey diminished. Only the provinces of New Brunswick and Nova Scotia benefitted from the continued hostilities. But even their war-induced prosperity proved too good to be true. Once economic pressure on American trade raised the stakes too high, the United States' war effort collapsed. Futile and inconclusive as a military exercise, the War of 1812 succeeded as a war against trade.

Table 6.1
A Comparison of Prize Tonnages Captured by Privateer and Royal Naval Vessels

	1812			1813			1814			1815		
	RN	Priv	Oth	RN	Priv	Oth	RN	Priv	Oth	RN	Priv	Oth
under 100t	29	15	0	69	78	1	45	50	2	1	5	0
Total t	1,681	1,243		4,425	4,976	12	2,606	2,593	100	65	293	
100 to 200t	22	6	0	59	27	1	36	7	0	4	1	0
Total t	3,244	753		8,637	3,335	135	5,356	974		559	172	
over 200t	43	3	1	45	4	0	33	0	0	2	0	0
Total t	12,570	907	270	13,710	1,047		8,455			469		
Tot #	94	24	1	173	189	2	114	57	2	7	6	
Tons	17,495	2,903	270	26,772	9,358	147	16,417	3,567	100	1,093	465	
Unkn t	25			41	4	5	38	3	2	2		5

Conclusion
Prizemaking Appraised

When the Treaty of Ghent brought the War of 1812 to an official close on Christmas Eve, 1814, it marked the end of privateering as an international weapon of war. Over the centuries privateering, also known as commerce raiding and guerre de course, had evolved well-understood procedures for seizing prizes and legally securing them through the courts. Seventeenth-century English jurisdictional wrangling had clarified the authority of the High Court of Admiralty and colonial vice-admiralty courts to adjudicate questions of prize. By the early nineteenth century prizemaking had become an accepted weapon in the naval arsenal, while privateering played a vital role in the war against trade. In examining the development of private armed warfare from its earliest known records to its role in Atlantic Canada in the War of 1812, this study has compared the prizemaking role of privateers from New Brunswick and Nova Scotia with that of Royal Navy vessels stationed along the American coast.

From 18 June 1812 to mid-February 1815, when the news of the peace finally reached Washington, hundreds of British and American privateers as well as naval vessels from both sides captured thousands of prizes. Compared to the prizes taken by larger, more numerous and heavily armed American privateers, provincial captures ran to smaller vessels with less valuable cargoes that would surrender without a fight. Investors in provincial privateering belonged to the maritime merchant class rather than the political or social elite. They were happy to combine patriotism with profit but did not reinvest unless there were gains to be made. Contrary to the stereotype of undisciplined freebooters covering their quasi-piratical activities with a letter of marque, the privateers of Atlantic Canada were well capitalized, law-abiding, business-like, generally well-behaved, and moderately successful.

The transformation of private armed warfare from a medieval expedient for resolving individual losses to a legally sanctioned act of war was a long, frequently contentious process. In Britain, maritime custom and judicial decisions resulted in the creation of a body of international prize law and a High Court of Admiralty to administer it. This legal tradition was exported to Britain's colonies in North America from which developed vice-admiralty courts. By the War of 1812, the vice-admiralty court of Halifax and the various American prize courts had established their jurisdiction over questions of prize so that all those involved in prizemaking respected their authority. The forty-five appeals from judgements of the Halifax vice-admiralty court noted in Appendix 1 indicate the overall satisfaction of the court's clients.[1]

The War of 1812 presents a useful case study of how privateering evolved from its dubious, sometimes lawless, origins to a respectable, legitimate, and effective means of maritime defence. Although privateering was consistently more popular than naval service, the independent nature of those who participated in it meant that its value as a

[1]Of the forty-five appeals, several were retracted and at least one was deserted. This represents only seven percent of all cases.

strategic weapon was limited. While most maritime historians recognize privateering as auxiliary to a national navy, its strategic value depends on their personal prejudices.

In 1812 privateering enabled merchants and shipowners to employ their vessels and crews when wartime conditions restricted their regular shipping trade. In the United States, the lack of a strong navy to defend American maritime rights against British insults prompted merchants to retaliate with private armed vessels. Along the coasts of New Brunswick and Nova Scotia, the presence of locally-owned private armed vessels provided a sense of security for coastal communities that the limited number of Royal Navy ships could not. Canadian historians such as Thomas Raddall, Janet E. Mullins, and C.H.J. Snider have only positive comments on the performance of Atlantic Canada's privateers.[2] The success of letter of marque vessels reported in American, British, and Canadian papers boosted morale in the maritime communities and encouraged others to participate or invest in privateering ventures.

During the course of the war, the Halifax Vice-Admiralty Court heard over 600 prize cases brought in by both privateers and naval crews. The one real weakness of the prize courts was the often long and always costly litigation that cut into the profits and eventual viability of prizemaking. For the court practitioners, however, the earnings of a judge, registrar, proctor, advocate, or court-appointed agent or appraiser could be very handsome. Once prizes and their cargoes were condemned, most were sold at auction, often to the same merchants who owned or backed the privateer that made the capture. In a neat economic cycle, the income from court-related activities contributed to the commercial life of the Atlantic provinces.

The business of privateering was very much part of the life of the community in which it took place.[3] For the inhabitants of Halifax, Liverpool, and Yarmouth, for example, a letter of marque offered a welcome alternative for investment, employment, and excitement. Privateering remained a popular activity in Atlantic Canada throughout the war despite the fact that almost half of all provincial letter-of-marque vessels failed to capture a prize, and a few privateers actually lost their lives. As part of a closely-linked mercantile fraternity, the privateers of New Brunswick and Nova Scotia preferred to cooperate rather than compete with each other. By supporting each others' ventures, they shared both the risks and the rewards. In this way, the profits made by the most successful privateers, the *Liverpool Packet*, *Sir John Sherbrooke*, and *Retaliation* circulated throughout the community and added to the overall prosperity.

While provincial privateers generally exchanged intelligence and even crew members among themselves, they competed with the Royal Navy for men, ships and prizes. Contributing to the preference for sailing under a letter of marque were reduced discipline, better food, shorter work shifts, and higher, more regular wages. Private armed vessels had little trouble securing crews at any time during the war, while the chronically short-handed navy was compelled to resort to impressment, occasionally from

---

[2]Thomas Raddall, *Halifax, Warden of the North* (Toronto, 1971); Janet E. Mullins, *Liverpool Privateering, 1756-1815* (1936; reprint, Liverpool, N.S., 1996); and C.H.J. Snider, *Under the Red Jack* (Toronto, 1927).

[3]Appendix 7 lists several hundred individuals and companies representing maritime communities in New Brunswick and Nova Scotia who were involved in at least one aspect of privateering.

the decks of privateers. Not only did impressment increase the traditional distrust that existed between the navy and privateers, it also reduced the incentive for information sharing that could have worked to their mutual benefit.

Privateers also had a distinct advantage when it came to prizes. Once a case was decided, their prize money was paid out promptly. In the case of naval prizes, agents for the officers and crews sometimes deliberately delayed payment or had difficulty determining who was aboard a certain ship at the time of capture and thereby entitled to share in the prize. Privateer crews in Atlantic Canada averaged forty to fifty men as compared to naval crews of several hundred or more. Although heavily armed naval vessels were able to attack larger, more profitable prizes, prize money had to be shared among everyone from the admiral to the cabin boy. Despite claims that the navy fought for the king first and prizes second, virtually every naval captain counted on prize money to supplement his wages. Orders to protect trade and defend shipping frustrated naval captains who were obliged to attack heavily armed privateers or American naval vessels with little prize potential, or bypass a likely prize if it meant leaving a convoy unprotected. The tendency of many naval historians to dismiss privateering as having limited influence on the conduct of a war reflects the rivalry and even jealousy fostered by such differences between privateering and naval service.

By most military standards the War of 1812 was a failure that should have been fought and forgotten. There were no decisive victories on land or at sea, both sides lacked strong political leadership, and few heroes emerged. The dramatic effect of the war on the participants elevated it beyond a minor footnote in North American history. Great Britain, which had never viewed the war as more than an annoying distraction from its efforts in Europe, was finally forced to acknowledge the superior skills of American naval crews and privateers.

Unfortunately for the United States, the war generated few economic benefits, even in the short term. Although it vindicated the independent nationhood of a new generation of Americans, the War of 1812 also revealed the deep regional differences that existed between New England and the South and the eastern seaboard and the West, which were to eventually split the nation. Britain's massive naval blockade of the entire American coast soon stifled any early profits made through licensed trading, smuggling and privateer captures. By 1814, trade had dried up and with it the flow of money needed to keep both banks and currency afloat. Neither the regular army nor the navy could drum up enough recruits to replace those lost or taken prisoner. Meanwhile in New England, people were so dissatisfied with the situation that there was serious discussion of separation! America's lack of a strong defensive naval capability enabled Britain's blockading squadron to confine several hundred privateers and almost the entire American navy to port. It was a lesson Americans never forgot.

Whether the capture of Canada had been part of American strategy or not, the success of provincial troops and the prowess of privateers from New Brunswick and Nova Scotia crushed forever the hopes of American expansionists. Economically, the Atlantic provinces made enormous gains at the expense of their American neighbours. Although the commercial bonanza did not last beyond the war, between 1812 and 1815 the provinces of New Brunswick and Nova Scotia enjoyed unprecedented prosperity. The exclusion of American vessels from the West Indies trade opened up lucrative Caribbean markets to colonial merchants, virtually without competition. Although they faced the threat of American privateers and naval vessels, most deemed the potential profits worth the risk. Military and naval contracts pumped up the local economy, especially in Halifax and Saint John, while creating jobs and investment opportunities. Wages rose to keep pace with rising prices and rents. Meanwhile, a long tradition of smuggling between New England and Canada's Atlantic provinces initiated a lively if illegal trade across the northeastern states. Maritime merchants on both sides engaged in a variety of stratagems to short-circuit government attempts to restrict British manufactures from entering the United States and American produce from reaching British markets. On the other hand, many patriotic ship owners and seamen from New Brunswick and Nova Scotia eagerly traded their coasting licences for letters of marque and engaged in a vigorous and often successful privateering war against American trade.

British fears of renewed hostilities in Europe and severe economic problems finally drove negotiators to make peace. An awkward end to an unsatisfactory war, the Treaty of Ghent failed either to transfer territory or proclaim a victor. It even ignored the issue of "Free Trade and Sailors' Rights" for which America went to war. Although neither Britain nor America acknowledged the demoralizing effect of ship captures on the political, social, and commercial lives of individuals, both sides were anxious for peace. After two and a half years, hundreds of prizes, and thousands of prisoners of war, naval prizemaking and privateering more than justified their role in the war that nobody wanted.

Appendix 1
Prize Cases Appearing in the Vice-Admiralty Court of Halifax from June 1812 to May 1815

The prizes listed here include vessels, cargoes, sundry articles, and HM Customs seizures, each of which is identified by a monition number [in square brackets]. These numbers appear on all relevant court documents and refer to the monition document that "admonished" all parties interested in the prize to prepare their arguments and submit their affidavits, petitions, or appeals to the vice-admiralty court within twenty-one days. A copy of the monition was usually affixed to the main mast of the prize. In cases where a vessel was lost or released, cargoes were stored in the customs house, and the monition was posted on the door.

Prizes recaptured by either the Royal Navy or privateers are identified with (Recap), and if known, the original captor from whom the prize was retaken is indicated. Prizes owned by allies or neutral flags like Sweden were usually restored upon the payment of salvage. Salvage awards to naval vessels and crews were one-eighth of the appraised value of the vessel and/or cargo while privateers were allowed one-sixth of the appraised value.

Known privateer or letter of marque vessels are identified by an asterisk *. British naval vessels have HMS before their names while USS denotes American naval vessels. The various types of prize vessels are identified as slp (sloop), brg (brig or brigantine), schnr (schooner), shp (ship), or bque (barque or barquentine). Tonnage is inserted where known. For several vessels, the tonnage is available only in Swedish lasts (Sw. last) or Spanish tons (Sp. t.).

The data for this Appendix were drawn from a variety of sources in Archives in Ottawa, Halifax, and London. In Ottawa, the National Archives of Canada preserves the records of the Vice-Admiralty Court of Halifax for the War of 1812 in RG8, IV, Vols. 73 -160. Since the British High Court of Admiralty heard all appeals from prize judgements, the Public Records Office in London supplied information on some vessels through HCA 46, Vols. 10 and 11 and HCA 46, Vol. 9. Finally, documentary evidence found in the RG1 series in the Public Archives of Nova Scotia was used to support or modify information gathered elsewhere. A 1911 publication edited by Georege Dow for the Essex Institute of Salem entitled *American Vessels Captured by the British during the Revolution and War of 1812* was particularly useful. Contemporary newspapers such as the *Nova Scotia Royal Gazette*, the London *Times*, and *Niles Weekly Register* of Baltimore corroborated some of the data.

1812 Date	Prize	Ship Type	Tons	Captor(s)	From	To	Cargo	Judgement & Costs
June 24	Malcolm [1]	brg	238 t.	HMS Belvidera	Madeira	Portland	wine	JC £410
25	Fortune [2]	shp	317 t.	HMS Belvidera	Bonavista	Boston	salt	JC £408
July 6	Minerva [3]	brg	256 t.	HMS Africa, Aeolus, Shannon Belvidera	Liverpool GB	Boston	salt, coal	JC £332
7	Enterprise [4]	brg	193 t.	HMS Ring Dove	St. Ubes	NY	salt	JC £386
8	George [5]	brg	148 t.	HMS Guerriere	La Rochelle, France	NY	brandy, wine, dry goods	C £9
8	Mary Elizabeth [78]	brg	167 t.	HMS Indian	St. Ubes	Portland ME	specie $2313	JC [NB] £190
9	William [20] (Recap)	bque	207 t.	HMS Indian (Dolphin* of Salem)	St. Andrews NB	Barnstable	lumber, dry goods	C £76 + £170 slvg
9	Benjamin Franklin [22]	shp	270 t.	Collector of Customs	Liverpool GB	Philadelphia	ballast	Detained under Prince Regent's Order JC (1813)
10	Marquis de Somer-uelas [6]	shp	359 t.	HMS Atalante	Civita Vecchia	Salem	brandy, wine, dry goods, hats, flowers, silks, feathers, art	JC, art R [21 paintings, 52 prints for Academy of Arts, Philadelphia] £457
11	Oroonoko [8]	shp	427 t.	HMS Shannon, Africa, Guerriere, Belvidera, Aeolus	Lisbon	NY	ballast	JC£439
11	Illuminator [11]	brg	255 t.	HMS Emulous	Havana	Boston	sugar, coffee, hides, molasses, specie	JC£696
12	Lively [16]	schnr	78 t.	HMS Emulous	St.Barthol-mew	Boston	molasses, rum, sugar	JC£379
12	Traveller [17]	schnr	109 t.	HMS Emulous	Georgia	Boston	timber	JC£215
13	Maria [9]	shp	344 t.	HMS Emulous	Cadiz	NY	bales of cloth, specie ($32,000)	JC£406

1812 Date	Prize	Ship Type	Tons	Captor(s)	From	To	Cargo	Judgement & Costs
July 15	Start [7](Recap)	brg	174 t.	HMS Spartan, Jupiter (Regulator*)	St. Ubes	Newburyport	salt	JC£309
15	Belleisle [14]	brg	119 t.	HMS Emulous	Havana	Salem	sugar, molasses	JC£434
16	Cordelia [13]	brg	168 t.	HMS Emulous	Figuera	Boston	ballast, specie $21,144	JC£368
16	USS Nautilus [42] (became new HMS Emulous)	US brg	200 t.	HMS Shannon, Africa, Belvidera, Guerriere, Aeolus	New York	on a cruise		JC(for HM Service)£126
16	Fair Trader* [73]	schnr	29 t.	HMS Indian	Salem	on a cruise		JC [NB]£104
16	Active*	schnr		HMS Spartan				
17	Nimrod [21] (Recap)	schnr	52 t.	HMS Paz (Polly* of Salem)	Liverpool NS	fishing		R (Salvage) £21 + £22 slvg
17	George [23]	brg	212 t.	HMS Emulous, Spartan	Messina	Salem	wines, brandy	JC £612
17	Argus* [74]	schnr	22 t.	HMS Indian	Boston	on a cruise in Bay of Fundy		JC [NB]£101
17	Mary [10]	brg	129 t.	HMS Spartan	Gibraltar	Boston	Malaga wine, currants, juniper berries, merino, wool	JC£432
18	Hiram [12]	schnr	97 t.	HMS Spartan, Emulous	Lisbon	Salem	fruit, specie $12,800	JC£420
18	Actress* [39] (became NS privateer Dart*)	slp	48 t.	HMS Spartan	New Haven	on cruise in Bay of Fundy		JC [NB] £103
18	Magnet [18] (became HMS prison ship)	shp	372 t.	HMS Ring Dove	Belfast	NY	passengers, ballast	JC (HM Service) £233
18	Martha [22] (Recap)	schnr	41 t.	HMS Paz	Halifax (Polly* of Salem)	Country Harbour Sable Island	militia arms & ammunition, provisions for Sable Island	R (Salvage) £20 + £ 31 slvg
18	Eliza [34] (Recap)	schnr		HMS Chubb (Buckskin*)		Halifax	Liverpool GB	R (Salvage) £19 slvg
18	Ann [36] (Recap)	brg		HMS Chubb (Teazer*)	Cadiz	St John NB	ballast	R (Salvage) £158 + £97 slvg

1812 Date	Prize	Ship Type	Tons	Captor(s)	From	To	Cargo	Judgement & Costs
19	Fanny [15] (Recap)	shp	400 t.	HMS Colibri (Teazer*)	Port Glasgow	St John NB	coal, drugs	R (Salvage) £144 + £975 slvg
19	Rover [19] (Recap)	schnr	98 t.	HMS Ring Dove (Regulator*)	Liverpool GB	Amelia Island	hardware, crockery, coals	JC£390
19	Four Sisters [24]	shp	204 t.	HMS Ring Dove	Lisbon	NY	ballast, $1,000	JC£407
19	Friendship* [72]	schnr	22 t.	HMS Indian	Charlestown	on a cruise in Bay of Fundy		JC [NB] £103
20	Hesper [26] (Recap)	brg	264 t.	HMS Ring Dove (Buck-skin*, taken from HMS Maidstone)	Liverpool GB	Norfolk	ballast	JC £355
22	George [30] (Recap)	brg		HMS Maidstone (Gleaner* of Kennebunk)	Poole	St. Andrews NB	ballast	R (Salvage) £118 + £63 slvg
22	Mariner [31] (Recap)	shp		HMS Colibri (Gleaner*)	Port Glasgow	St John NB	ballast	R (Salvage) £75 + 175 slvg
23	Mary Ann [28](Recap)	schnr		HMS Maidstone (Buck-) skin*)	Halifax	Québec City	tar	R (Salvage) £118 + £70 slvg
23	Gleaner* [25] (became NS provincial vessel)	slp	57 t.	HMS Colibri	Kennebunk	on a cruise		JC (HM Service) £87
24	Curlew* [27]	brg	279 t.	HMS Acasta	Boston	on a cruise		JC (HM Service) £244
26	Catherine* [29]	shp	281 t.	HMS Colibri	Boston	Archangel on a cruise		JC £368
30	Gossamer* [32]	brg	223 t.	HMS Emulous	Boston	on a cruise		JC (HM Service) £328
31	Eleanor [75]	schnr	66 t.	HMS Shannon, Africa	Puerto Rico	New Haven	rum [removed at sea]	Cargo JC [schnr burnt] £149
31	Prevoyante [33]	schnr		HMS Emulous (Orlando*)	Martinique	Halifax	sugar, molasses, rum	R (Salvage) £82 + £281 slvg
Aug 1	Zodiac [71]	shp	277 t.	HMS Alphea	NY	Portugal	flour, rice	R [captor pays costs]
1	Polly*	schnr	60 t.	HMS Maidstone, Spartan				[burnt]
1	Morning Star*	schnr	70 t.	HMS Maidstone, Spartan		Machias		[burnt]
3	Commodore Barry [201] [Brunswicker]	slp		HMS Maidstone, Spartan				
3	Madison	schnr		HMS Maidstone, Spartan		Little River		[NB]

1812 Date	Prize	Ship Type	Tons	Captor(s)	From	To	Cargo	Judgement & Costs
4	Concordia [55]	shp	386 t.	HMS Shannon, Africa, Belvidera, Aeolus, Guerriere	Liverpool GB	Baltimore	British dry	R (lic) £139
7	Grace [40] (Recap)	brg	164 t.	HMS Chubb (John*)	St. Mary's	England	pine planks, laths	R (Salvage) £57 + £106 slvg
8	Buckskin* [76]	schnr	40 t.	HMS Statira, Colibri	Salem	on a cruise		JC £87
9	Pythagoras* [77]	slp	43 t.	HMS Bream	Sacco MA	on a cruise		JC £47
10	Bolina [47]	shp	260 t.	HMS Morgiana	Gibraltar	Salem	wine, salt, capers, oil, specie $13,550	JC £478
10	Union Lass [35] (Recap)	schnr		HMS Chubb (unknown priv.)	St. John's, Nfld	Barrington NS	rum	R (Salvage) £47 + £176 slvg
10	Sally [58] (Recap)	brg	156 t.	HMS Morgiana (Benjamin Franklin* of NY)	Plymouth GB	Pictou NS	ballast	R (Salvage) £65 + £73 slvg
11	Henry [37] (Recap)	shp	282 t.	HMS Emulous (Lewis*)	Miramichi	Halifax	spars, lumber	R (Salvage) £77 + £371 slvg
11	Polly* [44]	schnr	34 t.	HMS Acasta, Colibri	Marblehead	on a cruise		JC £83
11	Prudence [46]	brg	158 t.	HMS Morgiana	Dublin	NY	sugar, linen	JC £319
11	Regulator* [43]	schnr	43 t.	HMS Colibri	Salem	on a cruise		JC £82
12	Dolphin* [38]	schnr	26 t.	HMS Earl of Moira	Porstsmouth MA	on a cruise		JC £84
13	Dolphin* [41]	schnr	43 t.	HMS Maidstone, Spartan, Indian, Colibri		Boston	on a cruise	JC £82
13	John [45]	brg	160 t.	HMS Maidstone	Liverpool GB	Portland	earthenware, salt	JC £358
13	Penelope [196] (Recap)	brg	291 t.	General Smyth* (Orlando*)	Demarera	Halifax	rum, sugar, coffee, molasses	JC [NB] £266 + £45 slvg
13	Apollo [102] (Recap)	shp		HMS Statira (John*)	Plymouth GB	Pictou	ballast	R (Salvage) £100 slvg
14	Union [50] (Recap)	brg		HMS Morgiana (Dolphin*)	Liverpool GB	Nfld	salt, coal, canvas	R (Salvage) £60 + £97 slvg
14	Lewis* [69]	schnr	36 t.	HMS Hope	Stonington CONN	on a cruise		JC £78

1812 Date	Prize	Ship Type	Tons	Captor(s)	From	To	Cargo	Judgement & Costs
16	Union [49]	shp	231 t.	HMS Emulous	Liverpool GB	Boston	British dry goods	R (lic) £215
17	Bainbridge [59]	shp	368 t.	HMS Belvidera	Liverpool GB	Philadelphia	dry goods, hardware	R (lic) £171
17	William [98] (Recap)	snow		HMS Statira (Dolphin*)	Britain	NB	lumber	R (Salvage) £49 + £94 slvg
17	Nancy [100] (Recap)	shp		HMS Statira (USS Essex)	Newfoundland	GB	salt	R (Salvage) £122 + £164 slvg
17	Eastern Star [56]	shp	217 t.	HMS Africa	Corunna	NY	ballast, specie $21,000	JC £380
18	Russel [101] (Recap)	brg		HMS Statira (John*)	Miramichi	Liverpool GB	timber	R (Salvage) £140 slvg
19	Osbourne [48] (Recap)	shp	465 t.	HMS Emulous (Teazer*)	Gibraltar	St. Andrews NB	ballast	R (Salvage) £87 + £8,313 slvg
19	Phoebe [51]	brg	203 t.	HMS Aeolus, Shannon	Civita Vecchia	Boston	brandy, oil, juniper berries, books, bronze furniture, porcelain	JC£471
21	Dolphin* [41]	schnr	91 t.	HMS Colibri, Shannon	Salem	on a cruise		JC [burnt]
21	Hare [53]	brg	246 t.	HMS Belvidera	Naples	Boston	silks, brandy	JC £725
21	Bunker Hill* [54] (became N.S. privateer Bunker Hill)	schnr	175 t.	HMS Belvidera	NY	on a cruise		JC £367
22	Monsoon [52]	shp		HMS Aeolus	Liverpool GB	Alexandria VA	salt, dry goods	R (lic) £177
22	James Madison	schnr					US Revenue Cutter	
23	Adeline [103] (Recap)	brg		HMS Statira (prize to USS Constitution from HMS Avenger)	London	Bath MA	dry goods	R (Salvage) $8000 slvg
23	Monk [61]	shp	253 t.	HMS Colibri	Rio de Janeiro	Salem	sugar, hides, horns	JC £422
24	Honestas [66]	shp	301 t.	HMS Nymph	St. Ubes	New Bedford	salt	JC £329
25	Science* [60]	slp	74 t.	HMS Emulous	Portsmouth NH	on a cruise in Bay of Fundy		JC £262

1812 Date	Prize	Ship Type	Tons	Captor(s)	From	To	Cargo	Judgement & Costs
25	Henrietta [62] (Recap)	brque		HMS Emulous (Dolphin*)	Miramichi	Liverpool GB	lumber	R (Salvage) £115 + £151 slvg
26	Patriot [81]	schnr	140 t.	HMS Acasta	Norfolk VA	Lisbon	flour, peas, beans	JC [R Appeal] £389
27	Jane [65]	shp		HMS Nymph	Liverpool GB	Philadelphia	dry goods, hardware	R (lic) £158
28	Merchant [63]	shp		HMS Nymph	Liverpool GB	NY	dry goods, paint, hardware	R (lic) £128
28	Georgiana [64]	shp		HMS Nymph	Liverpool GB	Norfolk		R (lic) £133
28	Fortune [131]	schnr	114 t.	General Smyth*	Machias NB	Boston	boards, rum	JC [NB] £406
28	Doris [79]	shp	202 t.	HMS Nymph	Londonderry	Philadelpia	ballast, passengers	JC £306
29	Merchant [67]	shp	270 t.	HMS Statira	Gottenburg	Portsmouth NH	iron	JC £331
30	Betsy [70]	schnr	127 t.	HMS Acasta	Naples	Boston	brandy	JC £366
30	Sophia [156]	brg	66 t.	HMS Plumper	Columbia MA	New Bedford	lumber	JC [NB] £659
30	Prince of Asturias [97] (Recap)	brg		HMS Statir (John*)	St. Mary's NS	Newcastle GB	lumber	R (Salvage) £71 + £121 slvg
31	Ceres [68]	shp	373 t.	HMS Spy (Storeship)	Liverpool GB	Boston	dry goods, crockery	R (lic) £136
Sept 2	Stockholm [82]	schnr	80 t.	HMS Maidstone, Spartan, Aeolus	St. Barthol-omew	Boston	rum, sugar, mollases, coffee	R £253
2	Planter [84] (Recap)	shp		HMS Shannon (Atlas*)	Surinam	London	coffee, cotton, sugar	R (Salvage) 368 + £1,236 slvg
3	Argo [121] (Recap)	snow brg		HMS Plumper (American squadron)	Pernambuco, Brazil	London	cotton, fustic, coconuts, small box of gold	R (Salvage) [NB] £483 slvg
4	Aristomenes [57]	shp	352 t.	HMS Shannon, Guerriere, Belvidera, Thetis, Aeolus	Liverpool GB	NY	dry goods, hardware	R (lic.) £168
4	Britannia [80] (Recap)	shp	211 t.	HMS Junon (Wily Rey-nard* of Boston)	Portsmouth	St. Andrews	in ballast	R (Salvage) £89 + £134 slvg

1812 Date	Prize	Ship Type	Tons	Captor(s)	From	To	Cargo	Judgement & Costs
5	Howe [154] (Recap)	brg	163 t.	HMS Plumper (Dart* of Portland)	Penzance	Pictou NS	in ballast	R (Salvage) [NB] £99 + £62 slvg
6	Hector [155] (Recap)	snow brg	258 t.	HMS Plumper	Dublin	Quebec	lumber	R (Salvage) [NB]
6	Charles Faucett [83]	brg	237 t.	HMS Emulous, Acasta, Statira, Nymph	Dublin	NY	linen, saltpeter, glass, glue, quills, cotton, passengers	R £141
6	Fabius [85]	shp	460 t.	HMS Shannon	St Mary's, Amelia Island	Portsmouth NH	timber	Ship JC £262 Cargo R £162
7	Factor [88]	shp	291 t.	Liverpool Packet*	Oporto	Norfolk, VA	wine, jewellery	Ship JC £256 Cargo R £145
8	Middlesex [87]	shp	325 t.	Liverpool Packet*	Liverpool GB	NY	salt, earthenware	R (lic) £53
11	Friendship [91]	schnr	98 t.	HMS Belvidera	Charleston SC	NY	cotton	JC £309
12	Ambition [107]	brg	140 t.	HMS Orpheus, Maidstone, Spartan, Emulous	Baltimore	Boston	flour	JC £318
12	Hiram [92]	schnr	95 t.	HMS Belvidera	Palermo	Philadelphia	brimstone, salt-peter, oil, soap feathers	Cargo JC Ship R £265
16	Sally Ann [86]	schnr	124 t.	HMS Statira	New London	St. Bartholomew	flour, tobacco, corn	JC (lic) [R Appeal] £729
17	Melantho [95]	shp	403 t.	HMS Spartan, Statira, Acasta, Nymph, Orpheus Maidstone, Emulous, Aoelus	Valparaiso,	Baltimore	copper, specie	JC £339 ($45,000), furs
17	Federal [104]	brg	115 t.	HMS Acasta	Prince's Island, Africa	Boston	coffee, ivory, palm oil, cane-, wood, gum, copal, old copper	JC £369
21	Diana [90] (Recap)	shp	250 t.	HMS San Domingo (Swordfish*)	Jamaica	Glasgow	coffee, sugar, ru, logwood	R (Salvage) £664 + £1,000 slvg
21	Abigail [89] (Recap)	shp	309 t.	HMS Poictiers (First Consul*)	Liverpool GB	Norfolk VA	salt, crockery, coal	R (lic) £331
23	Maria [94] (Recap)	ketch	80 t.	Liverpool Packet* (Marengo*)	St. Michael's	Gibraltar	wine, coffee, dye, wood	JC £176

1812 Date	Prize	Ship Type	Tons	Captor(s)	From	To	Cargo	Judgement & Costs
24	Packet [106]	ship	307 t.	HMS Orpheus	Liverpool GB	NY	dry goods, crockery	R (lic)
Oct 1	Elisia [93]	brg	120 t.	HMS Aeolus, Statira	Bath	St. Bartholomew	sheep, lumber, fish,soap	JC [R Appeal] £305
5	Pitt [96] (Recap)	brg		HMS Nymph (Thomas*)	Martinique	St. John's Nfld	rum, sugar, molasses, noyeau, tamarinds	R (Salvage) £59 + £205 slvg
5	El Rayo [99]	brg	100 t.	HMS Maidstone	Baltimore	Puerto Rico	flour, tobacco	R £527
10	Reward [132]	brg	182 t.	General Smyth*	Salem	Lisbon	flour, peas, potatoes, dried fish	JC [NB] [R Appeal] £693
11	Wily Reynard* [105]	schnr	23 t.	HMS Shannon	Boston	on a cruise		JC £73
14	Union [114]	schnr	105 t.	Liverpool Packet*	Philadelphia	Kennebunk	corn, flour	Droit [later C] £208
14	Polly [115]	schnr	85 t.	Liverpool Packet*	Charleston, SC	Boston	rice, cotton, sole leather, shoes	Droit [later C] £183
16	Four Brothers [112]	schnr	134 t.	Liverpool Packet*	Machias	NY	lumber	Droit [later C] £238
17	Blonde [108] (Recap)	schnr		HMS Acasta (John* of Salem)	Martinique	St John's Nfld	rum	R (Salvage) £356 slvg
17	Little Joe [111]	schnr	79 t.	Liverpool Packet*	Boston	NY	hops, pepper, alum gums, oil, sugar	Droit [later C] £273
18	Rapid [109]* (became HMS Nova Soctia)	brg	310 t.	HMS Maidstone, Spartan		Portland	on a cruise	JC (Salvage) £317
19	Union [110]	schnr	84 t.	HMS Maidstone	Labrador	Chatham	fish, oil	C
21	Anson [113]	schnr	97 t.	Liverpool Packet*	Boston	Baltimore	salt, cheese, earthenware, vinegar, cotton duck, bonnets	Droit [later C] £225
24	Lydia [133]	schnr	90 t.	General Smyth*	Buckstown	Baltimore	fish, lumber	Droit [later C] [NB]
31	Thorn* [116]	brg	291 t.	HMS Tenedos, Shannon, Nymph, Curlew		Marblehead	on a cruise	C

1812 Date	Prize	Ship Type	Tons	Captor(s)	From	To	Cargo	Judgement & Costs
Nov 10	Edward & Hiram [120]	schnr	109 t.	Liverpool Packet*	Nantucket	Kennebunk	ballast, passengers	Droit [later C] £177
11	New Forge [118]	schnr	47 t.	Liverpool Packet*	NY	Boston	sugar, earthen-ware, varnish, apples, old iron	Droit [later C] £182
11	Lucretia [119]	schnr	97 t.	Liverpool Packet*	Savannah	Boston	beef, pork, candles, soap, butter, lard, paper, shoes, fish line	Droit [later C] £223
13	Julian [117]	schnr	89 t.	Liverpool Packet*	Boston	NY	salt, oil, fish, paper	Droit [later C] £232
13	Economy [123]	brg	80 t.	Liverpool Packet*	Alexandria VA	Boston	flour, corn, rye	Droit [C] Appeal (lic)] £1,916
Dec 4	Revenge* [124]	schnr	65 t.	HMS Paz	Salem	on a cruise		C
9	Chase [125]	schnr	98 t.	Liverpool Packet*	Portland	Norfolk	lumber	Droit [later C] £166
12	Tulip* [130]	brg	195 t.	HMS Atalante	Philadelphia	Bordeaux	cotton, rice, fish	C
16	Fenelon [126]	schnr	109 t.	Liverpool Packet*	Baltimore	Boston	corn, flour, wheat	Droit [later 'C] £154
16	Eliza [136]	schnr	98 t.	Liverpool Packet*	Philadelphia	Boston	cannon, gun powder, sugar, flour, tobacco, iron, gin	Droit [later C] £143
17	Susan [128]	slp	40 t.	Liverpool Packet*	Alexandria	Boston	flour	Droit [later C] £152
17	Dove [135]	schnr	78 t.	Liverpool Packet*	Philadelphia	Boston	corn, oats	Droit [later C] £154
17	Two Friends [127]	schnr	32 t.	Liverpool Packet*	Baltimore	Boston	flour, tobacco	Droit [later C] £145
18	Columbia [134]	schnr	87 t.	Liverpool Packet*	Richmond VA	Boston	flour, tobacco, old iron	Droit [later C] £164
18	Three Friends [129]	schnr	66 t.	Liverpool Packet*	Baltimore	Boston	corn, flour, hemp	Droit [later C] (Sherbrooke lic) £198

1813 Date	Prize	Ship Type	Tons	Captor(s)	From	To	Cargo	Judgement & Costs
Jan 9	Highflyer* (became HMS tender High Flyer)	schnr	132 t.	HMS Acasta, Poictiers	Baltimore	on a cruise		C
Feb 9	Agnes [137] (Recap)	shp	135 t.	HM Customs (Hunter* of Boston)	Portsmouth	Nfld cruise	provisions	R (Salvage) £7 bonuses
17	Sarah [138]	brg	255 t.	HMS Tenedos	NY	Amsterdam	corn, potash, pipe staves	C N/A
Mar 4	Rising Sun [143]	schnr	75 t.	Sir John Sherbrooke*	Edentown NC	Barnstable	corn, tar, beans	C N/A
5	Friendship [139]	schnr	115 t.	Liverpool Packet*	Oporto	Boston	in ballast	C [R Appeal (lic)] N/A
8	General Green [145]	slp	83 t.	Liverpool Packet*	Boston	Albany NY	fish, wool, rum, cotton, sugar	C £61
9	Lawry [147]	schnr	104 t.	Liverpool Packet*	Boston	NY	iron, china, sugar	C N/A
10	Reliance [146]	slp	57 t.	Liverpool Packet*	Boston	NY	iron, tea, sugar, ashes, brimstone	C N/A
10	Bunker Hill [148]	schnr	29 t.	Liverpool Packet*	Newburyport	NY	plaster, candles, chocolate	C N/A
11	Hunter [150]	slp	83 t.	Retaliation*	Edgartown	Boston	corn, staves	C N/A
12	William [151]	schnr	103 t.	Retaliation*	Charleston	Lisbon	Indian corn	C N/A
13	Lucy [192]	schnr		HMS Rattler	Boston	Eastport	provisions, gin	R (lic) [9 puncheons [gin C] [NB] N/A
14	Swift [144]	brg	157 t.	Liverpool Packet*	Savannah GA	Providence RI	cotton, leather	C N/A
14	Nymph [149]	schnr	49 t.	Liverpool Packet*	Yorktown VA	Salem	corn, beans, skins	C N/A
18	Redbird [141]	slp	56 t.	Sir John Sherbrooke*	Murfreesboro	Boston	corn, tar	C N/A
19	Three Brothers [152]	schnr	40 t.	Retaliation*	Baltimore	Boston	flour, corn	C N/A
19	Victory [153]	brg	126 t.	Retaliation*	Lisbon	Boston	salt	R (lic) £1
20	Apollo [142]	slp	54 t.	Sir John Sherbrooke*	NC	Boston	corn	C N/A
23	Mary [140]	schnr	97 t.	Sir John Sherbrooke*	New Haven CONN	Bath	corn, "cidder", "cheas"	C N/A
26	Volant* [157]	shp	457 t.	HMS Curlew, La Hogue, Valiant	Bayonne	Boston	brandy, dry goods, muskets	C N/A

1813 Date	Prize	Ship Type	Tons	Captor(s)	From	To	Cargo	Judgement & Costs
Jan 9	Highflyer* (became HMS tender High Flyer)	schnr	132 t.	HMS Acasta, Poictiers	Baltimore	on a cruise		C
Feb 9	Agnes [137] (Recap)	shp	135 t.	HM Customs (Hunter* of Boston)	Portsmouth	Nfld cruise	provisions	R (Salvage) £7 bonuses
17	Sarah [138]	brg	255 t.	HMS Tenedos	NY	Amsterdam	corn, potash, pipe staves	C N/A
Mar 4	Rising Sun [143]	schnr	75 t.	Sir John Sherbrooke*	Edentown NC	Barnstable	corn, tar, beans	C N/A
5	Friendship [139]	schnr	115 t.	Liverpool Packet*	Oporto	Boston	in ballast	C [R Appeal (lic)] N/A
8	General Green [145]	slp	83 t.	Liverpool Packet*	Boston	Albany NY	fish, wool, rum, cotton, sugar	C £61
9	Lawry [147]	schnr	104 t.	Liverpool Packet*	Boston	NY	iron, china, sugar	C N/A
10	Reliance [146]	slp	57 t.	Liverpool Packet*	Boston	NY	iron, tea, sugar, ashes, brimstone	C N/A
10	Bunker Hill [148]	schnr	29 t.	Liverpool Packet*	Newburyport	NY	plaster, candles, chocolate	C N/A
11	Hunter [150]	slp	83 t.	Retaliation*	Edgartown	Boston	corn, staves	C N/A
12	William [151]	schnr	103 t.	Retaliation*	Charleston	Lisbon	Indian corn	C N/A
13	Lucy [192]	schnr		HMS Rattler	Boston	Eastport	provisions, gin	R (lic) [9 puncheons [gin C] [NB] N/A
14	Swift [144]	brg	157 t.	Liverpool Packet*	Savannah GA	Providence RI	cotton, leather	C N/A
14	Nymph [149]	schnr	49 t.	Liverpool Packet*	Yorktown VA	Salem	corn, beans, skins	C N/A
18	Redbird [141]	slp	56 t.	Sir John Sherbrooke*	Murfreesboro	Boston	corn, tar	C N/A
19	Three Brothers [152]	schnr	40 t.	Retaliation*	Baltimore	Boston	flour, corn	C N/A
19	Victory [153]	brg	126 t.	Retaliation*	Lisbon	Boston	salt	R (lic) £1
20	Apollo [142]	slp	54 t.	Sir John Sherbrooke*	NC	Boston	corn	C N/A
23	Mary [140]	schnr	97 t.	Sir John Sherbrooke*	New Haven CONN	Bath	corn, "cidder", "cheas"	C N/A
26	Volant* [157]	shp	457 t.	HMS Curlew, La Hogue, Valiant	Bayonne	Boston	brandy, dry goods, muskets	C N/A

1813 Date	Prize	Ship Type	Tons	Captor(s)	From	To	Cargo	Judgement & Costs
3	Dolphin	schnr		RD	Baltimore			C N/A
4	Defiance [172]	slp	104 t.	Liverpool Packet*	Wiscasset	NY	wood, spars, booms, poles	C N/A
4	Lydia [162]	schnr	113 t.	Liverpool Packet*	Warren MA	Havana	lumber	C N/A
4	Cossac* [182]	schnr	48 t.	HMS Emulous	Salem	Bay of Fundy on a cruise		JC [NB] £17 custody
4	Traveller [228]	slp	95 t.	HMS Rattler	Sedgewick	Salem	cordwood	C [NB] £89
5	John [168]	brg	131 t.	Liverpool Packet*	NY	Portland	flour	C N/A
5	Favorite [173]	schnr	68 t.	HMS Valiant	Plymouth	Eastport	corn, pease, lard, ham, tar, flax seed	C N/A
7	Belfast [169]	schnr	125 t.	Retaliation*	Boston	Penobscot	ballast	C N/A
8	Specie [174]	schnr	94 t.	HMS Nymph	Alexandria	Boston	flour	C [Appeal] N/A
9	Frederick Augustus [170]	shp	328 t.	Sir John Sherbrooke*	Cadiz	Newport	salt	R (lic) N/A
10	Packet [177]	slp	57 t.	HMS Valiant	Savannah	Providence	cotton, hides, old copper	C N/A
11	Expedition [185]	schnr	125 t.	HMS Rattler	Boston	Eastport	flour, rye, meal, rice, beef, tea, apples, wine cider, shoes	ship & part cargo C (lic) [Appeal Retraxit] [NB] N/A
12	Jennet [176]	brg	122 t.	HMS Junon, Statira, Belvidera, Maidstone, Laurestinus	Eastport	Chesapeake R.	lumber, beef, bread, soap, candles, herring, butter	C N/A
12	Flight [310]	schnr		HMS Spartan & Chesapeake Squadron	Bordeaux	Baltimore	bread, gloves, china, oil brandy, wine	Cargo C [schnr wrecked] £219
12	Caroline [171]	brg	195 t	HMS La Hogue	Wilmington DEL	Boston	tar, turpentine pitch, rosin	C [Appeal] N/A
15	Consolation [178]	slp	65 t.	Liverpool Packet*	NY	Nantucket	flour, gin, tobacco, salt	C N/A
16	Dispatch [175]	brg	168 t.	HMS La Hogue	Boston	Cadiz	flour, corn	R (lic) N/A
16	Plough Boy [180]	schnr	116 t.	HMS Orpheus	Charleston	Providence	cotton	C N/A

1813 Date	Prize	Ship Type	Tons	Captor(s)	From	To	Cargo	Judgement & Costs
16	Sally [193]	shp	194 t.	HMS La Hogue, Curlew, Nymph	Wiscasset	St. Bartholomew	lumber	R (lic) N/A
16	Portland Packet [190]	schnr	64 t.	Retaliation*	Newbern	Boston	tar, turpentine	C N/A
18	Patty [189]	schnr	76 t.	Retaliation*	Portland	Long Island	lumber	C N/A
18	Carline [194]	schnr	25 t.	Sir John Sherbrooke*	North Carolina	Manchester MA	corn, beans	C N/A
18	Bird [181]	schnr	80 t.	HMS Emulous	Frenchman's Bay	Spanish Main	staves, shingles	C [Appeal] [NB] £102
19	Richmond [191]	brg	150 t.	Retaliation*	NY	Saint John NB	flour	R (lic) N/A
19	Lark [229]	slp	70 t.	HMS Bream	Portsmouth MA	Penobscot	corn, wool, molasses, wheel-barrows	C [NB] £82
20	Paulina [188]	schnr	109 t.	Sir John Sherbrooke*	Norfolk Va	NY	coal, flour, tobacco	C N/A
20	Vivid* [179]	brg	186 t.	HMS Nymph	Boston	San Domingo	soap, candles, fish, swine, paper, calcutta goods	C N/A
20	Ulysses [195]	brg	156 t.	HMS Orpheus	St. Iago de Cuba	Newport RI	molasses, sugar	C N/A
20	Susannah [226]	slp	89 t.	HMS Bream	Deer Island	Boston	cordwood	C [NB] £77
23	Sibae [211]	brg	116 t.	Crown* (joint claim by HMS Atalante)	Savannah	Boston	cotton	C £235
23	Semiramis [224]	slp	85 t.	HMS Bream	Pleasant River	Boston	timber, cordwood	C [NB] £77
23	Racer [238] (lett of mque) (became HMS Shelburne)	schnr	230 t.	HMS Victorious, San Domingo, Rattler	Raphahanoc	Bordeaux	coffee, sugar, cotton	C £148
24	Sally [202]	brg	143 t.	HMS Curlew	Portland	St. Margaret's, Guadaloupe	lumber	R (lic) £81
25	Richmond [217]	schnr	94 t.	Retaliation*	Cuba	Rhode Island	molasses, coffee	C £107
26	Branch [223]	schnr	79 t.	HMS Bream	Boston	Deer Island	in ballast	C [NB] £73
28	Henry [198]	shp	192 t.	HMS La Hogue	Liverpool GB	Boston	salt, woolens, earthenware, glassware	R (lic) N/A

1813 Date	Prize	Ship Type	Tons	Captor(s)	From	To	Cargo	Judgement & Costs
28	Aeolus [197] (Recap)	brg	244 t.	HMS La Hogue (Alexander* of Boston)	Liverpool GB	Boston	salt, woolens, earthenware	R (Salvage) £615 slvg
30	Hector [203]	brg	156 t.	HMS Spartan	Havana	Newport RI	coffee, sugar, molasses	Cargo C Vessel R [Appeal] £230
May 1	Juana [208]	slp	54 Sp. t.	HMS Spartan, Martin	Havana	Newport RI	coffee, raisins, "campeachy wood	R £99
2	Susannah & Lucy [216]	schnr	117 t.	Liverpool Packet*	N. Yarmouth	Portsmouth NH	cordwood	C £94
2	Catherine [199] (Recap)	brg	132 t.	HMS La Hogue (Montgomery* of Salem)	St. Barthol-omew	London	rum	R (Salvage) £447 slvg
3	George Washington [215]	schnr	105 t.	Retaliation*	Bermuda	New Haven	ballast	R (lic) no fees
5	Montgomery* [204]	brg	160 t.	HMS Nymph, Shannon, Tenedos, Emulous	Salem	on a cruise		C £95
5	Ann [207] (Recap)	schnr	143 t.	HMS Nymph, Shannon, Tnedos, Emulous (Alexandra* of Salem)	New Orleans	Bordeaux	cotton, lead, skins	C £115
9	Young Phoenix [209] (Recap)	shp	200 t.	HMS Orpheus	Jersey	Arichat, Cape Breton	biscuits, shoes, boots, dry goods	R (Salvage) £107 + £397 slvg
10	Diomede [206]	brg	223 t.	HMS Nymph, La Hogue	Manilla	Salem	indigo, sugar, redwood, tea	C £178
10	Emperor [210] (Recap)	schnr	89 t.	HMS Ramilies, Orpheus (Holkar*)	North Carolina	Boston	Indian corn	C £92
10	Juliet [222]	slp	92 t.	HMS Paz	Matanzas, Cuba	Newport	molasses	C £80
10	Columbia [227] (Recap)	schnr	89 t.	HMS Rattler (Fame*)	Penobscot	Martinique	lumber, potatoes	C [NB] £89
11	Juliana Smith* [205] (became NS privateer Broke*)	schnr	37 t.	HMS Nymph	Boston	on a cruise		C £62
13	Sally [225]	schnr	85 t.	HMS Bream	Eastport	Boston	salt, fish	C £82

1813 Date	Prize	Ship Type	Tons	Captor(s)	From	To	Cargo	Judgement & Costs
15	Columbia [212]	brg	98 t.	Sir John Sherbrooke*	Savannah	Boston	cotton, reeds	C £92
16	Orion [232]	brg	196 t.	HMS La Hogue	NY	Lisbon	flour, Indian meal	R (lic) £224
18	Duck [214] (Recap)	shp	190 t.	HMS Bold (Governor Plumer*)	Cork	St. Lawrence, Nfld	provisions	R (Salvage) £62 + £944 slvg
18	Pilgrim [235]	brg	269 t.	HMS La Hogue	New Orleans	Cadiz	flour	C [R Appeal] £299
19	Alexander* [240]	shp	308 t.	HMS Rattler, Bream	Salem	on a cruise		C [NB] £100
19	Dolphin [231]	brg	217 t.	HMS La Hogue	NY	Oporto	pork, beef, flour, candles, staves, cider	R £136
19	Paragon [213] (Recap)	brg	157 t.	Sir John Sherbrooke* (American* of Salem)	Aberdeen	Saint John NB	ballast	R (Salvage) £59 + £233 slvg
19	General Hodgson [219] (Recap)	slp	61 t.	Sir John Sherbrooke* (Alexander")	Halifax	Martinique	fish, dry goods	R (Salvage) £49 + £138 slvg
19	San Gabriel [220] (Recap)	brg	110 Sp. t.	Sir John Sherbrooke* (Alexander*)	Havana	NY	molasses, sugar, coffee, hides	R (Salvage) £182
19	Fidelia [221]	shp	243 t.	HMS Orpheus, Ramilies	NY	Cadiz	flour, wheat, corn	R (lic) £215
20	Finland [276]	shp	240 t.	HMS Chesapeake squadron	Alexandria	Halifax	flour	R (lic) £197
20	Volador [263]	brg	217 t.	HMS Statira, Spartan, Martin	Philadelphia	Havana	silks, glass	C [R Appeal] £267
21	Enterprize* [218]	schnr	225 t.	HMS Tenedos, Curlew	Salem	on a cruise		C £81
24	Post Boy [239]	schnr	155 t.	HMS Rattler, Shannon, Tenedos	Salem	San Domingo	fish, bacon, brandy	C [NB] £142
26	Paragon [234] (Recap)	shp		HMS Tenedos (Grand Trunk* of Salem)	London	Buenos Ayres	dry goods	R (Salvage) £336 + £3,236 slvg
26	Lucy [237] (Recap)	brg		HMS Shannon (America*)	Halifax	Liverpool GB	cotton, wool, lumber	R (Salvage) £91 + £1,141 slvg
27	Governor Plumer* [233] (became NS privateer Lunenburg*)	schnr	91 t.	Sir John Sherbrooke*	Portsmouth NH	on a cruise		C £62
28	Harriet [416]	brg		HMS Victorious & blockading squadron			flour, corn	Cargo C [vessel burnt] £62

1813 Date	Prize	Ship Type	Tons	Captor(s)	From	To	Cargo	Judgement & Costs
28	Nancy [417]	schnr		HMS Victorious & blockading squadron			flour, corn,	Cargo C [vessel burnt] £62
30	Plough Boy [324]	slp		HMS Statira, Spartan, Martin	Delaware	Philadelphi	dye, tobacco cordwood	Cargo C [vessel ransomed for $1000] £59
30	Commerce [262]	brg	186 t.	HMS Spartan, Statira, Martin	Philadelphia	Gottenburg	cotton	C [Appeal] £278
31	William [243] (Recap)	brg		HMS Shannon (Yankee*)		Halifax	Jamaica	fish, lumberR (Salvage) £52 + £173 slvg
June 1	USS Chesapeake [241] (became HMS Chesapeake)	US frigate	1100 t.	HMS Shannon	Boston	on a cruise		C £132
1	Fanny [313]	brg		HMS Statira, Spartan, Martin	Madeira	Philadelphia	in ballast	C [$2,000 ransom] £69
1	Joanna [242]	schnr	48 t.	Dart*	Boston	Eastport	corn	C [NB] (lic) £73
2	Flor de Lisboa [258]	brg	110 Sp. t.	HMS Spartan, Statira, Martin	Porto Rico	Philadelphia	sugar, rice	C [R Appeal] £178
2	Carlotta [259]	brgtine	120 Sp. t.	HMS Spartan, Statira, Martin	Porto Rico	Philadelphia	rice, coffee, mahogany	C [Cargo R Appeal] £242
5	Washington [244]	schnr	66 t.	Dart*	Portland	Boston	lumber	C [NB] £51
6	Cuba [245]	shp	176 t.	Dart*	New Haven	Portland	flour	C [NB] (lic) £191
6	Betsey [253]	slp	93 t.	Retrieve*	Boston	Waldoborough	in ballast	C £40
8	Belle [257]	schnr	105 t.	HMS Spartan, Statira, Martin	Madeira	Egg Harbour	in ballast	C [Appeal deserted] £204
8	Hetty [261]	brg	158 t.	HMS Statira, Spartan, Martin	Madeira	Philadelphia	in ballast	C [Appeal] £115
11	Nymph [251]	schnr	20 t.	Matilda*	Boston	Machias	rye flour, corn, dall	R (lic) £41
12	Hero [264] (Recap)	brg	165 t.	HMS Martin, Spartan, Statira (Globe*)	Limerick	Lisbon	corn, provisions, army clothing	R (Salvage) £588
13	Morning Star [272]	slp		HMS Spartan Statira, Martin	Elizabeth Town	Egg Harbour	Indian corn	C [master abandoned] £80

1813 Date	Prize	Ship Type	Tons	Captor(s)	From	To	Cargo	Judgement & Costs
14	Del Carmen [260]	schnr	95 t.	HMS Spartan, Statira, Martin	NY	Havana	flour, corn, soap	R £213
14	Star [280]	shp	409 t.	HMS Victorious, Chesapeake Squadron	Alexandria	Lisbon	flour	C [R Appeal] £921
15	Lark [247] (Recap)	schnr	113 t.	HMS Borer (Teazer*)	Shelburne NS	Nfld.	lumber	R (Salvage) £39 + £64 slvg
16	Christiana [246] (Recap)	brg	129 t.	HMS Borer, Wasp (Retrieve* prize, re-captured by Teazer", retaken by RN)	Bath	Bermuda	boards, hoops, shingles	R (lic) £228
16	Roscio [311]	brg	180 t.	HMS Dover	Lisbon	Halifax	salt	Wrecked £118
16	Loyal Sam [250] (Recap)	shp	260 t.	Sir John Sherbrooke*, Matilda* (Gyro* of Baltimore)	New Providence	Glasgow	cotton, coffee, hides, specie	R (Salvage) £1,662
17	Porcupine* [248]	brg	330 t.	HMS Valiant, Acasta, Wasp	Bayonne	Boston	claret, brandy, silk, verdigris, hardware	C £183
18	Eunice [249]	schnr	139 t.	HMS Wasp	St. Ubes	Boston	salt	Ship R Cargo C [Appeal] £149
18	Protectress [277]	shp	292 t.	HMS Victorious & blockading squadron	Norfolk VA	Lisbon	flour	C [R Appeal] £906
19	Henry [252]	schnr	89 t.	Matilda*	Eastport	Boston	boards	C £51
19	Packet [268] (Recap)	shp	50 t.	Matilda* (Fly*)			cordwood, dry fish	C £40
22	Gustava [255]	brg	124 t.	HMS Sylph	Boston	Madeira	beef, pork, butter, gin, tar, pitch, staves	C [Appeal retraxit] £3,122
22	Thomas [254]	brg		HMS Wasp	Lisbon	Plymouth	ballast	R (lic) £52
24	North Star [256]	brg		HMS Tenedos	San Salvador	Boston	sugar, tea, hides, dry goods	C £154
24	Carl Gustaf [306]	shp	375 t.	HMS Martin, Statira	NY	Beaufort NC	ballast	R £320

1813 Date	Prize	Ship Type	Tons	Captor(s)	From	To	Cargo	Judgement & Costs
24	Herman [279] (formerly British ship Jamaica)	shp	413 t.	HMS Atalante & Chesapeake blockading squadron	Baltimore	Lisbon	flour	R (Salvage) [Appeal] £1,213
24	Maria [289]	brg	110 Swed	HMS Bold	Stockholm	Boston	iron, steel	C [NB] [R Appeal 1816] £430
24	Experiment [270]	slp	44 t.	Dart*	Boston	Bath	rum, gin, sugar, tobacco, coffee	C [NB] £51
26	Union [271]	shp	230 t.	Dart*	Cadiz	Boston	tin, salt, fruit	R [NB] £44
26	Carnarvon [267] [Santiago]	brg	265 t.	HMS Woolwich	Salem	Malaga	lumber, provisions	R £598
27	Young Teazer* [265]	schnr		HMS La Hogue	Portsmouth NH	on a cruise		[blown up in Mahone Bay] £58
27	Little Bill [278]	schnr	123 t.	HMS Loup Cervier	St. Bartholomew	Elizabeth City NC	sugar	R £273
27	Rebecca [290]	schnr	86 t.	HMS Boxer	NY	Cadiz	flour	C [NB] [Appeal] £354
28	Nancy [291]	schnr	15 t.	HMS Boxer	Little River ME		rum, brandy, "cyder"	C [NB] £85
28	Harriet [275] (Recap)	schnr	72 t.	HMS Dover (Fox*)	St. John's, Nfld	London	oil, seal skins	R Cargo £67+ £245 slvg
30	Minerva [269]	brg	180 t.	HMS La Hogue	Boston	Lisbon	beef, pork, staves	R £97
30	Thomas* [273] (became NS privateer Wolverine*)	schnr	122 t.	HMS Nymph	Portsmouth NH	on a cruise		C £80
30	Liverpool Packet [274]	shp	396 t.	HMS Dover	Lisbon	Boston	salt, fruit, dry goods	R £84
30	Ulysses* [314]	brg	249 t.	HMS Majestic, Ring Dove	Savannah	Bordeaux	cotton	C [Appeal] £147
July 3	Franklin [294]	schnr	91 t.	Weazle*	George's R.	Portland	lumber	C £65
4	Mary [281]	slp	44 t.	Retaliation*	Boston	Kennebunk	rum, molasses, vinegar, cider, nails	C £107
6	Valeria [283]	schnr	96 t.	Retrieve*	Bath	Providence RI	lumber, bark	C £46

1813 Date	Prize	Ship Type	Tons	Captor(s)	From	To	Cargo	Judgement & Costs
6	Calson [293]	schnr	108 t.	Weazle*	Kennebunk	St. Bartholomew	lumber	C £65
6	Two Brothers [343]	schnr	90 t.	HMS Boxer	Tannfield CONN	Eastport	flour, corn	R [NB] £80
7	Swift [285]	schnr	63 t.	HMS Curlew	Cape Cod	Ipswich	salt	C N/A
7	Two Brothers [286]	schnr	83 t.	HMS Curlew	Kennebunk	Ispwich	cordwood, bark	C £64+£186slvg
7	Ellen [288]	brg	186 Swed. lasts	HMS La Hogue	St. Bartholomew	Portland	molasses	R £117
7	Prudentia [292]	shp	190 t.	HMS Rattler	Ocracoke NC	Cadiz	flour, tobacco	R [NB] £109
7	Eunice [296]	slp	46 t.	HMS Curlew	Kennebunk	Ispwich	cordwood, bark	C £58
7	Friendship [345]	slp	101 t.	HMS Boxer	Block Island	Eastport	flour	C [NB] £99
7	Rose in Bloom [307]	slp	58 t.	Retaliation*	Scarborough	RI	board, shingles	C £68
7	Leonidas [295]	slp	76 t.	Weazel*	Frenchman's Bay	Boston	lumber	C £65
8	Fanny [284]	brg	146 t.	HMS La Hogue, Curlew	New Haven	Halifax	flour	C [Appeal] £174
8	Sea Flower [282] (Recap)	brg		HMS Fantome	Nfld	Barbados	codfish, salmon	R (Salvage) £65+ £156 slvg
8	Pilgrim [320]	schnr	22 t.	Matilda*	Portland	Eastport	in ballast	C £38
9	Priscilla [287]	schnr	60 t.	HMS Curlew	Chatham	Boston	fishing	C £58
9	Wasp [308]	schnr	99 t.	Retaliation*	Kennebunk	Falmouth	boards, shingles	C £80
10	Roxanna [333]	shp	330 t.	HMS La Hogue	Cadiz	Boston	block tin, fruit, cambric	R (lic) £60
10	Hannah [303]	shp	71 t.	Retrieve*	Frenchman's Bay	Nantucket	lumber	C £40
11	Republican* [299]	shp	280 t.	HMS Nimrod, Maidstone	NY	Santo Domingo	provisions, tobacco, fish lumber	C [Appeal] £428
11	John Adams [317]	brg	224 t.	HMS Rattler, Retrieve*	Portland MA	St. Bartholomew	lumber	R [NB] (lic) £74
11	Mentor [335]	slp	57 t.	HMS La Hogue	Provincetown	New Bedford	lumber	C £66
11	Jerusha [336]	slp	64 t.	HMS La Hogue	Provincetown		lumber	C £67
11	Friendship [402]	slp		HMS La Hogue		Provincetown	lumber	C £68
12	Ohio [297]	brg	191 t.	HMS Manly	Lisbon	New Haven	salt	R (lic) £128
12	Jefferson [318]	schnr	99 t.	HMS Bream	Boston	Prospect MA	in ballast	C £12
12	Sally [309]	schnr	34 t.	Retaliation*	Saco	Nantucket	lumber	C £75

1813 Date	Prize	Ship Type	Tons	Captor(s)	From	To	Cargo	Judgement & Costs
13	Harriett [321]	slp	38 t.	Matilda*	Penobscot	Portland	pickled fish	C £44
13	Friendship [322]	schnr	98 t.	Matilda*	Union R. ME	Beverly MA	cordwood, bark, shingles	C £44
13	Anna [298]	brgtne	113 Sp. t.	HMS Poictiers, Nimrod, Maidstone	New Haven	Laguiera	flour, gin, soap, butter, lard, beef	C [Appeal] £579
14	Betsey [316]	schnr	117 t.	HMS Bream, Rattler	Tortola	Cape Anne	rum	R [NB] (lic) £74
14	Triton [319]	schnr	122 t.	HMS Bream, Rattler	St. Thomas	Kennbunk	rum, molasses	R [NB] (lic) £71
14	Malaren [334]	brg	149 t.	HMS La Hogue	Plymouth NH	Antigua	staves, hoops, lumber	C £373
16	Venus [323]	schnr	72 t.	Matilda*	Rhode Island	Frenchman's Bay	pork, corn	C £44
17	York Town* [301]	shp	33 t.	HMS Maidstone, Poictiers, Nimrod	NY	on a cruise	captured cargo (Salvage) £89	Ship C Cargo R
18	Hope for Peace [315]	shallop	12 t.	Queen's City Militia		to Liverpool for licence but landed by mistake at Port Mouton NS		C £46
18	Lavinia [300] (Recap)	shp	212 t.	HMS Recruit (York Town*)	St. John's Nfld	Oporto	dry fish	R (Salvage) £164 + £736 slvg
18	Manchester [302] (Recap)	brg		HMS Maidstone, Poictiers, Nimrod (York Town*)	Falmouth		mail packet	R £61 + £213 slvg
20	Lively [305] (Recap)	schnr		HMS L'Epervier (Polly* of Salem)	St. Thomas	Halifax	oats, stone	R (Salvage) £23 + £55 slvg
22	Isabella [304]	brg	151 t.	HMS Pictou	Algeciras	Boston	wine, silk, oil	R £287
22	+Fanny [313]	brg		HMS Statira	Morris R.	Philadelphia		N/A
23	Randolph [331]	slp	33 t.	Fly*	Boston	Eastport	flour, pork, naval stores	C [Appeal] £101
24	Lively [341]	schnr	23 t.	Fly*	Boston	Penobscot	iron, turpentine, coffee, rum, gin, indigo	C £60
25	Fair Play [365]	slp		HMS Boxer	at anchor		lumber	C [NB] £71 slvg
25	Providence [312] (Recap)	schnr		HMS Nymph (Polly*)	St. Peter's NB	Halifax	fish	R £65 + £147

1813 Date	Prize	Ship Type	Tons	Captor(s)	From	To	Cargo	Judgement & Costs
27	Rebecca [347]	schnr	64 t.	Fly*	Penobscot	Marblehead	cordwood	C £67
28	Stamper [325] (Recap)	brg	191 t.	HMS Ring Dove (Polly*)	Poole GB	Halifax	salt	R (Salvage) £73 + £305
28	Polly [346]	slp	92 t.	Fly*	Boston	Friendship	corn, chairs	C £67
28	Friendship [348]	schnr	74 t.	Fly*	Provincetown	Penobscot	ballast	C £67
29	Mequait [361]	shp	76 t.	Dart*	Bath		corn, rye, fish	C [NB] £44
29	Dolphin [362]	schnr	67 t.	Dart*	Portland	Boston	cordwood	C [NB] £44
29	Mary [326] (Recap)	slp		HMS Nimrod (Polly*)	Newfoundland	Halifax	pickled & dry fish	R (Salvage) £49 +£90 slvg
31	Flor de Tejo [327]	brg	164 t.	HMS Manly	Lisbon	Boston	fruit, whalebone, bomb shells, wine, salt, verdigris	R £217 [14 casks wine condemned]
31	Porpoise [364]	schnr	32 t.	HMS Rattler	Cohasset	fishing	stores	C [NB] £74
31	William & Ann [329] (Recap)	slp	77 t.	HMS Nimrod (Fox*)	Scotland	Ireland	coal, blown glass	R (Salvage) £71 + £82 slvg
31	May Flower [339]	slp	19 t.	Matilda*	NY	Boston	flour, corn	C £47
July no date	Anaconda* [385]	brg		HMS Sceptre & squadron		Ocracoke SC		C £100
Aug 2	Hope [328] (Recap)	shp	300 t.	HMS Manly (Fox*)	Batavia	Providence RI	camphor, sugar, coffee, nutmeg, "dragons blood"	C £74
3	Luisa [340]	schnr	84 Sp.t	HMS Martin	Laguira, Venezuela	Providence RI	skins, indigo, coffee	Ship R Cargo C [Appeal] £539
3	Hannah [366]	schnr	47 t.	HMS Boxer	Boston	Thomas Town, MA	corn	C [NB] £75
3	Rebecca [367]	schnr	117 t.	HMS Boxer	Townshend MA	Boston	cordwood, bark	C [NB] £84
4	Four Brothers [330] (Recap)	schnr	40 t.	HMS Emulous (Polly*)	Arichat		rum	R (Salvage) £66 slvg
4	Freeport [379]	slp	58 t.	Broke*	Cohassit	Lynn	shingles, boards	C £58
4	Caravan [332]	brg	174 t.	Retrieve*	Antigua	Penobscot	molasses, rum	R (lic) £42
5	Amelia [338]	slp	79 t.	Matilda*	New Haven	NB	flour, corn	R £41
5	Minerva [351]	slp	43 t.	Matilda*	NY	Newport	flour, pork, snuff	C £67

1813 Date	Prize	Ship Type	Tons	Captor(s)	From	To	Cargo	Judgement & Costs
7	William [350]	slp	40 t.	Matilda*	Barnstable	fishing	cod	C £44
7	Mary [378] (ex Lilly of St. John, NB)	schnr	93 t.	Broke*	Boston	Portland	wool, liquors, wheat, Indian corn	C £62
7	Three Brothers [363]	schnr	94 t.	Dart*	Cape Ann	Portland	ballast	C [NB] £44
7	Lydia [352]	schnr	74 t.	Matilda*	Harwich	fishing	cod, oil	C £51
7	Alligator [349]	slp	28 t.	Matilda*	Sandwich MA	fishing	cod, stores	C £44
8	Wasp* [344]	slp	40 t.	HMS Bream	Salem	on a cruise		C [NB] £96
9	Dart [356]	schnr	14 t	Broke*	Boston	Portland	flour, rye, coffee	C £68
12	Don Carlos [337]	schnr	118 t.	Weazle*	Boston	Halifax	flour, beef, vinegar, shooks	R (lic) N/A
12	Gannet [358]	schnr	36 t.	HMS Curlew, Nymph	Hingham	Boston	fish	C £65
13	Paragon* [360]	schnr	167 t.	HMS Curlew, Nymph	Charleston SC	Boston	cotton, rice	C £117
13	Polly [342] (Recap)	schnr		HMS Statira (unknown*)	Halifax	St. Croix	fish, tar	R (Salvage) £49+ £75 slvg
16	Flor del Mar [353]	shp	311 t.	HMS La Hogue	Fayal, Madeira	Boston	wine, redwood	C [Appeal] £801
16	Dolphin [382]	slp	64 t.	Fly*	Portland	Boston	lumber, furniture	C £62
16	Diamond [383]	brg	229 t.	Fly*	Antigua & St. Bartholomew	Portland	molasses	R (lic) N/A
17	Endeavour [359]	slp	104 t.	HMS Curlew, Nymph	Castine	Boston	corn, cordwood	[wrecked] N/A
18	Morning Star [357]	schnr	33 t.	HMS Curlew, Nymph	Chincoteague Island	Eastport	corn	C £93
18	Chance [354] (Recap)	brg		HMS La Hogue, Tenedos* (unknown*)	Workington	Miramichi	ballast	R £37+ £88 slvg
18	King George [355] (Recap)	schnr	204 t.	HMS Recruit (Sunderland*)	Liverpool GB	Pillau	salt	R (Salvage) £22+ £250 slvg
20	Samuel [376]	schnr	71 t.	Broke*	Penobscot	Marblehead	firewood	C £58
20	John & Merriam [375]	schnr	77 t.	Broke*	Buckstown	Marblehead	firewood	C N/A
20	Industry [377]	schnr	26 t.	Broke*	Belfast MA	Boston	shingles, planks	C £58
24	Espozy y Mina [372]	schnr	45 t.	HMS Statira	Laguira	NY	indigo, hides	C [Appeal] £243

1813 Date	Prize	Ship Type	Tons	Captor(s)	From	To	Cargo	Judgement & Costs
25	Raven [369]	schnr	20 t.	HMS Manly	Newbury Port	Halifax	silks, cotton, grapes	R (lic) £61
25	Elizabeth [374]	slp		Star*	near Moose Island at anchor		ballast	C [NB] £60
26	Elizabeth [371] (Recap)	brg	170 t.	HMS Shelburne (Yankee*)	Brazil	Liverpool GB	cotton	R (Salvage) £139+ £1,425 slvg
27	Euphemia [370]	schnr	90 t.	HMS Majestic	Havana	Boston	copper, logwood	Shp R Cargo C £373
28	Hope [368]	shp	416 t.	HMS Loup Cervier	Lisbon	Newport	salt	R (Salvage) £60
29	Mariner [386] (Recap)	brg	230 t.	HMS Poictiers (Yankee of RI)	Kingston,	Belfast	sugar, rum, cotton, logwood	R (Salvage) £322+ £1,792 slvg
29	Hero [388]	schnr	84 t.	Dart*	Boston	Kennebeck	in ballast	C [NB] £42
30	Minerva [373]	schnr	136 t.	Weazle*	Barbados	Wiscasset MA	ballast, specie ($4,000)	R (lic) £73
31	Fortune [393]	schnr		HMS Boxer	Cohasset	fishing	mackerel, cod	C [NB] £86
31	Camden [389]	schnr	106 t.	Dart*	Boston	Penobscot	ballast	C [NB] £42
31	Divina Pastora [381]	shp	385 Sp.t	HMS Statira	Havana	NY	molasses, sugar, coffee, hides, ivory, dye wood	C [R Appeal] £2,303
Sept 1	Deborah [390]	schnr	49 t.	Dart*	cohassit	Saco	corn, apples, salt	C [NB] £42
2	Jerusalem [380]	shp	750 t.	HMS Majestic	Havana	Boston	copper, hides, sugar, coffee, "segar"	R [copper C] £314
2	Drake [424]	slp	13 t.	HMS Belvidera	Newburyport	NY	resin, turpentine	C £62
3	Watson [387] (Recap)	brg	230 t.	HMS Poictiers (Yankee*)	Brazil	Liverpool GB	cotton	R (lic) [part cargo C] £512 + £2,035 slvg
7	Resolution [413]	slp	58 t.	Star*	Mathias	Wareham	iron ore ballast	C [NB] £63
10	Mary [391]	schnr	37 t.	Wolverine*	Boston	Halifax	bread, flour, tobacco, cigars	1/3 R (lic) £72
11	Torpedo [392]	schnr	50 t.	HMS Plantagenet	New London		cheese, soap, nails, papers	C £93
11	Massachusetts [397]	shp	286 t.	HMS Canso	Lisbon	NY	salt	C [Appeal] £203

1813 Date	Prize	Ship Type	Tons	Captor(s)	From	To	Cargo	Judgement & Costs
11	Ocean [384] (Recap)	brg		HMS Borer (Frolic*)	St. John's, Nfld	Miramichi	in ballast	R (Salvage) £56+ £250 slvg
13	Elvira [404]	slp		HMS Orpheus, Valiant	Hartford		assorted goods	C £81
13	Mary [400] (Recap)	schnr	61 t.	HMS Sylph (originally owned by Americans)	Cape Henry, Haiti	Boston	sugar	2/3 Ship C 1/3 Cargo R £262+ £876 slvg
14	Santa Cecilia [398]	shp	222 t.	HMS Wasp	Lisbon	New Bedford	salt, dry goods	C [Appeal] £436
14	Flower [414]	schnr	26 t.	Star*	Rochester	Manchester	fish	C [NB] £60
15	Sally [406] (Recap)	schnr		Gleaner* (Industry*)	New Edinburgh NS		bricks, lumber, butter	R (Salvage) no fees
16	Catalana Patriota [394]			HMS Shannon				R [Appeal] £699
16	Alianza [395]			HMS Shannon				R [Appeal] £373
17	Queen Charlotte [396] (Recap)	schnr		HMS Shannon (Eldridge Gerry*)	Sydney NS	Nfld	cattle, sheep, butter	R (Salvage) £38+ £55 slvg
18	Little Sisters [401]	schnr	73 t.	HMS Belvidera, Statira	Trinidad, Cuba	Great Egg Harbour	sugar	C £105
19	Gamla Lodelse [403]	brg	190 t.	HMS High Flyer	Gottenburg	RI	iron, steel, glass, alum	R except $500 £221
20	Active [399]	shp		HMS L'Epervier	Gottenburg	Boston	iron	C [Appeal] £319
22	Ambition [411]	slp		HMS Statira	NY	Wilmington	iron mongery, wine, cheese	Cargo C £83
24	Venus [407]	shp	208 t.	HMS Borer	St. Iago de Cuba	Salem	sugar, molasses, coffee, "segars"	C £83+£164 slvg
25	Resolution [410]	shp	215 t.	HMS Majestic	Gottenburg	New Bedford	iron, deals	C [Appeal Retraxit] £600
27	Shannon [408] (Recap)	brg		HMS Manly (USS President)	St. Kitts	London	sugar, rum, molasses	R (Salvage) £267 slvg
29	Margarett [422] (Recap)	slp		HMS Martin (Starts* of Machias)	Saint John NB	West Indies	fish, lumber	R (Salvage) [NB] £30+ £61 slvg
29	San Domingo [421]	shp	97 t.	George*	Providence RI	Havana	sugar, coffee	wreck [surviving cargo C] £35

1813 Date	Prize	Ship Type	Tons	Captor(s)	From	To	Cargo	Judgement & Costs
Sept no date	Montezuma [420]	shp	320 t.	HMS La Hogue, Tenedos	Boston	Cadiz	candles, staves, cod, chairs, tar, turpentine, beef, tobacco, cloves	[C Appeal] £425
no date	Edward [409] (Recap)	brg		HMS Fantome (Whig*)			no cargo	R (Salvage) £55+£247 slvg
Oct 4	Charles [432]	shp	95 t.	HMS Paz	Elizabeth City	Ocracoke	flour	C £163
5	Medel Padria [423]	brg	103 t.	HMS Conflict, Paz	Ocracoke	Halifax	flour	R (lic) £149
5	Portsmouth Packet* [412]	schnr		HMS Fantome			cruizing	N/A
11	Charlotte [419]	shp	208 t.	HMS Comet	Carlskrona, Sweden	Newport	iron, steel, glass, linen	R £773
11	Richard de Stanley [405]	schnr	115 t.	HMS Paz		Boston	tar, pitch, turpentine, flour	[Appeal] N/A
11	Atlantic [415] (Recap)	brg	174 t.	HMS Maidstone, Poictiers (Argus*)	Trinidad	Cork	sugar, cotton	R (Salvage) £126+£875 slvg
13	Swallow [445]	schnr	24 t.	Shannon*	Bath	New Haven	dried fish	C £73
14	Randolph [439]	schnr	26 t.	HMS Paz	Newbern NC	NY	turpentine, paint, varnish, rosin, old copper	C £63
16	Baltic [418]	shp	261 t.	HMS La Hogue	St. Ubes	Boston	salt	R £78
16	Sally [425]	schnr	90 t.	HMS Loire, Ramilies	Georgetown SC	Halifax	corn, rice	C£111
19	Alert [431]	slp		HMS Borer	Nantucket	Falmouth	pitch, molasses	C £64
20	Ann [429]	brg	120 t.	Retrieve *	Cape Ann	St. Bartholomew	corn, bread, onions, potatoes	Part Cargo C [R Appeal] £349
20	Dispatch [430] (Recap)	brg		HMS Albion (Yankee*)	Liverpool GB	Quebec	rum, salt, coal	R (Salvage) £448+£1,331 slvg
21	Betsey & Jane [428]	schnr	76 t.	HMS Majestic	Kennebunk	Providence	lumber, butter	C £75

1813 Date	Prize	Ship Type	Tons	Captor(s)	From	To	Cargo	Judgement & Costs
25	Hoppett [426]	brg	150 t.	HMS Emulous	Gottenburg	Boston	iron, alum, glass, bale goods	R £368
25	Telemachus [427] (Recap)	brg	163 t.	HMS Narcissus (Yankee*)	Poole GB	Nfld	coal, salt	R (Salvage) £92+£473 slvg
27	William [433]	schnr		HMS Paz	NY	Charleston	provisions, rum, gin	C £84
28	Paris [434] (Recap)	bark		HMS Ring Dove (Yankee*)	Liverpool NS	Miramichi	in ballast	R (Salvage) £214+£156slvg
29	John & Mary [437] (Recap)	brg		HMS Loup Cervier (Yankee*)	Poole	Little Placentia Nfld	dry goods	R (Salvage) £524+£188
Nov 3	Industry* [435]	schnr	50 t.	HMS Arab	Marblehead	on a cruise		C £28
3	Peggy [436]	slp	91 t.	HMS L'Epervier, Fantome	St. George R.	Boston	timber, wood	C £30
4	Ann [438] (Recap)	brg		HMS Jaseur (Yankee*)	Liverpool GB	St. John's Nfld	salt, provisions	R (Salvage) £322+£764slvg
6	Rover [446]	schnr	42 t.	Shannon*	Penobscot	Chatham	lumber	C £71
7	Judith [444]	schnr	86 t.	Shannon*	Belfast	Boston	cordwood	C £69
8	Thorn [447]	schnr	101 t.	Shannon*	Kennebunk	Marblehead	cordwood	C £96
11	Huntress [442]	slp	99 t.	HMS Boxer, Valiant	NY	Newport RI	flour, rye, butter, paper, iron, stoves, dry goods	C £107
13	Financier [443]	schnr	57 t.	Shannon*	Kennebunk	Boston	cordwood	C £71
14	Husaren [440]	brg	57 Sw. lasts	HMS Jaseur, Narcissus	St. Bartholomew	New Haven	molasses, sugar	R £134
14	Hero [441]	schnr	90 t.	HMS Belvidera	Fairhaven	Savannah	in ballast	C £68
23	Franklin [448]	slp	80 t.	HMS Belvidera	Georgetown	NY	rice, cotton	C £86
24	Venus [449] (Recap)	schnr	100 t.	HMS Rifleman nearly wrecked when towed in	St. Bartholomew	Boston	rum, sugar, molasses	R (Salvage) £131+£138slvg

1813 Date	Prize	Ship Type	Tons	Captor(s)	From	To	Cargo	Judgement & Costs
27	Dove [485]	schnr	34 t.	HMS Martin	Newburyport MA	Eastport MA	cider	C [NB] no fees
Dec 1	General Marion [450]	schnr	241 t.	HMS Ramilies, Loire, Endymion	New Bedford	Charleston	salt, oil, nails	C £95
1	Rising Sun [469]	slp	34 t.	HMS Loire, Ramilies, Endymion	VA	Nantucket	corn, sweet potatoes	C £35
2	Chili [452]	shp	564 t.	HMS Nimrod	Nantucket	on whaling voyage		C £252
3	Manhattan [453]	slp	71 t.	HMS Nimrod	NY	Newport RI	flour, merchandise	Cargo C £116
4	Gardner [455]	shp	301 t.	HMS Loire, Ramilies	Nantucket	on whaling voyage		C £168
4	Catharine [470]	slp	38 t.	HMS Majestic, Junon	Bath		glass, linens, earthware cop-peras, "spelter"	cargo C [ship wrecked] £69
4	Policy [456] (Recap)	shp	276 t.	HMS Loire, Ramilies (USS Essex)	London	on whaling voyage		R (Salvage) £1,435 + £1,044 slvg
6	Jane [451]	slp	76 t.	HMS Junon, Majestic	Bath	Boston	cordwood, bark	C £66
8	West Indian [454]	schnr	96 t.	HMS Loire, Ramilies	Providence RI	Charleston SC	potatoes, apples, beets, onions, chocks, nails	C £76
8	Julian [471]	schnr	94 t.	HMS Martin	Boston	Machias	wood, assorted articles	C [NB] £36
8	Enterprise [457]	schnr	40 t.	Wolverine*	Boston	Philadelphia	salt	C £86
10	Betsy [464]	slp	98 t.	Wolverine*	Waldoborough	Boston	cordwood	C £65
10	Charles [461]	slp	75 t.	Wolverine*	Kennebunk	Boston	lumber	C £66
10	Laura Jane [460]	schnr	73 t.	Wolverine*	Scarborough	Boston	board, shingles	C £66
10	Jane [459]	schnr		Wolverine*	Cape Ann	Boston	cordwood	C £60
10	Polly [465]	schnr	89 t.	Wolverine*	Penobscot	Boston	lumber, fish	C £73
10	Rolla* [462] (became NS privateer Rolla*)	schnr	117 t.	HMS Loire, Ramilies	Baltimore	on a cruise		C £88
10	Trent [458]	schnr	70 t.	Wolverine*	British	Boston	cordwood	C £66
11	Erie [576] (became HMS tender)	schnr	76 t.	HMS Sophie	Havannah	Baltimore	sugar, coffee	C N/A

1813 Date	Prize	Ship Type	Tons	Captor(s)	From	To	Cargo	Judgement & Costs
13	Emeline [467]	slp	44 t.	HMS Boxer, Statira, Valiant, Loup Cervier	NY	Providence RI	flour	C £99
16	Enterprize [463]	schnr	119 t.	Shannon*	Boston	Bath	ballast	C £84
17	Rubicon [468]	schnr	98 t.	Shannon*	Boston	Belfast	ballast	C £89
17	Calmar [473]	slp		HMS Curlew				[Appeal C]
	(ex Rising States)							N/A
18	Nancy Sanders [472]	slp	49 t.	L'pool Packet*	RI	NY	barley, cheese	C £77
19	Patriot [474]	slp	49 t.	L'pool Packet*	NY	RI	flour, candles	C £81
22	Mary Ann [466]	slp	49 t.	L'pool Packet*	NY	RI	flour	C £16

1814 Date	Prize	Ship Type	Tons	Captor(s)	From	To	Cargo	Judgement & Costs
Jan 6	Mary [475]	slp	89 t.	Wolverine*	Penobscot	Boston	cordwood	C £42
6	Aurora [476]	schnr		Wolverine*	Mount Desert ME	Boston	cordwood	R £42
6	Victory [477]	schnr	52 t.	Wolverine*	Penobscot	Boston	planks, joist timer, rum	C £42
6	Ten Brothers [478]	schnr	105 t.	Wolverine*	Townshend	Salem	lumber	C £42
13	Hero [481]	slp	71 t.	Hare*	Penobscot	Portsmouth	cordwood	C [NB] £51
15	Recovery [484]	brg	190 t.	Hare*	Bermuda	Castine	ballast, specie taken off	C £55
21	Falun [479]	schnr	123 t.	Liverpool Packet*, Retaliation*	Halifax	Gardner's Bay	dry goods	R (lic) £256
22	Gustava [480] (ex General Hunter)	schnr	89 t.	Liverpool Packet*, Retaliation*	St. Bartholomew	Boston	molasses	R £126
Feb 23	Alfred* [482]	brg	217 t.	HMS Epervier, Junon	Salem	on a cruise		C £75
Mar 5	Lizard* [483]	schnr	60 t.	HMS Prometheus	Salem	on a cruise		C £68
16	Margaret [486] (Recap)	schnr		HMS Maidstone, Belvidera (Diomede*)	Martinique	Halifax	sugar, rum, molasses	R (Salvage) £66 + £370 slvg
23	San Joaquin [491]	brg	190 Sp.t	HMS Albion & squadron	Havana	Newport	molasses, sugar, honey, coffee	R £219
28	Holstein [488]	schnr	113 t.	HMS Belvidera	Cuba	RI	molasses, sugar	C £114
29	Esperanza [487]	schnr	70 t.	HMS Belvidera	Porto Rico	New London	copper, hides	R £30 + £248
30	Union [no #] (Recap)	ship	283 t.	HMS Curlew (Rambler* of Boston)	Jamaica	Liverpool GB	cotton, coffee, dyewood	[wrecked] N/A
April 9	Plutus [489] (Recap)	shp	182 t.	HMS Curlew (America*)	Gibraltar	London	rice, linen	R (Salvage) £110 + £892 slvg
18	Sarah [493]	schnr	69 Sw. lasts	HMS La Hogue, Maidstone, Sylph, Boxer	St. Bartholomew	Boston	molasses	R £205
21	New Zealander [492] (Recap)	shp	258 t.	HMS Belvidera (USS Essex)	Philadelphia	whaling		R (Salvage) £878 + £851 slvg

1814 Date	Prize	Ship Type	Tons	Captor(s)	From	To	Cargo	Judgement & Costs
21	Minerva [494]	brg	55 Sw.	HMS La Hogue, Sylph, Peacock, Boxer, Maidstone	Matanzas, Cuba	Boston	molasses, sugar	R £184
27	Pilgrim [490]	schnr	25 t.	HMS Bream	Boston	Eastport	gin, tobacco, flour	C [NB] £95
30	Hannah [495] (Recap)	brg		HMS Martin (Pyke*)	Bermuda	Little Egg Island	rum, molasses	C (Salvage) £85 + £170 slvg
May 4	Maria Francisca [509] (Recap)	brg	142 t	HMS Curlew (Diomede*)	Havana	Boston	molasses, coffee, sugar, rice	R £270
9	Dantzig [496]	brg	136 t.	HMS Fantome	Bath ME	Bermuda	lumber	C [NB [179]
13	Catalina [497]	brg	160 Sp t.	HMS Superb	San Domingo	New Bedford	molasses, hides	R £154
13	Victor [498]	brg	52 Sw lasts	HMS La Hogue, Maidstone, Sylph, Nimrod	Cape Francois, Haiti	New London	sugar	R £254
13	Experiment [503]	schnr	39 t.	HMS Bulwark	Barnstable	NY	fish, oil	C £85
14	Fame [504]	slp	35 t.	Liverpool Packet*	Sag Harbour	NY	beef, cheese	C £88
15	Amelia [499]	slp	49 t.	HMS Bulwark & Squadron	NY	Providence	rye flour, bread, ham, pork	C £85
15	Tejo [517]	shp	160 t.	HMS La Hogue	Demarera	Newport RI	rum, molasses, flour	C £162 + £23 slvg
18	John [515]	slp	60 t.	Shannon*	Salem	Wells MA	ballast	C £61
19	Ann [500]	slp	68 t.	Shannon*	Passamaquoddy Bay	Boston	earthenware, hardware, copper	C £61
19	Defiance [502]	schnr	97 t.	Shannon*	Prospect	Boston	fish, lumber	C £61
19	Sally [501]	slp	36 t.	Shannon*	Boston	Portland	gin, scythes	C £68
19	Candelaria [518]	slp	92 t.	HMS Superb	Havana	Boston	sugar, molasses	R £125
22	Dominica* [540]	schnr	212 t.	HMS Majestic, Morgiana, Dotterel	Charleston	St. Bartholomew	pitch, tar, rice, claret, rosin, tobacco, cheese	C £148
23	Quiz* [511]	schnr	214 t.	HMS Nieman	St. Iago de Cuba	Philadelphia	sugar, molasses, coffee	C £113

1814 Date	Prize	Ship Type	Tons	Captor(s)	From	To	Cargo	Judgement & Costs
23	Model [512]	schnr	250 t.	HMS Nieman	Little Egg Harbour	Cuba	flour	C [abandoned £113]
23	Clara [513]	schnr		HMS Nieman	Baltimore		salt	C £79
25	Two Brothers [506] (Recap)	ship	300 t.	HMS Curlew, Martin (Scourge*)	Liverpool GB	Heligoland	salt, coffee, porter, cheese raisins	R (Salvage) £450 + £264 slvg
25	Ontario [508] (Recap)	shp		HMS Curlew (Lawrence*)	Alicante	Greenock	wine, salt, cork	R (Salvage) £105 + £713 slvg
25	Hussar* [514]	schnr	211 t.	HMS Saturn	Baltimore	on a cruise		C £106
26	Thomas & Sally [505] (Recap)	brg		HMS Curlew, Martin (Grand Turk*)	Lisbon	London	fruit	R (Salvage) £63 + £113 slvg
28	Diomede* [510]	schnr	148 t.	HMS Rifleman	Salem	on a cruise		C £86
29	Success [507] (Recap)	brg	78 t.	HMS Charybdis (Scourge*)	Exeter	St John's Nfld	cordage, bread	R (Salvage) £156 + £371 slvg
31	Fame [516]	slp	86 t.	HMS Endymion	Nantucket	Ocracoke	spermaceti oil	C £108
May 22 - July 17	Sundry Articles [571] from stores and vessels (Julian, Brizi)			HMS Dragon & Chesapeake Squadron	Chesapeake Harbour		tobacco, flour, bread, beef, tar cigars	C N/A
June 1	Mary [531] (Recap)	shp	270 t.	HMS Martin (Diomede*)	Greenock	Quebec	flour, wine	R (Salvage) £133 + £1859 slvg
4	Francisca de Paula [525]	brg	90 t.	HMS Nimrod	Havana	Boston	molasses	C [Appeal deserted] £309
4	Betsy [520]	schnr	54 t.	HMS Recruit	Yarmouth MA	Barnstable	flour	cargo C £49
5	Magdalena [533]	schnr	62 t.	HMS Martin	Cape Ann	Halifax	flour, bread, apples	R (lic) £102
6	Herculaneum [519]	brg	111 t.	HMS La Hogue, Nimrod	San Domingo	Boston	molasses, sugar	C £229
7	Lively [522]	slp	70 t.	Shannon*	North Yarmouth	Boston	cordwood	C £62
7	Flash [526]	slp	20 t.	HMS Nieman, Saturn	New Bedford	Metonkin	salt	C £64
10	Eunice [523]	slp	57 t.	Shannon*	North Yarmouth	Boston	cordwood	C £62

1814 Date	Prize	Ship Type	Tons	Captor(s)	From	To	Cargo	Judgement & Costs
11	Two Friends [524]	schnr	65 t.	Shannon*	Provincetown	Saco	ballast	C £55
11	Orient [528]	schnr		HMS Bulwark, Nymph	in Scituate Harbour		codfish oil, sugar, vinegar, molasses	C £47
12	Armistice [527]	schnr	94 t.	Retaliation*	Boston	Eastport	food, shoes, candles, wine, gin, dry goods, earthenware	C £116
14	Janus [530]	slp	27 t.	Liverpool Packet*	New York	Newport	flour	R (lic) £226
14	Tickler [555]	slp	66 t.	HMS Saturn	New York	Machias	flour, beef, rye	C N/A
15	Adventure [538]	schnr	121 t.	Liverpool Packet*	San Domingo	Bristol RI	sugar, coffee, molasses	R £182
15	Strong [534]	schnr	22 t.	Shannon*	Gloucester MA	fishing		C £68
15	Four Friends [534]	schnr	28 t.	Shannon*	Gloucester MA	fishing		C N/A
16	Voador [521]	brg	156 t.	HMS La Hogue	St. Salvador	Boston	sugar, fustic	R £266
19	William [529] (Recap)	schnr		HMS Wasp (Snap Dragon*)	Halifax	West Indies	fish	R (Salvage) £60 + £244 slvg
22	Delesdernier [536]	schnr	95 t.	HMS Tenedos	Boston	St. Andrews NS	Indian meal, bread, tar, rosin, flour	C part cargo R £110
23	Ex-Bashaw [535]	slp	96 t.	HMS Bulwark	St. George's R.		fish, shingles, wood	C £53
23	Commerce [545] (Recap)	brg	195 t.	HMS Superb, Maidstone Sylph (Amelia*)	Liverpool GB	Halifax	British merchandise	R (Salvage) £476 + £1,658 slvg
26	Charles [539]	schnr	21 t.	Rolla*	Bath		dry goods, ballast	C £98
28	Voador [537]	brg	160 t.	HMS Nymph	St. Iago de Cuba	Boston	molasses, sugar	R £242
29	Hope [543] (Recap)	brg	149 t.	Rolla* (Lawrence*)	Tenarife	London	barilla, wine, orchilla	R (Salvage) £831 + £546 slvg
30	Snap Dragon* [532] (became NS privateer Snapdragon*)	schnr		HMS Martin	Newbern NC	on a cruise		C £84

1814 Date	Prize	Ship Type	Tons	Captor(s)	From	To	Cargo	Judgement & Costs
June no date	Nighthawk [589] (became HMS blockade tender)	schnr		HMS Superb, Maidstone, Sylph	Blockade of New London		tar, turpentine, oil, medical salts cotton	Cargo C N/A
June 11 - July 2	Morning Star [568]	slp		HMS Dragon, Chesapeake Squadron	harbour in Chesapeake		tobacco from stores and vessels	C [vessel only] N/A
July 2 - 10	Robust [569]	slp		HMS Dragon, Chesapeake Squadron	harbour in Chesapeake		bar iron, tobacco from stores & vessels	C N/A
July 2 - 10	Eclipse [570]	slp		HMS Dragon, Chesapeake Squadron	harbour in Chesapeake		tobacco from stores	C N/A
July 1	Eliza [541]	schnr	100 t.	HMS Armide, Endymion	Wilmington DEL	Halifax	flour, tar	N/A
3	Defiance [542]	slp	62 t.	Liverpool Packet*	New York	Newhaven	flour, cotton, wood, chairs	C £91
July 3	Eliza [566]	schnr	41 t.	HMS Rifleman	NY	Eastport	corn	C [NB] N/A
3	Bee [544]	schnr	27 t.	Rolla*	Newburyport	Kennebunk	gin, bread, cyder, flour	C £78
3	Hero [547]	schnr	31 t.	Retaliation*	Newburyport	Eastport	tar, vinegar	C £65
6	Bee [550]	schnr		HMS Nymph	Wellfleet	fishing		C no costs
8	Constellation [548]	schnr	31 t.	Retaliation*	Plymouth	fishing		C £59
8	Boxer [549]	schnr	25 t.	Rolla*	Cape Ann	fishing		C £61
10	Nelly [552] (Recap)	schnr	140 t.	HMS Bulwark (Yankee*)	New Providence	Greenock	coffee, sugar, logwood	R (Salvage) £569 + £5,884 slvg
10	Prudence [553]	schnr	17 t.	HMS Acasta	Washington NC	Barnstable	turpentine, tar, varnish	C N/A
11	Rattlesnake* [546] (became HMS vessel)	brg	280 t.	HMS Leander		Bay of Biscay on a cruise		Ship C Cargo R £107
11	Thorn [551]	schnr	74 t.	HMS Bulwark	Camden	Nantucket	Indian corn, flour	C £102
12	Henry Gilder* [562]	brg	194 t.	HMS Nieman	NY	Bordeaux on a cruise		C N/A

1814 Date	Prize	Ship Type	Tons	Captor(s)	From	To	Cargo	Judgement & Costs
13	Governor Shelby* [557] (lett of mque)	schnr	200 t.	HMS Narcissus, Saturn	NY	Amsterdam	tobacco	C N/A
13	Ranger [558]	schnr	34 t.	HMS Superb	NY	Providence	flour	C N/A
13	Union [609]	schnr	22 t.	HMS Rifleman	Camden	Moose Island	beef, butter, cheese	C [NB] N/A
14	Sundry Articles [692]			Army & Navy Forces	Moose Island		steel, cloth, tin, saddlery, specie (£29,464.14.4)	C £35
14	Maria Frederica [559]	shp		HMS Seahorse, Peruvian	Amsterdam	Boston	geneva juniper, berries, German steel, silks, madder	R £400
15	Sir Alexander Ball [556] (Recap)	shp	399 t.	HMS Nieman (General Armstrong*)	Bristol GB	Malta	potatoes, ale cheese, porter, hams, malt liquor	R (Salvage) £1,896 slvg
16	Stephanie* [560]	schnr	72 t.	HMS Acasta	Philadelphia	Havana	flour, onions, lard	C N/A
18	Antelope [561]	schnr	73 t.	HMS Tenedos	Elizabeth City NC	Portland	flour, tar	C N/A
19	Diana [565]	slp	70 t.	HMS Acasta	Philadelphia	Havana	flour	C N/A
19	Brizi [588] (became tender to HMS Dragon)	schnr		HMS Dragon, Chesapeake Blockade			tobacco (captured June 11 in Chesapeake)	C N/A
21	Tyger [563] (Recap)	brg	173 t.	HMS Bulwark (Yankee*)	Malaga	Stetin, Prussia	wine	R (Salvage) £252 + £1,137 slvg
23	Fame [564]	slp	48 t.	HMS Spencer, Nymph, Leander	Boston	Nantucket	beef, pork,	R £83
23	Unity [574]	slp	36 t.	HMS Asia	Washington NC	Philadelphia	spirits of turpentine, tar	C N/A
24	Hazard [575]	schnr	30 t.	HMS Acasta	Matomhen MD	Boston	corn, flour	C N/A
26	Cidade de Leira [554]	brg	230 t.	HMS Fantome	Lisbon	Boston	wool, salt, wine, sheep	Ship C Cargo R [NB] N/A

1814 Date	Prize	Ship Type	Tons	Captor(s)	From	To	Cargo	Judgement & Costs
28	Nancy [580]	slp	65 t.	Lively*	NY	Providence RI	flour, Indian corn	C N/A
29	Logan [583]	slp	32 t.	Lively*	New Haven	New London	flour	C N/A
29	Sukey [582]	schnr	44 t.	Lively*	NY	Seabrook	ballast	C N/A
July 20 - Aug. 14	Sundry Articles [625]			HMS Albion, Chesapeake Blockade	Potomac & Patuxent Rivers		turpentine, 105 hogsheads tobacco, flour	C N/A
30	Three Friends [567] (became HMS Pictou [ex US privateer Zebra*, and French cartel Bonne Foi])	schnr		HMS Pyramus took Zebra* and sold her in London. As Three Friends, captured by French and returned to GB as cartel; to Bermuda as Bonne Foi, prize to HMS Asia				R in Vice-Admiralty Court in Bermuda, sold to merchant, purchased for HM Transport R N/A
July no date	Defiance [573]	slp		HMS Superb, Sylph				N/A
July no date	Janus [572]	slp		HMS Nieman & Chesapeake Blockade				C £226
July no date	Tobacco cargo in Tucker (transport) [603]			in Chesapeake blockade			169 hogsheads tobacco, misc. cargo	C N/A
Aug 2	Delaware [578]	schnr	79 t.	HMS Acasta, Menalaus	Wilmington DEL	Cuba	flour, soap, crackers	C N/A
2	Jane [579]	slp	70 t.	HMS Acasta	Porto Rico	Wilmington DEL	sugar, hides	C N/A
3	Victory [585]	schnr	45 t.	HMS Leander	off Cape Cod	fishing		R N/A
3	Hibernia [604]	schnr	70 t.	HMS Nieman	Philadelphia	Havana	shooks, hoops	C N/A
3	Defiance [581]	slp	46 t.	Lively*	Chatham	fishing		C N/A
5	Dalkarlen [577]	brg	214 t.	HMS Leander	Amsterdam	Boston	iron, steel	R £480
6	Julian [598]	schnr	38 t.	HMS Borer	Boston	Machias	beef, pork, flour	C [NB] N/A
7	Old Carpenter [584]	schnr	22 t.	HMS Spencer	Halifax	Boston	dry goods	C N/A
7	Enigheton [586]	brg	180 t.	HMS Nieman	St. Andrews NB	Philadelphia	plaster of Paris, hardware	N/A
9	Anita [587]	brg	198 t.	HMS Leander	Boston	Havana	ballast	[Appeal deserted] N/A

1814 Date	Prize	Ship Type	Tons	Captor(s)	From	To	Cargo	Judgement & Costs
9	Ida* [602]	brg	278 t.	HMS Newcastle, Antelope	Boston	France	on cruise	C N/A
10	Victress [596]	slp	66 t.	Liverpool Packet*, Shannon	Bridgeport	NY	butter, cheese, whiskey	C N/A
10	Polly [599]	slp	44 t.	Liverpool Packet*	New Haven	NY	rum, molasses, cheese	C N/A
11	Minerva [597]	slp	44 t.	Shannon*, Liverpool Packet*	NY	Bridgeport	flour, fish	C N/A
15	Herald* [591]	schnr	231 t.	HMS Armide, Endymion	NY	on a cruise		C N/A
16	Invincible* [593] [ex Invincible Napoleon*] (Recap)	shp	331 t.	HMS Armide, Endymion, Pique	Charleston	NY	rice, sugar	C N/A
16	Helen [590] (Recap)	shp	237 t.	HMS Wasp (Invincible*)	Havana	Greenock	sugar, logwood	R (Salvage) £1,051 slvg
16	Hope [595]	schnr	33 t.	Liverpool Packet*	Boston	Machias	tobacco, flour, shoes	C N/A
19	Wanderer [594]	snow	100 t.	HMS Tenedos	Nfld	Corunna	dry fish	R (Salvage) £164 + £578 slvg
20	Conde dos Arcos [601]	shp	210 t.	HMS Superb, Forth, Loire	Bahia	New Haven	tea, sugar, wine, fustic	R £700
21	Judith [627]	slp		HMS L'Espoir	nr. Cape May		no papers, no cargo (cargo of iron, brandy, coffee, cotton, nails, tobacco from Hornet)	C N/A
24	Landrail [605] (Recap)	slp RN cutter	180 t.	HMS Wasp (Syren*)	England	Gibraltar	mail cutter	R (Salvage) £28 + £130 slvg
24	Peacock [621]	schnr		Pautuxent R. Squadron	lying ashore in Pautuxent R.		tobacco	C N/A
28	Dove [614]	schnr	32 t.	Lively*	NY	Providence RI	Indian corn, flour	C N/A

1814 Date	Prize	Ship Type	Tons	Captor(s)	From	To	Cargo	Judgement & Costs
28	Bee [632]	schnr	20 t.	HMS Rifleman, Peruvian	Halifax	Cape Ann	dry goods	C [NB] N/A
29	Hiland Hill [610]	slp	18 t.	Lively*	NY	Newport	Indian corn	C N/A
Aug 1-31	Eclipse, Peacock, Madixon [626]	schnrs		Army & Blockading Squadron	storehouses on shores of Potomac and Pautuxent R.		510 hogsheads tobacco	C N/A
30	Enterprize [608]	schnr	26 t.	HMS Nieman	Barnstable	Washington NC	oil, fish, beef	C N/A
31	Charlotte [606] (Recap)	brg	200 t.	HMS Wasp (Grand Turrk*) Prize to Mammoth*, recapt by HMS Canso, then Grand Turk*	Antigua	Glasgow	molasses, sugar, coffee	R (Salvage) £210 + £1,078 slvg
Aug 1 - Sept 20	Sundry Articles [655] (public stores)			Army & Navy on Potomac R.	Alexandria		25 hogsheads tobacco	C N/A
Sept 2	Favorite [607] (Recap)	brg	158 t.	HMS Alban (Hyderally*)	Calcutta	New South Wales	wheat, rice	R (Salvage) £452 + £488 slvg
2	Betsey [611]	slp	38 t.	Lively*	Nantucket	fishing		C N/A
2	Planter [612]	slp	48 t.	Lively*	Dartmouth	fishing		C N/A
2	Dromo [613]	schnr	27 t.	Lively*	Yarmouth	fishing		C N/A
3	William [628]	schnr		HMS Albion, Chesapeake Blockade			no papers	C N/A
3	Caledonia [629] (Recap)	shp	282 t.	HMS Nymph (Surprise*)	Greenock	Montreal	flour, bread, coal, British merchandise	R (Salvage) £1,892 slvg
4	Two Brothers [617]	schnr	17 t.	HMS Nieman	Philadelphia	Havana	flour, soap, onions, locks, Indian corn	C N/A
4	Maria [624]	schnr		HMS Nimrod	Newport	NY	salt, fish, oil	C N/A
5	James [622]	schnr	26 t.	HMS Nieman	Washington NC	NY	flour	C N/A

1814 Date	Prize	Ship Type	Tons	Captor(s)	From	To	Cargo	Judgement & Costs
6	Alexander [615] (Recap)	brg	207 t.	HMS Wasp (Mammoth*)	St. Thomas	Liverpool GB	sugar, rum, fustic	R (Salvage) £1,471 slvg
7	Betsey [616] (Recap)	shp	330 t.	HMS Pylades (Hyderally*)	Calcutta	Sumatra	rice	R (Salvage) N/A
8	Fox [631]	schnr		HMS Bacchante, Tenedos, Rifleman, Pictou	in Machias Harbour		beef, pork	C [NB] N/A
10	Industry [619]	schnr	21 t.	Lively*	Halifax	Newburyport	dry goods	C (lic) N/A
10	Betsy [620]	schnr		HMS Alban	Boston	Machias	flour, beef pork, butter	Cargo C Ship R N/A
10	Sandbird [635]	jebacco		Lunenburg*	Halifax	Boston	hardware, cloth	Cargo C (lic) N/A
13	Nancy [618] (Recap)	brg	126 t.	HMS Pylades (Portsmouth*)	Liverpool GB	Halifax	dry goods	R (Salvage) £241 slvg
14	Nancy [639]	brg		Forces at Penobscot	on Penobscot R		timber, lumber	C N/A
14	Victory [696] (Recap)	shp		Forces at Penobscot, Castine (Viper*)	Jamaica	Liverpool GB		R (Salvage) £286 + £175 slvg
15	Vestal [630] (Recap)	shp	247 t.	HMS Dragon (David Porter*)	Buenos Ayres	London	hides, tallow	R (Salvage) £2,450
15	Lucy [637]	schnr	30 t.	Lunenburg*	Newburyport	fishing		C N/A
16	Galloway [638]	shp		Army & Navy Forces	Penobscot		wine, spirits from Decatur and other vessels	[C Appeal] N/A
18	Daedalus* [623] (lett of mque)	schnr	137 t.	HMS Nieman	Port au Prince	NY	coffee	C N/A
18	Perserverance [642] (ex Franklin of NY [448]	slp	133 t.	HMS Bacchante	Moose Island	Castine	rum, dry goods, molasses	Part cargo C Ship R N/A
21	Albion [633] (Recap)	brg	133 t.	HMS Jaseur (Surprise*)	Lisbon	Bordeaux	cocoa, sugar	R (Salvage) £497 + £631 slvg
21	Dove [634]	schnr	24 t.	Lunenburg*	at Cape Ann	fishing		C N/A
26	Minerva [636]	schnr	136 t.	Lunenburg*	Wiscasset	Boston	timber, wood	C N/A
26	Good Hope [645]	schnr		HMS Loire	Philadelphia		turpentine, shingles	C N/A

1814 Date	Prize	Ship Type	Tons	Captor(s)	From	To	Cargo	Judgement & Costs
28	Sarah [640] (Recap)	schnr		HMS Maidstone (Spark*)	Saint John NB	Barbados	gin, fish, lumber	R (Salvage) £182 slvg
Sept 1 - 30	Vessels & Stores [641] goods found in woods & 7 vessels on stocks	shp schnr brg schnr shp schnr	230 t 45 t. 115 t 89 t. 500 t. 130 t.	Army & Navy Forces	Penobscot, Machias		Value of goods @ $20,000	JC N/A
	Sally	brg	110 t.	Army & Navy Forces	Penobscot,			
Sept 1 - 30	Vessels on stocks [644]	shp 3 brg 4 schnr slp		Army & Navy Forces	Penobscot,			C N/A
Sept 1 - 30	Victory [696] (Recap)	shp		Army & Navy Forces	Penobscot			R (Salvage) £286 + £175 slvg
Sept 1 - 30	Vessels, guns, stores	1 shp 36 schn 8 slp 11 brg 4 boat 2 small vessels		Army & Navy Forces	Penobscot		guns, ordnance stores	C N/A
Sept 1 - 30	Cod Hook [699] (Recap)	shp		HMS Spencer, Martin & Army				[R Appeal] N/A
Oct 1	Fylinda [646]	slp	40 t.	Liverpool Packet*	Fairfield CON	RI	corn, rye	C N/A
4	Tickler [648]	schnr	42 t.	HMS Nieman, Loire	Philadelphia	St. Bartholomew	flour, bread, soap	C N/A
6	Mary [643] (Recap)	schnr	92 t.	HMS Wasp (Portsmouth*)	Halifax	Martinique	fish, flour	R (Salvage) £68 + £231
11	William [647] (Recap)	brg	235 t.	HMS Armide	Rio de Janiero	London	sugar, coffee, fustic, ox horns, hides	N/A

1814 Date	Prize	Ship Type	Tons	Captor(s)	From	To	Cargo	Judgement & Costs
20	Saucy Jack [657] (became NS privateer Saucy Jack*)	schnr		HMS Saracen	Potomac R.		Indian corn	C N/A
22	Amazon [649] (Recap)	shp	233 t.	HMS Bulwark, HM transport ship (unknown*)	London	Quebec	flour, bread	R (Salvage) £5,000 slvg
23	Dolphin [653]	schnr	28 t.	Lunenburg*	Boston	Bath	iron	C N/A
23	Eagle [664]	schnr	70 t.	HMS Narcissus, Dispatch	in Long Island Sound		pistol stocks US Revenue Schnr	C N/A
23	Harlequin* [650]	schnr	232 t.	HMS Bulwark	Portsmouth	on a cruise		C N/A
24	Black Swan [652]	brg	126 t.	HMS Maidstone	Boston	Havana	lumber, dry goods	C N/A
26	Lively [654]	slp	41 t.	HMS St. Lawrence	New Bedford	Georgetown VA	salt, potatoes	C N/A
27	Mentor [651] (Recap)	shp	227 t.	HMS Maidstone	Portsmouth	Quebec	beef, bread, pork, rum	R (Salvage) £7,000 bond
30	Halifax Packet [656] (Recap)	brg	188 t.	HMS Bulwark (Harpy*)	Aberdeen	Halifax	dry goods, flour, oatmeal, cordage	R (Salvage) £803 slvg
Nov 1	Macdonough* [659]	brg	180 t.	HMS Bacchante	Portsmouth	on a cruise		C N/A
1	Eliza Ann [669]	slp	50 t.	Minerva*	New Bedford	NY	Indian corn	C N/A
3	Rachel [663]	brg	150 t.	Rover*	Portland	Wilmington SC	salt, potatoes	C N/A
5	Charles [658] (Recap)	brg	131 t.	HMS Saturn (David Porter*)	Saint John NB	Barbadoss	fish, lumber, oil	R (Salvage) £196 slvg
5	Theodore [661] (Recap)	brg	237 t.	HMS Saturn (Chasseur*)	Marinam, Brazil	Liverpool GB	cotton	R (Salvage) £3,351 slvg
5	Ranger [666]	schnr	85 t.	Lunenburg*	Friendship	Bristol	cordwood, scantlings	C N/A
8	General Putnam* [662]	schnr	170 t.	HMS Leander	Salem	on a cruise		C N/A
9	Jane [660] (Recap)	brg	224 t.	HMS Maidstone (Gen. Putnam*)	Liverpool GB	Saint John NB	salt	R (Salvage) £235
9	Julian [665] (Recap)	schnr	70 t.	Own Crew (David Porter*)	St. Vincent	London	rum	R (Salvage) N/A
9	Ruth [670]	schnr	22 t.	Rover*	Portland	Portsmouth	dry fish	C N/A

1814 Date	Prize	Ship Type	Tons	Captor(s)	From	To	Cargo	Judgement & Costs
11	Goods Seized [685]			HM Customs	Castine		cigars, tobacco, soap, beef, pork gin, shoes, nails	C [Instance Court] N/A
12	Three Friends [667]	schnr	25 t.	Lunenburg*	Kittery	Boston	fishing	C N/A
12	Jane [668]	slp	66 t.	Rover*	Boston	Harpswell	ballast, stores	C N/A
19	Hero [671]	slp	44 t.	HMS Tenedos			potatoes, onions, apples, cheese	C N/A
23	Fermina [674]	shp	260 t.	HMS Maidstone, Junon, Arab, Curlew	Boston	Amelia Island	ballast	R N/A
24	Superb [673]	brg	115 t.	HMS Spencer	Charleston	Philadelphia	rice	C (Salvage) £394 + £92 slvg
Dec no date	Three Williams [676] (Recap)	brg	95 t.	HMS Arab (Grand Turk*)	Nfld	Portugal	fish	R (Salvage) £277 + £256 slvg
2	Cynthia [675]	schnr	90 t.	Rolla*	NY	New Providence	rye, grain, flour, lumber, cotton, wool, juniper berries	C N/A
Dec 3	Lucia [695]	slp		Liverpool Packet*, Rolla* (later taken by HMS Curlew)	NY	New Bedford		[Wrecked] N/A
3	Gleaner [679]	slp	70 t.	Rolla*	NY	Hartford	flour, rye, tea, whiskey, iron, crockery, glass, Franklin stoves	C N/A
4	Hope [678]	slp	42 t.	Liverpool Packet*	Providence	NY	salt, candles, cod	C N/A
5	Fox [684]	slp	53 t.	Rover*	Newburyport	Elizabeth NC	salt	N/A
6	Fair Trader [680]	schnr	30 t.	Rolla*, Liverpool Packet*	New Bedford	NY	rice, wine, salt, candles, fish	C N/A
8	Lady Prevost [677] (Recap)	brg	146 t.	HMS Nimrod (Yankee*)	Lisbon	St. John's Nfld	salt	R (Salvage) £171 slvg

1814 Date	Prize	Ship Type	Tons	Captor(s)	From	To	Cargo	Judgement & Costs
14	Fame* [672]	slp	30 t.	Militia of Yarmouth	Salem	on a cruise		C N/A
24	Armistice [681] (became NS privateer Rover*)	schnr	140 t.	HMS Junon	Charleston	NY	rice, cotton, oranges, copper	C N/A
31	Goods seized at Windsor [682]			HM Customs			cotton, silk, etc.	[R Instance Court] N/A

1815 Date	Prize	Ship Type	Tons	Captor(s)	From	To	Cargo	Judgement & Costs
Jan 3	Guerriere* [683]	brg	169 t.	HMS Junon	Portsmouth	on a cruise		C N/A
13	Comet [690]	schnr	80 t.	Rolla*	New Bedford	Elizabeth City NC	salt, dry goods	C N/A
15	Industry [687]	slp	36 t.	Rover*	NY	Sag Harbour	flour, cyder	Cargo C N/A
21	Experiment [689]	slp	96 t.	Lunenburg*	NY	Nantucket	flour, corn, oats	R (lic) N/A
22	Tomahawk* [688]	schnr	202 t.	HMS Bulwark	Boston	on a cruise		C N/A
24	Joseph & Mary [693] (Recap)	brg	267 t.	HMS Bulwark (Leo*)	PEI	Falmouth	timber	C £453
26	Gift [686]	schnr	41 t.	Rover*	Boston	Charleston	beef, pork, provisions	N/A
Feb 9	Atlas [691]	schnr	40 t.	Dove*	Elizabeth City NC	Newburyport	flour, rice	C N/A
16	George [692]	brg	172 t.	Dove*	Georgetown SC	Boston	rice, cotton, molasses	C N/A
23	Margaret [694] (Recap)	brg		HMS Bulwark (Champlain*)	Saint John NB	West Indies	fish, oil, lumber	R (Salvage) £205 slvg
26	Rhoda [697] (Recap)	schnr	129 t.	HMS Bulwark (Brutus*)	Bermuda	Liverpool GB	sugar, coffee, cotton, sarsaperilla	R (Salvage) £383 slvg
Mar 7	Legal Tender [698] (Recap)	brg	160 t.	HMS Spencer (David Porter8)	St. Johns Nfld	Lisbon	fish, oil	No Salvage £334
19	Thistle [701] (Recap) (ex Belle [259])	schnr	101 t.	HMS Cossack (America*)	Malaga	Halifax	wine, fruit	R (Salvage) £647 + £17 Appeal [Appeal retraxit]
26	Louisa [702] (Recap)	brg	65 t.	HMS Maidstone (Harpy* but taken after peace)	Gibraltar	Greenock	wine, fruit	R (Salvage) £340
Mar no date	Tudor [700]	brg		HM Customs				[Instance Court] N/A
May 15 - June 1	Goods Seized at Halifax and Castine [706]			HM Customs			food, wool, tobacco, shoes purses, gloves, brooms	C [Instance Court] N/A
no date	Petition of C.S. Hill [703]							[Instance Court] 22 May, 1815 N/A

1815 Date	Prize	Ship Type	Tons	Captor(s)	From	To	Cargo	Judgement & Costs
no date	Sherbrooke [704]	brg		HM Customs				[Instance Court] 26 May, 1815 N/A
no date	Blockade [705]	schnr		HM Customs				N/A

Appendix 2
Standing Interrogatories

Eighteenth-century efforts to regularize the adjudication of prize led the British Admiralty Court to develop standardized questions for members of captured crews. Known as the Standing Interrogatories, these questions elicited detailed information on the act of capture, the vessel and cargo seized, the behaviour of the prize maker, any extenuating circumstances (such as a licence), and whatever other shipping intelligence the subject could contribute.

By the War of 1812, colonial prize courts had adopted a fairly elaborate list of thirty-four questions that were put to one or more representative crew members from every prize. In the documents of the Vice-Admiralty Court of Halifax, 443 cases, or 62 percent of files contain at least one and as many as seven responses to the Standing Interrogatories. Sworn under oath, the information gathered from these documents provides a profile of American and foreign shipping along the eastern coast of North America during the War of 1812 and a testament to the activities of prizemakers, whether navy or provincial privateers.

Dr. Christopher Robinson recorded the following list of questions in 1812 and it was published subsequently in the legal series, *English Reports*, Vol. 165. They are described as:

> STANDING INTERROGATORIES, to be administered on behalf of Our Sovereign Lord George the Third by the grace of God, of Great Britain, France and Ireland, King, Defender of the Faith. To all commanders, masters, officers, mariners, and other persons found on board any ships and vessels, which have been or shall be seized or taken as prize by any of His Majesty's ships or vessels of war, or by merchants ships or vessels which have or shall have commissions or letters of marque and reprisals, concerning such captured ships, vessels, or any goods, wares, and merchandise on board the same, examined as witnesses in preparatory, during the present hostilities.

1. Where were you born and where have you lived for these seven years last past? Where do you live now, and how long have you lived in that place? To what prince or state, or to whom are you, or have you ever been a subject, and of what cities or towns have you been admitted a burgher or freeman, and at what time and in what manner were you admitted a burgher or freeman, and at what time and in what manner were you so admitted? How long have you resided there since you were admitted a burgher or a freeman, or where have you resided since? What did you pay for your admission? Are you a married man, and if married, where do your wife and family reside?

2. Were you present at the time of taking and seizing the ship or her lading, or any of the goods or merchandises concerning which you are now examined? Had the ship, concerning which you are now examined any commission? What, and from whom?

3. In what place, latitude or port, and in what year, month, and day was the ship and goods, concerning which you are now examined, taken and seized? Upon what pretence and for what reason were they seized? Into what place or port were they carried, and under what colours did the said ship sail? What other colours had you on board, and for what reason had you such other colours? Was any resistance made at the time when the said ship was taken; and if yea, how many guns were fired, and by whom, and by what ship or ships were you taken? Was such a vessel a ship of war, or a vessel acting without any commission, as you believe? Were any other, and what ships, in sight at the time of the capture?

4. What is the name of the master or commander of the ship or vessel taken? How long have you known the said master, and who appointed him to the command of the said ship? Where did such master take possession of her, and at what time, and what was the name of the person who delivered the possession to the said master? Where doth he live? Where is the said master's fixed place of abode? if he hath no fixed place of abode, then let him be asked, where was his last place of abode, and where does he generally reside? How long has he lived there? Where was he born, and of whom is he now a subject? Is he married, if yea, where does his wife and family reside?

5. Of what tonnage or burthen is the ship which has been taken? What was the number of mariners, and of what country were the said seamen or mariners? Did they all come on board at the same port, or at different ports, and who shipped or hired them, and when and where?

6. Had you or any of the officers or mariners belonging to the ship or vessel concerning which you are now examined, any and what part, share, or interest in the said ship, or her lading? If yea, set forth who and what goods or interest you or they have? Did you belong to the said ship or vessel at the time she was seized and taken? In what capacity did you belong to her? How long have you known her? When and where did you first see her, and where was she built?

7. What is the name of the ship? How long hath she been so called? Do you know of any other name or names by which he hath been called? If yea, what were they? Had she any passport or sea-brief on board, and from whom? To what ports and places did she sail during her said voyage before she was taken? Where did her last voyage begin, and where was the said voyage to have ended? Set forth the quality of every cargo the ship has carried to the time of her capture, and what ports such cargoes have been delivered at? From what parts and at what time particularly, from the last clearing port, did the said ship sail, previous to the capture?

8. What lading did the said ship carry at the time of her first setting sail in her last voyage, and what particular sort of lading and goods had she on board at the time when she was taken? In what year and in what month was the same put on board? Set forth the different species of the lading and the quantities of each sort?

9. Who were the owners of the ship or vessel, concerning which you are now examined, at the time when she was seized? How do you know that they were the owners of the said ship at that time? Of what nation and country are such owners by birth? Where do they reside, and where do their wives and families reside? How long have they resided there? Where did they reside before, to the best of your knowledge? To whom are they subject?

10. Was any bill of sale made, and by whom, to the aforesaid owners of the said ship; and if any such was made, in what month and year? Where and in the presence of what witnesses, was such a bill of sale made? Was any and what engagement entered into concerning the purchase farther than what appears upon the bill of sale? If yea, was it verbal or in writing? Where did you last see it, and what has become of it?

11. Was the said lading put on board in one port and at one time, or at several ports and at several times, and at what ports, by name? Set forth what quantities of each sort of goods were shipped at each port?

12. What are the names of the respective laders or owners, or consignees, of the said goods? What countrymen are they? Where do they now live and carry on their business or trade? How long have they resided there? Where did they reside before, to the best of your knowledge? And where were the said goods to be delivered, and for whose real account, risk, or benefit? Have any of the said consignees or laders any, and what interest, in the said goods? If yea, whereon do you found your belief that they have such interest? Can you take upon yourself to swear that you believe, that at the time of the lading the cargo, and at the present time, and also if the said goods shall be restored and unladen at the destined ports, the goods did, do, and will belong to the same persons, and to none others?

13. How many bills of lading were signed for the goods seized on board the said ship? Were any of those bills of lading false or colourable, or were any bills of lading signed which were different in any respect from those which were on board the ship at the time she was taken? What were the contents of such other bills of lading, and what became of them?

14. Are there, in Great Britain, any bills of lading, invoices, letters, or instruments, relative to the ship and goods concerning which you are now examined? If yea, set forth where they are, and in whose possession, and what is the purport thereof, and when they were brought or sent to this kingdom?

15. Was there any charter party signed for the voyage, in which the ship, concerning which you are now examined, was seized and taken? What became thereof? When, where and between whom, was such charter-party made? What were the contents of it?

16. What papers, bills of lading, letters, or other writings, were on board the ship at the time she took her departure from the last clearing port, before her being taken as prize? Were any of them burnt, torn, thrown overboard, destroyed, or cancelled, concealed or attempted to be concealed, and when, and by whom, and who was then present?

17. Has the ship, concerning which you are now examined, been at any time, and when, seized as prize, and condemned as such? If yea, set forth into what port she was carried and by whom, and by what authority, and on what account she was condemned?

18. Have you sustained any loss by the seizing and taking of the ship concerning which you are now examined? If yea, in what manner do you compute such your loss? Have you already received any indemnity, satisfaction, or promise of satisfaction for any part of the damage which you have sustained or may sustain by this capture and detention, and when, and from whom?

19. Is the said ship or goods, or any, and what part, insured? If yea, for what voyage is such insurance made, and at what premium, and when and by what persons, and in what country was such insurance made?

20. In case you had arrived at your destined port, would your cargo, or any part thereof, on being unladen, have immediately become the property of the consignees, or any other person, and whom? Or was the lader to take the chance of the market for the sale of his goods?

21. Let each witness be interrogated of the growth, produce, and manufacture of what country and place was the lading of the ship or vessel, concerning which you are examined, or any part thereof?

22. Whether all the said cargo, or any and what part thereof, was taken from the shore or quay, or removed or transhipped from one boat, barque, vessel, or ship, to another? From what and to what shore, quay, boat, barque, vessel, or ship, and when and where was the same so done?

23. Are there in any country, besides Great Britain, and where, or on board any and what ship or ships, vessel or vessels, other than the ship and vessel concerning which you are now examined, any bills of lading, invoices, letters, instruments, papers or documents, relative to the said ship or vessel and cargo, and of what nature are such bills of lading, invoices, letter, instruments, papers, or documents, and what are the contents?

24. Were any papers delivered out of the said ship or vessel, or carried away in any manner whatsoever? And when, and by whom, and to whom, and in whose custody, possession, or power, do you believe the same now are?

25. Was bulk broken during the voyage in which you were taken, or since the capture of the said ship? And when, and where, by whom, and by whose orders? And for what purpose, and in what manner?

26. Were any passengers on board the aforesaid ship? Were any of them secreted at the time of the capture? Who were the passengers by name? Of what nation, rank, profession, or occupation? Had they any commission? For what purpose, and from whom? From what place were they taken on board, and when? To what place were they finally destined, and upon what business? Had any, and which, of the passengers any, and what property, or concern, or authority, directly or indirectly regarding the ship and cargo? Were there any officers, soldiers, or mariners secreted on board, and for what reason were they secreted? Were any of His Britannic Majesty's subjects on board, or secreted, or confined at the time of the capture? How long and why?

27. Were, and are, all the passports, sea-briefs, charter-parties, bills of sale, invoices and papers, which were found on board entirely true and fair? Or are any of them false and colourable? Do you know of any matter or circumstance to affect their credit? By whom were the passports or sea briefs obtained, and from whom? Were they obtained for this ship only? And upon the oath, or affirmation of the persons therein described, or where they were delivered to, or on behalf of the person or persons who appear to have been sworn, or to have affirmed thereto, without their having ever, in fact, made any such oath or affirmation? How long a time were they to last? Was any duty or fee payable and paid for the same? And is there any duty or fee to be paid on the renewal thereof? Have such passports been renewed, and how often? and has the duty or fee been paid for such renewal? Was the ship in a port in the country where the passports and sea-briefs were granted? And if not, where was the ship at the time? Had any person on board any let-pass or letters of safe-conduct? If yea, from whom, and for what business?

28. If it should appear that there are in Ireland, or the British American colonies, or in any place or country, besides Great Britain, any bills of lading, invoices, instruments, or papers relative to the ship and goods, concerning which the witness is now examined; then interrogate, how they were they brought into such place and country? In whose possession are they, and do they differ from any of the papers on board, or in Great Britain or Ireland, or elsewhere, and in what particular do they differ? Have you written or signed any letters or papers, concerning the ship and her cargo? If yea, what was their purport? To whom were they written and sent, and what is become of them?

29. Toward what port or place was the ship steering her course at the time of her being first pursued and taken? Was her course altered upon the appearance of

the vessel by which she was taken? Was her course at all times, when the weather would permit, direct to the place or port for which she appears to have been destined by the ship papers? Was the ship before, or at the time of her capture, sailing beyond or wide of the said place or port to which she was destined by the said ship papers? At what distance was she therefrom? Was her course altered at any, and what time, and to what other port or place, and for what reason?

30. By whom, and to whom hath the said ship been sold or transferred, and how often? At what time and at what place, and for what sum or consideration, hath such sum or consideration been paid or satisfied? Was the sum paid, or to be paid, a fair and true equivalent? or what security or securities have been given for the payment of the same, and by whom, and where do they live now? Do you know or believe in your conscience, such sale or transfer has been truly made?
And not for the purpose of covering or concealing the real property? Do you verily believe that if the ship should be restored, she will belong to the persons now asserted to be the owners, and to none others?

31. What guns were mounted on board the ship, and what arms and ammunition were belonging to her? Why was she so armed? Were there on board any other guns, mortars, howitzers, balls, shells, handgrenades, muskets, carbines, fuzees, halberts, spontoons, swords, bayonets, locks for muskets, flints, ramrods, belts, cartridges, cartridge-boxes, pouches, gun-powder, salt-petre, nitre, camp-equipage, military tools, uniforms, soldiers cloathing(sic) or accoutrements, or any sort of warlike or naval stores? Were any of such warlike or naval stores, or things, thrown overboard to prevent suspicion at the time of capture? And were, and are any such warlike stores, before described, concealed on board under the name merchandise, or any other colourable appellation, in the ship papers? If yea, what are the marks on the casks; bails, and packages, in which they were concealed? Are any of the before named articles, and which, for the sole use of any fortress or garrison in the port or place to which such ship was destined? Do you know, or have you heard of any ordinance, placart, or law existing, in such kingdom or state, forbidding the exportation of the same by private persons without licence? Were such warlike or naval stores put on board by any public authority? When and where were they put on board?

32. What is the whole which you know or believe, according to the best of your knowledge and belief, regarding the real and true property and destination of the ship and cargo, concerning which you are now examined, at the time of capture?

ADDITIONAL INTERROGATORIES

33. Did the said ship, on the voyage in which she was captured, or on or during any, and what former voyage or voyages, sail under the convoy of any ship or ships of war, or other armed vessel or vessels? If yea, interrogate for what reason or purpose did she sail under such convoy? Of what force was or were such convoying ship or ships? And to what state or country did such ship or ships belong? What instructions or directions had you, or did you receive on each and every of such voyages, when under convoy, respecting your sailing or keeping in company with such armed or convoying ship or ships; and rom whom did you receive such instructions or directions? Had you any and what instructions or directions, and from whom, for resisting or endeavouring to avoid or escape from capture, or for destroying, concealing or refusing to deliver up your ship's documents and papers? Or any and what other papers that might be, or were put on board your said ship? If yea, interrogate particularly as to the tenor of such instructions, and all particulars relating thereto. Let the witness be asked if he is in possession of such instructions, or copies thereof; if yea, let him be directed to leave the same with the examiner, to be annexed to his deposition.

34. Did the said ship, during the voyage in which she was captured, or on doing any and what former voyage or voyages, sail to or attempt to enter any port under blockade by the arms or forces of any, and which of the belligerent powers? If yea, when did you first learn or hear of such port being so blockaded, and were you at any and what time, and by whom warned not to proceed to, or to attempt to enter such blockaded port? What conversation or other communication passed thereon? And what course did you pursue upon, and after, being so warned off?

Appendix 3
Nova Scotia and New Brunswick
Letter of Marque Vessels, 1812-1815

Ship	Size & Type	Date of Marque	Crew	Guns	Prz
1. **Caledonian**	623 t. shp	17 July/12	40	14	--
		[Letter of marque against France and the Batavian Republic]			
2. **General Smyth** [NB]	cutter				4
3. **Liverpool Packet**	67 t. schnr	i) 20 Aug./12	40	5	21
		[Letter of marque against France and enemies of the Crown]			
		ii) 5 Feb./13			12
		[Letter of marque against the U.S.]			
		iii) 20 Nov./13			14
[Captured by *Thomas* of Portsmouth, N.H., 11 June/13. As *Portsmouth Packet*, captured by HMS *Fantome* and bought by Enos Collins to return to privateering as the *Liverpool Packet*]					
		iv) 11 Nov./14			3
4. **Union**[NB]				1	
5. **Sir John Sherbrooke** [NB]	187 t. brgtn	23 Nov./12	30	10	--
[Former American brg *Vernon*]					
6. **Hunter** [NB]	schnr	Dec./12			
[Armed vessel on loan from the Superintendant of Trade and Fisheries]					
7. **Retaliation**	71 t. schnr	i) 3 Feb./13	50	5	10
		ii) 25 May/13	30	5	4
		iii) 20 Dec./13	35	5	5
[Former American privateer *Revenge*, Salem. Captured in Dec./14]					
8. **Sir John Sherbrooke**	273 t. brgtn	11 Feb./13	150	18	18
[Former American privateer *Thorn*, Marblehead, Mass. Captured by American privateer *Saucy Jack*, Charleston]					

Ship		Size & Type	Date of Marque	Crew	Guns	Prz
9.	**Rattler**	27 t.				1
	[Former American jebacco boat, tender for **Sir John Sherbrooke.**]					
10.	**Crown**	22 t. schnr	14 Apr./13	35	1	1
	[Captured off Waldoborough by local volunteers in a sloop, May/13]					
11.	**Dart** [NB]	74 t. slp	i) 4 May/13	25	4	5
			ii) 14 July/13	--	-	6
	[Former American privateer *Actress*, New Haven, Conn. Captured by Rhode Island Revenue Cutter *Vigilant*, Oct./13]					
12.	**Matilda**	50 t. schnr	11 May/13	40	5	14
13.	**Retrieve**	55 t. schnr	i) 21 May/13	40	2	5
			ii) 21 Sept./13	45	4	1
			iii) 8 July/14	20	2	0
	[Burnt at sea]					
14.	**Weazle**	45 t. schnr	28 May/13	35	5	5
15.	**Fly**	50 t. schnr	i) 28 May/13	35	3	0
			ii) 6 July/13	35	3	7
	[Captured by U.S. brig *Enterprize*, 20 Aug./13]					
16.	**Bunker Hill**	179 t. schnr	17 June/13	15	3	--
	[Former American privateer *Bunker Hill*, New York]					
17.	**Broke**	52 t. schnr	i) 6 July/13	35	5	6
			ii) 27 Sept./13		--	
	[Former American privateer *Juliana Smith*, Boston]					
18.	**Gleaner**	67 t. slp	9 July/13	20	5	1
	[Former American privateer *Gleaner*, Kennebunkport, Me., taken into provincial service]					
19.	**George**	123 t. schnr	11 Aug./13	60	6	1
20.	**Wolverine**	143 t. schnr	i) 20 Aug./13	80	12	1
			ii) 8 Nov./13	80	10	11
	[Former American privateer *Thomas*, Portsmouth, N.H., captor of the *Liverpool Packet*]					
21.	**Star** [NB]	schnr		3		
22.	**Brunswicker** [NB]	slp				
	[Former American Revenue cutter, *Commodore Barry*, taken into provincial service]					

Ship	Size & Type	Date of Marque	Crew	Guns	Prz
23. **Shannon**	146 t. schnr	2 Sept./13	50	5	18
[Former American privateer *Growler*, Salem]					
24. **Herald**	279 t. shp	8 Sept./13	25	10	--
25. **Edward**	322 t. brgtn	25 Sept./13	25	9	--
26. **Eleanor**	192 t. brgtn	27 Sept./13	25	12	--
27. **Intrepid**	67 t. lugger	20 Oct./13	16	6	--
28. **Hare**	38 t. slp	29 Nov. 13	25	2	2
[Captured, 1814]					
29. **Rolla**	132 t. schnr	8 June/14	60	5	9
[Former American privateer *Rolla*, Baltimore. Lost at sea, 1815]					
30. **Dolphin**	tender for *Rolla*				1
31. **Lively**	30 t. schnr	4 July/14	30	5	10
[Captured by the American privateer *Surprise*, Salem]					
32. **Lunenburg**	93 t. schnr	i) 18 Aug./14	45	5	8
		ii) 29 Nov./14		--	
[Former American privateer *Governor Plumer*, Portsmouth, N.H.]					
33. **Sherbrooke**	205 t. brgtn	27 Aug./14	15	11	--
34. **Rover**	85 t. schnr	23 Sept./14	50	5	6
[Former American privateer *Armistice*]					
35. **Ann**	57 t. schnr	24 Sept./14	20	1	--
[Recaptured by two American privateers]					
36. **Saucy 16**	schnr				$19,000 -Mullins
37. **Minerva**	64 t. slp	3 Oct./14	45	3	1
38. **Snapdragon** [NB]	167 t. schnr	9 Nov./14	30	6	--
[Former American privateer *Snap Dragon*, Newbern, Conn.]					
39. **Saucy Jack**	100 t. schnr	14 Dec./14	45	3	(1) -Snider
[Former American privateer *Saucy Jack*, Charleston]					

Ship	Size & Type	Date of Marque	Crew	Guns	Prz
40. **Dove**	30 t. schnr	24 Jan./15	20	1	2
41. **Telegraph**	schnr				(1)-Snider
42. **Comet [NB]**			14		-Snider

C.H.J. Snider, *Under the Red Jack* (Toronto, 1927) lists a number of privateer or letter of marque vessels for which no documentation has been found. These include:

Ship	Size & Type	Date of Marque	Prz
1. **Nonsuch** (Halifax)	schnr	Aug./12	(2)
2. **Fly** (St. John's, Nfld.)	schnr	1812	(3)
3. **Amelia** (Pictou, N.S.)	brigantine		(0)
4. **Dart** (Liverpool, N.S.)	slp	Nov./13	(6)
5. **Thinks-I-to-Myself** (Castine)	jebacco		(0)

Note: The number of prizes credited to each privateer includes prizes that were joint captures with other privateers or naval vessels.

Appendix 4
Investment in Privateering

Name of Vessel	Bond	Owners
1. **Caledonian** Thomas Boag (Master)	17 July 1812 - £1500 John Black - Merchant, Halifax John Brown - Merchant, Halifax James Thorn - Merchant, Halifax	George Robertson, Greenock, N.S. William Forsyth, Greenock, N.S. James Hunter, Greenock, N.S. William Smith, Liverpool, U.K. John Black, Halifax
2. **General Smyth**	Summer 1812	Province of New Brunswick
3. **Liverpool Packet** (U.S. slaver *Black Joke*) John Freeman (Master)	24 August 1812 - £1500 Enos Collins - Merchant, Halifax John Moody - Merchant, Halifax Joseph Freeman - Liverpool, N.S.	Enos Collins, Halifax Benjamin Knaut, Liverpool, N.S. John & James Barss, Liverpool, N.S.
Joseph Barss, Jr. (Master)	10 February 1813 - £1500 John Moody - Merchant, Liverpool, N.S. John Barss - Merchant, Liverpool, N.S. Joseph Freeman - Merchant, Liverpool, N.S.	Enos Collins, Halifax Benjamin Knaut, John & James Barss Liverpool, N.S.
Caleb Seely (Master)	25 November 1813- £1500 John Moody - Merchant, Halifax John Barss - Merchant, Liverpool, N.S. Joseph Freeman - Merchant, Liverpool, N.S.	Enos Collins, Halifax Benjamin Knaut, Liverpool, N.S. John & James Barss, Liverpool, N.S.

Name of Vessel	Bond	Owners
Lewis Knaut (Master)	20 October 1814 - £1500 Enos Collins - Merchant, Halifax Joseph Allison - Merchant, Halifax	Enos Collins, Halifax Joseph Allison, Halifax
4. **Union**	20 November 1812 - £1500 William Ward - Merchant, St. John, N.B. John Atkinson - Merchant, St. John, N.B.	George Younghusband, St. John, N.B. Samuel Miles, St. John, N.B. William R. Boyd, St. John, N.B. John Atkinson, St. John, N.B.
5. **Sir John Sherbrooke** (U.S. brig *Vernon*) Thomas Robson (Master)	23 November 1812 - £1500 William Lawson - Merchant, Halifax Enos Collins - Merchant, Halifax Joseph Allison - Merchant, Halifax	Andrew Sterling Ritchie, St. John, N.B. William Pagan, St. John, N.B. Robert Pagan, St. Andrews, N.B.
6. **Hunter**	December 1812	Province of New Brunswick
7. **Retaliation** (Ex U.S. schooner *Revenge*) Thomas Freeman (Master)	10 February 1813 - £1500 Charles Hill - Merchant, Halifax William K. Reynolds - Merchant, Halifax	Snow Parker, Liverpool, N.S. Thomas Freeman, Liverpool, N.S.
Benjamin Ellenwood (Master)	27 May 1813 - £1500 John Brown - Merchant, Halifax William K. Reynolds - Merchant, Halifax	Snow Parker, Liverpool, N.S. Thomas Freeman, Liverpool, N.S. John Roberts, Liverpool, N.S. James Gorham, Liverpool, N.S.
Harris Harrington (Master)	22 December 1813 - £1500 John Brown - Merchant, Halifax William K. Reynolds - Merchant, Halifax	Snow Parker, Liverpool, N.S. Thomas Freeman, Liverpool, N.S. Gordon Dewolf, Liverpool, N.S.

Name of Vessel	Bond	Owners
8. **Sir John Sherbrooke** (Ex. U.S. privateer *Thorn*) Joseph Freeman (Master)	15 February 1813 - £1500 Enos Collins - Merchant, Halifax Joseph Allison - Merchant, Halifax	Enos Collins, Halifax Joseph Freeman, Liverpool, N.S. Joseph & James Barss, Liverpool, N.S. Benjamin Knaut, Liverpool, N.S.
9. **Rattler** (Ex. U.S. jebacco boat)	Tender for *Sir John Sherbrooke*	Same as *Sir John Sherbrooke*
10. **Crown** Solomon Jennings (Master)	14 April 1813 - £1500 Thomas Smith - Merchant, Halifax William O'Bryan - Merchant, Halifax	Samuel Harris, Halifax Solomon Jennings, Halifax
11. **Dart** (Ex U.S. privateer *Actress*) John Harris (Master)	7 May 1813 - £1500 Samuel Cunard - Merchant, Halifax John Owen - Merchant, Halifax	Robert Shires, St. John, N.B. James Hay, Jr., St. John, N.B. James Thorpe Hanford, St. John, N.B.
James Ross (Master)	15 July 1813 - £1500 John Roy - Merchant, Halifax Samuel Cunard - Merchant, Halifax	Robert Shires, St. John, N.B. James Hay, Jr., St. John, N.B. James Thorpe Hanford, St. John, N.B.
12. **Matilda** John Burkett (Master)	11 May 1813 - £1500	Richie, Barlie, Robinson, Burkett, Annapolis Royal, N.S.
13. **Retrieve** Silas Crane (Master)	28 May 1813 - £1500 John Starr - Merchant, Halifax William Young - Mariner, Falmouth, N.S.	Silas Crane, Halifax William Young, Falmouth, N.S.
William Allen (Master)	21 September 1813 - £1500 Thomas Leonard - Merchant, Halifax William Church - Halifax	Thomas Leonard, Halifax Starr & Shannon, Halifax

Name of Vessel	Bond	Owners
William Young (Master)	9 July 1814 - £1500 William K. Reynolds - Merchant, Halifax Elisha DeWolf - Merchant, Horton, N.S.	Thomas H. Woodward, Halifax William K. Reynolds, Halifax James Coggswell, Halifax
14. **Weazle** George William Anderson (Master)	31 May 1813 - £1500 William Bond - Grocer, Halifax Francis Muncey - Grocer, Halifax	Joseph Hamilton, Halifax William Bond, Halifax Francis Muncey, Halifax
15. **Fly** Enoch Stanwood (Master)	3 June 1813 - £1500 William Murphy - Trader, Halifax John Thomas Hill - Attorney, Halifax	Israel Harding, Halifax Enoch Stanwood, Halifax Charles Hill, Halifax
Elkanah Clements (Master)	6 July 1813 - £1500 Arthur Brymer - Merchant, Halifax John Thomas Hill - Attorney, Halifax	Charles Hill, Halifax Israel Harding, Halifax
16. **Bunker Hill** (Ex. U.S. privateer) James Chadwick (Master)	19 June 1813 - £1500 John Pryor - Halifax Henry Yeomans - Merchant, Halifax	John Pryor, Halifax
17. **Broke** (Ex. U.S. schooner *Juliana Smith*) Daniel Waid (Master)	6 July 1813 - £1500 William Rudolph - Merchant, Halifax John Osborne - Merchant, Halifax	Phineas Lovett, Jr., Annapolis Royal, N.S.
William Smith (Master)	1 October 1813 - £1500 William Rudolph - Merchant, Halifax John Osborne - Merchant, Halifax	P. Lovett, Jr., Annapolis Royal, N.S.

Name of Vessel	Bond	Owners
18. **Gleaner** (Ex. U.S. privateer) Prince Kinney (Master)	10 July 1813 - £1500 Prince Kinney - Merchant, Halifax John George Pyke - Merchant, Halifax	John George Pyke "is the owner on behalf of the Province,"
19. **George** John Gilchrist (Master)	13 August 1813 - £1500 George Haim - Trader, Halifax Thomas Smith - Baker, Halifax	Thomas H. Mason, Halifax George Haim, Halifax Thomas Smith, Halifax Joseph Schofield, Halifax
20. **Wolverine** (Ex U.S. schooner *Thomas*) Shea (Master)	21 August 1813 - £1500 John Moody - Merchant, Halifax William Rudolph - Merchant, Halifax	Joseph, Thomas & John Barss, Joseph Freeman, Benjamin Knaut, Charles William Liverpool, N.S.
John Roberts, Jr. (Master)	10 November 1813 - £1500 William Rudolph - Merchant, Halifax John Moody - Merchant, Halifax	Joseph, Thomas & James Barss, Joseph Freeman, Benjamin Knaut, Liverpool, N.S.
21. **Star** Caleb Seely (Master)	1813	St. John, N.B.
22. **Brunswicker** (Ex. U.S. Revenue Cutter)	Province of New Brunswick	Province of New Brunswick
23. **Shannon** (Ex U.S. Privateer *Growler*) Benjamin Ellenwood (Master)	4 September 1813 - £1500 John Moody - Merchant, Halifax William K. Reynolds - Merchant, Halifax	Snow Parker, Liverpool, N.S.
24. **Herald** Charles Simonds (Master)	11 September 1813 - £1500 Michael Tobin - Merchant, Halifax William Donald - Merchant, St. John, N.B.	Hugh Johnson & Son, St. John, N.B. Thomas Milledge, St. John, N.B.

Name of Vessel	Bond	Owners
25. **Edward** James H. Tidmarsh (Master)	30 September 1813 - £1500 William Lawson - Merchant, Halifax Michael Tobin - Merchant, Halifax	Messrs. Belcher and Wright, Halifax
26. **Eleanor** Alexander Anderson (Master)	30 September 1813 - £1500 William Lawson - Merchant, Halifax Michael Tobin - Merchant, Halifax	Messrs. Belcher and Wright, Halifax
27. **Intrepid** John Lenfesty (Master)	22 October 1813 - £1500 James Forman - Merchant, Halifax Henry Yeomans - Merchant, Halifax	Peter LeLacheur, Guernsey, U.K.
28. **Hare** James Reid (Master)	30 November 1813 - £1500 John Moody - Merchant, Halifax Noah Desbrow - Merchant, St. John, N.B.	Noah Desbrow, St. John, N.B. John Clark, St. John, N.B. Hugh Doyle, St. John, N.B.
29. **Rolla** (Ex. U.S. privateer) John Freeman (Master)	10 June 1814 -£1500 Enos Collins - Merchant, Halifax Joseph Allison - Merchant, Halifax	Joseph Freeman, James R. DeWolf John & James Barss, Benjamin Knaut, Liverpool, N.S. Enos Collins, Halifax Joseph Allison, Halifax
30. **Dolphin**	Tender for *Rolla*	Same as *Rolla*
31. **Lively** Joseph Barlett (Master)	July, 1814	Samuel Dexter, Liverpool, N.S. Stephen Gardner, Liverpool, N.S.

Name of Vessel	Bond	Owners
32. **Lunenburg** (Ex U.S. privateer *Governor Plumer*) Joseph Falt (Master)	19 August 1814 - £1500 John Clark - Merchant, Halifax Henry Moser - Merchant, Lunenburg, N.S.	Philip Rudolph, John N. Oxner, Henry Wollenhaup, Henry Moser, Lunenburg, N.S.
Thomas Chamberlain (Master)	30 November 1814 - £1500 John Clark - Merchant, Halifax John Pendergast - Merchant, Halifax	Henry Moser, Lunenburg, N.S. Philip Rudolph, Lunenburg, N.S, John N. Oxner, Lunenburg, N.S. Henry Wollenhaup, Lunenburg, N.S.
33. **Sherbrooke** William Corken (Master)	27 August 1814 - £1500 John Dougan - Merchant, Halifax Garret Miller - Merchant, Halifax	James Cavan, Barbados
34. **Rover** (Ex. U.S. Privateer *Armistice*) John Brown (Master)	24 September 1814 - £1500 William K. Reynolds - Merchant, Halifax John Brown - Merchant, Halifax	Snow Parker, Liverpool, N.S.
35. **Ann** Randall McDonald (Master)	30 September 1814 - £750 Samuel Cunard - Merchant, Halifax Frederick Major - Merchant, Halifax	John Osborn, Halifax
36. **Saucy Sixteen**		16 investors, Liverpool, N.S.
37. **Minerva** Joseph Bartlett (Master)	3 October 1814 - £750 John Moody - Merchant, Halifax Joseph Boyle - Merchant, Halifax	Joseph & Thomas Barss, Liverpool, N.S. Joseph Bartlett, Liverpool, N.S. Andrew Webster, Liverpool, N.S.

Name of Vessel	Bond	Owners
38. **Snapdragon** (Ex. U.S.privateer) James Reid (Master)	11 November 1814 - £1500 John Roy - Merchant, Halifax Samuel Cunard - Merchant, Halifax	Messrs. Curry & Handford, St. John, N.B.
39. **Saucy Jack** Joseph Bartlett (Master)	16 December 1814 - £1500 Joseph Boyle - Merchant, Halifax Thomas Barss - Merchant, Liverpool, N.S.	Joseph Boyle, Halifax Thomas Barss, Liverpool, N.S. Joseph Bartlett, Liverpool, N.S.
40. **Dove** James Harrington (Master)	24 January 1815 - £1500 John Moody - Merchant, Halifax Charles Hill, Jr. - Merchant, Halifax	Joseph Cottingham Bates, Liverpool, N.S.
41. **Telegraph**		Liverpool, N.S.
42. **Comet**		St. John, N.B.

Appendix 5
Royal Naval Vessels and Their Prizes

Ship (rate, tons, guns, dates)	Master	JC+	Recapts	Capts
Acasta (5th) 1142t, 44g (1797 - 1821)	Capt. Alexander Robt Kerr	4+½+1/8	1	4+3/2 +1/3+¼
Aeolus (5th) 910t, 32g (1802 - 1817)	Lord James Townshend	2/2+¼+2/5 1/8		2+1/3 +2/5
Africa (3rd) 1415t, 64g (1781 - 1814)	Capt. John Bastard	1+½+¼+ 2/5		1/5
Alban (schnr) 253t, 14g (1813 - 1822) [Wrecked, 18 Dec./12, replaced by ex-US vessel]	Lt. Robert F. Gibson		1	2
Albion (3rd) 1743t, 74g (1802 - 1836)	Capt. John F. Devonshire		1	3
Alert (slp) 303t, 16g (1804 - 1812) [Nfld. Station, capured by USS *Essex*]	T.L.P. Laugharne		1	
Alphea (schnr) 112t, 10g (1806 - 1813) [blown up in action with *Wily Reynard**, 10 Sept./13]	Lt. Thomas William Jones			1
Antelope (4th) 50g (1803 -) [Newfoundland Station]	James Carpenter			½
Arab (brg) 390t, 18g (1812 - 1823) [wrecked]	Lt. Henry Jane	1	1	2+¼
Armide (5th) 1104t, 38g (1806 - 1815)	Sir Thomas Troubridge	1+½	½+1/3	
Asia (3rd) 1763t, 74g (1811 - 1819)	Alexander Skene		1	2

Ship (rate, tons, guns, dates)	Master	JC+	Recapts	Capts
Atalante (slp) 416t, 18g	Frederick Hickey	1		4½
(1808 -1813) [wrecked off Halifax, 10 Nov./13]				
Bacchante (5th) 1077t, 38g	Francis Stanfell			2+¼
(1811 -1858)				
Barbadoes (6th) 755t, 28g	Capt. Thomas Huskisson			
(1803-1812) {ex-Fr. *Le Brave*} [wrecked off Sable Island]				
(1813) (brg) 315t,	Capt John Fleming			
{ex-U.S. lett of mque *Herald*}				
+ **JC** indicates condemned to the crown *jurae coronae*; * indicates privateer or letter of marque				
Barossa (5th) 947t, 36g	William H. Shirreff			1/7
(1812 -1841)				
Belvidera (5th) 946t, 36g	Capt. Richard Byron	5+¼+2/5	1+½	8+½+3/5
(1809 -1906)				
Bold (gun brg) 182t, 12g	Lt. John Skekel		1	1
(1812 -1813) [wrecked off Prince Edward Island, 27 Sept./13]				
Borer (gun brg) 184t, 12g	Lt. Richard Coote		2+½	3
(1812 -1815)				
Boxer (gun brg) 182t, 12g	Samuel Blyth			8+½+¼
(1812 -1813) [captured by USS *Enterprise*, 5 Sept./13]				+1/5
Bream (schnr) 80t, 4g	Lt. John Simpson (1812)	1		11+6/2
(1807 - 1816)	Lt. Hare (1813)			
Bulwark (3rd) 1940t, 74g	Capt. David Milne		7	6+½
{ex-*Scipio*} (1807 -1826)				
Canso (schnr) 225t, 12g	Lt. Wentworth P. Croke			1
(1813 - 1816) {ex-US *Lottery*}				
Centurion (4th, recg shp) 50g	Lt. John K. Kinsman (1812)			
(1808 -)	Lt. William A. Brand (1813)			
Charybdis (brg) 385t, 18g	Lt. James Cliphan			1
(1809 -1819)				

Ship (rate, tons, guns, dates)	Master	JC+	Recapts	Capts
Chubb (schnr) 80t, 4g (1807 -1812) [wrecked]	Lt. Samuel Nisbett		4	1
Colibri (slp) 365t, 16g (1809 -1813) {ex-Fr. *Colibri*} [wrecked]	Capt. John Thompson		2	4+3/2+¼
Comet (slp) 427t, 18g (1807 -1815)	George William Blaney			1
Conflict (gun brg)181t, 12g (1812 -1840)	Capt. Henry Baker			½
Cossack (6th) 546t, 22g (1806-1816) {ex-*Pandour*}	Hon. Robert Rodney			1
Curlew (brg/slp) 386t, 18g (1812 - 1822) Cruizer {ex US priv.}	Michael Head			9+7/2 +2/3+2/4
Dispatch (brg/slp)388t, 18g (1812 - 1836) Cruizer	Richard Galway			½
Dominica (slp) 203t, 14g (1807 - 1815) {ex-Fr.} [captured by *Decatur**, 5 Aug./13, recapt., wrecked 15 Aug./15]	R. Hockings			
Dotterell (brg/slp)387t, 18g (1808 - 1848) Cruizer	William W. Daniel			1/3
Dover (troopship) 692t, 38g (1811 -1836)	Augustus Drury		1	2
Dragon (3rd) 1815t, 74g (1798 - 1824)	Robert Barrie			6
Earl of Moira (ordnce tnder) 14g [sent to Great Lakes 1812]	James K. White	1		
Emulous (slp) 384t, 18g (1806 - 1812) Cruizer [wrecked 7 Aug./12]	William Howe Mulcaster	9+½+¼	4 +1/8	1+¼
New Emulous (slp) 213t, 14g (1812 - 1817) {ex-USS *Nautilus*}	William Godfrey		2	2+2/4
Endymion (4th) 1277t, 50g (1797 - 1868)	Henry Hope			1+2/2 +4/3

Ship (rate, tons, guns, dates)	Master	JC+	Recapts	Capts
Epervier (brg/slp) 388t, 18g	Richard Wales		1	1+2/2
(1812 - 1814) Cruizer [captured by USS *Peacock*, 29 Apr./14]				
Espoir (brg/slp) 385t, 18g	Norwich Duff			1
(1804 -1821) Cruizer				
Fantome (brg/slp) 385t, 18g	John Lawrence/ T.S. Sykes		2	3+½+2/6
(1810 - 1814) {ex-Fr. priv.} [wrecked off Halifax]				
Forth				1/3
Goree (slp) 18g	H.D. Byng			
Guerriere (5th) 1092t, 38g	Capt. James R. Dacres	2/5		1+2/5
(1806 - 1812) {ex-Fr.} [burnt by USS *Constitution*, Nov./12]				
Highflyer (schnr) 144t, 5g	Lt. W. Hutchinson			1
(1813) tender to HMS *San Domingo*				
{ex-Am. priv.}[recaptd by USS *President*, 9 Sept./13]				
Hogue (3rd) 1750t, 74g	Commodore Hotham		3+½	18+3/2+
(1811 -1848)	& Hon. Thomas B. Capel			3/3+2/4 +1/5
Hope (brg/slp) 237t, 10g	John Scott	1		
(1809 - 1819) Tender from Bermuda Dockyard				
Indian (slp) 400t, 18g	Henry Jane	4¼	1	
(1805 - 1817)				
Jaseur (brg/slp) 387t, 18g	George Edward Watts		1	1+½
(1813 - 1845)				
Java (5th) 1000t, 38g	Henry Lambert			
(1811 - 1812) {ex-Fr. *Renommee*}[captd off Brazil by USS *Constitution*, 29 Dec./12]				
Juniper (schnr) 150t, 8g	Lt. Nathaniel Vassal	1½		
(1808 - 1814)				

Ship (rate, tons, guns, dates)	Master	JC+	Recapts	Capts
Junon (5th) frigate 38g (1810 -1817) {ex-Fr. *Bellone*}	Capt. James Saunders		1	2+3/2+¼ +1/5
Lacedemonian (5th) 38g ?(18)	Samuel Jackson			
Laura (schnr) 112t, 10g (1806-1812) [captd by Fr. priv. 8 Sept./12]	Lt. N.C. Hunter			
Laurestinus (6th) 526t, 24g (1806 - 1813) {ex-Fr. *Laurel*} [captd by Fr., recaptd, renamed, wrecked 22 Oct./13]	Thomas Graham			1/5
Leander (4th) 1572t, 58g (1813-1830)	Sir George Collier			5+1/3
Loire (5th) 1100t, 40g (1798 - 1818) {ex-Fr.}	Thomas Brown		½	2+3/2 +3/3
Loup Cervier (slp) (1813 -) {ex-USS *Wasp*}	William B. Mends		1	2+¼
Macedonian (5th) 1082t, 38g (1810-1812) [captd by USS *United States*, 25 Oct./12]	Capt. John S. Carden			
Magnet (brg/slp) 285t, 16g (1809-1812) {ex-Fr. priv. *Joseph*} [wrecked]	F.M. Maurice			
Maidstone (5th) 947t, 36g (1811 -1865)	George Burdett, William Skipsey	1+½+2/4 +1/8	2+2/2+1/3	7+2/2+ 5/3+2/4 +2/5+2/6
Majestic (3rd) 1623t, 74g (1785 - 1816)	John Hayes			4+3/2 +1/3
Manly (gun brg) 180t, 14g (1812 - 1833)	Edward Collier		2	3
Marlborough (3rd)1754t, 74g (1807 - 1835)	R Admiral Cockburn & R. Honyman			2/6+1/7
Martin (slp) 399t, 18g (1809 1817) [wrecked]	J. Evans (1812) Humphrey Senhouse (1813)		3	7+4/3 +3/2

Ship (rate, tons, guns, dates)	Master	JC+	Recapts	Capts
Menelaus (5th) 1077t, 38g (1810 -1832)			1/2	
Minerva (5th) 32g (1804 -)	Richard Hawkins			
Mohawk (gun brg) 148t, 10g (1810 - 1814 - possibly *Viper* of 1810)	Henry Litchfield			2/6+1/7
Morgiana (slp) 400t, 18g (1811 - 1825)	David Scott (1812) W.B. Mends (1813)	2	2	1/3
Musquedoboit (schnr) 225t, (1812 -) {ex-lett of mque *Lynx*}	Lt. John Murray			
Narcissus (5th) 894t, 32g (1801 - 1837)	Capt. John R. Lumley		1	3/2
Newcastle (4th) 1556t, 60g (1813 - 1850)	Lord George Stuart			½
Nieman (5th) 1093t, 38g ((1809 - 1815) {ex-Fr.}	Capt. Samuel Pym			12+½
Nimrod (brg/slp) 384t, 18g (1812 - 1827) [wrecked] Cruizer	Nathaniel Mitchell (1812) George R. Hilton (1813)		2+1/3	5+2/2 +2/3+¼
Nova Scotia (brg) 310t, 12g (1812 -) {ex-US priv. *Rapid*}	Lt. Bartholomew Kent			
Nymph (5th) 1087t, 38g {ex-*Nereid*)	Farmery P. Epsworth	2+1/8	2	12+6/2+(1812-1875) +1/3+4/4
Orpheus (5th) 947t, 36g (1809 -1819)	Capt. Hugh Piggott	1+¼+1/8		4+2/2
Paz (schnr) ? 10g (1807 - 1814) {ex-Spanish)	Lt. Perry Dumaresq		2	6+½
Peacock (brg/slp) 434t,18g (1812 - 1814){ex-*Wasp*} [capt by USS *Hornet*, 24 Feb./13, wrecked 29 Aug./14]	William Peake			1/5

Ship (rate, tons, guns, dates)	Master	JC+	Recapts	Capts
Peruvian (brg/slp)383t, 18g (1808 - 1830) Cruizer	George Keppen			2/2
Pictou (brg/slp) 215t, 16g (1813 - 1814) {ex-*Syren*} [captured by USS *Constitution*, 14 Feb./14]	Edward Stephens			1 + ¼
Pique (5th) 1028t, 36g (1800 - 1809) {ex-Fr.}	Capt. Maitland			
Plantagenet (3rd)1777t, 74g (1801 - 1817)	Robert Lloyd			1
Plumper (gun brg)181t, 10g (1812) [wrecked in Bay of Fundy with £70,000 specie, Dec./12]	Lt. James Bray	1	3	
Poictiers (3rd) 1765t, 74g (1810 - 1857)	Sir J. P. Beresford		3 + ½ + 1/3	½ + 2/3
Prometheus (fireshp) 432t, 18g (1807 - 1819)	Hercules Robinson			1
Pylades (slp) 367t, 16g (1794 - 1815)	J. G. Roberts			2
Ramilies (3rd) 1670t, 74g (1785 - 1850)	Sir Thomas Hardy		½	5/2 + 2/3
Rattler (slp) 360t, 18g (1795 - 1815)	Alexander Gordon (1812) H.D. Byng (1813)			+2/3
Recruit (brg/slp) 383t, 18g (1806 -1822) Cruizer	Henry F. Senhouse (1812) George R. Pechell (1813)		2	1
Rifleman (brg/slp) 387t, 18g (1809 - 1836) Cruizer	Joseph Pearce		1	3 + ½ + ¼
Ring Dove (brg/slp) 385t, 18g (1806 - 1829) Cruizer	William Dowers		5	2
Romulous (5th) 879t, 36g ((1785 - 1816)	George W.H. Knight		1	
St. Lawrence (schnr) 240t,12g (1813-1815) {ex-US priv. *Atlas*}[recapt by Am priv *Chasseur*, recapt by HMS *Acasta*]	David Bond			1

Ship (rate, tons, guns, dates)	Master	JC+	Recapts	Capts
San Domingo (3rd) 1820t, 74g (1809 - 1816)	S.J. Pechell		1	1/3+2/6
Saracen (brg/slp) 387t, 18g (1812 - 1819) Cruizer	Alexander Dixie			1
Saturn (3rd) 1646t, 74g (1786 - 1868)	James Nash		2	2+2/2
Sceptre (3rd) 1727t, 74g (1802 - 1821)	Charles B.H. Ross		1	
Seahorse (5th) 998t, 38g (1794 - 1819)	Capt. Alexander Gordon		½	
Shannon (5th) 1066t, 38g (1806 - 1832)	B. Philip de Vere Broke	2+3/2 +¼+1/5	2	4+1/3 3/4+2/5
Shelburne (schnr) 221t, 14g (1813 - 1817) {ex-US priv. *Racer*}	Lt. David Hope		1	
Sophie (brg/slp) 387t, 18g (1809 -1825) Cruizer	Nicholas Lockyer			1
Spartan (5th) 1084t, 38g (1806 - 1822)	Edward P. Brenton	3+4/2 +2/4+1/8	2+2/2 +1/3	1+½+10/3 1/3
Spencer (3rd) 1917t, 74g (1800 - 1822)	Richard Ragget			3+1/3
Spy (storeshp) 227t, 16g (1804 - 1812) {ex-*Comet*} [captd by Fr.]	Richard Anderson			1
Statira (5th) 1080t, 38g (1807 - 1815) [wrecked 26 Feb./14]	Hazard Stackpole	1+2/2+1/8	8 +9/3+¼	6+2/2 1/5+2/6
Superb (3rd) 1919t, 74g (1798 - 1826)	Hon. Charles Paget			1+½+3/3
Sylph (brg/slp) 400t, 18g (1812 - 1815) [wrecked]	W. Evans (1812) G. Dickens /Lt. C.P Brown			2+½+2/3 +¼+1/5
Tartarus (6th) 20g (1806 -)	John Pasco		1	

Ship (rate, tons, guns, dates)	Master	JC+	Recapts	Capts
Tenedos (5th) 1083t, 38g (1812 - 1843)	Capt. Hyde Parker			7+3/2 +1/3+4/4
Thetis (gun brg) 185t, 10g (1810 - 1836)	William H. Byam			1/5
Thistle (gun brg) 185t, 12g (1812 - 1823)	J.K. White			
Union (2nd) 2149t, 98g (1811 - 1833)			½	
Valiant (3rd) 1718t, 74g (1807 - 1823)	Capt. R.D. Oliver			2+2/2+ 3/3+¼
Victorious (3rd) 1724t, 74g (1808 - 1862)	John Talbot			4+1/3
Wasp (brg/slp) 387t, 18g (1812 - 1847) Cruizer	Lt. Richard Crawford		½	9+½+1/3
Woolwich (storeshp) 908t, 40g (5th en flute) (1785-1814) [wrecked off Barbuda, 6 Nov./13]	Thomas Ball Sullivan			1

TOTAL: 118 vessels

(Data from J.J. Colledge, *Ships of the Royal Navy* (London, 1987), and W.P. Gosset *The Lost Ships of the Royal Navy, 1793-1815* (London, 1986.)

Appendix 6
Letters of Agency - RN Ships

According to the documents found in NAC, RG 8, IV, Vols. 73-150, most of the British naval vessels active on the North American station appointed agents to act on their behalf in matters of prize. Sometimes they appointed agents in both England and Nova Scotia. When an agent was replaced, a new letter of agency was signed and filed with the admiralty and vice-admiralty court. The list below indicates the agent(s) for each vessel, the location of their agency responsibility, and the dates of their letter of appointment, where known.

Ship	Agent	Date
Acasta	1. Thomas Maynard	26 June/13
	2. John Dougan	1 July/14
Aeolus	Thomas Heavyside	
Africa		
Alban	Charles Martyr, Thomas Heavyside	14 July/14
Albion	1. George Redmond Hulbert (NS)	5 Oct/13
	Messrs Cook & Halford (London)	
	2. John Dougan, John Robert Glover	7 Feb/14
Alert		
Alphea	Richard Tremain	
Antelope		
Arab	1. Charles Martyr, Lawrence Hartshorne	Nov./13
	Thomas Boggs, Lawrence Hartshorne Jr.	
	2. Thomas Heavyside, Charles Martyr	July/14
Armide	John Dougan (NS), William Elybrook (London)	Jan./14
Asia	John Dougan, William Balhetchet	22 Mar./14
Atalante	1. Andrew Wright	30 Mar./13
	2. Geo. R. Hulbert, Thomas Heavyside	14 Aug./13
Bacchante	1. John Dougan, William Balhetchet	10 Sept./14
	2. John Dougan, Charles Martyr (for captures at Castine, Hampden, Machias)	no date
Barbadoes		
Barossa	John Dougan, John Barnett	29 Apr./13
Belvidera	Hartshorne, Boggs & Co. (NS), James Sykes (London)	1 Apr./13
Bold	1. Thomas Heavyside, John Barnett	24 May/13
	2. John Dougan, John Barnett (NS), William Black (Saint John, NB)	14 July/13

Ship	Agent	Date
Borer	1. Wm Standert, Wm Stewart (London) Geo. R. Hulbert, James Fraser (NS)	18 June/13
	2. John Robinson (Saint John, NB)	29 May/14
Boxer	John Barnett, John Dougan (NS) M. Evans (London)	29 May/13
Bream		
Bulwark	1. Chas. Martyr, Hartshorne, Boggs & Co.	29 May/14
	2. Thomas Maynard	24 Dec./14
	3. Thomas Maynard, Hartshorne, Boggs & Co.	"
Canso		
Centurion		
Charybdis	James Fraser	30 May/14
Chubb	Hartshorne, Boggs & Co.	
Colibri	Hartshorne, Boggs & Co.	
Comet		
Conflict	John Dougan, John Barnett (NS), Wm. Standert (London)	29 Oct./13
Cossack	James Sykes (London), Thos. Maynard	Mar./13
Curlew	1. Geo. R. Hulbert, Hartshorne, Boggs & Co., Samuel Head	3 Apr./13
	2. Samuel Head, Hartshorne, Boggs & Co., James Fraser	3 Apr./13
Dispatch	John Dougan, William Balhetchet	29 July/14
Dominica		
Dotterell	John Dougan	14 Apr./15
Dover	Lawrence Hartshorne, Thos. Boggs, Lawrence Hartshorne, Jr.	9 July/13
Dragon	John Dougan	14 Nov./13
Earl of Moira		
Emulous		
New Emulous	1. Wm Black (Saint John, NB)	6 Apr./13
	2. Hartshorne, Boggs & Co.	1 Nov./12
Endymion	Thos. Maynard, Geo. R. Hulbert	26 Nov./14
Epervier	Geo. R. Hulbert, James Fraser	25 Aug./13
Espoir	John Dougan, Wm. Balhetchet	16 June/14
Fantome	1. Geo. R. Hulbert	22 Feb./13
	2. Wm Black (Saint John, NB), Henry Sark, Joseph Woodhead (London)	18 July/14
Forth		
Goree		
Guerriere	Thomas Heavyside (1812), James Fraser (NS), Cowburn & Lowe (London)	July/14
Highflyer		
Hogue	James Fraser (1813), Geo. R. Hulbert	
Hope		

Ship	Agent	Date
Indian	Thomas Heavyside (1812)	
Jaseur	John Dougan, Hartshorne, Boggs & Co.	30 Oct./13
Java		
Juniper		
Junon	1. Geo. R. Hulbert, John Lowden McAdam (Bristol)	7 Dec./12
	2. Geo. R. Hulbert, Ommanny & Druce (London)	6 Oct./13
	3. James Fraser (NS), Ommanny & Druce (London)	26 July/14
Lacedemonium	J. Dougan	
Laurestinus		
Leander	Charles Martyr, James Fraser	
Loire	1. Geo. R. Hulbert, Wm. J. Sykes (London)	21 Sept./13
	2. John Dougan, Wm. Balhetchet	15 Apr./14
Loup Cervier	James Fraser, Geo. R. Hulbert	27 July/13
Macedonian		
Maidstone	1. Geo. R. Hulbert	28 Dec./12
	2. Thos. Maynard (NS), Toulman & Coapland (London)	June-Dec./13
	3. Charles Martyr, John Dougan	6 Sept./14
Magnet		
Majestic	1. Chas. Martyr, Lawrence Hartshorne, Thos. Boggs	3 June/13
	2. Geo. R. Hulbert	Aug./13
	3. John Dougan, James Brown (Bristol)	10 Mar./14
Manly	1. John Dougan, John Barnett	23 July/13
	2. John Dougan, Wm. Balhetchet	2 July/14
Marlborough	James Fraser	
Martin	1. Geo. R. Hulbert	19 Feb./13
	2. Wm. Ayre, John Owen	19 Apr./13
	3. John Owen, Chas. Martyr (NS), John Hawker (Plymouth)	29 Apr./14
	4. John Dougan	15 Aug./14
Menelaus	Dougan & Barnett (NS), Messrs North & Creed (London)	15 Aug./14
Minerva		
Mohawk	James Fraser, Geo. R. Hulbert	
Morgiana	1. James Fraser, Geo. R. Hulbert	7 Mar./13
	2. John Dougan	
Narcissus	Geo. R. Hulbert, James Fraser	9 Feb./13
	James and Michael Tobin	
Newcastle	1. John Dougan	13 Apr./13
	2. John Dougan	duplicate

Ship	Agent	Date
Nieman	1. John Dougan	9 Mar./14
	2. Charles Martyr	9 Aug./14
Nimrod	1. Geo. R. Hulbert	20 Apr./13
	2. Geo. R. Hulbert, Lawrence Hartshorne Thos. Boggs, Lawrence Hartshorne, Jr.	13 Dec./13
	3. Hartshorne, Boggs & Co.	June/14
	4. Hartshorne, Boggs & Co.	3 Oct./14
Nova Scotia		
Nymph	Thos. Maynard	20 Mar./14
Orpheus	John Dougan, Geo. R. Hulbert	
Paz	Thos. Heavyside	20 Jan./13
Peacock		
Peruvian	John Dougan, Wm. Balhetchet Thomas Heavyside	18 Oct./14
Pictou	Thomas Boggs	
Pique		
Plantagenet	Hartshorne, Boggs & Co., Geo. R. Hulbert	
Plumper	Wm. Black (Saint John, NB)	
Poictiers	Hartshorne, Boggs & Co.	
Prometheus		
Pylades		
Ramilies		
Rattler	Wm. Black (NB)	
Recruit	Thomas Heavyside	
Rifleman	Dougan & Barnett	
Ring Dove	John Dougan, Chas. Martyr	
Romulous	John Dougan	
St. Lawrence		
San Domingo	Geo. R. Hulbert	
Saracen		
Saturn	John Dougan	
Sceptre		
Seahorse	Thomas Heavyside	
Shannon	Thomas Heavyside	
Shelburne		
Sophie		
Spartan	John Dougan, Andrew Wright	
Spencer	Chas. Martyr, Thos. Maynard	
Spy	Andrew Wright	
Statira	Geo. R. Hulbert, Thos. Maynard	
Success	Hartshorne, Boggs & Co.	
Superb		
Sylph	Geo. R. Hulbert, James Fraser	
Tartarus		
Tenedos	Thos. Heavyside	

Ship	Agent	Date
Thetis		
Thistle		
Union		
Valiant	James Fraser	
Victorious	Geo. R. Hulbert	
Wasp	Dougan & Barnett	
Woolwich	Thos. Heavyside	

117 vessels, 80 with at least one letter of agency.

Appendix 7
Prize-Related Activity Among Merchants in Nova Scotia and New Brunswick

Investment in privateering activities in New Brunswick and Nova Scotia took the form of ownership (O) or provision of bond money for a cruise (B). Other members of the maritime commercial establishment served as agents for privateer or naval captains and crew members (A), or worked as appraisers for the court of vice-admiralty to determine the salvage value of a ship or cargo (E) or whether it had contravened the rules regarding contraband. A profile of merchant activities for the main ports of Atlantic Canada is listed below.

Name		Activity
HALIFAX, NS		
1. John Albro (1764-1839)	E - 1	
2. William Ayre	A - 1	HMS *Martin*
3. Joseph Allison	O - 1	*Rolla*
	B - 4	*Liverpool Packet* (2), *Sir John Sherbrooke, Rolla*
	E - 1	
4. William Balhetchet	A - 12	HMS *Asia, Bacchante, Dispatch, Espoir, Loire, Manly, Peruvian*
5. John Barnett	A - 11	HMS *Barossa, Bold* (2), *Boxer, Conflict, Manly, Menelaus*
6. John Bartlett	O - 2	*Minerva, Saucy Jack*
7. A. Belcher (1763-1841) & Wright	O - 2	*Edward, Eleanor*
8. John Black (1764-1823)	O - 1	*Caledonia*
	B - 1	"
	E - 1	
9. Charles Boggs (1775-1858)	E - 9	
10. Thomas Boggs (1871-1859)	A - 5	HMS *Arab, Dover, Majestic, Nimrod, Pictou*
11. William Bond	O - 1	*Weazel*
	B - 1	"
12. Joseph Boyle	O - 1	*Saucy Jack*
	B - 2	*Minerva, Saucy Jack*
13. John Boyd	E - 19	
14. John Brown	B - 4	*Caledonian, Retaliation* (2), *Rover*
	E - 8	
15. Arthur Brymer	B - 1	*Fly*
16. Elisha Calkin	E - 1	
17. William Church	B - 1	*Retrieve*

Name		Activity
18. John Clark	**B** - 2	*Lunenburg* (2)
	E - 1	
19. Enos Collins (1774-1871)	**O** - 6	*Liverpool Packet* (4), *Sir John Sherbrooke, Rolla*
	B - 5	*Liverpool Packet* (2), *Sir John Sherbrooke* (2 privateers), *Rolla*
20. Silas Crane (1743- ?)	**O** - 1	*Retrieve*
21. James Creighton	**E** - 1	
22. Samuel Cunard (1788-1864)	**B** - 4	*Dart* (2), *Ann, Snapdragon*
	E - 1	
23. James Dewolf (1787-1835)	**E** - 1	
24. Thomas Dewolf (b.1785)	**A** - 16	
26. Thomas Dobson	**E** - 1	
27. John Dougan	**B** - 1	*Sherbrooke*
	A - 31	HMS *Acasta, Albion, Armide, Asia, Bacchante* (2), *Barossa, Bold, Boxer, Conflict, Dispatch, Dotterell, Dragon, Espoir, Jaseur, Lacedemonium, Loire, Maidstone, Majestic, Manly* (2), *Martin, Morgiana, Newcastle* (2), *Nieman, Orpheus, Peruvian, Ring Dove, Romulous, Saturn, Spartan*
28. Dougan & Barnett	**A** - 3	HMS *Menelaus, Rifleman, Wasp*
29. Ebenezer Dyer	**E** - 1	
30. James Forman (1795-1873)	**B** - 1	*Intrepid*
	E - 5	
31. James Fraser (1759-1822)	**A** - 15	HMS *Borer, Charybdis, Curlew, Epervier, Guerriere, La Hogue, Junon, Leander, Loup Cervier, Marlborough, Mohawk, Morgiana, Narcissus, Sylph, Valiant*
	E - 4	
32. John Robert Glover	**A** - 1	HMS *Albion*
33. George Haim	**O** - 1	*George*
	B - 1	*George*
34. Joseph Hamilton	**O** - 1	*Dove*
35. Israel Harding	**O** - 2	*Fly* (2)
36. Hartshorne, Boggs & Co.	**A** - 14	HMS *Belvidera, Bulwark* (2), *Chubb, Colibri, Curlew* (2), *New Emulous, Jaseur, Nimrod* (2), *Plantagenet, Poictiers, Success*
37. Lawrence Hartshorne, Sr. (1755-1822)	**A** - 5	HMS *Arab, Chubb, Dover, Majestic, Nimrod*
38. Lawrence Hartshorne, Jr.	**A** - 3	HMS *Arab, Dover, Nimrod*

Name		Activity
39. Samuel Harris	**O** - 1	*Crown*
40. Samuel Head (1773-1837)	**A** - 2	HMS *Curlew* (2)
41. Thomas Heavyside	**A** - 14	HMS *Aeolus, Alba, Arab, Atalante, Bold, Guerriere, Indian, Paz, Peruvian, Recruit, Seahorse, Shannon, Tenedos, Woolwich*
	E - 2	
42. Charles Hill (1747-1825)	**O** - 2	*Fly* (2)
	B - 1	*Retaliation*
	E - 1	
43. John Thomas Hill	**B** - 2	*Fly* (2)
44. William Hughes (1745-1813)	**O** - 1	
	B - 1	
	E - 1	
45. George Redmond Hulbert	**A** - 24	HMS *Albion, Atalante, Borer, Curlew, Endymion, Epervier, Fantiome, Junon* (2), *Loire, Loup Cervier, Maidstone, Majestic, Martin, Mohawk, Morgiana, Narcissus, Nimrod* (2), *Orpheus, Plantagenet, San Domingo, Statira, Sylph, Victorious*
46. James Hutchins	**E** - 1	
47. Solomon Jennings	**O** - 1	*Crown*
48. Richard Kidston	**E** - 1	
49. John Lawson (1749-1828)	**E** - 9	
50. Jesse Lean	**E** - 1	
51. Thomas Leonard	**O** - 1	*Reprieve*
	B - 1	
52. Anthony Lockwood	**E** - 2	
53. Frederick Major	**B** - 1	
54. Charles Martyr	**A** - 12	HMS *Alban, Arab* (2), *Bacchante, Bulwark, Leander, Maidstone, Majestic, Martin, Nieman, Ring Dove, Spencer*
55. Thomas Mason	**O** - 1	*George*
56. Capt. Thomas Maynard (1768-1857)	**A** - 9	HMS *Acasta, Bulwark* (2), *Cossack, Endymion, Maidstone, Nymph, Spencer, Statira*
57. William McCorken	**O** - 1	*Sherbrooke*
58. R. McDonald	**O** - 1	*Ann*
59. William McLean	**E** - 2	
60. Garret Miller (1770-1840)	**B** - 1	
	E - 2	
61. John Milloy	**A** - 1	
62. Alexander Mitchell	**E** - 1	

Name		Activity
63. John Moody	B - 9	
	E - 25	
64. John Morris	E - 1	
65. Francis Muncy	O - 1	*Weazel*
	B - 1	
66. William Murphy	B - 1	
67. William O'Bryan	O - 1	*Weazel*
	B - 1	
68. John Osborne	O - 1	
	B - 2	
	E - 1	
69. John Owen (1778-1824)	B - 1	
70. John Pendergast	B - 1	
71. Kinney Prince	B - 1	
72. John Pryor	O - 1	*Bunker Hill*
	E - 13	
73. John G. Pyke (1743-1828)	B - 1	
74. William King Reynolds	O - 1	
	B - 5	
75. J. Reid	O - 1	*Snapdragon*
76. David Ridgeway	E - 1	
77. John Roy	B - 2	
78. William Rudolph	B - 4	
79. Joseph Schofield	O - 1	*George*
80. Thomas Smith	O - 1	*George*
	B - 2	
81. Enoch Stanwood	O - 1	*Fly*
82. John Starr (1775-1827)	B - 1	
83. Starr & Shannon	O - 1	*Retrieve*
84. Hugh Somerville	A - 1	
85. James Thom	B - 1	
	E - 8	
86. Joseph Thomas	E - 1	
87. James Thompson	E - 1	
88. James Tidmarsh	E - 1	
89. Michael Tobin (1776?-1843)	B - 2	
	A - 1	HMS *Narcissus*
	E - 17	
90. Richard Tremaine (1774-1854)	A - 1	HMS *Alphea*
	E - 14	
91. Thomas Wallace	E - 1	
92. William Ward	B - 1	
93. Walter Wilkie	E - 1	
94. James Woodward	E - 1	

Name		Activity
95. Jesse Woodward	**E** - 1	
96. Thomas Woodward	**E** - 1	
97. Andrew Wright	**A** - 3	HMS *Atalante, Spartan, Spy*
98. Henry Yeomans	**B** - 2	
LIVERPOOL, NS		
1. James Barss (1782-1863)	**O** - 7	*Liverpool Packet, Sir John Sherbrooke, Wolverine, Rolla*
2. John Barss (d. 1851)	**O** - 6	As above
	B - 2	
3. Joseph Barss	**O** - 3	*Wolverine, Minerva*
4. Thomas Barss (1789-1816)	**O** - 4	*Wolverine, Minerva*
	B - 1	
5. Joseph Bartlett	**O** - 3	*Lively, Saucy Jack, Minerva*
6. Joseph Cottingham Bates	**O** - 1	*Dove*
7. Gordon Dewolf (1784-1819)	**O** - 1	*Retaliation*
8. James Dewolf (1787-1835)	**O** - 1	*Rolla*
9. Samuel Dexter (1771-1831)	**O** - 1	*Rolla*
10. Joseph Freeman	**O** - 4	*Sir John Sherbrooke, Rolla, Wolverine* (2)
	B - 3	*Liverpool Packet* (3)
11. Thomas Freeman (1775-1842)	**O** - 2	*Retaliation, Rolla*
12. Stephen Gardner	**O** - 1	
13. John Gorham (1771-	**O** - 1	*Retaliation*
14. Benjamin Knaut	**O** - 5	*Liverpool Packet, Sir John Sherbrooke, Wolverine, Rolla*
15. Snow Parker	**O** - 4	*Retaliation, Rover, Shannon*
	E - 3	
16. John Perkins	**E** - 3	
17. John Roberts (1881-1839)	**O** - 1	
18. Caleb Seely	**O** - 1	*Liverpool Packet*
19. William Smith	**O** - 1	*Caledonia*
20. Dr. Andrew Webster (1778-1855)	**O** - 1	*Minerva*
LUNENBURG, NS		
1. T. Chamberlain	**O** - 1	*Lunenburg*
2. J. Fault	**O** - 1	*Lunenburg*
3. William Henry Maser	**O** - 2	*Lunenburg*
	B - 1	
4. John Oxner	**O** - 2	*Lunenburg*
5. Philip Rudolph	**O** - 2	*Lunenburg*
6. Henry Wollenhaup	**O** - 2	*Lunenburg*

Name		Activity
ANNAPOLIS ROYAL, NS		
1. Phineas Lovett, Jr. (1745-1828)	O - 2	*Broke*
2. Thomas Richie	O - 1	*Matilda*
3. William Bailie	O - 1	*Matilda*
4. John Robinson (1781-1839)	O - 1	*Matilda*
5. John Berkett	O - 1	*Matilda*
GREENOCK, NS		
1. William Forsyth	O - 1	*Caledonia*
2. James Hunter	O - 1	*Caledonia*
3. George Robertson	O - 1	*Caledonia*
HORTON, NS		
1. William Young	O - 1	*Retrieve*
	B - 1	
ST. JOHN, NB		
1. John Atkinson	O - 1	
	B - 1	
2. William Black	A - 5	HMS *Bold, New Emulous, Fantome, Plumper, Rattler*
3. William Robert Boyd	O - 1	
4. John Clarke	O - 1	*Hare*
5. Andrew Crookshank	E - 3	
6. Messrs Curry & Hanford	O - 1	
7. Noah Desbrow	O - 1	*Hare*
	B - 1	
8. William Donald	B - 1	
9. Hugh Doyle	O - 1	*Hare*
10. James Thorpe Hanford	O - 2	*Dart*
11. James Hay Jr.	O - 2	*Dart*
12. Hugh Johnson & Son	O - 1	*Herald*
13. Samuel Mills	O - 1	
14. Thomas Milledge	O - 1	*Herald*
15. Robert Pagan (1750-1821)	O - 1	*Sir John Sherbrooke*
16. A.S. Ritchie	O - 1	
17. John Robinson	E - 1	
	A - 1	HMS *Borer*
18. Robert Shires	O - 2	*Dart*
19. Andrew Sterling	O - 1	
20. Zalman Wheeler	E - 1	
21. George Younghusband	O - 1	

Bibliography

PRIMARY SOURCES:

1. **Vice-Admiralty Court Records**

English Reports, CLXV, Ecclesiastical, Admiralty and Probate and Divorce V, Edinburgh: W. Green and Son Ltd., 1923.

National Archives of Canada, RG 8, IV, Vice-Admiralty Court, Halifax, 1784 - 1818, Prize Court Records (Vols. 73-150).

Provincial Archives of Nova Scotia

RG 1, Vol. 501, Vessels captured 1812-1818

Vol. 375, Sales of property by the Vice-Admiralty Court 1811-1816

MG 1, Vol. 233, W.R. Copp Family papers

MG 100, Vol. 16, Articles on privateering

Vol. 175, Names of vessels and commanders receiving letters of marque, 1803-1814.

Vol. 210, Notes on privateering

Public Records Office, Chancery Lane, London

ADM 1, HCA Vol. 42 - Prize Appeal Records

HCA Vol. 44 - 74 - Assignation Books

HCA Vol. 45, 64 - 67 - Prize Appeals Case Books

HCA Vol. 46, 10 - 11 - Prize Appeal Interlocutories

HCA Vol. 49, 99 - List of Adjudications from Halifax

Halsbury's Laws of England, Viscount Hailsham, ed., London: Butterworth & Co. Ltd., 1938, Vol. XXVI, XXVIII.

Roscoe, E.S., ed. *Reports of Prize Cases determined in the High Court of Admiralty before the Lords High Commissioners of Appeals in Prize Causes and before the Judicial Committee of the Privy Council from 1745 to 1859*. 2 vols. London: Stevens & Sons Limited, 1905.

Stewart, James. *Reports of cases argued and determined in the Court of Vice-Admiralty at Halifax, in Nova Scotia from the commencement of the war, in 1803, to the end of the year 1813, in the time of Alexander Croke LLD., Judge of that Court*. Halifax, N.S., 1813.

Stockton, Alfred A. *Report of Cases Decided in the Vice-Admiralty Court of New Brunswick from 1879 to 1891 with a Digest of all Canadian Vice-Admiralty Cases*. Saint John, N.B.: J. and A. McMillan, 1894.

2. **Statutes:**

28 Hen. VIII, c. 15 - The Offences at Sea Act, 1536

11 Will. III, c. 7 - Suppression of Piracy, 1698-1699

6 Ann, c. 37 - An Act for the Encouragement of the Trade to America, 1708

4 Geo. I, c. II - The Piracy Act, 1717

8 Geo. I, c. 24 - The Piracy Act, 1721

13 Geo. II, c. 4 - An Act for the more effectual securing and encouraging the Trade of his Majesty's British subjects to America and for the Encouragement of Seamen to enter into his Majesty's Service, 1740

17 Geo. II, c. 34 - An Act for the better Encouragement of Seamen in His Majesty's Service and Privateers to annoy the Enemy, 1744

18 Geo. II, c. 30 - The Piracy Act, 1745

26 Geo. III, c. 60 - An Act for the further Increase and Encouragement of Shipping and Navigation, 1787

33 Geo. III, c. 65-68 - An Act for the further encouragement of British Marines; and for other purposes therein, 1793

39 Geo. III, c. 37 - The Offences at Sea Act, 1799

41 Geo. III, c. 95, 96 - An Act for the better Regulation of his Majesty's Prize Courts in the West Indies and America, and for giving a more speedy and effectual Execution to the Decrees of the Lords Commissioners of Appeals, 2 July 1801

45 Geo. III, c. 71 - An Act for the Encouragement of Seamen, and for the better and more effectually manning his Majesty's Navy during the present war, 27 June 1805

46 Geo. III, c. 72 - The Offences at Sea Act, 1806

49 Geo. III, c. 123 - An Act to explain and amend an Act made in the Forty fifth Year of His present Majesty for the Encouragement of Seamen, and for the better and more effectually manning His Majesty's Navy during the present War; and for the further Encouragement of Seamen and for the better and more effectually providing for the Interest of the Royal Hospital for Seaman at Greenwich and the Royal Hospital for Soldiers at Chelsea; and to extend the Provisions of the said Act to the said Act to cases arising in consequence of Hostilities commenced since the passing of the said Act, 1809

53 Geo. III, c. 63 - An Act to extend Two Acts of the Forty fifth and Forty ninth Years of His present Majesty to American Prizes, 1813

3. Newspapers:

Nova Scotia Royal Gazette, Halifax, 17 June 1812 - 12 April 1815

Niles' *Weekly Register*, Baltimore, September 1811-1815

London *Times*, London, 1 June 1812 - 1 May 1815.

4. Personal Accounts

Brenton, E.B. (Attrib.) *Some Account of the Public Life of the Late Lieutenant-General Sir George Prevost, Bart*. London: T. Cadell, 1823.

Bryant, William M. *The Old Sailor: A Thrilling Narrative of the Life and Adventures of Elias Hutchins, during 40 Years on the Ocean*. 1853. Reprint. Cape Porpoise, Maine: Atlantic Firemen's Educational Association, 1973.

Durand, James. *James Durand, An Able Seaman of 1812*. George S, Brooks, ed. 1820. Reprint. New Haven: Yale University Press, 1926.

Fergusson, Charles Bruce, ed. *The Diary of Simeon Perkins 1797-1803*. 3 vols., Toronto: Champlain Society, 1967.

Johnson, Noah. (A Wanderer). *Journals of Two Cruises aboard the American Privateer Yankee*. 1812. Reprint. New York: The Macmillan Company, 1967.

5. Published Documents

Dudley, William S., ed. *The Naval War of 1812, A Documentary History*. Washington, D.C.: Naval Historical Center, Vol. I, 1985; Vol. II, 1992.

Ells, Margaret, ed. *A Calendar of Official Correspondence and Legislative Papers, Nova Scotia, 1802-15*. Halifax: Public Archives of Nova Scotia, Publication No. 3, 1936.

Hattendorf, John B., R.J.B. Knight, A.W.H. Pearsall, N.A.M. Rodger, and G. Till, eds. *British Naval Documents 1204-1960*. Washington, D.C.: Naval Records Society, 1993.

Harlow, Vincent and Frederick Madden, eds., *British Colonial Developments, 1774-1834: Select Documents*. Oxford: Clarendon Press, 1953.

Instructions for Private Armed Vessels of the United States. Twelfth Congress. Sess. I, XLIX, 1812.

Jameson, J. Franklin, ed. *Privateering and Piracy in the Colonial Period: Illustrative Documents*. 1923. Reprint. New York: Augustus M. Kelley, 1970.

Labaree, Leonard Woods, ed. *Royal Instructions to British Colonial Governors, 1670-1776*. I. New York: Octagon Books, 1967.

Marsden, R.G., ed. *Documents relating to Laws and Customs of the Sea*. 2 vols. London: Naval Records Society, 1915.

____________. *Select Pleas in the Court of Admiralty*. Vol. I, The Court of Admiralty of the West, A.D. 1390-1404, and Vol. II, The High Court of Admiralty, A.D. 1547-1602. London: Selden Society, 1897.

Naish, G.P.B., ed. *Nelson's Letters to his Wife and Other Documents 1758-1831*. London: Routledge & Kegan Paul, 1958.

Piracy and Privateering, National Maritime Museum, Catalogue of the Library, IV. London: H.M. Stationery Office, 1972.

Pritchard, M.J. and D.E.C. Yale, eds., *Hale and Fleetwood on Admiralty Jurisdiction*. London: Selden Society, 1993.

Treaties and Agreements Affecting Canada - 1814-1925. Ottawa: Department of External Affairs, Queen's Printer, 1927.

Twiss, Sir Travers, Q.C, D.C.L., ed. *Monumenta Juridica - The Black Book of the Admiralty*. 1857. Reprint. Weisbaden: Lessing Druckerei, 1965.

Vattel de, Emerich. *The Law of Nations or Principles of the Law of Nations Applied to the Conduct of Affairs of Nations and Sovereigns*. Joseph Chitty, ed., Philadelphia: T & J.W. Johnson & Co., 1857.

Vezian, Peter. "Journal of a Privateersman," *The Atlantic Monthly*, VII (1861), 353-424.

Wood, W., ed., *Select British Documents of the Canadian War of 1812*, 3 vols. Toronto: Champlain Society, XIII-XV, 1920-1926. Reprint. New York: Greenwood Press, 1968.

SECONDARY SOURCES:

Albion, Robert Greenhalgh. *Makers of Naval Policy 1798-1947*. Annapolis, Md.: Naval Institute Press, 1980.

Allen, Gardner Weld. *Papers of Isaac Hull*. Boston: The Boston Athaneum, 1929.

Allen, H.C. *The Anglo-American Relationship Since 1783*. London: Adam & Charles Black, 1959.

Anderson, Peggy, "Enos Collins 1774-1871." *Canadian Antiques and Art Review*, III, (1981), 29-32.

Andrews, Kenneth R., ed. *English Privateering Voyages to the West Indies, 1588-1595*. Cambridge: Hakluyt Society, 1959.

Archibald, Hon. Adams G. "Sir Alexander Croke." *Nova Scotia Historical Society*. Halifax, N.S. (1880), 110-128.

Armstrong, John. "The Significance of Coastal Shipping in British Domestic Transport, 1550-1830." *International Journal of Maritime History*, III (1991), 70-76.

Auchinleck, G. *A History of the War between Great Britain and the U.S.A. During the Years 1812, 1813 & 1814*. 1855. Reprint. Toronto: Arms & Armour Press, 1972.

Barnes, James. *Naval Actions of the War of 1812*. New York: Harper & Brothers Publishers, 1896.

Blake, Gordon. *Customs Administration in Canada*. Toronto: University of Toronto Press, 1957.

Bonnel, Ulane. *La France, Les États-Unis et la guerre de course (1797-1815)*. Paris: Nouvelles Éditions Latines, 1961.

Bonnet, Stanley. *The Price of Admiralty*. London: Robert Hale Ltd., 1968.

Bourne, Edward E., LL.D. *The History of Wells and Kennebunk*. Portland, Me.: B. Thurston & Co., 1875.

Brebner, J.B. "Nova Scotia's Remedy for the American Revolution." *Canadian Historical Review*, XV (1934), 171-181.

Bromley, J.S. *Corsairs and Navies, 1660-1770*. London: Hambledon Press, 1987.

________. "Duguay Trouin: The Financial Background." *Mariner's Mirror*, LXXI (1985), 259-285.

________. Review of Elizabethan Privateering by Kenneth R. Andrews. *Mariner's Mirror*, LI, 1965, 282-285.

Brooks, F.W. "The Cinq Ports." *Mariner's Mirror*, XV (1929), 142-191.

Buckner, Phillip, "The Colonial Office and British North America." *Dictionary of Canadian Biography*, Vol. VIII (1850-1861) Toronto: University of Toronto Press, 1985, xxiii-xxxvii.

Caffrey, Kate. *The Lion and the Union: The Anglo-American War, 1812-1815*. London: André Deutsch Ltd., 1978.

Carson, Edward A. "The Customs Plantation Records." *Journal of the Society of Archivists*, IV (1971), 212-217.

Chapelle, Howard I. *The History of American Sailing Ships*. 1935. Reprint. New York: Bonanza Books, 1982.

Chapin, Howard M. *Privateering in King George's War, 1739-1748*. Providence, R.I.: Rhode Island Historical Society, 1928.

__________. *Rhode Island Privateers in King George's War, 1739-1748*. Providence, R.I.: Rhode Island Historical Society, 1926.

Cheyette, Frederic L. "The Sovereign and the Pirates, 1332." *Speculum: A Journal of Medieval Studies*, XLV (1970), 40-68.

Chowdharay-Best, G. "Ancient Maritime Law." *Mariner's Mirror*, LXII (1976), 81-91.

Clark, P.D. "Beamish Murdoch. Nova Scotia's National Historian." *Acadiensis*, XXI (1991), 85-109.

Clark, G.N., "English and Dutch Privateers under William II." *Mariner's Mirror*, VII (1921), 162-195.

Coggleshall, George. *The American Privateers*. New York: G. Coggleshall, 1861.

Colledge, J.J. *Ships of the Royal Navy*. London: Greenhill Books, 1987.

Colombos, C. John. *A Treatise on the Law of Prize*. Grotius Society Publications, No. 5. London: Longmans, Green & Co., 1949.

Commission Internationale d'Histoire Maritime. *Course et Piraterie: Études présentées à la Commission Internationale d'Histoire Maritime à l'occasion de son XVe colloque international pendant le XVe Congrès International des Sciences historiques* (San Francisco, août 1975). 2 vols. Paris: Institut de Recherche et d'Histoire de Textes Édition du Centre National de la Recherche Scientifique, 1975.

Copp, Walter Ronald. "Military Activities in Nova Scotia During the War of 1812." *Collections of the Nova Scotia Historical Society*. XXIV (1938), 57-74.

__________. "Nova Scotian Trade During the War of 1812." *Canadian Historical Review*, XVIII (1937), 141-155.

Crane, W.B. and J.P. Cranwell. *Men of Marque*. New York: W.W. Norton & Co., 1940.

Crawford, Michael J. "The Navy's Campaign against the Licensed Trade in the War of 1812." *American Neptune*, XLVI (1986), 165-172.

Crimmin, P.K., "The Prisoner of War Registers, 1793-1815: a Possible Archival Source for Maritime History." *Mariner's Mirror*, LXXX (1994), 469-472.

Crowell, Clement W. *Novascotiaman*. Halifax, N.S.: Nova Scotia Museum, 1979.

Crowhurst, Patrick. *The French War on Trade: Privateering 1793-1815*. Brookfield, Conn.: Gower Publishing, 1989.

__________. "The Admiralty and the Convoy System in the Seven Years War." *Mariner's Mirror*, LVII (1971), 163-173.

Crump, Helen J. *Colonial Admiralty Jurisdiction in the Seventeenth Century*. London: Longmans Green, 1931.

Cuthbertson, Brian. *The Old Attorney General*. Halifax: Nimbus Publishing, 1980.

Deane, James Parker, D.C.L. *Effect of War upon the Trade and Property of Neutrals and Maritime Capture and Prize*. London: Wildy and Sons, 1854.

Dickens, Charles. *David Copperfield*. 1850. Reprint. New York, Rand McNally & Co., n.d.

Doty, Joseph D. *The British Admiralty Board as a Factor in Colonial Administration, 1689-1763*. Philadelphia: 1930.

Doull, Hon. John. *Sketches of Attorney Generals of Nova Scotia, 1750-1926*. Halifax, N.S.: 1964.

Dow, George Francis, ed. *American Vessels captured by the British during the Revolution and War of 1812*. Salem, Mass.: The Essex Institute, 1911.

Dye, Ira. *The Fatal Cruise of the Argus. Two Captains in the War of 1812*. Washington, D.C.: Naval Institute Press, 1994.

Eastman, Ralph. *Some Famous Privateers of New England*. Boston: State Street Trust Co., 1928.

Fergusson, Charles Bruce. "The Establishment of the Consulate of the United States of America in Halifax." *Nova Scotia Historical Quarterly*, III (1973), 57-73.

Fish, Peter G. "International Crises, American Neutrality, and Prize Cases in U.S. Courts on the Atlantic Maritime Frontier from Baltimore to Charleston: 1793-1916." Paper presented at the annual meeting of the North American Society for Oceanic History, Wilmington, N.C., 1995.

Forester, C.S. *The Naval War of 1812*. London: Michael Joseph Ltd., 1957.

Fraser, D.G.L. "The Origin and Function of the Court of Vice-Admiralty in Halifax, 1749-1759." *Nova Scotia Historical Society*, XXXIII (1961), 57-80.

Garitee, Jerome R. *The Republic's Private Navy: The American Privateering Business as Practiced by Baltimore during the War of 1812*. Middletown, Conn.: Wesleyan University Press, 1977.

Gilroy, Marion. "Customs Fees in Nova Scotia." *Canadian Historical Review*, XVII (1936), 9-22.

Gosset, W.P. *The Lost Ships of the Royal Navy*. London: Mansell Publishing Ltd., 1986.

Graham, Gerald S. "The Origin of Free Ports in British North America." *Canadian Historical Review*, XXII (1941), 25-34.

Gutridge, Tony. "Aspects of Naval Prize Agency." *Mariner's Mirror*, LXXX (1994), 43-53.

Gwyn, Julian. *The Enterprising Admiral: The Personal Fortune of Admiral Sir Peter Warren*. Montreal: McGill-Queen's University Press, 1974.

Halpenny, Frances, ed. *Dictionary of Canadian Biography* Vol. VIII (1850-1861), Barss, 62-63; Vol. IX (1861-1870). Sir Samuel Cunard, 172-177; Vol. X (1870-1881), Enos Collins, 188-190. Toronto: University of Toronto Press.

Hannay, James, D.C.L. "The War of 1812." *Collections of the Nova Scotia Historical Society*, XI (1901), 1-396.

Harlow, V.T. *The Founding of the Second British Empire, 1763-1793*. Vol. 1. London: Longman's Green & Co., 1952.

Harman, Joyce. *Trade and Privateering in Spanish Florida, 1732-1763*. St. Augustine, Fla.: St. Augustine Historical Society, 1969.

Hickey, Donald P. *The War of 1812 - A Forgotten Conflict*. Urbana, Ill.: University of Illinois Press, 1989.

__________. *The War of 1812: A Short History*. Urbana, Ill.: University of Illinois Press, 1995.

Hitsman, J. Mackay. *Safeguarding Canada 1763-1871*. Toronto: University of Toronto Press, 1968.

__________. *The Incredible War of 1812*. Toronto: University of Toronto Press, 1965.

Hodgson, Godfrey. *Lloyd's of London*. London: Penguin Books, 1986.

Holdsworth, Sir William. *A History of English Law*. 16 vols. 1938. Reprint. London: Methuen & Co. Ltd., 1966.

Horsman, Reginald. *The War of 1812*. London: Eyre & Spottiswoode, 1969.

Jackson, Melvin H. *Privateers in Charleston, 1793-1796*. Washington, D.C.: U.S. Govt. Printing Office, 1969.

Jacobs, Major James Ripley and Glenn Tucker. *The War of 1812 - A Compact History*. New York: Hawthorn Books, Inc., 1969.

Jenkins, H.J.K. "Privateers, Picaroons, Pirates: West Indian Commerce Raiders, 1793-1801." *Mariner's Mirror*, LXXIII (1987), 181-186.

Jordan, William B., Jr. *A History of Cape Elizabeth, Maine*. Portland, Me.: House of Falmouth, 1965.

Kendall, Charles Wye. *Private Men-of-War*. London: Philip Allen & Co. Ltd., 1931.

Kennedy, Paul M. *The Rise and Fall of the Great Powers: Economic Change and Military Conflict from 1500 to 2000*. New York: Random House, 1987.

__________. *The Rise and Fall of British Naval Mastery*. London: Allen Lane, 1976.

Kilby, William Henry. *Eastport and Passamaquoddy*. 1888. Reprint. Eastport, Moose Island, Me.: Border History Fathom Series, Number 2, 1982.

Laing, Lionel H. "Nova Scotia's Admiralty Court as a Problem of Colonial Administration." *Canadian Historical Review*, XVI (1935), 151-161.

Lawrence, J. W. *Foot-Prints; or, Incidents in Early History of New Brunswick*. Saint John, N.B.: J. & A. McMillan, 1883.

Leefe, John. *The Atlantic Privateers*. Halifax: Penthouse Press, 1978.

________. "A Bluenose Privateer of 1812." *Nova Scotia Historical Quarterly*, III (1973), 1-18.

________. "The Atlantic Privateers, Part 1 and Part 2." *Nova Scotia Historical Quarterly*, VIII (1978), 1-17; (1978), 109-125.

Lemmon, Sarah McCulloh. "Dissent in North Carolina during the War of 1812." *The North Carolina Historical Review*, XLIX (1972), 104-118.

_______________. *North Carolina and the War of 1812*. 1971. Reprint. Raleigh, N.C.: Division of Archives and History, North Carolina Department of Cultural Resources, 1984.

Lohnes, Barry J. "British Naval Problems at Halifax During the War of 1812." *Mariner's Mirror*, LIX (1973), 317-333.

Lord, G. de Forest and G.C. Sprague. *Cases on the Law of Admiralty*. St. Paul, Minn.: West Publishing Co., 1939.

Lushington, Godfrey. *A Manual of Prize Law*. London: Butterworths, 1866.

Lydon, James G. *Pirates, Privateers, and Profits*. Upper Saddle River, N.J.: The Gregg Press, 1970.

Lynch, Peter, Q.C. "Early Reminiscences of Halifax." *Collections of the Nova Scotia Historical Society*, XVI (1912), 171-204.

Macintyre, Capt. Donald. *The Privateers*. London: Paul Elek, 1975.

Maclay, E.S. *A History of American Privateers*. New York: D. Appleton & Co., 1899.

MacMechan, Archibald McKellar. *Nova Scotia Privateers*. Toronto: The Ryerson Press, 1930.

MacNutt, W.S. *The Atlantic Provinces: The Emergence of Colonial Society, 1712-1857*. Toronto: McClelland and Stewart Ltd., 1968.

________. *New Brunswick, A History: 1784-1867*. Toronto: Macmillan of Canada, 1963.

Mahan, Alfred Thayer. *The Influence of Sea Power upon History, 1660-1783*. 1890. Reprint. London: Methuen, 1965.

_______. *Sea Power in its Relations to the War of 1812*, Vols. 1 & 2. Boston: Little Brown & Co., 1905.

Mahon, John K. *The War of 1812*. Gainesville, Fla.: University of Florida Press, 1972.

Marsden, R.G. "Early Prize Jurisdiction and Prize Law in England." *English Historical Review*, XXIV (1909), 675-697.

Martel, J.S. "Halifax During and After the War of 1812." *The Dalhousie Review*, XXIII (1943), 289-304.

_______ "Nova Scotia's Contribution to the Canadian Relief Fund in the War of 1812." *Canadian Historical Review*, XXIII (1942), 297-302.

Matthews, Keith and Gerald Panting, eds. "Ships and Shipbuilding in the North Atlantic Region." *Proceedings of the Conference of the Atlantic Canada Shipping Project*. St. John's, Nfld.: Memorial University of Newfoundland, 1978.

Meyer, W.R. "English Privateering in the War of the Spanish Succession, 1702-1713." *Mariner's Mirror*, LXIX (1983), 435-446.

_______. "English Privateering in the War of 1688 to 1697." *Mariner's Mirror*, LXVII (1981), 259-272.

McFee, William. *The Law of the Sea*. Philadelphia: J.B. Lippincott Co., 1950.

McKee, Christopher. *A Gentlemanly and Honourable Profession: The Creation of the U.S. Naval Officer Corps, 1794-1815*. Annapolis, Md.: Naval Institute Press, 1991.

McIntosh, Dave. *The Collectors: A History of Canadian Customs and Excise*. Toronto: N.C. Press Ltd. and DSS Canada, 1984.

Minchinton, Walter E. and David J. Starkey. "Characteristics of Privateers Operating from the British Isles Against America, 1777-1783." in *Ships, Seafaring and Society: Essays in Maritime History*, Timothy J. Runyan, ed., 251-274. Detroit: Wayne State University Press, 1987.

Morison, Samuel Eliot. *The Maritime History of Massachusetts, 1783-1860*. 1921. Reprint. Boston: Houghton Mifflin Co., 1961.

Morrison, James H. and James Moreira, eds. *Tempered by Rum*. Halifax, N.S.: Pottersfield Press, 1988.

Mouzon, Harold Alwyn. *Privateers of Charleston in the War of 1812*. Charleston, S.C.: The Historical Commission of Charleston, 1954.

Mullins, Janet E. *Some Liverpool Chronicles*. 1941. Reprint. Liverpool, N.S.: Lancelot Press, 1980.

__________. *Liverpool Privateering, 1756-1815*, 1936. Reprint. Liverpool, N.S.: Queen's County Historical Society, 1996.

__________. "The Liverpool Packet". Reprint. Liverpool, N.S.: Queen's County Historical Society, 1966.

Murdoch, Beamish. *A History of Nova Scotia or Acadie*. 3 vols., Halifax, N.S.: James Barnes, 1867.

__________. *Epitome of the Laws of Nova Scotia*, IV, Halifax, N.S., 1833.

Nelson, George A. "The First Cruise of the Privateer *Harpy*." *American Neptune*, I (1941), 116-122.

Nichols, George E.E. "Notes on Nova Scotia Privateers." *Nova Scotia Historical Society*, XX, 1908. Reprint. Canadiana House (1981), 111-152.

North, P.M. *Cheshire's Private International Law*. London: Butterworth's, 1974. [9th ed.]

Nova Scotia Museum, *The Simeon Perkins House*. leaflet, no date.

O'Connell, D.P. *The Influence of Law on Sea Power*. Manchester: Manchester University Press, 1975.

Pack, A.J. "A Naval Sidelight in the 1812 War with America." *Mariner's Mirror*, LXXIII (1987), 287-291.

Packard, Aubigne Lermond. *A Town that Went to Sea*. Portland, Me.: Falmouth Publishing House, 1950.

Pares, Richard. *Colonial Blockade and Neutral Rights, 1739-1763*. Oxford: The Clarendon Press, 1938.

Payne, A. Martin. "Life of Sir Samuel Cunard." *Collections of the Nova Scotia Historical Society*, XIX (1918), 75-91.

Perkins, Bradford, ed., *The Causes of the War of 1812*. New York: Holt, Rinehart & Winston, 1962.

Petrie, Donald A. "The Ransoming of Eliza Swan." *American Neptune*, LIII (1993), 98-108.

__________. "Forbidden Prizes." *American Neptune*, LIV (1994), 165-174.

Potter, E.B., ed. *Sea Power - A Naval History*. New York: Prentice Hall Inc., 1960.

Pullen, H. E. *The Shannon and the Chesapeake*. Toronto: McClelland & Stewart Ltd., 1970.

Raban, Peter. "Channel Island Privateering, 1739-1763." *International Journal of Maritime History*, I (1989), 287-299.

Raddall, Thomas H. *Halifax, Warden of the North*. 1948. Reprint. Toronto: McClelland & Stewart, 1971.

__________. *The Path of Destiny: Canada from the British Conquest to Home Rule: 1763-1850*. Toronto: Doubleday Canada Ltd., 1957.

Rawlyk, K.G., ed. *Historical Essays on the Atlantic Provinces*. Toronto: MacMillan & Stewart Ltd., 1967.

Reed, Seth O. "The Trade between Providence, Rhode Island, and the Caribbean and South America in 1796." *American Neptune*, XLV, (1985), 166-173.

Rediker, Marcus. *Between the Devil and the Deep Blue Sea: Merchant Seamen, Pirates, and the Anglo-American Maritime World, 1700-1750*. Cambridge: Cambridge University Press, 1987.

Reynolds, Clark G., ed., *Global Crossroads and the American Seas*. Missoula, Mont., Pictorial Histories Publishing Co., 1988.

Rice, George Wharton. *The Shipping Days of Old Boothbay*. Boothbay Harbour, Me., 1938.

Robertson, Marion. *King's Bounty: A History of Early Shelburne, Nova Scotia*. Halifax, N.S.,: Nova Scotia Museum, 1983.

Robinson, Howard. *Carrying British Mails Overseas*. London: George Allen & Unwin, 1964.

Robinson, William Morrison, Jr. *The Confederate Privateers*. 1928. Reprint. Columbia, S.C.: University of South Carolina Press, 1990.

Rodger, N.A.M. *Wooden World: An Anatomy of the Georgian Navy*. London: Collins, 1986.

Roosevelt, Theodore. *The Naval War of 1812 or the History of the United States Navy during the Last War with Great Britain to Which is Appended an Account of the Battle of New Orleans*. 1882. Reprint. Annapolis, Md., Naval Institute Press, 1987.

Rosas, Allan. *The Legal Status of Prisoners of War*. Helsinki: 1976, 43-69.

Roscoe, E.S. *A History of the English Prize Court*. London: Lloyd's, 1924.

Rothery, H.C. *Prize Droits*. London: HMSO, 1915.

Rowe, William Hutchinson. *Shipbuilding Days and Tales of the Sea in Old North Yarmouth and Yarmouth, Maine*. Portland, Me.: Marks Printing House, 1924.

Runyan, Timothy J., ed., *Ships, Seafaring, and Society: Essays in Maritime History*. Detroit, Mich., Wayne State University Press, 1987.

____________. *Merchants, Privateers and the Law: The Anglo-American Experience*. offprint.

____________. "The Rolls of Oleron and the Admiralty Court in the Fourteenth Century." *American Journal of Legal History*, XIX, (1975).

____________. *Mariners and the Law of the Sea in Later Medieval England*, paper presented at the annual meeting of the International Commission of Maritime History, August 1980.

Ryerson, Egerton. *The Loyalists of America and their Times: From 1620-1816*. Vol. II. Toronto: William Briggs, 1880.

Sanborn, Frederic Rockwell. *Origins of the Early English Maritime and Commercial Law*. New York: The Century Co., 1930.

Savage, Carleton. *Policy of the United States toward Maritime Commerce in War*. Washington, D.C.: U.S. Govt. Printing Office, 1934.

Senior, William. *The History of Maritime Law*. Maritime Miscellany Series, No. 8, 260-275.

Sheffield, William P. *Rhode Island Privateers and Privateersmen*. Newport, R.I.: John P. Sanborn, 1883.

Smith, Gene A. *"For the Purposes of Defense": The Politics of the Jeffersonian Gunboat Program*. Newark: University of Delaware Press, 1995.

__________. "A Means to an End: Gunboats and Thomas Jefferson's Theory of Defense." *American Neptune*, LV (1995), 11-121.

Snider, C.H.J. *Under the Red Jack*. Toronto: The Musson Book Co. 1927.

Sprague, Alan B. "Some American Influences on the Law and Law Courts of Nova Scotia, 1849-1853." *Nova Scotia Historical Review*, XII (1992), 1-31.

Stagg, J.C.A. *Mr. Madison's War: Politics, Diplomacy, and Warfare in the Early American Republic, 1783-1830*. Princeton, N.J.: Princeton University Press, 1983.

Stanley, George F.G. *The War of 1812 - Land Operations*. Toronto: Macmillan of Canada, National Museums of Canada, 1983.

Starkey, David J. *British Privateering Enterprise in the Eighteenth Century*. Exeter: University of Exeter Press, 1990.

____________. "Eighteenth Century Privateering Enterprise." *International Journal of Maritime History*, I (1989), 279-286.

____________. "Pirates and Markets." *Research in Maritime History*, VII, Lewis R. Fischer, ed., St. John's, Nfld.: International Maritime Economic History Association (1994), 59-80.

Stewart, Walter. *Towers of Gold - Feet of Clay*. Toronto: Totem Books, 1983.

Stone, Arthur J. "The Admiralty Court in Colonial Nova Scotia." *Dalhousie Law Journal* (1994), 363-429.

Stuart, Reginald C. "Special Interests and National Authority in Foreign Policy: American-British Provincial Links During the Embargo and the War of 1812." *Diplomatic History*, no date.

Swanson, Carl E. *Predators and Prizes: American Privateering and Imperial Warfare, 1739-1748*. Columbia, S.C.: University of South Carolina Press, 1991.

__________. "Pirates and Markets." *Research in Maritime History*, No. 7. St. John's, Nfld.: International Maritime Economic History Association (1994), 59-80.

__________. "Privateering in Early America." *International Journal of Maritime History*, I (1989), 253-278.

Symonds, Craig L. *Navalists and Antinavalists, The Naval Policy Debate in the United States, 1785-1827*. Newark, N.J.: University of Delaware Press, 1980.

Tanner, Dwight."Young Teazer, The Making of a Myth." *Nova Scotia History Quarterly*, VI (1976), 405-412.

Taylor, George Rogers, ed. *The War of 1812: Past Justifications and Present Interpretations*. Boston: D.C. Heath & Co., 1963.

Timewell, H.C. "Guernsey Privateers." *Mariner's Mirror*, LVI (1970), 199-218.

Tracy, Nicholas. *Attack on Maritime Trade*. Toronto: University of Toronto Press, 1991.

Tucker, Spencer C. *The Jeffersonian Gunboat Navy*. Columbia, S.C.: University of South Carolina Press, 1993.

__________. "The Jeffersonian Gunboats in Service." *American Neptune*, LV (1995), 97-110.

Ubbelohde, Carl. *The Vice-Admiralty Courts and the American Revolution*. Chapel Hill, N.C.: University of North Carolina Press, 1960.

Uden, Grant and Richard Cooper, eds. *A Dictionary of British Ships and Seamen*. New York: St. Martin's Press, 1980.

Von Pivka, Otto. *Navies of the Napoleonic Era*. London: David & Charles, 1980.

Waite, Peter, Sandra Oxner, Thomas Barnes, eds. *Law in a Colonial Society: the Nova Scotia Experience*. Toronto: The Caswell Co. Ltd., 1984. [Dalhousie/Berkeley Lectures on Legal History.

Wehberg, Hans, Dr. Jur. *Capture in War on Land and Sea*. London: P.S. King & Son, 1911.

Whitelaw, W.M. *The Maritimes and Canada before Confederation*. Toronto: Oxford University Press, 1966.

Williams, Gomer. *History of the Liverpool Privateers*. London: William Heinemann, 1897.

Williams, Neville. *Contraband Cargoes, Seven Centuries of Smuggling*. London: Longmans, Green & Co., 1959.

Wiswall, F.L. Jr. *The Development of Admiralty Jurisdiction and Practice since 1800*. London: Cambridge University Press, 1970.

Yale, D.E.C., ed. *Sir Matthew Hale's The Prerogatives of the King*. London: The Selden Society, 1976.

Printed and bound by CPI Group (UK) Ltd, Croydon, CR0 4YY

16/09/2026

14963458-0005